IN
A
NEW
LAND

IN A NEW LAND

An Anthology of Immigrant Literature

Sari Grossman
Joan Brodsky Schur

 National Textbook Company
a division of *NTC Publishing Group* • Lincolnwood, Illinois USA

To Our Families and Students

Acknowledgments

Grateful acknowledgment is given authors, publishers, and agents for permission to reprint or reproduce the following copyrighted material. Every effort has been made to determine copyright owners. In the case of any omissions, the publisher will be pleased to make suitable acknowledgment in future editions.

"Memories of Korea" by Piers Kim Bolnick; written as a student at the Village Community School, New York City. Reprinted by permission of the author.

Excerpt from "In a Room and a Half" from LESS THAN ONE by Joseph Brodsky. Copyright © 1986 by Joseph Brodsky. Reprinted by permission of Farrar, Straus & Giroux, Inc.

"Ellis Island" by Joseph Bruchac. Reprinted by permission of the author, from THE REMEMBERED EARTH, Red Earth Press, Albuquerque, NM, 1979.

From MY ÁNTONIA by Willa Cather. Copyright 1918 by Willa Sibert Cather. Copyright renewed 1946 by Willa Sibert Cather. Reprinted by permission of Houghton Mifflin Company. All rights reserved.

This passage first appeared in DONALD DUK by Frank Chin. Coffee House Press, 1991. Reprinted by permission of the publisher. Copyright © 1991 by Frank Chin.

"How to Rent an Apartment Without Money" from A PUERTO RICAN IN NEW YORK AND OTHER SKETCHES by Jesus Colon. Reprinted by permission of International Publishers.

"Los New Yorks" by Victor Hernandez Cruz is reprinted with permission of the publisher from RHYTHM, CONTENT AND FLAVOR (Houston: Arte Publico Press—University of Houston, 1989).

Lorraine Duggin's poem, "Learning My Father's Language," first appeared in LOOKING FOR HOME: WOMEN WRITING ABOUT EXILE, Milkweed Editions, Ed. Keenan and Lloyd, Dec. 1989. Reprinted by permission of the author.

"Emigrant/Immigrant I" and "Emigrant/Immigrant II" from LOOKING FOR HOME by Rina Ferrarelli, Milkweed Editions, 1990. Reprinted by permission of the author.

"Bananas" from JEWS WITHOUT MONEY by Michael Gold. Avon Books, 1966. Reprinted by permission of the Evelyn Singer Literary Agency.

"Delia" from TEMPORARY SHELTER by Mary Gordon. Copyright © 1987 by Mary Gordon. Reprinted by permission of Random House, Inc.

"Prelude" by Albert Halper: copyright 1938 by Harper's Magazine, Inc., copyright renewed 1966 by Albert Halper. Reprinted by permission of Thomas Halper and Lorna Halper.

Acknowledgments continue on pages 333-334, which represent a continuation of this copyright page.

1996 Printing

CONTENTS

INTRODUCTION

IN A NEW LAND IS AN ANTHOLOGY OF PROSE, POETRY, fiction, and drama based on the American immigrant experience. America has always been a land of immigrants, never more so than today. The complete range of this enormous and rich ethnic diversity could never be captured in any anthology. What we hope to do here is to acquaint the reader with some of the common threads and transforming experiences which touched the lives of the newly arrived, whether they came nearly four hundred years ago by sail or yesterday by jet plane.

The book is organized neither according to countries of origin nor by chronology. Rather it is organized thematically. The themes of the immigrant experience such as dreams of the future, feelings of displacement, the search for a new identity, and the longing for what was left behind speak to us all powerfully and personally. Reading about the lives of others always increases empathy and understanding. The selections in this book make clear that our diversity, inherent from the start, continues to enrich us. This thematic approach is inherently multicultural, as is America itself.

The writers represented in this anthology come from almost every continent and include both literary prize winners and contemporary high school students. They range from William Bradford to Gustavus Vassa to Richard Rodriguez to David Hwang, Jamaica Kincaid, Amy Tan, and Mary Gordon.

The range of genres is equally diverse. We include journals, essays, speeches, personal memoirs, and autobiographies, as well as plays, novels, poems, short stories, folktales, and songs. Throughout the book readers are encouraged to write in all of these forms—as well as many others—in the Writer's Workshop.

We felt it so important to acknowledge the Native American cultures who preceded by thousands of years those who immigrated that we have chosen to begin our book with their voices. Our prologue addresses issues which reverberate throughout our history; it comprises selections which date back to the early 1800s and continue to the present. A speech by Creek Chief Speckled Snake uses rhetoric with consummate mastery to express his people's anger at the usurpation of their land. Zitkala-Ša, a Yankton Sioux writing in the 1920s, recalls how she was made to feel like a stranger in her own land. Contemporary authors such as poet Joseph Bruchac are faced with the dilemma of fitting into the world of American society while reaffirming the values of their own native cultures. These are themes which connect their lives to the immigrants who displaced them. These authors remind us that literature can transform history into something that touches our lives.

In our first unit we deal with that moment of arrival when both hope and anxiety color the vision of those literally—"Fresh Off the Boat." The pilgrims' faith in America as "the Promised Land," as expressed by William Bradford, became an archetype for later arrivals. The relentless optimism of these newcomers helps them to overcome many obstacles. From George Papashvily, who is made to part with his Astrakhan cap, to David Hwang's "FOB," who is ridiculed about the style of his trousers, these immigrants are able to cope with the need to conform. Their good humor and hopeful innocence protect them even when being taken advantage of.

In "New Words for a New Land" we encounter the challenges faced by immigrants learning English for the first time. We begin with Leo Rosten's famous character H*Y*M*A*N K*A*P*L*A*N, whose "fresh off the boat" confidence sees him through his night school education. He is ever unaware of the humor his fractured English affords the reader. Richard Rodriguez, in his memoir about becoming fluent in English, reminds us of the loss and pain of this transition. Later in the unit a variety of authors from W. S. Merwin to Leroy Quintana communicate in poetry the power that language unlocks.

"American Dream/American Reality," our longest unit, highlights the tension between the dream and the actuality. In this unit we get both the account of the nightmarish voyage of an African slave as well as the dream-come-true account of the young Andrew Carnegie. Adrienne Rich and Emma Lazarus provide the contrast between the reality and the dream in their metaphors of America as threshold. Women, who often had less control over their lives to begin with, were in many cases able to negotiate roles for themselves superior to the ones they left. Kate Simon, Willa Cather, Mitsuye Yamada, and Yoshiko Uchida all deal with this topic of female negotiation. Some immigrants are able to control their fate; others are overwhelmed by hostility and exploitation. The greenhorn naivete left many unprepared for the prejudice still confronting immigrants to this day. Albert Halper's story "Prelude" is set on the eve of World War II, as a Jewish family discovers bigotry in America. Despite the fact that reality does not always match the dream, Martin Luther King, Jr., affirms for all Americans the power of a vision shared.

Whether recent immigrants or not, we all have a "World Left Behind" as we move on in life. For the immigrant what is recalled has peculiar potent impact. Memories are often all that remain, and writing becomes a way to document what otherwise exists only in the mind. Joseph Brodsky, a political exile, remembers the parents he will never see again. Eva Hoffman, who came as a young girl, treasures her idealized vision of a childhood interrupted. Also included are the accounts of several contemporary immigrant students from Asia who are able to express and preserve their recollections of their homelands with impressive eloquence. We hope that these works will inspire readers to preserve and share their own memories through writing.

Our final unit, "Transplantings," deals with the process by which families take root in America. Some newcomers, from the start, are able to do this with greater ease than others. Some are able to integrate more successfully than others the past and the present. Langston Hughes in "The Negro Speaks of Rivers" feels he has brought to America the strengths of African history and that his "soul has grown deep like the rivers" in both Africa and America. Amy Tan's Waverly Jong and her immigrant mother combine Chinese wisdom with the "new American rules" to win a place in this culture. For some families, the conflict between the old ways and the new is divisive. This is true for Donald Duk, Frank Chin's fictional adolescent, as well as for Mary Gordon's sisters in "Delia." The title of Victor Hernandez Cruz's poem "Los New Yorks" speaks for itself.

Though America is a "nation of immigrants," not until now have traditional American literature anthologies reflected the wide diversity of American voices. As we chose selections for this book, we rediscovered the ability of great writing to transcend time, place, and culture. The eloquence of these writers enables us, from whatever background, to appreciate the ways in which we are both alike and different. It is our hope that these selections will enable contemporary readers to make personal and powerful connections with the lives of those Americans who preceded them. Understanding others helps us understand ourselves.

Sari Grossman
Joan Brodsky Schur

PEOPLE OF THE BEGINNINGS

Aしthough *In a New Land* is a literary anthology based on the immigrant experience, we thought it appropriate to begin our book with the voices of the people who came here first, the Native Americans. They lived on the continent for perhaps 30,000 years, in as many as 600 different cultural groups, before being "discovered" by European explorers.

The Native Americans had no name for themselves as a whole. Rather, a group often had a name which reflected the pride it took in its culture and values.

Beginning with the European landings on this continent, these first inhabitants were dispossessed of their lands and forced into involuntary migrations. Over time almost all of the territories familiar to them were usurped and put to different uses. The Native Americans who survived were made to feel like aliens, strangers in their own land. As such they found the new America as bewildering and as difficult to understand as did many of the waves of the newly arrived.

The difficulties of learning the language, assimilating into mainstream life, and the longing for a lost heritage are themes for those who have been here the longest as well as for the newest waves of immigrants to reach our shores.

The selections here include Native American voices dating back to the early 1800s up to the present. What endures of their cultures? How do individuals hold fast to values and lifestyles the dominant culture has at worst extinguished and at best ignored? These are some of the questions posed by the poems, speeches, and personal accounts in this prologue to *In a New Land*.

★ *Ellis Island* ★

JOSEPH BRUCHAC

Poet and editor and writer, Joseph Bruchac is an Abnaki Indian on his mother's side and Czechoslovakian on his father's. Here he writes about his dual heritage and the mixed feelings it arouses.

Beyond the red brick of Ellis Island[1]
where the two Slovak[2] children
who became my grandparents
waited the long days of quarantine,[3]
after leaving the sickness,   5
the old Empires of Europe,
a Circle Line[4] ship slips easily
on its way to the island
of the tall woman, green
as dreams of forests and meadows   10
waiting for those who'd worked
a thousand years
yet never owned their own.

Like millions of others,   15
I too come to this island,
nine decades the answerer
of dreams.

Yet only one part of my blood loves that memory.
Another voice speaks   20

[1]*Ellis Island:* site where U.S. Immigration and Naturalization Service examined and
  processed immigrants from 1892 to 1943. It is now a national park.
[2]*Slovak:* Slavic people of eastern Czechoslovakia.
[3]*quarantine:* isolation of newly arrived immigrants to ensure they had no communicable
  diseases before they were released.
[4]*Circle Line:* company that runs ferries to Liberty Island, Ellis Island, and around Manhattan Island.

of native lands
within this nation.
Lands invaded
when the earth became owned.
Lands of those who followed   25
the changing Moon,
knowledge of the seasons
in their veins.

Talking It Through

This poem is written in free verse, a form that depends for its effects on flowing rhythms and striking imagery, and has no regular pattern of rhyme and rhythm. The poet directs the reading of his work by means of line breaks—how the phrases and sentences are arranged on the page—and by the visual spacing of sections of his poem.

1. In "Ellis Island," the first and longest portion describes a boat trip to "the island of the tall woman." Can you tell by Bruchac's description of her, "green as dreams . . . ," who this woman is? What does the poet mean when he says "waiting for those who'd worked/ a thousand years/ yet never owned their own"?

   This passage is rich with metaphorical language, which compares unlike things to create strong images and feelings. A simile is a kind of metaphor, using *like* or *as* to connect the items compared. "Green as dreams" is an example of simile. Look for others as you read the poetry in this text.

2. The middle section, or stanza of this poem, tells you that for "nine decades" or ninety years (from the writing of the poem) this place has been "the answerer of dreams."

   Explain the poet's meaning here. What draws him to this island?

3. In the third stanza "another voice speaks." Whose voice is it? In what way does the author contrast the experiences of the "two Slovak children" at the beginning of the poem with the other part of his heritage? How does he regard his mixed ancestry?

4. What does Bruchac mean when he talks about "native lands within this nation"? Immigrants often look back with sentimental longing (nostalgia) toward their "native land," the one left behind. In what ways have Bruchac's other ancestors had to leave theirs behind? What do you think remains? Is there an Ellis Island experience for Native Americans?

Writer's Workshop

1. Write a poem of two voices that contrast with each other in their view of a single subject. It could be something like City Night, Country Night or A Cat Lover, A Cat Hater. It might be a poem that contrasts the views and impressions of a young person and an older person listening to the same piece of music.

   Change stanzas to emphasize the different voices as Bruchac does. Try to use similar line patterns and rhythms in each stanza.

2. How do similes make you "see" in original ways? The comparisons should be *fresh*. (An example of a trite, or stale, simile is "fresh as a daisy" because it is so overused that it becomes uninteresting or commonplace, or what is called a cliché.)

   Make your own list of similes, starting with the following: fresh as _____, tired as _____, green as _____, shiny as _____, happy as _____, sweet as _____, small as _____, fierce as _____, cold as _____. Share these with classmates, discarding any that another student also has come up with or that many people have heard before.

   You may use a word or phrase, as Bruchac did, to complete your simile. Try for a comparison that you really think is valid, yet which makes the reader appreciate a new relationship between ordinarily unlike things. When you get several that you like, take your favorite simile and use the adjective as the title of your poem. Then use the simile as a springboard to other images to convey your feelings about the subject.

3. If you had an "answerer of dreams," what would you ask for? Write a series of requests to the answerer of dreams.

Brothers: We
★ *Have Heard* ★
the Talk . . .

SPECKLED SNAKE

In 1829 the aged Creek chief Speckled Snake spoke to his people about President Andrew Jackson's advice that they move west of the Mississippi River.

BROTHERS: WE HAVE HEARD THE TALK OF OUR GREAT FATHER;[1] IT IS VERY kind. He says he loves his red children. . . .

When the first white man came over the wide waters, he was but a little man . . . very little. His legs were cramped by sitting long in his big boat, and he begged for a little land. . . .

When he came to these shores the Indians gave him land, and kindled fires to make him comfortable. . . .

But when the white man had warmed himself at the Indian's fire, and had filled himself with the Indian's hominy,[2] he became very large. He stopped not at the mountain tops, and his foot covered the plains and the valleys. His hands grasped the eastern and western seas. Then he became our Great Father. He loved his red children, but he said: "You must move a little farther, lest by accident I tread on you."

With one foot he pushed the red men across the Oconee, and with the other he trampled down the graves of our fathers. . . .

On another occasion he said, "Get a little farther; go beyond the Oconee

---

[1]*Great Father:* Native American description of the President of the United States.

[2]*hominy:* food made from corn, a crop unknown in Europe at the time and native to the American continent.

and the Ocmulgee[3]—there is a pleasant country." He also said, "It shall be yours forever."

Now he says, "The land you live upon is not yours. Go beyond the Mississippi; there is game; there you may remain while the grass grows and the rivers run."

Will not our Great Father come there also? He loves his red children, and his tongue is not forked.[4]

Brothers! I have listened to a great many talks from our Great Father. But they always began and ended in this—"Get a little farther; you are too near me." I have spoken.

★ ★ ★ ★ ★

Talking It Through

1. Oratory is skill or eloquence in delivering a speech. What about this piece lets you know that it is a speech? How does it begin and end? What is the speaker's purpose? What qualities of oratory do you notice that would make it an effective speech?

2. How does Speckled Snake use his image of the "first white man" to ridicule those who took over Native American lands? How does this "little man" become the "Great Father"?

3. According to Speckled Snake, when the Great Father told the Native Americans to settle west of the Oconee and Ocmulgee, he gave them the land forever. What is the Great Father telling them now?

4. When Speckled Snake tells us that the Great Father's tongue "is not forked," he is using irony. Irony is a mode of expression in which the writer says one thing, but actually means something different. How does Speckled Snake make it clear that the Great Father's tongue is forked, that he lied before and that he is lying now?

5. What other uses of irony can you find in this speech? For example, look at how Speckled Snake uses the term "Great Father." How should a father act? How does this one behave?

6. You may have noted in your first reading of this speech that Speckled Snake uses repetition (repeating words and phrases) as a literary device.

---

[3] *the Oconee and the Ocmulgee:* Indian settlements in what is now South Carolina and Georgia.

[4] *tongue is not forked:* does not lie or deceive.

Why is repetition an especially powerful device for Speckled Snake to use to deliver his particular message?

Writer's Workshop

1. Speckled Snake makes use of irony in his speech. To understand the effect, rewrite the ironic parts of the speech in a literal, direct way. For example, you might begin:

   > Brothers: We have heard the talk of the President; it is very cruel. He really hates us. . . .

   Speckled Snake also makes use of caricature. He ridicules the white man by exaggerating a physical characteristic. The white man was "very little" when he arrived on these shores. He "became very large" after the Indian gave him shelter and food. Rewrite those parts of the speech that use caricature.

   When you have finished, write a brief essay comparing your version of Speckled Snake's speech with the original. Describe the different effects on an audience. Which version is more interesting? Why? More persuasive? Why? Which expresses a deeper anger? Why do you think so?

2. Imagine that you are a Creek listening to Speckled Snake in 1829. What would be your thoughts and feelings? How might you express them? Write your own speech to be given after Speckled Snake's. Address your audience directly in as persuasive a manner as possible. Use repetition.

from American Indian Stories

★ ★

Z I T K A L A - Š A

Zitkala-Ša, a Dakota Sioux of the Yankton reservation, was born in 1876. At the age of eight, she traveled with other children of her tribe to White's Manual Institute in Wabash, Indiana. The purpose of this Quaker missionary school was to convert Indians to Christian beliefs and to teach them the ways of white society. In the process, the Indians were required to give up tribal beliefs, cultures, customs, and languages. It was three years before she would return home and see her mother again. In these passages, she records her first experiences in a bewildering alien environment.

THE CUTTING OF MY LONG HAIR

THE FIRST DAY IN THE LAND OF APPLES WAS A BITTER-COLD ONE; FOR THE snow still covered the ground, and the trees were bare. A large bell rang for breakfast, its loud metallic voice crashing through the belfry overhead and into our sensitive ears. The annoying clatter of shoes on bare floors gave us no peace. The constant clash of harsh noises, with an undercurrent of many voices murmuring an unknown tongue, made a bedlam[1] within which I was securely tied. And though my spirit tore itself in struggling for its lost freedom, all was useless.

A paleface woman, with white hair, came up after us. We were placed in a line of girls who were marching into the dining room. These were Indian girls, in stiff shoes and closely clinging dresses. The small girls wore sleeved aprons and shingled hair. As I walked noiselessly in my soft moccasins, I felt like sinking to the floor, for my blanket had been stripped from my shoulders. I looked hard at the Indian girls, who seemed not to care that they were even more immodestly dressed than I, in their tightly fitting clothes. While we marched in, the boys entered at an opposite door.

[1]*Bedlam:* a scene of wild uproar and confusion. St. Mary of Bethlehem was a London insane asylum popularly called "Bedlam."

I watched for the three young braves who came in our party. I spied them in the rear ranks, looking as uncomfortable as I felt.

A small bell was tapped, and each of the pupils drew a chair from under the table. Supposing this act meant they were to be seated, I pulled out mine and at once slipped into it from one side. But when I turned my head, I saw that I was the only one seated, and all the rest at our table remained standing. Just as I began to rise, looking shyly around to see how chairs were to be used, a second bell was sounded. All were seated at last, and I had to crawl back into my chair again. I heard a man's voice at one end of the hall, and I looked around to see him. But all the others hung their heads over their plates. As I glanced at the long chain of tables, I caught the eyes of a paleface woman upon me. Immediately I dropped my eyes, wondering why I was so keenly watched by the strange woman. The man ceased his mutterings, and then a third bell was tapped. Every one picked up his knife and fork and began eating. I began crying instead, for by this time I was afraid to venture anything more.

But this eating by formula was not the hardest trial in that first day. Late in the morning, my friend Judéwin gave me a terrible warning. Judéwin knew a few words of English, and she had overheard the paleface woman talk about cutting our long, heavy hair. Our mothers had taught us that only unskilled warriors who were captured had their hair shingled by the enemy. Among our people, short hair was worn by mourners, and shingled hair by cowards!

We discussed our fate some moments, and when Judéwin said, "We have to submit, because they are strong," I rebelled.

"No, I will not submit! I will struggle first!" I answered.

I watched my chance, and when no one noticed I disappeared. I crept up the stairs as quietly as I could in my squeaking shoes,—my moccasins had been exchanged for shoes. Along the hall I passed, without knowing whither I was going. Turning aside to an open door, I found a large room with three white beds in it. The windows were covered with dark green curtains, which made the room very dim. Thankful that no one was there, I directed my steps toward the corner farthest from the door. On my hands and knees I crawled under the bed, and cuddled myself in the dark corner.

From my hiding place I peered out, shuddering with fear whenever I heard footsteps near by. Though in the hall loud voices were calling my name, and I knew that even Judéwin was searching for me, I did not open my mouth to answer. Then the steps were quickened and the voices became excited. The sounds came nearer and nearer. Women and girls entered the room. I held my breath and watched them open closet doors and peep behind large trunks. Some one threw up the curtains, and the room was filled with sudden light. What caused them to stoop and look under the bed

I do not know. I remember being dragged out, though I resisted by kicking and scratching wildly. In spite of myself, I was carried downstairs and tied fast in a chair.

I cried aloud, shaking my head all the while until I felt the cold blades of the scissors against my neck, and heard them gnaw off one of my thick braids. Then I lost my spirit. Since the day I was taken from my mother I had suffered extreme indignities.[2] People had stared at me. I had been tossed about in the air like a wooden puppet. And now my long hair was shingled like a coward's! In my anguish I moaned for my mother, but no one came to comfort me. Not a soul reasoned quietly with me, as my own mother used to do; for now I was only one of many little animals driven by a herder.

THE SNOW EPISODE

A SHORT TIME AFTER OUR ARRIVAL WE THREE DAKOTAS[3] WERE PLAYING IN the snowdrift. We were all still deaf to the English language, excepting Judéwin, who always heard such puzzling things. One morning we learned through her ears that we were forbidden to fall lengthwise in the snow, as we had been doing, to see our own impressions. However, before many hours we had forgotten the order, and were having great sport in the snow, when a shrill voice called us. Looking up, we saw an imperative hand beckoning us into the house. We shook the snow off ourselves, and started toward the woman as slowly as we dared.

Judéwin said: "Now the paleface is angry with us. She is going to punish us for falling into the snow. If she looks straight into your eyes and talks loudly, you must wait until she stops. Then, after a tiny pause, say, 'No.' " The rest of the way we practiced upon the little word "no."

As it happened, Thowin was summoned to judgment first. The door shut behind her with a click.

Judéwin and I stood silently listening at the keyhole. The paleface woman talked in very severe tones. Her words fell from her lips like crackling embers, and her inflection ran up like the small end of a switch. I understood her voice better than the things she was saying. I was certain we had made her very impatient with us. Judéwin heard enough of the words to realize all too late that she had taught us the wrong reply.

"Oh, poor Thowin!" she gasped, as she put both hands over her ears.

---

[2]*indignities:* slighting or humiliating treatment; insulting one's dignity or worthiness.

[3]*Dakotas:* The Dakotas were an offshoot of the Sioux Indians whose former habitat was in the region of North and South Dakota.

Just then I heard Thowin's tremulous[4] answer, "No."

With an angry exclamation, the woman gave her a hard spanking. Then she stopped to say something. Judéwin said it was this: "Are you going to obey my word the next time?"

Thowin answered again with the only word at her command, "No."

This time the woman meant her blows to smart, for the poor frightened girl shrieked at the top of her voice. In the midst of the whipping the blows ceased abruptly, and the woman asked another question: "Are you going to fall in the snow again?"

Thowin gave her bad password another trial. We heard her say feebly, "No! No!"

With this the woman hid away her half-worn slipper, and led the child out, stroking her black shorn head. Perhaps it occurred to her that brute force is not the solution for such a problem. She did nothing to Judéwin nor to me. She only returned to us our unhappy comrade, and left us alone in the room.

During the first two or three seasons misunderstandings as ridiculous as this one of the snow episode frequently took place, bringing unjustifiable frights and punishments into our little lives.

Within a year I was able to express myself somewhat in broken English. As soon as I comprehended a part of what was said and done, a mischievous spirit of revenge possessed me. One day I was called in from my play for some misconduct. I had disregarded a rule which seemed to me very needlessly binding. I was sent into the kitchen to mash the turnips for dinner. It was noon, and steaming dishes were hastily carried into the dining-room. I hated turnips, and their odor which came from the brown jar was offensive to me. With fire in my heart, I took the wooden tool that the paleface woman held out to me. I stood upon a step, and, grasping the handle with both hands, I bent in hot rage over the turnips. I worked my vengeance upon them. All were so busily occupied that no one noticed me. I saw that the turnips were in a pulp, and that further beating could not improve them; but the order was, "Mash these turnips," and mash them I would! I renewed my energy; and as I sent the masher into the bottom of the jar, I felt a satisfying sensation that the weight of my body had gone into it.

Just here a paleface woman came up to my table. As she looked into the jar, she shoved my hands roughly aside. I stood fearless and angry. She placed her red hands upon the rim of the jar. Then she gave one lift and strode away from the table. But lo! the pulpy contents fell through the crumbled bottom to the floor! She spared me no scolding phrases that I had

---

[4]*tremulous:* timid, fearful; trembling from fear or nervousness.

earned. I did not heed them. I felt triumphant in my revenge, though deep within me I was a wee bit sorry to have broken the jar.

As I sat eating my dinner, and saw that no turnips were served, I whooped in my heart for having once asserted the rebellion within me.

★ ★ ★ ★ ★

Talking It Through

The Cutting of My Long Hair

1. We use the expression "culture shock" to describe differences in customs, values, or ideas experienced by those who encounter a sharp shift in their accustomed environment. How does the author of the piece experience this? What can you tell about her past life from her reactions to the new setting?

   What are her first sensory impressions? How do they affect her? What contrasts between the Indian ways and her own circumstances does she speak of?

2. What is Judéwin's warning? Why does Zitkala-Ša consider this to be such a calamity? In your opinion, is her effort to resist worthwhile? Give your reasons.

3. How does the author use descriptive language to dramatize her feelings? Find passages which for you are especially meaningful. Discuss these with the class.

The Snow Episode

4. How does the language barrier add to the difficulties of life at the Indian boarding school? Do those in authority seem, from the children's point of view, sympathetic or arbitrary?

5. How does Zitkala-Ša avenge one of the "frights and punishments" that the children were subjected to?

6. A *symbol* is a word, phrase, or image having a number of associated meanings which may itself stand for that which it represents. What symbolic value or meaning does the jar of turnips have for the author?

7. To the Native American children, the demands of the authorities seem bewildering. How might the missionary school staff justify their rules and expectations?

Writer's Workshop

1. Zitkala-Ša says that she heard the scissors "gnaw" off one of her thick braids and that as it did so, she lost her "spirit." She became "only one of many little animals driven by a herder."

   Write an essay to explain what the author means by "spirit," and what you think is the cost of conforming to prevailing social customs. Does her experience apply to life situations today? Use examples to illustrate your point of view.

2. In both of these chapters, the author's recollections are strengthened by her strong sensory impressions of remembered events. Sounds and odors, as well as visual images, make her writing vivid for the reader.

   Delve into your own memory for moments or incidents where one or more of your senses strongly imprinted an event or experience. Try to bring back the feelings and impressions triggered by such small details as Zitkala-Ša recalls. Use them to shape a personal essay.

★ *This We Know* ★

CHIEF SEATTLE

There are many versions of the speech made by Suquamish Chief Seattle in 1855 when he was forced to sell his tribal lands. Historians have recently pointed out that interpretations have not always given a true picture of Chief Seattle's way of life.

THE PRESIDENT IN WASHINGTON SENDS WORD THAT HE WISHES TO BUY our land. But how can you buy or sell the sky? The land? The idea is strange to us. If we do not own the freshness of the air and the sparkle of the water, how can you buy them?

Every part of this earth is sacred to my people. Every shining pine needle, every sandy shore, every mist in the dark woods, every meadow, every humming insect. All are holy in the memory and experience of my people.

We know the sap which courses through the trees as we know the blood that courses through our veins. We are part of the earth and it is part of us. The perfumed flowers are our sisters. The bear, the deer, the great eagle, these are our brothers. The rocky crests, the juices in the meadow, the body heat of the pony, and man, all belong to the same family.

The shining water that moves in the streams and rivers is not just water, but the blood of our ancestors. If we sell you our land, you must remember that it is sacred. Each ghostly reflection in the clear water of the lakes tells of events and memories in the life of my people. The water's murmur is the voice of my father's father.

The rivers are our brothers. They quench our thirst. They carry our canoes and feed our children. So you must give to the rivers the kindness you would give any brother.

If we sell you our land, remember that the air is precious to us, that the air shares its spirit with all the life it supports. The wind that gave our grandfather his first breath also receives his last sigh. The wind also gives our children the spirit of life. So if we sell you our land, you must keep it apart and sacred, as a place where man can go to taste the wind that is sweetened by the meadow flowers.

Will you teach your children what we have taught our children? That the earth is our mother? What befalls the earth, befalls all the sons of the earth.

This we know: The earth does not belong to man, man belongs to the earth. All things are connected like the blood which unites us all. Man did not weave the web of life, he is merely a strand in it. Whatever he does to the web, he does to himself.

One thing we know: Our god is also your god. The earth is precious to him and to harm the earth is to heap contempt on its creator.

Your destiny is a mystery to us. What will happen when the buffalo[1] are all slaughtered? The wild horses tamed? What will happen when the secret corners of the forest are heavy with the scent of many men and the view of the ripe hills is blotted by talking wires?[2] Where will the thicket be? Gone! Where will the eagle be? Gone! And what is it to say goodbye to the swift pony and the hunt? The end of living and the beginning of survival.

When the last Red Man has vanished with his wilderness and his memory is only the shadow of a cloud moving across the prairie, will these shores

[1] *buffalo:* The buffalo provided the Plains Indians with food, clothing, and tools. It was hunted nearly to extinction by white settlers.

[2] *talking wires:* telegraph poles.

and forests still be here? Will there be any of the spirit of my people left?

We love this earth as a newborn loves its mother's heartbeat. So, if we sell you our land, love it as we have loved it. Care for it as we have cared for it. Hold in your mind the memory of the land as it is when you receive it. Preserve the land for all children and love it, as God loves us all.

As we are part of the land, you too are part of the land. This earth is precious to us. It is also precious to you. One thing we know: There is only one God. No man, be he Red Man or White Man can be apart. We *are* brothers after all.

★ ★ ★ ★ ★

Talking It Through

1. Chief Seattle structures his speech through a series of questions and answers. He first asks, "But how can you buy or sell the sky? The land?" In the first two paragraphs, he uses many poetic images. How do they function to support his view that it is difficult to sell the land?

2. Chief Seattle believes the "earth is our mother." In the next few paragraphs he also talks about nature as a brother and sister. Here he is using metaphor, a figure of speech in which two things are compared without the use of *like* or *as*. What are some of the specific images he uses to help us see the earth and humanity's relationship to it as his culture does?

3. There are many places in this speech where the speaker repeats a word, or series of words, in a question or answer. Find some of the words or phrases he repeats. Why do you think he uses repetition?

4. What is it that Chief Seattle is asking us to do with the land? Have we done it? What does he mean by "The end of living and the beginning of survival"? In your opinion are we and the other animals on the earth living in such a time? Explain.

5. Although Chief Seattle could end on a note of anger and sadness because he is being forced to cede his people's land, he chooses to end on a note of reconciliation. What are some of the reasons he might do so?

6. The last question posed by Chief Seattle is, "Will there be any of the spirit of my people left?" Chief Seattle is probably speaking of his specific tribe and, of course, many Native American cultures are now extinct. But taking the question in its broader meaning, what legacy do you think the native peoples of America have left us in general? In what ways is their culture still alive and part of our heritage as well as their own?

Writer's Workshop

1. Write an essay comparing the speeches of Chief Speckled Snake and Chief Seattle. Speckled Snake is trying to convince his people not to trust the white man and therefore not to sell their land. Chief Seattle, speaking nearly thirty years later, may seem more resigned to the fate in store for his people and their land. In what way is the tone (angry, earnest, prophetic, sarcastic, poetic) of their speeches different? What literary devices do both make use of, and to what effect? (Consider the use of repetition, irony, metaphor, caricature.) In what way has each chosen a style and tone effective for his particular message?

2. In an essay discuss the quote, "What befalls the earth, befalls all the sons of the earth." Do you agree with this statement? Why or why not? Find examples to defend your point of view.

3. Write a poem or poetic description which has been inspired by Chief Seattle. You could choose to develop new images and metaphors for Mother Earth, or to contrast the land Chief Seattle describes to what it has become today. Think of how repetition can be an effective technique.

★ *Grandfather* ★

SHIRLEY CRAWFORD

Shirley Crawford belongs to the Kalistel tribe. This poem was written when the author was a student at the Institute of American Indian Arts in Santa Fe, New Mexico.

Grandfather sings, I dance.
Grandfather speaks, I listen.
Now I sing, who will dance?
I speak, who will listen?

Grandfather hunts, I learn.   5
Grandfather fishes, I clean.
Now I hunt, who will learn?
I fish, who will clean?

Grandfather dies, I weep.
Grandfather buried, I am left alone.   10
When I am dead, who will cry?
When I am buried, who will be alone?

Talking It Through

1. What do you feel the Grandfather represents or symbolizes in this poem? A symbol is a word for something concrete which also suggests a more abstract meaning.

2. In the previous selection Chief Seattle asks, "Will you teach your children what we have taught our children?" In what way is this poem also concerned with preserving culture and passing it on to future generations?

3. A stanza is a group of lines forming one of the divisions of a poem. It is usually several lines long and typically has a regular pattern in the number of lines and the arrangement of the words. How has the poet carefully arranged the way words repeat within each stanza? How is each stanza the same as or different from the one preceding? Why do you think the poet has chosen three stanzas for this poem? How do the repeated phrases enhance the author's message?

4. What are the verbs in this poem? In what tenses are the verbs? What is the only verb in the past tense? How do these verbs convey the poet's meaning?

5. What feelings does this poem convey to you? Why?

Writer's Workshop

1. Write a poem or essay about what a grandparent (or another elder person) has meant to you. What has this person been able to share with you?

2. In the poem "Grandfather," Shirley Crawford has used a grandparent as a *symbol*. The grandfather is not just an elderly relative, but may stand for something else. Write a poem about something which has become a symbol to you, or to many people in our society, such as the Statue of Liberty.

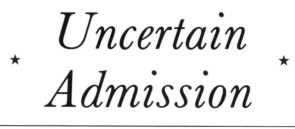

Uncertain Admission

★ ★

FRANCES BAZIL

Frances Bazil, a Coeur d'Alene Indian, wrote this poem while studying at the Institute of American Indian Arts.

The sky looks down on me in aimless blues
The sun glares at me with a questioning light
The mountains tower over me with uncertain shadows
The trees sway in the bewildered breeze
The deer dance in perplexed rhythms   5
The ants crawl around me in untrusting circles
The birds soar above me with doubtful dips and dives
They all, in their own way, ask the question, Who are
you, who are you?
I have to admit to them, to myself,   10
I am an Indian.

Talking It Through

1. What question is the world of nature asking the poet in this poem? How does the poet convey not being able to escape answering the question?

2. The poet takes inanimate objects (the mountains, sky, sun) and animals (deer, ants, birds) and makes it seem as if they are all posing a direct question. How does Bazil create this effect? What are some of the key words the poet chooses?

3. How many different ways might the poet have answered the question, "Who are you?" Why do you think the author has chosen to answer, "I am an Indian"?

4. Alliteration is the repetition of the first consonant sound in two or more closely adjoining words. Can you find an example of alliteration in this poem?

Writer's Workshop

1. Write a poem of your own in which you or another subject is asked "Who are you?" Who or what will ask the question in your poem? What will be the answer? (If modern appliances asked the question—a TV, a computer, a cassette player—how would you answer?)

2. Write an essay in which you use themes in this poem and compare them to the issues and themes in one other selection in "People of the Beginnings." Here are two choices:
   a. The role of identity in "Uncertain Admission" and "The Cutting of My Long Hair" by Zitkala-Ša.
   b. The theme of nature and identity in "Ellis Island" and "Uncertain Admission."

FRESH OFF THE BOAT

★ ★ ★ ★ ★
★ ★ ★ ★ ★
★ ★ ★ ★ ★
★ ★ ★ ★ ★
★ ★ ★ ★ ★
★ ★ ★ ★ ★

THIS UNIT CHARTS THE IMMIGRANT EXPERIENCE FROM THE moment of arrival, that hopeful time of wonder and anticipation, awe and anxiety, when the vast expanse of ocean traveled became a one-way passage to a place that was both a "promised land" and a land full of promise.

We begin with the account of William Bradford, who describes the terrors of the Pilgrims' voyage and first landing off Cape Cod when nothing but wilderness and unknown danger lay ahead and there was no turning back. Bradford speaks eloquently of his faith as one of those "chosen" by God to build a new life in America.

Succeeding immigrants voiced a similar optimism, lured by stories of freedom, wealth, and glory that drifted back to the "old country." Michael Pupin, who first heard of America as a peasant schoolboy in Europe and eventually became a celebrated inventor here, never for a moment doubted he would succeed, despite his penniless arrival and lack of English. For George Papashvily, being "fresh off the boat" afforded the opportunity to trade old ways for new. More contemporary arrivals, like Jamaica Kincaid's Lucy, and David Hwang's Steve still have their dreams, but their awkwardness in an unfamiliar setting may lead to misunderstanding or even ridicule. A common question arises in each of these selections: What does it feel like to be a stranger?

Of Their Voyage and Safe Arrival at Cape Cod

★   ★

WILLIAM BRADFORD

The Pilgrims came to America from England seeking religious freedom. William Bradford was on board the Mayflower when it landed, after sixty-five days at sea, at Cape Cod in 1620. Only half the settlers survived the first brutal winter in America. Bradford became the second governor of the colony, a post which he held for more than thirty years. In this excerpt from The History of Plymouth Plantation, *he describes their arrival.*

THESE TROUBLES BEING OVER, AND ALL BEING TOGETHER IN THE ONE SHIP, they put to sea again on September 6th with a prosperous wind, which continued for several days and was some encouragement to them, though, as usual, many were afflicted with seasickness. I must not omit to mention here a special example of God's providence.[1] There was an insolent and very profane[2] young man—one of the sailors,[3] which made him the more overbearing—who was always harassing the poor people in their sickness, and cursing them daily with grievous execrations[4] and did not hesitate to tell them that he hoped to help throw half of them overboard before they came to their journey's end . . . But it pleased God, before they came half

---

[1] *providence:* an example of the good guidance and care of God.

[2] *profane:* showing disrespect or contempt for religious things.

[3] *sailors:* The sailors were not members of the Separatist sect as were the Pilgrims who had hired them for the journey.

[4] *execrations:* curses.

seas over, to smite[5] the young man with a grievous disease, of which he died in a desperate manner, and so was himself the first to be thrown overboard. Thus his curses fell upon his own head, which astonished all his mates for they saw it was the just hand of God upon him.

After they had enjoyed fair winds and weather for some time, they encountered cross winds and many fierce storms by which the ship was much shaken and her upper works made very leaky. . . . But at length all opinions, the captain's and others' included, agreed that the ship was sound under the water-line. . . .

So they committed themselves to the will of God, and resolved to proceed. In several of these storms the wind was so strong and the seas so high that they could not carry a knot of sail, but were forced to hull[6] for many days . . . But to be brief, after long beating at sea, on November 11th they fell in with a part of the land called Cape Cod at which they were not a little joyful. . . .

Having found a good haven and being brought safely in sight of land, they fell upon their knees and blessed the God of Heaven who had brought them over the vast and furious ocean, and delivered them from all the perils and miseries of it, again to set their feet upon the firm and stable earth, their proper element. . . .

But here I cannot but make a pause, and stand half amazed at this poor people's present condition; and so I think will the reader, too, when he considers it well. Having thus passed the vast ocean . . . they now had no friends to welcome them, nor inns to entertain and refresh their weatherbeaten bodies, nor houses—much less towns—to repair[7] to. . . .

[The] savage barbarians when they met them were readier to fill their sides full of arrows than otherwise! As for the season, it was winter, and those who have experienced the winters of the country know them to be sharp and severe, and subject to fierce storms, when it is dangerous to travel to known places—much more to search an unknown coast. Besides, what could they see but a desolate wilderness, full of wild beasts and wild men; and what multitude there might be of them they knew not! Neither could they, as it were, go up to the top of Pisgah,[8] to view from this wilderness a more goodly country to feed their hopes; for which way soever they turned their eyes (save upward to the heavens!) they could gain little solace[9] from

---

[5]*smite:* to punish or destroy.

[6]*hull:* to float or drift with sails furled.

[7]*repair:* to go.

[8]*Pisgah:* The mountain from which Moses was permitted by God to view the Promised Land of Canaan.

[9]*solace:* comfort, relief.

any outward objects. Summer being done, all things turned upon them a weatherbeaten face; and the whole country, full of woods and thickets, presented a wild and savage view.

If they looked behind them, there was the mighty ocean which they had passed, and was now a gulf separating them from all civilized parts of the world. . . .

What, then, could now sustain them but the spirit of God, and his Grace? Ought not the children of their fathers rightly to say: Our fathers were Englishmen who came over the great ocean, and were ready to perish in this wilderness; but they cried unto the Lord and He heard their voice, and looked on their adversity.[10] . . . Let them therefore praise the Lord, because He is good and His mercies endure forever. Yea, let them that have been redeemed of the Lord, show how He hath delivered them from the hand of the oppressor. When they wandered forth into the desert wilderness . . . and found no city to dwell in, both hungry and thirsty, their soul was overwhelmed in them. Let them confess before the Lord His loving kindness, and his wonderful works before the sons of men!

★ ★ ★ ★ ★

Talking It Through

1. In the first paragraph, Bradford tells about a sailor who dies and whose body is thrown overboard. Why does Bradford believe the sailor died, and what does it tell us about the beliefs and attitudes of the Pilgrims? What kind of language does Bradford use to describe the event? How do these words give it added power?

2. The Pilgrims spent two-and-a-half months at sea on board the *Mayflower.* How does Bradford describe being at sea? What do the Pilgrims first do when they land?

3. How does Bradford describe the land? Make a list of the new hardships the Pilgrims must face. Which elements are to you most frightening? What words are repeated in this description and what is their effect?

4. Why does Bradford turn our view back to the ocean, after describing the land ("If they looked behind them . . .")?

5. After describing many hardships, Bradford ends with a prayer of Thanksgiving. Why do you think he does so? How does his prayer, which is based

---

[10]*adversity:* suffering.

on Psalm 107, summarize all that he has described before? What comparison is he making between the Pilgrims and the ancient Hebrews? In what way is America seen as a Promised Land?

6. Bradford himself was on the voyage he describes. Yet he never mentions his personal hardships or fears. Why do you think he might have described these events as an observer, rather than a participant? Does he win our sympathy by being further removed?

Writer's Workshop

1. Write a story or autobiographical account about the experience of being uprooted, of ending one life and beginning another. It could be about coming to a new country, or simply moving to a new town. If you prefer, set your story in the future and write a science fiction piece. What is being left behind? What is being hoped for in the "New World" ahead? Is there any symbol you can incorporate which dramatizes the moment of separation? The Statue of Liberty, Ellis Island, Plymouth Rock, all lie at the edge of the sea and beginning of land, marking the moment when one journey ends and a new one begins.

2. Imagine you are a Pilgrim with Bradford aboard the *Mayflower*. Write your own account of the events from a more personal point of view. What family members are with you? What are your fears and dreams? Try to use the language and outlook of the Pilgrims, describing events as *you* might have experienced them.

The
Hardships
★   ★
# of a Greenhorn

MICHAEL PUPIN

As a young Serbian immigrant, Michael Pupin, having sold his schoolbooks, watch, and a precious sheepskin coat to pay for his passage, left the port of Hamburg, Germany, in March 1874, and arrived at Castle Garden in New York City two weeks later. He had only five cents in his pocket, but persuaded the examiners to let him stay. Pupin later became a noted scientist and inventor in the field of electro-mechanics, and an honored and respected professor, proud of his American citizenship. Pupin won the Pulitzer Prize for From Immigrant to Inventor, *from which "The Hardships of a Greenhorn" is taken.*

MY FIRST NIGHT UNDER THE STARS AND STRIPES WAS SPENT IN CASTLE Garden.[1] It was a glorious night, I thought; no howling of the gales, no crashing of the waves, and no tumbling motion of the world beneath my feet, such as I had experienced on the immigrant ship. The feeling of being on *terra firma*[2] sank deep into my consciousness and I slept the sound sleep of a healthy youth, although my bed was a bare floor. The very early morning saw me at my breakfast, enjoying a huge bowl of hot coffee and a big chunk of bread with some butter, supplied by the Castle Garden authorities at Uncle Sam's expense. Then I started out, eager to catch a glimpse of great New York, feeling, in the words of the psalmist, "as a strong man ready to run a race." An old lady sat near the gate of Castle

---

[1] *Castle Garden:* was originally a fort built to defend New York during the War of 1812. In 1855 it became an immigration station. In 1896, it was put to use as an aquarium. Now it is a monument supervised by the National Park Service. It was replaced as a debarkation station by Ellis Island.

[2] *terra firma:* Latin, meaning firm or solid earth; dry land.

Garden offering cakes and candies for sale. A piece of prune pie caught my eye, and no true Serb[3] can resist the allurements of prunes. It is a national sweetmeat. I bought it, paying five cents for it, the only money I had, and then I made a bee-line across Battery Park, at the same time attending to my pie. My first bargain in America proved a failure. The prune pie was a deception; it was a prune pie filled with prune pits, and I thought of the words of my fellow passenger on the immigrant ship who had said: "No matter who you are or what you know or what you have you will be a greenhorn[4] when you land in America." The prune-pie transaction whispered into my ear: "Michael, you are a greenhorn; this is the first experience in your life as a greenhorn. Cheer up! Get ready to serve your apprenticeship as a greenhorn before you can establish your claim to any recognition," repeating the words of my prophetic fellow passenger who had served his apprenticeship in America. No prophet ever uttered a truer word.

The old Stevens House, a white building with green window-shutters, stood at the corner of Broadway and Bowling Green. When I reached this spot and saw the busy beehive called Broadway, with thousands of telegraph-wires stretching across it like a cobweb between huge buildings, I was overawed, and wondered what it meant. Neither Budapest, nor Prague, nor Hamburg had looked anything like it. My puzzled and panicky expression and the red fez[5] on my head must have attracted considerable attention, because suddenly I saw myself surrounded by a small crowd of boys of all sizes, jeering and laughing and pointing at my fez. They were newsboys and bootblacks, who appeared to be anxious to have some fun at my expense. I was embarrassed and much provoked, but controlled my Serbian temper. Presently one of the bigger fellows walked up to me and knocked the fez off my head. I punched him on the nose and then we clinched. My wrestling experiences on the pasturelands of Idvor came to my rescue. The bully was down in a jiffy, and his chums gave a loud cheer of ringing laughter. I thought it was a signal for general attack, but they did not touch me nor interfere in any way. They acted like impartial spectators,

---

[3]*Serb:* a native of Serbia, a former kingdom in southeastern Europe which at one point was the frontier of the Ottoman Empire. Serbians are a Slavic people with their own language and traditions. At one time they were part of the Austro-Hungarian Empire. After World War I they were incorporated as part of Yugoslavia.

[4]*greenhorn:* a raw, inexperienced person; originally applied to cattle with green (young) horns. Just-arrived immigrants were disparagingly referred to as "greenhorns."

[5]*fez:* a cone-shaped felt cap, usually red, ornamented with a long black tassel. Formerly the national headdress of the Turks, it was adopted by Serbians, according to Pupin, because they lived adjacent to Turks along the eastern border of their territory.

anxious to see that the best man won. Suddenly I felt a powerful hand pulling me up by the collar, and when I looked up I saw a big official with a club in his hand and a fierce expression in his eye. He looked decidedly unfriendly, but after listening to the appeals of the newsboys and bootblacks who witnessed the fight he softened and handed me my fez. The boys who a little while before had jeered and tried to guy[6] me, evidently appealed in my behalf when the policeman interfered. They had actually become my friends. When I walked away toward Castle Garden, with my red fez proudly cocked on my head, the boys cheered. I thought to myself that the unpleasant incident was worth my while, because it taught me that I was in a country where even among the street urchins there was a strong sentiment in favor of fair play even to a Serbian greenhorn. America was different from Austria-Hungary. I never forgot the lesson and never had a single reason to change my opinion.

A gentleman who had witnessed the fight joined me on my return trip to Castle Garden, and when we reached the employment bureau he offered me a job. When I learned that one of my daily duties would be to milk a cow, I refused. According to Serb traditions, milking a cow is decidedly a feminine job. Another gentleman, a Swiss foreman on a Delaware farm, offered me another job, which was to drive a team of mules and help in the work of hauling things to the field preparatory for spring planting. I accepted gladly, feeling confident that I knew all about driving animals, although I had never even seen a mule in all my experiences in Idvor. We left for Philadelphia that forenoon and caught there the early afternoon boat for Delaware City, where we arrived late in the afternoon.

As we passed through Philadelphia I asked the Swiss foreman whether that was the place where a hundred years before famous Benjamin Franklin flew his kite, and he answered that he had never heard of the gentleman, and that I must have meant William Penn. ''No,'' said I, ''because I never heard of this gentleman.'' ''You have still to learn a thing or two about American history,'' said the Swiss foreman, with a superior air. ''Yes, indeed,'' I said, ''and I intend to do it as soon as I have learned a thing or two about the English language''; and I wondered whether the Swiss foreman who had never heard of Benjamin Franklin and his kite had really learned a thing or two in American history, although he had lived some fifteen years in the United States.

There were quite a number of farmers on the Delaware boat, every one of them wearing a long goatee but no mustache; such was the fashion at that time. Every one of them had the brim of his slouch hat turned down, covering his eyes completely. As they conversed they looked like wooden

[6]*guy:* tease, make fun of.

images; they made no gestures and I could not catch the expression of their hidden eyes; without these powerful aids to the understanding of the spoken word I could not make out a single syllable in their speech. The English language sounded to me like an inarticulate mode of speech, just as inarticulate as the joints of those imperturbable Delaware farmers. I wondered whether I should ever succeed in learning a thing or two in this most peculiar tongue. I thought of the peasants at the neighborhood gatherings in Idvor, and of their winged words, each of which found its way straight into my soul. There also appeared before my mental vision the image of Baba Batikin, with fire in his eye and a vibratory movement of his hand accompanying his stirring tales of Prince Marko. How different and how superior those peasants of Idvor appeared to me when I compared them with the farmers on that Delaware boat! ''Impossible,'' said I, ''that a Serb peasant should be so much superior to the American peasant!'' Something wrong with my judgment, thought I, and I charged it to my being a greenhorn and unable to size up an American farmer.

At the boat-landing in Delaware City a farm-wagon was awaiting us, and we reached the farm at supper-time. The farm-buildings were fully a mile from the town, standing all by themselves; there was no village and there were no neighbors, and the place looked to me like a camp. There was no village life among American farmers, I was told, and I understood then why those farmers on the Delaware boat were so devoid of all animation. The farm-hands were all young fellows, but considerably older than myself, and when the foreman introduced me to them, by my Christian name, I found that most of them spoke German with a Swiss accent, the same which the foreman had who brought me from New York. One of them asked me how long I had been in the country, and when I told him that I was about twenty-four hours in the country, he smiled and said that he thought so, evidently on account of the unmistakable signs of a greenhorn which he saw all over me.

The first impression of an American farm was dismal. In the messroom, however, where supper was served, everything was neat and lovely, and the supper looked to me like a holiday feast. I became more reconciled to the American farm. The farm-hands ate much and spoke very little, and when they finished they left the dining-room without any ceremony. I was left alone, and moved my chair close to a warm stove and waited for somebody to tell me what to do next. Presently two women came in and proceeded to clear the supper-table; they spoke English and seemed to pay no attention to me. They probably thought that I was homesick and avoided disturbing me. Presently I saw a young girl, somewhat younger than myself. She pretended to be helping the women, but I soon discovered that she had another mission. Her appearance reminded me of a young Vila, a Serbian fairy, who in the old Serbian ballads plays a most wonderful part. No hero ever perished through misfortune who had the good fortune to win the friendship of a Vila. Supernatural both in intelligence and in physical skill, the Vilae could always find a way out of every difficulty. I felt certain that if there ever was a Vila this young girl was one. Her luminous blue eyes, her finely chiselled features, and her graceful movements made a strange impression upon me. I imagined that she could hear the faintest sound, that she could see in the darkest night, and that, like a real Vila, she could feel not only the faintest breezes but even the thoughts of people near her. She certainly felt my thoughts. Pointing to a table in a corner of the dining-room, she directed my attention to writing-paper and ink, placed there for the convenience of farm-hands. I understood her meaning, although I did not understand her words. I spent the evening writing a letter to my mother. This was my wish, and the Vila must have read it in my face.

One of the farm-hands, a Swiss, came in after a while in order to remind me that it was bedtime and to inform me that early in the morning he would wake me up and take me to the barn, where my job would be assigned to me. He kept his word, and with lantern in hand he took me long before sunrise to the barn and introduced me to two mules which he put in my charge. I cleaned them and fed them while he watched and directed; after breakfast he showed me how to harness and hitch them up. I took my turn in the line of teams hauling manure to the fields. He warned me not to apply myself too zealously to the work of loading and unloading, until I had become gradually broken in, otherwise I should be laid up stiff as a rod. The next day I was laid up, stiffer than a rod. He was much provoked, and called me the worst ''greenhorn'' that he ever saw. But, thanks to the skilled and tender care of the ladies on the farm, I was at my job again two days later. My being a greenhorn appealed to their sympathy; they seemed to have the same kind of soul which I had first observed in my American friends who paid my fare from Vienna to Prague.

One of my mules gave me much trouble, and the more he worried me the more amusement he seemed to furnish to the other farm-hands, rough immigrants of foreign birth. He did not bite, nor did he kick, as some of the mules did, but he protested violently against my putting the bridle on his head. The other farm-hands had no advice to offer; they seemed to enjoy my perplexity. I soon discovered that the troublesome mule could not stand anybody touching his ears. That was his ticklish spot. I finally got around it; I never took his bridle off on working-days, but only removed the bit, so that he could eat. On Sunday mornings, however, when I had all the time I wanted, I took his bridle off, cleaned it, and put it on, and did not remove it again for another week. The foreman and the superintendent discovered my trick and approved of it, and so the farm-hands lost the amusement which they had had at my expense every morning at the har-nessing hour. I noticed that they were impressed by my trick and did not address me by the name of greenhorn quite so often. They were also sur-prised to hear me make successful attempts to speak English. Nothing counts so much in the immigrant's bid for promotion to a grade above that of a greenhorn as the knowledge of the English language. In these efforts I received a most unexpected assistance, and for that I was much indebted to my red fez.

On every trip from the barnyard to the fields, my mules and I passed by the superintendent's quarters, and there behind the wall of neatly piled-up cord-wood I observed every now and then the golden curls of my American Vila. She cautiously watched there, just like a Serbian Vila at the edge of a forest. My red fez perched up on a high seat behind the mules obviously attracted and amused her. Whenever I caught her eye I saluted in regular Balkan fashion, and it was a salute such as she had never seen before in the State of Delaware. Her curiosity seemed to grow from day to day, and so did mine.

One evening I sat alone near the warm stove in the messroom and she came in and said: "Good evening!" I answered by repeating her greeting, but pronounced it badly. She corrected me, and, when I repeated her greeting the second time, I did much better, and she applauded my genuine effort. Then she proceeded to teach me English words for everything in the dining-room, and before that first lesson was over I knew some twenty English words and pronounced them to her satisfaction. The next day I repeated these words aloud over and over again during my trips to the fields, until I thought that even the mules knew them by heart. At the second lesson on the following evening I scored a high mark from my teacher and added twenty more words to my English vocabulary. As time went on, my vocabulary increased at a rapid rate, and my young teacher was most enthusiastic. She called me "smart," and I never forgot the word. One evening she brought in her mother, who two weeks previously had taken care of me when I was laid up from overzealous loading. At that time she could not make me understand a single word she said. This time, however, I had no difficulty, and she was greatly surprised and pleased. My first examination in English was a complete success.

At the end of the first month on the Delaware farm my confidence in the use of the English language had grown strong. During the second month I grew bold enough to join in lengthy conversations. The superintendent's wife invited me often to spend the evening with the family. My tales of Idvor, Panchevo, Budapest, Prague, Hamburg, and the immigrant ship interested them much, they said. My pronunciation and grammar amused them even more than they were willing to show. They were too polite to indulge in unrestrained laughter over my Serbian idioms. During these conversations the Vila sat still and seemed to be all attention. She was all eyes and ears, and I knew that she was making mental notes of every mistake in my grammar and pronunciation. At the next lesson she would correct every one of these mistakes, and then she watched at the next family gathering to see whether I should repeat them. But I did not; my highest ambition was to show myself worthy of the title "smart" which she had given me.

One evening I was relating to the superintendent's family how I had refused the first offer of a job at Castle Garden, because I did not care to accept the daily duty of milking a cow, which, according to my Serbian notions, was purely a feminine job. I admitted that Serbian and American notions were entirely different in this particular respect, because, although over a hundred cows were milked daily on the farm, I never saw a woman in any one of the many barns, nor in the huge creamery. I confessed also that both the Vila and her mother would be entirely out of place not only in the cow-barns but even in the scrupulously clean creamery, adding that if the Vila had been obliged to attend to the cows and to the creamery, she would not have found the time to teach me English, and, therefore, I preferred the American custom. Vila's mother was highly pleased with this remark and said: "Michael, my boy, you are beginning to understand our American ways, and the sooner you drop your Serbian notions the sooner you will become an American."

She explained to me the position of the American woman as that of the educator and spiritual guide of the coming generation, emphasizing the fact that the vast majority of teachers in American primary schools were women. This information astonished and pleased me, because I knew that my mother was a better teacher than my schoolmaster, an old man with a funny nasal twang. Her suggestion, however, that I should drop my Serbian notions and become an American as soon as possible disturbed me. But I said nothing; I was a greenhorn only and did not desire to express an opinion which might clash with hers. I thought it strange, however, that she took it for granted that I wished to become an American.

★ ★ ★ ★ ★

Talking It Through

1. How is Michael Pupin's optimism about America revealed in his first experiences "off the boat"? What impresses him about New York compared with Austria-Hungary?

2. What bias does he have against milking cows? How can you tell Pupin

already thinks he knows something about America despite his lack of English?

3. To what does Pupin attribute the differences between an American farmer and a Serbian peasant?

4. The young farm girl who clears the supper table reminds Pupin of a *Vila*. What do you learn from his description that gives you some insight into his personality? Is the comparison valid?

5. *Tone* is a particular style or manner of writing expressing mood. Often it reflects the audience for whom the author intends his work. In this selection Michael Pupin clearly communicates his own tone. How would you describe it?

   What does Pupin view as his major accomplishments during the course of his first employment in Delaware? Would the same series of events be subject to different interpretations if the author had a different tone?

Writer's Workshop

1. The term "greenhorn" is used by Michael Pupin to refer to himself. What does this seem to mean to him? Look for his observations about his condition throughout the selection. Use these to write an essay comparing his attitude with that of Americans he encounters. Emphasize similarities and difficulties in outlook.

   Could one be a greenhorn without being an immigrant? You might want to consider this point in your concluding paragraph.

2. Write the letter Michael Pupin sends to his mother. What would he choose to tell her about? What might he omit? Think about your *tone*.

3. Write about Michael Pupin's adventures as if he were depressed, missed his family terribly, and was pessimistic about his prospects. Write in the first person and use the events of the selection.

⋆ *The First Day* ⋆

GEORGE AND HELEN
WAITE PAPASHVILY

George Papashvily and his American wife collaborated on Anything Can
Happen, *a book recounting George's experiences as an immigrant from Georgia,
one of the republics of the former Soviet Union, to the United States shortly after
World War I (1914–1918).*

AT FIVE IN THE MORNING THE ENGINES STOPPED, AND AFTER THIRTY-SEVEN
days the boat was quiet.

We were in America.

I got up and stepped over the other men and looked out the porthole.
Water and fog. We were anchoring off an island. I dressed and went on
deck.

Now began my troubles. What to do? This was a Greek boat and I was
steerage,[1] so of course by the time we were half way out I had spent all my
landing money for extra food.

Hassan, the Turk, one of the six who slept in the cabin with me, came
up the ladder.

"I told you so," he said as soon as he saw me. "Now we are in America
and you have no money to land. They send you home. No money, no going
ashore. What a disgrace. In your position, frankly, I would kill myself."

Hassan had been satisfied to starve on black olives and salt cheese all the
way from Gibraltar, and he begrudged every skewer of lamb I bribed away
from the first-cabin steward.

We went down the gangplank[2] into the big room. Passengers with pictures in their hands was rushing around to match them to a relative. Before
their tables the inspectors was busy with long lines of people.

The visitors' door opened and a fellow with big pile of caps, striped blue
and white cotton caps with visors and a top button, came in. He went first

---

[1]*steerage:* the part of an ocean passenger ship occupied chiefly by immigrants. The
cheapest berths were in the hold, which was crowded, lacking in fresh air, sanitary
facilities, and headroom.

[2]*gangplank:* a temporary walkway for passengers from a ship to the dock or pier.

to an old man with a karakul[3] hat near the window, then to a Cossack[4] in the line. At last he came to me.

"Look," he said in Russian, "look at your hat. You want to be a green-horn all your life? A karakul hat! Do you expect to see anybody in the U.S.A. still with a fur hat? The customs inspector, the doctor, the captain—are they wearing fur hats? Certainly not."

I didn't say anything.

"Look," he said. "I'm sorry for you. I was a greenhorn once myself. I wouldn't want to see anybody make my mistakes. Look, I have caps. See, from such rich striped material. Like wears railroad engineers, and house painters, and coal miners." He spun one around on his finger. "Don't be afraid. It's a cap in real American style. With this cap on your head, they couldn't tell you from a citizen. I'm positively guaranteeing. And I'm trading you this cap even for your old karakul hat. Trading even. You don't have to give me one penny."

Now it is true I bought my karakul *coudie* new for the trip. It was a fine skin, a silver lamb, and in Georgia[5] it would have lasted me a lifetime. Still—

"I'll tell you," the cap man said. "So you can remember all your life you made money the first hour you were in America, I give you a cap and a dollar besides. Done?"

I took off my *coudie* and put on his cap. It was small and sat well up on my head, but then in America one dresses like an American and it is a satisfaction always to be in the best style. So I got my first dollar.

Ysaacs, a Syrian, sat on the bench and smoked brown paper cigarettes and watched all through the bargain. He was from our cabin, too, and he knew I was worried about the money to show the examiners. But now, as soon as the cap man went on to the next customer, Ysaacs explained a way to get me by the examiners—a good way.

Such a very good way, in fact, that when the inspector looked over my passport and entry permit I was ready.

"Do you have friends meeting you?" he asked me. "Do you have money to support yourself?"

I pulled out a round fat roll of green American money—tens, twenties—a nice thick pile with a rubber band around.

---

[3]*karakul:* a valuable, tightly curled fur from young lambs of the Astrakhan region of Russia. The skins were often made into a distinctively shaped hat.

[4]*Cossack:* member of a Russian group noted for horsemanship that provided irregular cavalry for the Russian army.

[5]*Georgia:* an independent republic of the former Soviet Union whose southern border is the shore of the Black Sea.

"O.K.," he said. "Go ahead." He stamped my papers.

I got my baggage and took the money roll back again to Ysaacs' friend, Arapouleopolus, the money lender, so he could rent it over again to another man. One dollar was all he charged to use it for each landing. Really a bargain.

On the outer platform I met Zurabeg, an Ossetian,[6] who had been down in steerage too. But Zurabeg was no greenhorn coming for the first time. Zurabeg was an American citizen with papers to prove it, and a friend of Gospadin Buffalo Bill[7] besides. This Zurabeg came first to America twenty years before as a trick show rider, and later he was boss cook on the road with the Gospadin Buffalo Bill. Every few years, Zurabeg, whenever he saved enough money, went home to find a wife—but so far with no luck.

"Can't land?" he asked me.

"No, I can land," I said, "but I have no money to pay the little boat to carry me to shore." A small boat went chuffing back and forth taking off the discharged passengers. "I try to make up my mind to swim, but if I swim how will I carry my baggage? It would need two trips at least."

"Listen, donkey-head," Zurabeg said. "This is America. The carrying boat is free. It belongs to my government. They take us for nothing. Come on."

So we got to the shore.

And there—the streets, the people, the noise! The faces flashing by— and by again. The screams and chatter and cries. But most of all the motion, back and forth, back and forth, pressing deeper and deeper on my eyeballs.

We walked a few blocks through this before I remembered my landing cards and passport and visas. I took them out and tore them into little pieces and threw them all in an ash can. "They can't prove I'm not a citizen, now," I said. "What we do next?"

"We get jobs," Zurabeg told me. "I show you."

We went to an employment agency. Conveniently, the man spoke Russian. He gave Zurabeg ticket right away to start in Russian restaurant as first cook.

"Now, your friend? What can you do?" he asked me.

"I," I said, "am a worker in decorative leathers particularly specializing in the ornamenting of crop handles according to the traditional designs."

---

[6]*Ossetian:* person from the Caucasus region of southeastern Russia.

[7]*Buffalo Bill:* (William Frederick Cody, 1846–1917). An American scout, Indian fighter, bison hunter, and guide, who in 1883 started a series of famous Wild West shows. Cowboys, Indians, animals, and personalities like Chief Sitting Bull and Annie Oakley were featured.

"My God!" the man said. "This is the U.S.A. No horses. Automobiles. What else can you do?"

Fortunately my father was a man of great foresight and I have two trades. His idea was that in the days when a man starves with one, by the other he may eat.

"I am also," I said, "a swordmaker. Short blades or long; daggers with or without chasing; hunting knives, plain or ornamented; tempering, fitting, pointing—" I took my certificate of successful completion of apprenticeship out of my *chemidon*.

"My God! A crop maker—a sword pointer. You better take him along for a dishwasher," he said to Zurabeg. "They can always use another dishwasher."

We went down into the earth and flew through tunnels in a train. It was like the caves under the Kazbeck where the giant bats sleep, and it smelled even worse.

The restaurant was on a side street and the ladyowner, the *hasaika*, spoke kindly. "I remember you from the tearoom," she said to Zurabeg. "I congratulate myself on getting you. You are excellent on the *piroshkis*,[8] isn't it?"

"On everything, madame," Zurabeg said grandly. "On everything. Buffalo Bill, an old friend of mine, has eaten thirty of my *piroshkis* at a meal. My friend—" he waved toward me— "will be a dishwasher."

I made a bow.

The kitchen was small and hot and fat—like inside of a pig's stomach. Zurabeg unpacked his knives, put on his cap, and, at home at once, started to dice celery.

"You can wash these," the *hasaika* said to me. "At four we have party."

It was a trayful of glasses. And such glasses—thin bubbles that would hardly hold a sip—set on stems. The first one snapped in my hand, the second dissolved, the third to tenth I got washed, the eleventh was already cracked, the twelfth rang once on the pan edge and was silent.

Perhaps I might be there yet, but just as I carried the first trayful to the service slot, the restaurant cat ran between my feet.

When I got all the glass swept up, I told Zurabeg, "Now, we have to eat. It's noon. I watch the customers eat. It makes me hungry. Prepare a *shashlik*[9] and some cucumbers, and we enjoy our first meal for good luck in the New World."

"This is a restaurant," Zurabeg said, "not a *duquani* on the side of the Georgian road where the proprietor and the house eat with the guests

---

[8]*piroshkis:* dumplings or tarts of dough enclosing meat, potatoes, or vegetable filling.
[9]*shashlik:* skewered meat, frequently lamb, usually broiled over charcoal.

together at one table. This is a restaurant with very strict organization. We get to eat when the customers go, and you get what the customers leave. Try again with the glasses and remember my reputation. Please.''

I found a quart of sour cream and went into the back alley and ate that and some bread and a jar of caviar which was very salty—packed for export, no doubt.

The *hasaika* found me. I stood up. ''Please,'' she said, ''please go on. Eat sour cream. But after, could you go away? Far away? With no hard feelings. The glasses—the caviar—it's expensive for me—and at the same time I don't want to make your friend mad. I need a good cook. If you could just go away? Quietly? Just disappear, so to speak? I give you five dollars.''

''I didn't do anything,'' I said, ''so you don't have to pay me. All in all, a restaurant probably isn't my fate. You can tell Zurabeg afterward.''

She brought my cap and a paper bag. I went down through the alley and into the street. I walked. I walked until my feet took fire in my shoes and my neck ached from looking. I walked for hours. I couldn't even be sure it was the same day. I tried some English on a few men that passed. ''What watch?'' I said. But they pushed by me so I knew I had it wrong. I tried another man. ''How many clock?'' He showed me on his wrist. Four-thirty.

A wonderful place. Rapidly, if one applies oneself, one speaks the English.

I came to a park and went in and found a place under a tree and took off my shoes and lay down. I looked in the bag the *hasaika* gave me. A sandwich from bologna and a nickel—to begin in America with.

What to do? While I decided, I slept.

A policeman was waking me up. He spoke. I shook my head I can't understand. Then with hands, with legs, rolling his eyes, turning his head, with motions, with gestures (really he was as good as marionettes I saw once in Tiflis), he showed me to lie on the grass is forbidden. But one is welcome to the seats instead. All free seats in this park. No charge for anybody. What a country.

But I was puzzled. There were iron arm rests every two feet along the benches. How could I distribute myself under them. I tried one leg. Then the other. But when I was under, how could I turn around? Then, whatever way I got in, my chin was always caught by the hoop. While I thought this over, I walked and bought peanuts for my nickel and fed the squirrels.

Lights began to come on in the towers around the park. It was almost dark. I found a sandy patch under a rock on little bluff above the drive. I cut a *shashlik* stick and built a fire of twigs and broiled my bologna over it and ate the bread. It lasted very short. Then I rolled up my coat for a pillow like the days during the war and went to sleep.

I was tired from America and I slept some hours. It must have been almost midnight when the light flashed in my face. I sat up. It was from the head lamp of a touring car choking along on the road below me. While I watched, the engine coughed and died. A man got out. For more than an hour he knocked with tools and opened the hood and closed it again.

Then I slid down the bank. In the war there were airplanes, and of course cars are much the same except, naturally, for the wings. I showed him with my hands and feet and head, like the policeman: "Give me the tools and let me try." He handed them over and sat down on the bench.

I checked the spark plugs and the distributor, the timer and the coils. I looked at the feed line, at the ignition, at the gas. In between, I cranked. I cranked until I cranked my heart out onto the ground. Still the car wouldn't move.

I got mad. I cursed it. I cursed it for a son of a mountain devi. I cursed it for the carriage of the diavels in the cave. I cursed it by the black-horned goat, and when I finished all I knew in Georgian I said it again in Russian to pick up the loose ends. Then I kicked the radiator as hard as I could. The car was old Model T,[10] and it started with a snort that shook the chassis like an aspen.

The man came running up. He was laughing and he shook my hands and talked at me and asked questions. But the policeman's method didn't work. Signs weren't enough. I remembered my dictionary—English-Russian, Russian-English—it went both ways. I took it from my blouse pocket and showed the man. Holding it under the headlights, he thumbed through.

"Work?" he found in English.

I looked at the Russian word beside it and shook my head.

"Home?" he turned to that.

"No," again.

I took the dictionary. "Boat. Today."

"Come home—" he showed me the words—"with me—" he pointed to himself. "Eat. Sleep. Job." It took him quite a time between words. "Job. Tomorrow."

"Automobiles?" I said. We have the same word in Georgian.

"Automobiles!" He was pleased we found one word together.

We got in his car, and he took me through miles and miles of streets with houses on both sides of every one of them until we came to his own. We went in and we ate and we drank and ate and drank again. For that, fortunately, you need no words.

---

[10]*Model T:* Henry Ford's first assemblyline automobile. In 1908, the first year of its production, 10,000 were sold. By 1912, Ford factories produced 75,000 identical cars.

Then his wife showed me a room and I went to bed. As I fell asleep, I thought to myself: Well, now, I have lived one whole day in America and—just like they say—America is a country where anything, anything at all can happen.

And in twenty years—about this—I never changed my mind.

★ ★ ★ ★ ★

Talking It Through

1. Compare Papashvily's fresh-off-the-boat experience of greenhornism with that of Michael Pupin. In each, the headgear they wear marks them as different, foreign, somewhat absurd in the eyes of Americans. Their ways of dealing with this are rather different. What argument helps to persuade George to trade his fine fur hat for a striped workman's cap of small value (and size)?

2. How does Papashvily deal with the problem of being denied landing for lack of adequate funds?

   The newcomers come from a long line of traders. Papashvily comments, "Really a bargain," after his first exchange involving U.S. currency. Compare this with Pupin's first expenditure in America. Who got the better deal? How do their attitudes compare?

3. When Papashvily meets his shipboard friend Zurabeg, he tells him, "I have no money to carry me to shore," and then explains how he *might* reach land. What device does he use to express his concerns? Is the tone serious?

4. Once ashore, what are George's very first impressions? Are they comparable to Michael Pupin's?

   How do their first experiences in the city compare? Could an immigrant's needs be so quickly satisfied today? What would be different?

5. What job skills does the author proudly offer? What does he discover about them? How does his first job turn out? How does he handle this?

6. Note Papashvily's first attempts to communicate in English. How are they similar to Pupin's? In what ways do they differ?

   The author's attempts to sleep on a park bench are frustrated. How does he cope?

7. Like Michael Pupin, George Papashvily has an upbeat attitude and is optimistic about his encounters. He is undaunted by his language difficulties and he exudes confidence.

How does the author let the reader know something about the state of his English at the time of the writing of these memoirs (about twenty years later)? How proficient is he? What effect does this have on the narrative?

Writer's Workshop

1. Papashvily's ability to perceive himself and his circumstances with detachment and good-natured objectivity gives this narrative a humorous style that engages the reader. Analyze the ways the authors accomplish this. Then think of a personal experience with a potential for embarrassment. Write about it so that the reader will both sympathize with and find humor in your plight.

2. Write a short piece using dialogue based on the incident in which George offers to fix the car as if the encounter were happening today. How successful would your protagonist (hero) be? How would he be treated? What outcome will your contemporary incident have?

3. In what sense does George Papashvily mean "Anything Can Happen"? Why do you think he gave that title to the book from which this selection was taken? Explain in an essay. Draw on materials from the selection for examples to back up your thesis or point of view.

★ *A Ship Unloads Her Cargo* ★

VILHELM MOBERG

Vilhelm Moberg is the author of a four-part saga, The Emigrants, *about a Swedish family who arrives in America in 1850. Like other immigrants seeking farmland, the Nilssons cross a treacherous ocean, only to begin a vast trek across the American continent in search of land as yet unclaimed by European settlers.*

Captain Lorentz, himself a Swede, is ". . . like a father with his children," eager to protect his charges from the unscrupulous cheats who prey on the newly arrived in the New York harbor. But he has his own problems as well. He is responsible for posting a three-hundred-dollar bond for any incurably sick immigrant aboard his ship.

THE PASSENGERS WERE NOW COMING TO THE CABIN TO COLLECT THEIR MONEY. A tall, husky man hit his forehead against the cabin ceiling as he came down the ladder. The captain said, "Look out for your skull! You might need it in America."

An unusually large nose protruded from the man's face; Captain Lorentz need not ask the name of this farmer, he remembered him well. One night during the voyage—while the worst tempest was raging—he had stanched a hemorrhage for this man's wife. The peasant had thanked him and said that his wife owed her life to the *Charlotta*'s captain.

He consulted the passenger list: "Karl Oskar Nilsson. Paid 515 rdr. bko."

At the exchange rate of one dollar for each two and a half daler, the farmer had two hundred and six dollars coming to him. But from this sum the captain must deduct the exchange fee and the landing fees for man, wife, brother and three children.

He told the farmer, "You have to pay thirty-seven and a half daler for six people."

"Is that the entrance fee to America?"

"We might call it that. There is also the exchange fee. Four dollars— that is, ten daler."

Lorentz counted and deducted: Balance to pay—a hundred and eighty-seven dollars. He counted out this sum in twenty-, ten-, and one-dollar coins, gold and silver, which he gave to the young farmer, who himself counted the money slowly and carefully. Then he put the coins, one at a time, into a homemade sheepskin belt which he carried around his waist under his shirt. The captain gave the hiding place a nod of approval.

The big-nosed farmer, having received his money, still remained standing in the cabin.

"Do you think you've been cheated in the exchange?" the captain asked.

"No. No, it isn't that. But I would like to ask you about something, Mr. Captain."

"Yes?"

Karl Oskar Nilsson continued: There were fifteen of them, eight full grown and seven children, all from Ljuder Parish in Smaland, who had undertaken the voyage together to this new country. Now they had been delayed at sea, the summer was already far advanced, and they were anxious to reach their destination as soon as possible, so as to be able to find land and get something planted before winter set in. All of those from Ljuder Parish intended to go to Minnesota, where land was said to be reasonably priced for people with little money. Now they wanted to continue their journey without delay; would the captain be kind enough to advise them how to get started inland?

"Have you any definite place in mind?"

"Yes. Here is the name."

From his purse Karl Oskar took out a soiled, worn piece of paper, once part of an envelope:

> Mister Anders Mansson
> Taylors Falls Past Offis
> Minnesota Territory
> North-America.

"Who gave you this address?" asked the captain.

"An old woman on board the ship. Mansson is her son. She's going to him and we'll all be in the same company; they say there's good land where her son lives."

"You rely on the woman? What's her name?"

"Fina-Kajsa. She is from Oland; her husband died in the first storm."

Captain Lorentz suddenly straightened. "You mean the old woman who is so sick?"

"She is better now, she says; she feels so well in her body she'll be able to go with the rest of us."

"Then you'll take the old woman in your company and be responsible for her?"

"Yes. She has money for her journey. And we'll look after her as best we can. When we get there, perhaps her son will help us find land."

The captain's face had suddenly lightened; it was not the first time Providence[1] had helped him out of a difficult dilemma. This time, apparently, Providence had chosen the farmer to get him out of his difficulty with Fina-Kajsa Andersdotter, and thus save his company three hundred dollars.

He handed the important piece of paper back to Karl Oskar.

"It's a long way to the territory of Minnesota. About fifteen hundred English miles, I believe."

"Is it so . . . so . . . far away?" Karl Oskar's face fell, and he scratched his head with its unkempt hair, yellow as barley straw, grown very long during the voyage from Sweden.

---

[1]*Providence:* an example of the care and good guidance of God.

"Of course, it's only two hundred and fifty Swedish miles," the captain hastened to assure him. He did not wish to frighten the farmer by dwelling on the journey's length, but rather to encourage him to undertake it. He continued: Every time he had transported farmers in search of land he had advised them to go as deep as possible into America; the farther west they went, the richer the soil was, and the broader were the regions to choose from. Most of the distance they could travel on river steamboats.

"Two hundred and fifty miles! It isn't exactly next door."

The infinitely long road which had worried Karl Oskar at first had shrunk to one-sixth, but it was still two hundred and fifty times the distance from Korpamoen to Ljuder church. He thought to himself, he must be careful how he spoke of the distance to others in his company; it might dishearten them.

"I will arrange the contract for the journey," Captain Lorentz assured him. "Including the Widow Andersdotter, there will be sixteen in your company?"

Karl Oskar had never seen this taciturn, unobliging man so talkative and willing to help as he was today. The captain spoke almost as to an equal: Yes, he often arranged contracts with honest companies for transportation inland. His conscience bade him help immigrants leave New York as soon as possible; they couldn't stay here in the harbor, they couldn't settle in Battery Park. And he knew an honest Swedish man in New York whom he often asked to guide the immigrants and act as their interpreter. The man's name was Landberg, he had once been carpenter on this very ship, the best carpenter Lorentz had ever had. But several years ago, when the captain was transporting a group of religious fanatics from Helsingland, followers of the widely known prophet Erik Janson, Landberg had been so taken by their religion that he left the ship in New York and joined the group. After half a year, Landberg had lost faith in the prophet, who had plundered him. The poor man had been forced to flee from Janson's tyranny penniless and practically naked. Landberg now earned his living by acting as interpreter and guide for Swedish immigrants. He spoke English fluently, and it was Captain Lorentz's custom to send for him as soon as the ship docked in New York. This time also he had notified the one-time carpenter, and Landberg had been given a pass by the health officer to come aboard the brig.

"How much would the interpreter cost?" Karl Oskar asked.

"It depends on the distance he must accompany you. I believe he charges three dollars for each grown person as far as Chicago."

"Hmmm . . . Well, we can't manage by ourselves. None of us can speak this tongue."

The captain thought, to leave these poor, helpless peasants to shift for themselves would be almost like driving a flock of sheep into a forest full of wolves. He said, "If you would like speedy transport inland, you must take the steam wagon from Albany. Landberg will get contracts with all the companies concerned."

"Thank you, Captain, for your great help."

It had been reported to the captain during the voyage that this big-nosed peasant had been dissatisfied with his quarters, had complained of the small ration of water, and had been insubordinate to the ship's officers. But Lorentz no longer disliked the man: Karl Oskar undoubtedly had a good head; and then, he was the tool of Providence.

". . . And you think the old woman is strong enough to be moved?"

"She says she is. She was on her feet again today."

It was indeed strange; a few days ago the Widow Andersdotter had been shaking in every limb with the ague, fallen off to the very bones from diarrhea. But such miraculous recoveries had happened before, and even though Lorentz had little use for the customs of the North American Republic, he had to admit that the mere sight of the country worked like magic on people; one day they were lying in their bunks sighing and crying and ready to die, unable to lift head from pillow, and the next day they were on their feet again. When semi-corpses saw the shores of America, they returned to life.

★ ★ ★ ★ ★

Talking It Through

1. What can we infer about the difficulties suffered by immigrants on board the *Charlotta*? What has the relationship between the Captain and Nilsson, the passenger, been like during the journey?

2. Captain Lorentz is a good man who has honestly exchanged his passengers' Swedish money for American dollars. Yet he does dupe Nilsson. How does he trick him, and why? Is there any humor in the ploy? Do you feel that Lorentz has been destructive or helpful in duping Nilsson?

3. Landberg, the Swedish interpreter and guide, has also been the victim of a hoax. What was it? Is there anyone in America, Swedish or otherwise, whom you feel the Nilssons will be able to trust completely? What other immigrants in "Fresh Off the Boat" have been taken advantage of?

4. What is the tone of this episode? Is it any less optimistic than Pupin's or Papashvily's arrival in America? If so, why or why not? Explain your reasons.

Writer's Workshop

1.   Write a brief continuation of the Nilssons' journey, as they seek to reach Minnesota. You may wish to do some research about the available modes of transportation in the 1850s. Later on Moberg writes, "Since leaving their home the immigrants had traveled by flat-wagon and sailing ship, by river boat and steam wagon, by canal boat and steamer." In your account, focus on Karl Oskar Nilsson's memories of the Captain. How do Nilsson's further adventures put into focus the Captain's advice? Is Nilsson, in retrospect, grateful or angry for the Captain's help?

2.   As the Nilssons cross the continent, Moberg writes: "The immigrants had passed through the portals of the West. They were on a new ship, and on the new ship they met a new sea, a sea unlike any they had ever seen or traversed: the prairie's own sea of grass."

   Write a poem or description in which you compare the American prairie to the sea. As you write about the landscape, incorporate images of the sea, thereby creating similes and metaphors.

★ *Poor Visitor* ★

JAMAICA KINCAID

Jamaica Kincaid grew up in Antigua, an island in the Caribbean, not far from Puerto Rico, and now lives in Vermont. "Poor Visitor" is the first chapter of her novel Lucy *which is about a teenaged girl from the Caribbean who comes to New England to work as an* au pair *(mother's helper). Jamaica Kincaid is also the author of* Annie John.

IT WAS MY FIRST DAY. I HAD COME THE NIGHT BEFORE, A GRAY-BLACK AND cold night before—as it was expected to be in the middle of January, though I didn't know that at the time—and I could not see anything clearly on the way in from the airport, even though there were lights everywhere. As we drove along, someone would single out to me a famous building, an important street, a park, a bridge that when built was thought to be a spectacle. In a daydream I used to have, all these places were points of happiness to me; all these places were lifeboats to my small drowning soul, for I would imagine myself entering and leaving them, and just that— entering and leaving over and over again—would see me through a bad feeling I did not have a name for. I only knew it felt a little like sadness but heavier than that. Now that I saw these places, they looked ordinary, dirty, worn down by so many people entering and leaving them in real life, and it occurred to me that I could not be the only person in the world for whom they were a fixture of fantasy. It was not my first bout with the disappointment of reality and it would not be my last. The undergarments that I wore were all new, bought for my journey, and as I sat in the car, twisting this way and that to get a good view of the sights before me, I was reminded of how uncomfortable the new can make you feel.

I got into an elevator, something I had never done before, and then I was in an apartment and seated at a table, eating food just taken from a refrigerator. In the place I had just come from, I always lived in a house, and my house did not have a refrigerator in it. Everything I was experiencing—the ride in the elevator, being in an apartment, eating day-old food that had been stored in a refrigerator—was such a good idea that I could imagine I would grow used to it and like it very much, but at first it was all so new that I had to smile with my mouth turned down at the corners. I slept soundly that night, but it wasn't because I was happy and comfortable—quite the opposite; it was because I didn't want to take in anything else.

That morning, the morning of my first day, the morning that followed my first night, was a sunny morning. It was not the sort of bright sun-yellow making everything curl at the edges, almost in fright, that I was used to, but a pale-yellow sun, as if the sun had grown weak from trying too hard to shine; but still it was sunny, and that was nice and made me miss my home less. And so, seeing the sun, I got up and put on a dress, a gay dress made out of madras cloth—the same sort of dress that I would wear if I were at home and setting out for a day in the country. It was all wrong. The sun was shining but the air was cold. It was the middle of January, after all. But I did not know that the sun could shine and the air remain cold; no one had ever told me. What a feeling that was! How can I explain? Something I had always known—the way I knew my skin was the color brown of a nut rubbed repeatedly with a soft cloth, or the way I knew my own name—something I took completely for granted, "the sun is shining, the air is warm," was not so. I was no longer in a tropical zone, and this realization now entered my life like a flow of water dividing formerly dry and solid ground, creating two banks, one of which was my past—so familiar and predictable that even my unhappiness then made me happy now just to think of it—the other my future, a gray blank, and overcast seascape on which rain was falling and no boats were in sight. I was no longer in a tropical zone and I felt cold inside and out, the first time such a sensation had come over me.

In books I had read—from time to time, when the plot called for it—someone would suffer from homesickness. A person would leave a not very nice situation and go somewhere else, somewhere a lot better, and then long to go back where it was not very nice. How impatient I would become with such a person, for I would feel that I was in a not very nice situation myself, and how I wanted to go somewhere else. But now I, too, felt that I wanted to be back where I came from. I understood it, I knew where I stood there. If I had had to draw a picture of my future then, it would have been a large gray patch surrounded by black, blacker, blackest.

What a surprise this was to me, that I longed to be back in the place that I came from, that I longed to sleep in a bed I had outgrown, that I longed to be with people whose smallest, most natural gesture would call up in me such a rage that I longed to see them all dead at my feet. Oh, I had imagined that with my one swift act—leaving home and coming to this new place—I could leave behind me, as if it were an old garment never to be worn again, my sad thoughts, my sad feelings, and my discontent with life in general as it presented itself to me. In the past, the thought of being in my present situation had been a comfort, but now I did not even have this to look forward to, and so I lay down on my bed and dreamt I was eating a bowl of pink mullet[1] and green figs cooked in coconut milk, and it had been cooked by my grandmother, which was why the taste of it pleased me so, for she was the person I liked best in all the world and those were the things I liked best to eat also.

The room in which I lay was a small room just off the kitchen—the maid's room. I was used to a small room, but this was a different sort of small room. The ceiling was very high and the walls went all the way up to the ceiling, enclosing the room like a box—a box in which cargo traveling a long way should be shipped. But I was not cargo. I was only an unhappy young woman living in a maid's room, and I was not even the maid. I was the young girl who watches over the children and goes to school at night. How nice everyone was to me, though, saying that I should regard them as my family and make myself at home. I believed them to be sincere, for I knew that such a thing would not be said to a member of their real family.

---

[1]*mullet:* a type of fish.

After all, aren't family the people who become the millstone[2] around your life's neck? On the last day I spent at home, my cousin—a girl I had known all my life, an unpleasant person even before her parents forced her to become a Seventh-Day Adventist—made a farewell present to me of her own Bible, and with it she made a little speech about God and goodness and blessings. Now it sat before me on a dresser, and I remembered how when we were children we would sit under my house and terrify and torment each other by reading out loud passages from the Book of Revelation, and I wondered if ever in my whole life a day would go by when these people I had left behind, my own family, would not appear before me in one way or another.

There was also a small radio on this dresser, and I had turned it on. At that moment, almost as if to sum up how I was feeling, a song came on, some of the words of which were "Put yourself in my place, if only for a day; see if you can stand the awful emptiness inside." I sang these words to myself over and over, as if they were a lullaby, and I fell alseep again. I dreamt then that I was holding in my hands one of my old cotton-flannel nightgowns, and it was printed with beautiful scenes of children playing with Christmas-tree decorations. The scenes printed on my nightgown were so real that I could actually hear the children laughing. I felt compelled to know where this nightgown came from, and I started to examine it furiously, looking for the label. I found it just where a label usually is, in the back, and it read "Made in Australia." I was awakened from this dream by the actual maid, a woman who had let me know right away, on meeting me, that she did not like me, and gave as her reason the way I talked. I thought it was because of something else, but I did not know what. As I opened my eyes, the word "Australia" stood between our faces, and I remembered then that Australia was settled as a prison for bad people, people so bad that they couldn't be put in a prison in their own country.

My waking hours soon took on a routine. I walked four small girls to their school, and when they returned at midday, I gave them a lunch of soup from a tin, and sandwiches. In the afternoon, I read to them and played with them. When they were away, I studied my books, and at night I went to school. I was unhappy. I looked at a map. An ocean stood between me and the place I came from, but would it have made a difference if it had been a teacup of water? I could not go back.

Outside, always it was cold, and everyone said that it was the coldest winter they had ever experienced; but the way they said it made me think they said this every time winter came around. And I couldn't blame them for not really remembering each year how unpleasant, how unfriendly

---

[2]*millstone:* heavy burden.

winter weather could be. The trees with their bare, still limbs looked dead, and as if someone had just placed them there and planned to come back and get them later; all the windows of the houses were shut tight, the way windows are shut up when a house will be empty for a long time; when people walked on the streets they did it quickly, as if they were doing something behind someone's back, as if they didn't want to draw attention to themselves, as if being out in the cold too long would cause them to dissolve. How I longed to see someone lingering on a corner, trying to draw my attention to him, trying to engage me in conversation, someone complaining to himself in a voice I could overhear about a God whose love and mercy fell on the just and the unjust.

I wrote home to say how lovely everything was, and I used flourishing words and phrases, as if I were living life in a greeting card—the kind that has a satin ribbon on it, and quilted hearts and roses, and is expected to be so precious to the person receiving it that the manufacturer has placed a leaf of plastic on the front to protect it. Everyone I wrote to said how nice it was to hear from me, how nice it was to know that I was doing well, that I was very much missed, and that they couldn't wait until the day came when I returned.

One day the maid who said she did not like me because of the way I talked told me that she was sure I could not dance. She said that I spoke like a nun, I walked like one also, and that everything about me was so pious it made her feel at once sick to her stomach and sick with pity just to look at me. And so, perhaps giving way to the latter feeling, she said that we should dance, even though she was quite sure I didn't know how. There was a little portable record-player in my room, the kind that when closed up looked like a ladies' vanity case, and she put on a record she had bought earlier that day. It was a song that was very popular at the time—three girls, not older than I was, singing in harmony and in a very insincere and artificial way about love and so on. It was very beautiful all the same, and it was beautiful because it was so insincere and artificial. She enjoyed this song, singing at the top of her voice, and she was a wonderful dancer—it amazed me to see the way in which she moved. I could not join her and I told her why: the melodies of her song were so shallow, and the words, to me, were meaningless. From her face, I could see she had only one feeling about me: how sick to her stomach I made her. And so I said that I knew songs, too, and I burst into a calypso about a girl who ran away to Port-of-Spain, Trinidad, and had a good time, with no regrets.

The household in which I lived was made up of a husband, a wife, and the four girl children. The husband and wife looked alike and their four children looked just like them. In photographs of themselves, which they placed all over the house, their six yellow-haired heads of various sizes were bunched as if they were a bouquet of flowers tied together by an unseen string. In the pictures, they smiled out at the world, giving the impression that they found everything in it unbearably wonderful. And it was not a farce, their smiles. From wherever they had gone, and they seemed to have been all over the world, they brought back some tiny memento, and they could each recite its history from its very beginnings. Even when a little rain fell, they would admire the way it streaked through the blank air.

At dinner, when we sat down at the table—and did not have to say grace (such a relief; as if they believed in a God that did not have to be thanked every time you turned around)—they said such nice things to each other, and the children were so happy. They would spill their food, or not eat any of it at all, or make up rhymes about it that would end with the words "smelt bad." How they made me laugh, and I wondered what sort of parents I must have had, for even to think of such words in their presence I would have been scolded severely, and I vowed that if I ever had children I would make sure that the first words out of their mouths were bad ones.

It was at dinner one night not long after I began to live with them that they began to call me the Visitor. They said I seemed not to be a part of things, as if I didn't live in their house with them, as if they weren't like a family to me, as if I were just passing through, just saying one long Hallo!, and soon would be saying a quick Goodbye! So long! It was very nice! For look at the way I stared at them as they ate, Lewis said. Had I never seen anyone put a forkful of French-cut green beans in his mouth before? This made Mariah laugh, but almost everything Lewis said made Mariah happy and so she would laugh. I didn't laugh, though, and Lewis looked at me, concern on his face. He said, "Poor Visitor, poor Visitor," over and over, a sympathetic tone to his voice, and then he told me a story about an uncle he had who had gone to Canada and raised monkeys, and of how after a while the uncle loved the monkeys so much and was so used to being around them that he found actual human beings hard to take. He had told me this story about his uncle before, and while he was telling it to me this time I was remembering a dream I had had about them: Lewis was chasing me around the house. I wasn't wearing any clothes. The ground on which I was running was yellow, as if it had been paved with cornmeal. Lewis was chasing me around and around the house, and though he came close he could never catch up with me. Mariah stood at the open windows saying, Catch her, Lewis, catch her. Eventually I fell down a hole, at the bottom of which were some silver and blue snakes.

When Lewis finished telling his story, I told them my dream. When I finished, they both fell silent. Then they looked at me and Mariah cleared her throat, but it was obvious from the way she did it that her throat did not need clearing at all. Their two yellow heads swam toward each other and, in unison, bobbed up and down. Lewis made a clucking noise, then said, Poor, poor Visitor. And Mariah said, Dr. Freud[3] for Visitor, and I wondered why she said that, for I did not know who Dr. Freud was. Then they laughed in a soft, kind way. I had meant by telling them my dream that I had taken them in, because only people who were very important to me had ever shown up in my dreams. I did not know if they understood that.

★ ★ ★ ★ ★

Talking It Through

1. Lucy comes to New England from a tropical island. Make a list of some of the things that Lucy finds strange about her new surroundings. In what ways is she a greenhorn or, as her hosts call it, a "Poor Visitor"? Explain.

2. Why do you think Lucy has left her native Antigua? Does she have any dreams and hopes about what her life in America will bring her? Because the narrator never tells us outright, you may have to read between the lines and make inferences.

3. Although Lucy arrives by plane, Kincaid uses many images of water to describe the separation from her homeland. Find at least two of these images. Why might Kincaid have used them, even in this day of air travel?

4. Kincaid describes many physical sensations in this account. What are some that captured your attention? In what way have these descriptions enhanced the feeling that Lucy has entered a "new world"? What do you associate with warmth? With cold?

5. How do the other people in this story react to Lucy? Even though Lucy speaks English, do they always understand each other? Do they ever laugh at her strange ways? What other immigrants in this chapter were laughed at? Explain.

Writer's Workshop

1. Lucy has chosen to leave her homeland, yet in some ways she misses it. In an essay, compare and contrast her feelings for Antigua and New England. What did she seem to dislike about her life in Antigua? What does she now

[3]*Dr. Freud:* Sigmund Freud, the German founder of psychoanalysis who developed theories of dream interpretation.

miss about it? What does she like and dislike about America? Before you write, make lists of her reactions to both places. In your essay discuss how Kincaid's use of imagery and sensory descriptions enhances your appreciation of Lucy's reactions.

2. Lucy says, "I wrote home to say how lovely everything was, and I used flourishing words and phrases, as if I were living life in a greeting card . . ." Write the letter Lucy might have written describing New England, her work, and the people she has met.

3. Jamaica Kincaid is writing about an immigrant today. Yet Lucy's experience and those of earlier immigrants have some striking similarities. How would you compare Lucy's first few days in America to either Michael Pupin's or George Papashvily's? Who had the harder situation? How did the immigrants cope? Think of comparing the following:
   a. The experience of culture shock, of being a lone newcomer in a new land.
   b. The reactions of Americans to the newcomer.
   c. How the immigrant coped. What strategies did he or she bring to the situation to make the transition easier?

★ *from* FOB ★

D A V I D   H E N R Y   H W A N G

Chinese American playwright David Hwang won the 1981 Best Play Obie Award for FOB, *a work in which two Asian-American college students meet a "Fresh Off the Boat" immigrant. The play mixes Oriental stagecraft with contemporary theatre to comment on the predicament of how to come to terms with one's ethnic identity and the desire to "fit in" an adopted society.*

The characters in FOB *are Dale, a second-generation American of Chinese descent, Grace, his cousin, a first-generation Chinese American, and Steve, a friend, who is a Chinese newcomer. All three are in their early twenties.*

Mr. Hwang, a graduate of Stanford University and the Yale School of Drama, is also the author of M. Butterfly.

PROLOGUE

Lights up on a blackboard. Enter DALE, *dressed preppie. The black-board is the type which can flip around so both sides can be used.* HE *lectures like a university professor, using the board to illustrate his points.*

DALE: F-O-B. Fresh Off the Boat. FOB. What words can you think of that characterize the FOB? Clumsy, ugly, greasy FOB. Loud, stupid, four-eyed FOB. Big feet. Horny. Like Lenny[1] in "Of Mice and Men." Very good. A literary reference. High water pants. Floods, to be exact. Someone you wouldn't want your sister to marry. If you are a sister, someone you wouldn't want to marry. That assumes we're talking about boy FOBs, of course. But girl FOBs aren't really as . . . FOBish. Boy FOBs are the worst, the . . . pits. They are the sworn enemies of all ABC—Oh, that's "American-Born Chinese"—Of all ABC girls. Before an ABC girl will be seen on Friday night with a boy FOB in Westwood, she would rather burn off her face. (HE *flips around the board. On the other side is written: "1. Where to find FOBs 2. How to spot a FOB"*) FOBs can be found in great numbers almost anyplace you happen to be, but there are some locations where they cluster in particularly large swarms. Community colleges, Chinese-club discos, Asian sororities, Asian fraternities, Oriental churches, shopping malls, and, of course, Bee Gee concerts. How can you spot a FOB? Look out! If you can't answer that, you might be one. (HE *flips back the board, reviews*) F-O-B. Fresh Off the Boat. FOB. Clumsy, ugly, greasy FOB. Loud, stupid, four-eyed FOB. Big feet. Horny. Like Lenny in "Of Mice and Men." Floods. Like Lenny in "Of Mice and Men." F-O-B. Fresh Off the Boat. FOB.

Lights fade to black. We hear American pop music, preferably in the funk-R&B-disco area.

ACT I

Scene 1

The back room of a small Chinese restaurant in Torrance, California. Single table, with tablecloth; various chairs, supplies. One door leads outside, a back exit, another leads to the kitchen. Lights up on GRACE, *at the table. The music is coming from a*

---

[1]*Lenny:* Lenny is a character in John Steinbeck's *Of Mice and Men*. He is a tenderhearted, retarded adult, unaware of his own strength.

small radio. On the table is a small, partially wrapped box, and a huge blob of discarded scotch tape. As Grace *tries to wrap the box, we see what has been happening: The tape she's using is stuck; so, in order to pull it out, she must tug so hard that an unusable quantity of tape is dispensed. Enter* Steve, *from the back door, unnoticed by* Grace. He *stands, waiting to catch her eye, tries to speak, but his voice is drowned out by the music.* He *is dressed in a stylish summer outfit.*

Grace: Aaaai-ya!

Steve: Hey! *(No response;* He *turns off the music)*

Grace: Huh? Look. Out of tape.

Steve: *(In Chinese)* Yeah.

Grace: One whole roll. You know how much of it got on here? Look. That much. That's all.

Steve: *(In Chinese)* Yeah. Do you serve chong you bing[1] today?

Grace: *(Picking up box)* Could've skipped the wrapping paper, just covered it with tape.

Steve: *(Chinese)* Excuse me!

Grace: Yeah? *(Pause)* You wouldn't have any on you, would ya?

Steve: *(English from now onward)* Sorry? No. I don't have a bing. I want to buy bing.

Grace: Not bing! Tape. Have you got any tape?

Steve: Tape? Of course I don't have tape.

Grace: Just checking.

Steve: Do you have bing?!

Pause.

Grace: Look, we're closed 'til five . . .

Steve: Idiot girl.

Grace: Why don't you take a menu?
Steve: I want you to tell me!

Pause.

---

[1]*chong you bing:* a kind of scallion pancake.

GRACE: *(Ignoring* STEVE*)* Working in a Chinese restaurant, you learn to deal with obnoxious customers.

STEVE: Hey! You!

GRACE: If the customer's Chinese, you insult them by giving forks.

STEVE: I said I want you to tell me!

GRACE: If the customer's Anglo, you starve them by not giving forks.

STEVE: You serve bing or not?

GRACE: But it's always easy just to dump whatever happens to be in your hands at the moment. *(*SHE *sticks the tape blob on* STEVE*'s face)*

STEVE: I suggest you answer my question at once!

ACT I

Scene 2

Lights up on DALE *and* STEVE *eating. It is a few minutes later and food is on the table.* DALE *eats Chinese style, vigorously shoveling food into his mouth.* STEVE *picks.* GRACE *enters carrying a jar of hot sauce.* STEVE *sees her.*

STEVE: *(To* GRACE*)* After eating, you like to go dance?

DALE: *(Face in bowl)* No, thanks. I think we'd be conspicuous.

STEVE: *(To* GRACE*)* Like to go dance?

GRACE: Perhaps. We will see.

DALE *(To* STEVE*)* Wait a minute. Hold on. How can you just . . .? I'm here, too, you know. Don't forget I exist just 'cuz you can't understand me.

STEVE: Please repeat?

DALE: I get better communication from my fish. Look, we go see movie. Three here. See? One, two, three. Three can see movie. Only two can dance.

STEVE: *(To* GRACE*)* I ask you to go dance.

GRACE: True, but . . .

DALE: *(To* GRACE*)* That would really be a screw, you know? You invite me down here, you don't have anyone for me to go out with, but you decide to go dancing.

GRACE: Dale, I understand.

DALE: Understand? That would really be a screw. *(To* STEVE*)* Look, if you wanna dance, go find yourself some nice FOB partner.

STEVE: ''FOB?'' Has what meaning?

GRACE: Dale . . .

DALE: F-O-B. Fresh Off the Boat. FOB.

GRACE: Dale, I agree.

DALE: See, we both agree. *(To* GRACE*)* He's a pretty prime example, isn't he? All those foreign students—

GRACE: I mean, I agree about going dancing.

DALE: —go swimming in their underwear and everything—What?

GRACE: *(To* STEVE*)* Please understand. This is not the right time for dancing.

STEVE: Okay.

DALE: ''Okay.'' It's okay when *she* says it's okay.

STEVE: *(To* DALE*)* ''Fresh Off Boat'' has what meaning?

DALE: *(To* GRACE*)* Did you ever hear about Dad his first year in the US?

GRACE: Dale, he wants to know . . .

DALE: Well, Gung Gung[2] was pretty rich back then, so Dad must've been a pretty disgusting . . . one, too. You know, his first year here, he spent, like, $13,000. And that was back 'round 1950.

GRACE: Well, Mom never got anything.

STEVE: FOB means what?

DALE: That's probably 'cause women didn't get anything back then. Anyway, he bought himself a new car—all kinds of stuff, I guess. But then Gung Gung went bankrupt, so Dad had to work.

GRACE: And Mom starved.

DALE: Couldn't hold down a job. Wasn't used to taking orders from anyone.

GRACE: Mom was used to taking orders from everyone.

STEVE: Please explain this meaning.

[2]*Gung Gung:* Chinese for Grandfather.

DALE: Got fired from job after job. Something like fifteen in a year. He'd just walk in the front door and out the back, practically.

GRACE: Well, at least he had a choice of doors. At least he was educated.

STEVE: *(To* DALE*)* Excuse!

DALE: Huh?

GRACE: He was educated here. In America. When Mom came over, she couldn't quit just 'cuz she was mad at her employer. It was work or starve.

DALE: Well, Dad had some pretty lousy jobs, too.

STEVE: *(To* DALE*)* Explain, please!

GRACE: Do you know what it's like to work eighty hours a week just to feed yourself?

DALE: Do you?

STEVE: Dale!

DALE *(To* STEVE*)* It means you. You know how, if you go to a fish store or something, they have the stuff that just came in that day? Well, so have you.

STEVE: I do not understand.

DALE: Forget it. That's part of what makes you one.

Pause.

STEVE: *(Picking up hot sauce, to* DALE*)* Hot. You want some?

Pause.

DALE: Well, yeah. Okay. Sure.

STEVE *puts hot sauce on* DALE's *food.*

DALE: *(Continued)* Hey, isn't that kinda a lot?

GRACE: See, Steve's family comes from Shanghai.

DALE: Hmmmm. Well, I'll try it (HE *takes a gulp, puts down his food)*

GRACE: I think perhaps that was too much for him.

DALE: No.

GRACE: Want some water?

DALE: Yes.

GRACE *exits.*

DALE: *(Continued)* You like hot sauce? You like your food hot? All right—here. (HE *dumps the contents of the jar on* STEVE's *plate, stirs*) Don't you ever worry about your intestines falling out?

GRACE *enters, gives water to* DALE. STEVE *sits shocked.*

DALE: Thanks. FOBs can eat anything, huh? They're specially trained. Helps maintain the characteristic greasy look.

STEVE, *cautiously, begins to eat his food.*

DALE *(Continued)* What—? Look, Grace, he's eating that! He's amazing! A freak! What a cannibal!

GRACE: *(Taking* DALE's *plate)* Want me to throw yours out?

DALE: *(Snatching it back)* Huh? No. No, I can eat it.

DALE *and* STEVE *stare at each other across the table. In unison,* THEY *pick up as large a glob of food as possible, stuff it into their mouths.* THEY *cough and choke.* THEY *rest, repeat the face-off a second time.* THEY *continue in silent pain.* GRACE, *who has been watching this, speaks to us.*

GRACE: Yeah. It's tough trying to live in Chinatown. But it's tough trying to live in Torrance, too. It's true. I don't like being alone. You know, when Mom could finally bring me to the US, I was already ten. But I never studied my English very hard in Taiwan, so I got moved back to the second grade. There were a few Chinese girls in the fourth grade, but they were American-born, so they wouldn't even talk to me. They'd just stay with themselves and compare how much clothes they all had, and make fun of the way we all talked. I figured I had a better chance of getting in with the white kids than with them, so in junior high I started bleaching my hair and hanging out at the beach—you know, Chinese hair looks pretty lousy when you bleach it. After a while, I knew what beach was gonna be good on any given day, and I could tell who was coming just by his van. But the American-born Chinese, it didn't matter to them. They just giggled and went to their own dances. Until my senior year in high school—that's how long it took for me to get over this whole thing. One night I took Dad's car and drove on Hollywood Boulevard, all the way from downtown to Beverly Hills, then back on Sunset. I was looking and listening—all the time with the window down, just so I'd feel like I was part of the city. And that Friday, it was—I guess—I said, "I'm lonely. And I don't like it. I don't like being alone." And that was all. As soon as I said it, I felt all of the breeze—it was really cool on my face—and I heard all of the radio—and the music sounded really good, you know? So I drove home.

Pause. DALE *bursts out coughing.*

GRACE: *(Continued)* Oh, I'm sorry. Want some more water, Dale?

DALE: It's okay. I'll get it myself. *(*HE *exits)*

STEVE: *(Looks at* GRACE*) Good, huh?*

STEVE *and* GRACE *stare at each other, as lights fade to black.*

★ ★ ★ ★ ★

Talking It Through

1. A monologue by Dale opens the play and sets forth its theme. The action then moves to a small Chinese restaurant, owned by Grace's father, in Torrance, California.

    What is the tone of the monologue? What do you think is responsible for Dale's derisive description of an FOB? How does this attitude differ from that of the knowledgeable acquaintance who helps George Papash- vily land his first job? What would account for the difference?

2. Would a contemporary FOB have an easier or harder time assimilating American culture than one who came several generations ago? Give your reasons. What are some of the attributes that mark someone as an FOB, according to Dale? Do these fall into the same categories as those which would have marked one in the past?

3. Dale says "girl FOBs aren't so FOBish." Would you agree that a woman would fit into a new society more smoothly? Does Jamaica Kincaid's Lucy bear this out? Explain. List some advantages and disadvantages of being male or female in a new cultural environment. Do your results corroborate Dale's statement?

4. FOB is meant for the stage. It makes use of props, lighting, and other dramatic devices to engage its audience (including passages that echo traditional Chinese theater in style). What is the function of the lecture format of the prologue? What limitations are placed on an author by the play form? What *can't* a playwright rely on?

5. This selection contrasts traditional Chinese attitudes toward men and women. How was the immigrant experience different for Dale's father and Grace's mother? They were members of the same family. With whom would you sympathize more? Why?

6. How would you explain Dale's put-downs of Steve? Are there any fresh insights in these exchanges?

7. Look for examples of humor in this scene. How does this humor differ from that in the Papashvily piece?

8. What does the battle of the hot sauce stand for here? What might it be symbolic of? Why do Dale and Steve continue eating despite their pain? How might this episode connect them with traditional Chinese dramatic heroes?

9. Grace's monologue at the end of Scene 2 reveals things about her previously unknown to the audience. What do we learn? What factors affected her ability to blend in here? How successful was she in assimilating? What finally made Grace able to feel truly American? How does her own experience help her to empathize with Steve, the FOB?

Writer's Workshop

1. Instead of Dale's lecture-prologue, write an essay explaining what he means by an FOB. Elaborate on his sketchy descriptions. "High water pants," for example, would be the opposite look to long low-on-the-hip jeans. Lenny, in John Steinbeck's *Of Mice and Men*, was a retarded adult who was both tenderhearted and clumsy and unaware of his physical strength. The Bee Gees were a popular musical group in the 1970s. Dale's economical "shorthand" images quickly tell the audience what the play's subject and theme will be. Give your essay a serious, high-minded tone to convey similar ideas.

2. A play compresses time and uses space in more limited ways than a novel. A set may be impressionistic, realistic, or abstract. Yet a play can engage the imagination and interest very rapidly. From conversation alone we get our cues to character.

   If you were a novelist writing the character of Steve (David Hwang gives little descriptive background for casting him in either the stage directions or cast list), what would you tell us about him? Invent a biography for Steve and write his life story to the time he arrives by plane to Los Angeles from Hong Kong.

3. Grace is a complex and interesting character, pivotal to the action of *FOB*. Write a poem to compare her outer manner with her inner feelings. Use stanzas or line breaks to direct the reader's progress through your work. Traditional Chinese poetry uses succinct imagery to convey feeling. Try creating word pictures to capture Grace's emotions.

NEW WORDS FOR A NEW LAND

★ ★ ★ ★ ★
★ ★ ★ ★ ★
★ ★ ★ ★ ★
★ ★ ★ ★ ★
★ ★ ★ ★ ★
★ ★ ★ ★ ★

NOT KNOWING ENGLISH MARKED ANY IMMIGRANT AS "FRESH off the boat." In "New Words for a New Land" we look at the problems immigrants face learning a new language. We begin the unit with the humorous account of Mr. Kaplan, a night-school student in the 1930s. In the early decades of the twentieth century, all immigrant children were taught in English, and no effort was made to preserve their native language. The goal was to "Americanize" all newcomers as quickly as possible. Richard Rodriguez, a Mexican American writer, teacher, and television correspondent, grew up in more recent times when bilingual education was thought to be preferable.

However the immigrant learned English, the process was not easy. What is involved in learning a language? Does the person acquire a new identity along with a new language? Must the old one be given up? As writers and poets especially sensitive to the importance of language in our lives, these authors make us look at language itself with a new eye.

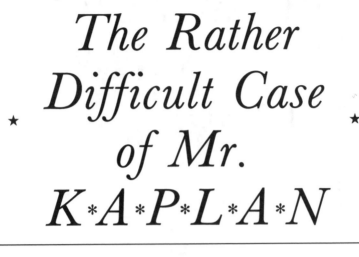

The Rather Difficult Case of Mr. K*A*P*L*A*N

LEO ROSTEN

Learning English was one of the hardest tasks the new immigrant had to face. This humorous story is set in the 1930s at a time when thousands of adult immigrants attended night schools. There they were taught English, American customs, and civics. Leo Rosten (Leonard Q. Ross) is best known for his book The Joys of Yiddish.

In the third week of the new term, Mr. Parkhill was forced to the conclusion that Mr. Kaplan's case was rather difficult. Mr. Kaplan first came to his special attention, out of the thirty-odd adults in the beginners' grade of the American Night Preparatory School for Adults ("English—Americanization—Civics—Preparation for Naturalization"), through an exercise the class had submitted. The exercise was entitled "Fifteen Common Nouns and Their Plural Forms." Mr. Parkhill came to one paper which included the following:

house	makes	houses
dog	"	dogies
libary	"	Public libary
cat	"	Katz

Mr. Parkhill read this over several times, very thoughtfully. He decided that here was a student who might, unchecked, develop into a "problem case." It was clearly a case that called for special attention. He turned the page over and read the name. It was printed in large, firm letters with red crayon. Each letter was outlined in blue. Between every two letters was a star, carefully drawn, in green. The multi-colored whole spelled, unmistakably, H*Y*M*A*N K*A*P*L*A*N.

This Mr. Kaplan was in his forties, a plump, red-faced gentleman, with wavy blond hair, *two* fountain pens in his outer pocket, and a perpetual smile. It was a strange smile, Mr. Parkhill remarked: vague, bland, and consistent in its monotony. The thing that emphasized it for Mr. Parkhill was that it never seemed to leave the face of Mr. Kaplan, even during Recitation and Speech period. This disturbed Mr. Parkhill considerably, because Mr. Kaplan was particularly bad in Recitation and Speech.

Mr. Parkhill decided he had not applied himself as conscientiously as he might to Mr. Kaplan's case. That very night he called on Mr. Kaplan first.

"Won't *you* take advantage of Recitation and Speech practice, Mr. Kaplan?" he asked, with an encouraging smile.

Mr. Kaplan smiled back and answered promptly, "Vell, I'll tell abot Prazidents United States. Fife Prazidents United States is Abram Lincohen; Hodding, Coolitch, Judge Vashington, an' Banjamin Frenklin."

Further encouragement revealed that in Mr. Kaplan's literary Valhalla[1] the "most famous tree American wriders" were Jeck Laundon, Valt Viterman, and the author of "Hawk L. Barry-Feen," one Mocktvain. Mr. Kaplan took pains to point out that he did not mention Relfvaldo Amerson because "He is a poyet, an' I'm talkink abot wriders."

Mr. Parkhill diagnosed the case as one of "inability to distinguish between 'a' and 'e.' " He concluded that Mr. Kaplan *would* need special attention. He was, frankly, a little disturbed.

Mr. Kaplan's English showed no improvement during the next hard weeks. The originality of his spelling and pronunciation, however, flourished—like a sturdy flower in the good, rich earth. A man to whom "Katz" is the plural of "cat" soon soars into higher and more ambitious endeavor. As a one-paragraph "Exercise in Composition," Mr. Kaplan submitted:

When people is meating on the boulvard, on going away one is saying, "I am glad I mat you," and the other is giving answer, "Mutual."

Mr. Parkhill felt that perhaps Mr. Kaplan had overreached himself, and should be confined to the simpler exercises.

Mr. Kaplan was an earnest student. He worked hard, knit his brows regularly (albeit with that smile), did all his homework, and never missed a class. Only once did Mr. Parkhill feel that Mr. Kaplan might, perhaps, be a little more *serious* about his work. That was when he asked Mr. Kaplan to "give a noun."

[1]*Valhalla:* the final resting place for the souls of heroes in Norse mythology.

"Door," said Mr. Kaplan, smiling.

It seemed to Mr. Parkhill that "door" had been given only a moment earlier, by Miss Mitnick.

"Y-es," said Mr. Parkhill. "Er—and another noun?"

"Another door," Mr. Kaplan replied promptly.

Mr. Parkhill put him down as a doubtful "C." Everything pointed to the fact that Mr. Kaplan might have to be kept on an extra three months before he was ready for promotion to Composition, Grammar, and Civics, with Miss Higby.

One night Mrs. Moskowitz read a sentence, from "English for Beginners," in which "the vast deserts of America" were referred to. Mr. Parkhill soon discovered that poor Mrs. Moskowitz did not know the meaning of "vast." "Who can tell us the meaning of vast'?" asked Mr. Parkhill lightly.

Mr. Kaplan's hand shot up, volunteering wisdom. He was all proud grins. Mr. Parkhill, in the rashness of the moment, nodded to him.

Mr. Kaplan rose, radiant with joy. " 'Vast!' It's commink fromm *diraction*. Ve have four diractions: de naut, de sot, de heast, and de vast."

Mr. Parkhill shook his head. "Er—that is 'west,' Mr. Kaplan." He wrote "vast" and "west" on the blackboard. To the class he added, tolerantly, that Mr. Kaplan was apparently thinking of "west," whereas it was "vast" which was under discussion.

This seemed to bring a great light into Mr. Kaplan's inner world. "So is 'vast' vat you eskink?"

Mr. Parkhill admitted that it was "vast" for which he was asking.

"Aha!" cried Mr. Kaplan. "You minn *'vast*,' not"—with scorn— " 'vast.' "

"Yes," said Mr. Parkhill, faintly.

"Hau Kay!" said Mr. Kaplan, essaying the vernacular.[2] "Ven I'm buyink a suit clothes, I'm gattink de cawt, de pents, an' de vast!"

Stunned, Mr. Parkhill shook his head, very sadly.

"I'm afraid that you've used still another word, Mr. Kaplan."

Oddly enough, this seemed to give Mr. Kaplan great pleasure.

Several nights later Mr. Kaplan took advantage of Open Questions period. This ten-minute period was Mr. Parkhill's special innovation in the American Night Preparatory School for Adults. It was devoted to answering any questions which the students might care to raise about any difficulties which they might have encountered during the course of their adventures with the language. Mr. Parkhill enjoyed Open Questions. He liked to clear up *practical* problems. He felt he was being ever so much more constructive

[2]*essaying the vernacular:* trying ordinary, everyday speech.

that way. Miss Higby had once told him that he was a born Open Questions teacher.

"Plizz, Mr. Pockheel," asked Mr. Kaplan as soon as the period opened. "Vat's de minnink fromm—" It sounded, in Mr. Kaplan's rendition, like "a big department."

" 'A big department,' Mr. Kaplan?" asked Mr. Parkhill, to make sure.

"Yassir!" Mr. Kaplan's smile was beauteous to behold. "In de stritt, ven I'm valkink, I'm hearink like 'I big de pottment.' "

It was definitely a pedagogical[4] opportunity.

"Well, class," Mr. Parkhill began. "I'm sure that you have all—"

He told them that they had all probably done some shopping in the large downtown stores. (Mr. Kaplan nodded.) In these large stores, he said, if they wanted to buy a pair of shoes, for example, they went to a special *part* of the store, where only shoes were sold—a *shoe* department. (Mr. Kaplan nodded.) If they wanted a table, they went to a different *part* of the store, where *tables* were sold. (Mr. Kaplan nodded.) If they wanted to buy, say, a goldfish, they went to still another part of the store, where goldfish . . . (Mr. Kaplan frowned; it was clear that Mr. Kaplan had never bought a goldfish.)

"Well, then," Mr. Parkhill summed up hastily, "each article is sold in a different *place*. These different and special places are called *departments*." He printed "D-E-P-A-R-T-M-E-N-T" on the board in large, clear capitals. "And a *big* department, Mr. Kaplan, is merely such a department which is large—*big!*"

He put the chalk down and wiped his fingers.

"Is that clear now, class?" he asked, with a little smile. (It was rather an ingenious explanation, he thought; it might be worth repeating to Miss Higby during the recess.)

It *was* clear. There were thirty nods of approval. But Mr. Kaplan looked uncertain. It was obvious that Mr. Kaplan, a man who would not compromise with truth, did *not* find it clear.

"Isn't that clear *now*, Mr. Kaplan?" asked Mr. Parkhill anxiously.

Mr. Kaplan pursed his lips in thought. "It's a *fine* haxplination, Titcher," he said generously, "but I don' unnistand vy I'm hearink de voids de vay I do. Simms to me it's used in annodder minnink."

"There's really only one meaning for 'a big department.' " Mr. Parkhill was definitely worried by this time. "*If* that's the phrase you mean."

Mr. Kaplan nodded gravely. "Oh, dat's de phrase—ufcawss! It sonds like dat—or maybe a leetle more like '*I* big de pottment.' "

Mr. Parkhill took up the chalk. ("*I* big department" was obviously a

[4]*pedagogical:* teaching.

case of Mr. Kaplan's own curious audition.) He repeated the explanation carefully, this time embellishing the illustrations with a shirt department, a victrola section, and "a separate part of the store where, for example, you buy canaries, or other birds."

Mr. Kaplan sat entranced. He followed it all politely, even the part about "canaries, or other birds." He smiled throughout with consummate reassurance.

Mr. Parkhill was relieved, assuming, in his folly, that Mr. Kaplan's smiles were a testimony to his exposition.[5] But when he had finished, Mr. Kaplan shook his head once more, this time with a new and superior firmness.

"Is the explanation *still* not clear?" Mr. Parkhill was genuinely concerned by this time.

"Is de haxplination clear!" cried Mr. Kaplan with enthusiasm. "Ha! I should live so! Soitinly! Clear like *gold!* So clear! An' netcheral too! But Mr. Pockheel—"

"Go on, Mr. Kaplan," said Mr. Parkhill, studying the white dust on his fingers. There was, after all, nothing more to be done.

"Vell! I tink it's more like '*I* big de pottment.' "

"Go on, Mr. Kaplan, go on." (*Domine, dirige nos.*)[6]

Mr. Kaplan rose. His smile was broad, luminous, transcendent; his manner was regal.

"I'm hearink it in de stritt. Somtimes I'm stendink in de stritt, talkink to a frand, or mine vife, mine brodder—or maybe only stendink. An' somvun is pessink arond me. An' by hexident he's givink me a bump, you know, a *poosh!* Vell, he says, 'Axcuse me!' no? But somtimes, an' *dis* is vat I minn, he's sayink, '*I big de pottment!*' "

Mr. Parkhill studied the picture of "Abram Lincohen" on the back wall, as if reluctant to face reality. He wondered whether he could reconcile it with his conscience if he were to promote Mr. Kaplan to Composition, Grammar, and Civics—at once. Another three months of Recitation and Speech might, after all, be nothing but a waste of Mr. Kaplan's valuable time.

★ ★ ★ ★ ★

---

[5]*exposition:* a detailed explanation.
[6]*Domine, dirige nos:* Lord, direct us.

Talking It Through

1. Describe Mr. Kaplan and his personality. What do we learn about him from the way he dresses, writes his name, smiles, and answers questions?

2. Many of Mr. Parkhill's students have difficulty learning English. Why does Mr. Parkhill regard Mr. Kaplan as such a special problem? What does he plan to do about Mr. Kaplan at the end of the story?

3. Correct Mr. Kaplan's list of plural nouns. Why is his list so funny? What is funny about his list of five presidents? Who are Jeck Laundon, Valt Viterman, Mocktvain and Relfvaldo Amerson? What are people really saying when they say "I big de pottment"?

4. Comedy often arises from situations in which characters misunderstand each other. Here, Mr. Kaplan's mispronunciation of English creates problems. Give some examples in this story where humor arises from misunderstandings.

5. Based on the story, what do you think Mr. Parkhill is like? How would you describe him? Is he condescending or caring?

Writer's Workshop

1. Write another episode in the life of Kaplan in which a confusion over English leads to a funny misunderstanding. It could involve Mr. Parkhill as well as several other night school students. Be sure to keep Mr. Kaplan behaving "in character."

2. We often find the mistakes that children make when learning their language funny or endearing. As a child, can you remember any misunderstandings you had about what words meant in your native language? Or, if you have recently learned English, did any mistakes you made create unusual problems? If so, write an autobiographical account, giving us your view of the confusion the misunderstanding created. How was it finally resolved?

3. Analyze the humor in Rosten's writing and compare it to a television comedy you enjoy. Humor often arises when adults behave, or are seen to behave, like children. Many funny situations arise when characters misunderstand each other. Choose one episode from a TV show and compare it to "The Education of H*Y*M*A*N K*A*P*L*A*N."

from Hunger
of Memory

RICHARD RODRIGUEZ

Richard Rodriguez is the son of parents who emigrated to the United States from Mexico. Before he went to school, he and his family spoke Spanish in their home. Going to school exposed him for the first time to the sounds and meanings of American English. He writes here of coming to terms with that process.

Supporters of bilingual education today imply that students like me miss a great deal by not being taught in their family's language. What they seem not to recognize is that, as a socially disadvantaged child, I considered Spanish to be a private language. What I needed to learn in school was that I had the right—and the obligation—to speak the public language of *los gringos*. The odd truth is that my first-grade classmates could have become bilingual, in the conventional sense of that word, more easily than I. Had they been taught (as upper-middle-class children are often taught early) a second language like Spanish or French, they could have regarded it simply as that: another public language. In my case such bilingualism could not have been so quickly achieved. What I did not believe was that I could speak a single public language.

Without question, it would have pleased me to hear my teachers address me in Spanish when I entered the classroom. I would have felt much less afraid. I would have trusted them and responded with ease. But I would have delayed—for how long postponed?—having to learn the language of public society. I would have evaded—and for how long could I have afforded to delay?—learning the great lesson of school, that I had a public identity.

Fortunately, my teachers were unsentimental about their responsibility. What they understood was that I needed to speak a public language. So their voices would search me out, asking me questions. Each time I'd hear them, I'd look up in surprise to see a nun's face frowning at me. I'd mumble, not really meaning to answer. The nun would persist, "Richard, stand up. Don't look at the floor. Speak up. Speak to the entire class, not just to me!"

But I couldn't believe that the English language was mine to use. (In part, I did not want to believe it.) I continued to mumble. I resisted the teacher's demands. (Did I somehow suspect that once I learned public language my pleasing family life would be changed?) Silent, waiting for the bell to sound, I remained dazed, diffident, afraid.

Because I wrongly imagined that English was intrinsically a public language and Spanish an intrinsically private one, I easily noted the difference between classroom language and the language of home. At school, words were directed to a general audience of listeners. ('Boys and girls.') Words were meaningfully ordered. And the point was not self-expression alone but to make oneself understood by many others. The teacher quizzed: "Boys and girls, why do we use that word in this sentence? Could we think of a better word to use there? Would the sentence change its meaning if the words were differently arranged? And wasn't there a better way of saying much the same thing?" (I couldn't say. I wouldn't try to say.)

Three months. Five. Half a year passed. Unsmiling, ever watchful, my teachers noted my silence. They began to connect my behavior with the difficult progress my older sister and brother were making. Until one Saturday morning three nuns arrived at the house to talk to our parents. Stiffly, they sat on the blue living room sofa. From the doorway of another room, spying the visitors, I noted the incongruity—the clash of two worlds, the faces and voices of school intruding upon the familiar setting of home. I overheard one voice gently wondering, "Do your children speak only Spanish at home, Mrs. Rodriguez?" While another voice added, "That Richard especially seems so timid and shy."

That Rich-heard!

With great tact the visitors continued, "Is it possible for you and your husband to encourage your children to practice their English when they are home?" Of course, my parents complied. What would they not do for their children's well-being? And how could they have questioned the Church's authority which those women represented? In an instant, they agreed to give up the language (the sounds) that had revealed and accentuated our family's closeness. The moment after the visitors left, the change was observed. *"Ahora, speak to us en inglés,"* my father and mother united to tell us.

At first, it seemed a kind of game. After dinner each night, the family gathered to practice "our" English. (It was still then *inglés,* a language foreign to us, so we felt drawn as strangers to it.) Laughing, we would try to define words we could not pronounce. We played with strange English sounds, often overanglicizing our pronunciations. And we filled the smiling gaps of our sentences with familiar Spanish sounds. But that was cheating, somebody shouted. Everyone laughed. In school, meanwhile, like my brother and sister, I was required to attend a daily tutoring session. I needed a full year of special attention. I also needed my teachers to keep my attention from straying in class by calling out, *Rich-heard*—their English voices slowly prying loose my ties to my other name, its three notes, *Ri-car-do*. Most of all I needed to hear my mother and father speak to me in a moment of seriousness in broken—suddenly heartbreaking—English. The scene was inevitable: One Saturday morning I entered the kitchen where my parents were talking in Spanish. I did not realize that they were talking in Spanish however until, at the moment they saw me, I heard their voices change to speak English. Those *gringo* sounds they uttered startled me. Pushed me away. In that moment of trivial misunderstanding and profound insight, I felt my throat twisted by unsounded grief. I turned quickly and left the room. But I had no place to escape to with Spanish. (The spell was broken.) My brother and sisters were speaking English in another part of the house.

Again and again in the days following, increasingly angry, I was obliged to hear my mother and father: "Speak to us *en inglés.*" *(Speak.)* Only then did I determine to learn classroom English. Weeks after, it happened: One day in school I raised my hand to volunteer an answer. I spoke out in a loud voice. And I did not think it remarkable when the entire class understood. That day, I moved very far from the disadvantaged child I had been only days earlier. The belief, the calming assurance that I belonged in public, had at last taken hold.

Shortly after, I stopped hearing the high and loud sounds of *los gringos.* A more and more confident speaker of English, I didn't trouble to listen to *how* strangers sounded, speaking to me. And there simply were too many English-speaking people in my day for me to hear American accents anymore. Conversations quickened. Listening to persons who sounded eccentrically pitched voices, I usually noted their sounds for an initial few seconds before I concentrated on *what* they were saying. Conversations became content-full. Transparent. Hearing someone's *tone* of voice—angry or questioning or sarcastic or happy or sad—I didn't distinguish it from the words it expressed. Sound and word were thus tightly wedded. At the end of a day, I was often bemused, always relieved, to realize how "silent," though crowded with words, my day in public had been. (This public silence measured and quickened the change in my life.)

At last, seven years old, I came to believe what had been technically true since my birth: I was an American citizen.

But the special feeling of closeness at home was diminished by then. Gone was the desperate, urgent, intense feeling of being at home; rare was the experience of feeling myself individualized by family intimates. We remained a loving family, but one greatly changed. No longer so close; no longer bound tight by the pleasing and troubling knowledge of our public separateness. Neither my older brother nor sister rushed home after school anymore. Nor did I. When I arrived home there would often be neighborhood kids in the house. Or the house would be empty of sounds.

Following the dramatic Americanization of their children, even my parents grew more publicly confident. Especially my mother. She learned the names of all the people on our block. And she decided we needed to have a telephone installed in the house. My father continued to use the word *gringo*. But it was no longer charged with the old bitterness or distrust. (Stripped of any emotional content, the word simply became a name for those Americans not of Hispanic descent.) Hearing him, sometimes, I wasn't sure if he was pronouncing the Spanish word *gringo* or saying gringo in English.

Matching the silence I started hearing in public was a new quiet at home. The family's quiet was partly due to the fact that, as we children learned more and more English, we shared fewer and fewer words with our parents. Sentences needed to be spoken slowly when a child addressed his mother or father. (Often the parent wouldn't understand.) The child would need to repeat himself. (Still the parent misunderstood.) The young voice, frustrated, would end up saying, "Never mind"—the subject was closed. Dinners would be noisy with the clinking of knives and forks against dishes. My mother would smile softly between her remarks; my father at the other end of the table would chew and chew at his food, while he stared over the heads of his children.

My *mother!* My *father!* After English became my primary language, I no longer knew what words to use in addressing my parents. The old Spanish words (those tender accents of sound) I had used earlier—*mamá and papá*—I couldn't use anymore. They would have been too painful reminders of how much had changed in my life. On the other hand, the words I heard neighborhood kids call *their* parents seemed equally unsatisfactory. *Mother* and *Father; Ma, Papa, Pa, Dad, Pop* (how I hated the all-American sound of that last word especially)—all these terms I felt were unsuitable, not really terms of address for *my* parents. As a result, I never used them at home. Whenever I'd speak to my parents, I would try to get their attention with eye contact alone. In public conversations, I'd refer to "my parents" or "my mother and father."

My mother and father, for their part, responded differently, as their children spoke to them less. She grew restless, seemed troubled and anxious at the scarcity of words exchanged in the house. It was she who would question me about my day when I came home from school. She smiled at small talk. She pried at the edges of my sentences to get me to say something more. (What?) She'd join conversations she overheard, but her intrusions often stopped her children's talking. By contrast, my father seemed reconciled to the new quiet. Though his English improved somewhat, he retired into silence. At dinner he spoke very little. One night his children and even his wife helplessly giggled at his garbled English pronunciation of the Catholic Grace before Meals. Thereafter he made his wife recite the prayer at the start of each meal, even on formal occasions, when there were guests in the house. Hers became the public voice of the family. On official business, it was she, not my father, one would usually hear on the phone or in stores, talking to strangers. His children grew so accustomed to his silence that, years later, they would speak routinely of his shyness. (My mother would often try to explain: Both his parents died when he was eight. He was raised by an uncle who treated him like little more than a menial servant. He was never encouraged to speak. He grew up alone. A man of few words.) But my father was not shy, I realized, when I'd watch him speaking Spanish with relatives. Using Spanish, he was quickly effusive. Especially when talking with other men, his voice would spark, flicker, flare alive with sounds. In Spanish, he expressed ideas and feelings he rarely revealed in English. With firm Spanish sounds, he conveyed confidence and authority English would never allow him.

The silence at home, however, was finally more than a literal silence. Fewer words passed between parent and child, but more profound was the silence that resulted from my inattention to sounds. At about the time I no longer bothered to listen with care to the sounds of English in public, I grew careless about listening to the sounds family members made when they spoke. Most of the time I heard someone speaking at home and didn't distinguish his sounds from the words people uttered in public. I didn't even pay much attention to my parents' accented and ungrammatical speech. At least not at home. Only when I was with them in public would I grow alert to their accents. Though, even then, their sounds caused me less and less concern. For I was increasingly confident of my own public identity.

I would have been happier about my public success had I not sometimes recalled what it had been like earlier, when my family had conveyed its intimacy through a set of conveniently private sounds. Sometimes in public, hearing a stranger, I'd hark back to my past. A Mexican farmworker approached me downtown to ask directions to somewhere. "*Hijito . . .* ?" he said. And his voice summoned deep longing. Another time, standing beside my mother in the visiting room of a Carmelite convent, before the dense screen which rendered the nuns shadowy figures, I heard several Spanish-speaking nuns—their busy, singsong overlapping voices—assure us that yes, yes, we were remembered, all our family was remembered in their prayers. (Their voices echoed faraway family sounds.) Another day, a dark-faced old woman—her hand light on my shoulder—steadied herself against me as she boarded a bus. She murmured something I couldn't quite comprehend. Her Spanish voice came near, like the face of a never-before-seen relative in the instant before I was kissed. Her voice, like so many of the Spanish voices I'd hear in public, recalled the golden age of my youth. Hearing Spanish then, I continued to be a careful, if sad, listener to sounds. Hearing a Spanish-speaking family walking behind me, I turned to look. I smiled for an instant, before my glance found the Hispanic-looking faces of strangers in the crowd going by.

★ ★ ★ ★ ★

Talking It Through

1. At the beginning of this selection Richard Rodriguez speaks of a "public" versus a "private" language. What does he mean by this? Do even families whose native language is English have a private language they speak at home? Discuss.

   List the differences between public and private language as enumerated by Rodriguez. Can you think of others?

   Are there instances in your own language-learning experience that are comparable? Share them with the class.

2. The nuns visit the Rodriguez home to encourage Richard and his brother and sister to use English at home. At first the family's efforts to comply seem humorous to them, but gradually the progress of the children contrasts with the less successful efforts of their parents. Rodriguez describes their efforts as "heartbreaking"—and feels alienated from their intimacy when they speak Spanish.

   Why do you think he comes to feel grief instead of joy at his own progress?

3. What happens to turn "Ricardo" into "Rich-heard"? What changes in his perceptions take place as he becomes fluent in the new language? How old is he when this happens?

4. How does the Americanization of their children change Mr. and Mrs. Rodriguez? How does their home life change? Does this alter the relationships within the family? Try to explain how each family member would feel.

5. Rodriguez speaks of his dissatisfaction with both Spanish and informal American terms of address for his parents. What causes his discomfort? How does he resolve this?

What forms of parental address do you use? How do you refer to your family members to others? Do your names for family members vary? When? Why?

6. Richard Rodriguez says that he and his brother and sister grew accustomed to their father's silence, which was attributed to shyness. Was the father truly shy? When did he appear confident?

7. What does Rodriguez mean when he says that Spanish voices he heard recalled "the golden age" of his youth?

8. What has Richard gained in exchange for the loss of intimacy of his native language? When does public language serve our needs?

Writer's Workshop

1. Write an essay taking the opposite point of view from that of Richard Rodriguez. Make a case for bilingual education—being taught subjects in one's native tongue while learning English as another subject. What will be accomplished? What will be easier? What will be preserved?

2. Write a series of monologues for the different members of the Rodriguez family (Richard, his mother, and his father) brought about by the nuns' visit or Richard's becoming an "American Citizen" at age seven. Have them speak about their feelings and the roles that each now play in the family.

3. Write about an event or a personal experience in private language and public language. How will your word choice differ in each account? What vernacular or conversational words would be appropriate to either or both accounts? How will you report conversation in each? What might be censorable in both accounts? Make each account one to two pages long. Try reading each aloud to determine the impact on your audience.

Learning
★ My Father's ★
Language

LORRAINE DUGGIN

Lorraine Duggin teaches creative writing and literature at Creighton University in Omaha. In this poem she describes how her immigrant father was ridiculed as a child for mispronouncing a word.

The accent is always on the first syllable:
in the word of more than three syllables,
there is a secondary accent on the third syllable.
                    —Instructional Manual In Czech

He tells me about the time
his schoolmates laugh so hard,
laugh him under the desk, red-faced,
out of the room, embarrassed, down
the halls, humiliated,   5
of Jungmann School.

First generation American son
of Bohemian[1] immigrants,
how was he to know

this language of different rules,   10
this country which found
humor in foreignness,
this vocabulary ludicrous[2]

[1]*Bohemian:* Czech.
[2]*ludicrous:* ridiculous, absurd.

when accent falls upon
em, as in "emigré,"[3] which   15
his parents are, or "eminent,"[4]
which they aren't,

accent falling again on gen
as in "gentle" or "gentlemen,"
neither of which howling   20
classmates pretend to be

when the boy who becomes my father
sounds out, broken, aloud,
pronouncing from his first year
reader a word he sees on the page: 25

emÍ -er -geń -cy.

Talking It Through

1. Why do you think the poet begins this poem with instructions from a manual in Czech?

2. In the first stanza, or group of lines, what effect does the laughter of his classmates have on Duggin's father? What words does the poet emphasize in describing it?

3. In trying to pronounce "emergency" the father incorrectly emphasizes the first syllable, "em." What words are associated in the poem with "em"? Why do you think the poet has chosen them? What do they tell us about her father?

4. Again, in the word "emergency," the father wrongly emphasizes "gen." What words in the poem begin with "gen"? How do the "gen" words separate the father from his American classmates?

5. Why do you think the poet based this poem around the word "emergency"?

6. How is the word "language" used in the poem? What has the daughter learned about "my father's language"? What do you think the poet means when English is referred to as "this language of different rules"?

[3] *emigré:* the French word for emigrant.
[4] *eminent:* well-known.

Writer's Workshop

1. In poetry, words are often used for their associations. Some words remind us of other words, evoke certain images which remind us of other words or images. In "Learning My Father's Language" the poet has explored the meaning of "emergency" in her father's life, syllable for syllable. Choose a word that has meaning for you. Play with the word—what associations does it bring to mind? Look it up in the dictionary. What are the roots of the word? Then write a poem based on that word.

2. The father in "Learning My Father's Language" is very much a greenhorn. He does not know the "rules"; he is a "first generation American" reading from his "first year reader." Write a short essay in which you compare his experience to other greenhorns in "Fresh Off the Boat."

★ *Emigrant/ Immigrant I & Emigrant/ Immigrant II* ★

RINA FERRARELLI

Rina Ferrarelli came to America when she was fifteen. She is a poet who teaches English at the University of Pittsburgh. An emigrant is a person who leaves his or her original country. An immigrant is a person who settles in a new country.

Emigrant/Immigrant I

From the people
beyond reckoning of generations
a town whose customs and tongue
defined you as much as your name
your occupation.   5

But you're adaptable.
You stand alone in your new country
your new town, the old one
an obscure alllusion[1]
with a newly-minted   10
easier-to-pronounce name,
given or chosen,
new clothes
and the latest American haircut.

Neither color, nor shape or size,   15
nor the face you were born with
can you take for granted anymore.
People talk around you
point things out
syl-lab-i-cate slowly   20
or raise their voices
but you smile, grateful,
eager to please.
You're learning to read lips
they're helping you cross the street.   25
YOU, who are you?
They don't know, do you?

Emigrant/Immigrant II

A slight accent.
    Forming
each phrase before
delivery
and never a slur.   5

---

[1]*obscure allusion:* a reference to something little known.

Checking
every move,
prepared
for all contingencies.[1]
Close,   10
yet not quite.

Insisting
on a knife and fork
when your fingers
would do as well.   15

Almost there.
The place sighted,
but out of reach.
Destined never to cross

into the interior.   20
A bridge, a border town.

Talking It Through

Emigrant/Immigrant I

1. How can a person be both an emigrant and an immigrant? How do other people determine which one a person is? On what basis do you think a person defines him- or herself as one or the other?

2. According to the poet, what defined a person in the old country? Could you choose your identity there? Could you escape it?

3. In the second stanza the old names become "newly-minted" ones which are easier for Americans to pronounce. Why do you think the poet has used the phrase "newly-minted"? What else is "new" in the second stanza? In the second stanza, are "you" an emigrant or an immigrant, in your opinion?

4. The poet seemed quite confident in the second stanza stating "But you're adaptable." In what ways is the emigrant/immigrant compared to a blind and deaf person by the third stanza? Why would the poet make such a comparison?

[1]*contingencies:* emergencies.

5. Why don't other people know who you are? Is a foreigner more unknown than any other stranger, in your opinion? By the end of the poem is the "you" in the poem an emigrant, an immigrant—neither or both? Explain your answer.

EMIGRANT/IMMIGRANT II

1. Why do you think the poet titled the poem "Emigrant/Immigrant II?" In what ways does it represent a second stage in the process of adapting to a new country? In what ways has language been important in this process?

2. What is the emigrant/immigrant striving for? What is "The place sighted, but out of reach"?

3. In what ways is "A bridge, a border town" like the emigrant/immigrant?

Writer's Workshop

1. In poetry, the placement of each word in a line and the grouping of lines into stanzas are very important. A poet can emphasize a certain word by placing it carefully on the page—at the beginning of a line, at the end of a line, or even by making one word a line in itself. Reading the poem aloud can sometimes help us "hear" these emphases.

   In both of Ferrarelli's poems, the poet uses free verse: unrhymed lines with irregular rhythmic patterns. In both, words are grouped into stanzas, which form divisions in the poem. But in "Emigrant/Immigrant I" there are clearly three stanzas, whereas in "Emigrant/Immigrant II" the stanzas are less clearly defined—perhaps intentionally. Just glancing at both poems, we can see that she has arranged her words differently in order to enhance the meaning of each poem.

   In an essay, compare Ferrarelli's use of free verse in "Emigrant/Immigrant I" and "Emigrant/Immigrant II." Show how she has carefully chosen her word arrangements in both poems, and give detailed examples.

2. In her poems, Ferrarelli has described what it is like to be an outsider striving to cross "into the interior." Language has been an important element in this struggle. In an autobiographical account or a short story, write about a person struggling to "fit in." How do clothes, hair, and use of the "right" words become an important factor? How is the person defined by the "in group"? How does he or she define him or herself?

3. Write a poem titled, "Emigrant/Immigrant III." What other struggles might the person face in the next phase of adjustment? How might language continue to play a role?

★ *Emigré* ★

W. S. M E R W I N

W. S. Merwin is a prize-winning poet and translator who lived in Europe for many years and who has taught at a number of American colleges and universities. He currently resides in Hawaii where he is active in environmental causes. Many of his poems first appeared in The New Yorker *magazine.*

You will find it is
much as you imagined
in some respects
which no one can predict
you will be homesick   5
at times for something you can describe
and at times without being able to say
what you miss
just as you used to feel when you were at home

some will complain from the start   10
that you club together
with your own kind
but only those who have
done what you have done
conceived of it longed for it   15
lain awake waiting for it
and have come out with

no money no papers nothing
at your age
know what you have done   20
what you are talking about
and will find you a roof and employers

others will say from the start
that you avoid
those of your country   25
for a while
as your country becomes
a category in the new place
and nobody remembers the same things
in the same way   30
and you come to the problem
of what to remember after all
and of what is your real
language
where does it come from what does it   35
sound like
who speaks it

if you cling to the old usage
do you not cut yourself off
from the new speech   40
but if you rush to the new lips
do you not fade like a sound cut off
do you not dry up like a puddle
is the new tongue to be trusted

what of the relics of your childhood   45
should you bear in mind pieces
of dyed cotton and gnawed wood
lint of voices untranslatable stories
summer sunlight on dried paint
whose color continues to fade in the   50
growing brightness of the white afternoon
ferns on the shore of the transparent lake
or should you forget them
as you float between ageless languages
and call from one to the other who you are   55

Talking It Through

1. What is the "it" in the first stanza? Note how line three, ("in some respects"), because of the lack of punctuation can modify the meaning of the lines preceding it as well as of those that follow, resulting in two or more possible meanings.

2. Who does Merwin say will come to the aid of the new arrival? Who might complain about immigrants clubbing together with their own kind? What kind of emigré comes out "with no money no papers nothing at your age"? What does the poet admire about the emigré in this stanza?

3. The second stanza begins "some will complain from the start," while the third begins "others will say from the start," continuing the account of how an immigrant begins to settle into his or her new surroundings. What is the effect of beginning each stanza with similar words? What does Merwin mean when he says "nobody remembers the same things/in the same way"? Why is what to remember a "problem"?

4. Stanzas three and four deal with the trials of learning a new language and giving up the old. The dilemma of loss is present with either choice. Merwin says movingly, ". . . if you rush to new lips/"do you not fade like a sound cut off/do you not dry up like a puddle." What does he mean when he adds "is the new tongue to be trusted"? Trusted to do what or say what?

5. The last stanza of this poem contain its most vivid imagery as the poet calls upon the emigré to remember the past in the other land. He enumerates "relics" of a childhood—"pieces of dyed cotton and gnawed wood," "lint of voices," "summer sunlight on dried paint," the "brightness of a white afternoon," "ferns on the shore of the transparent lake." All of these suggest a time of tranquility and happiness. A *relic* was originally an object owned by or a remain of a venerated person or saint. How do the items in Merwin's list function as relics? The poet questions whether it would be better to bear in mind or to forget these sense memories. Which would you advise?

    The ending lines of the poem deal with one's sense of identity. Merwin sees the emigré as a displaced person who floats "between ageless languages/calling from one to the other who you are." What is the effect of the verb "float" in the closing lines of "Emigré"?

Writer's Workshop

1. W. S. Merwin carefully constructs "Emigré" so that each stanza makes its own argument. The poem builds to a climax that makes use of striking

visual images. Could auditory sense memory be as evocative? Try writing a poem where remembered *sounds* are vividly recalled and described to bring back times of pleasure in your own life. Reach back as far as you can in your own experience. Divide your poem into stanzas to show time breaks.

2. What is the effect of addressing each stanza in "Emigré" to an unnamed "you" who is an emigré? How does it personalize the poem? Write a poem to a "you" of your own about something this "you" should care about. Give advice, or ask questions to give your poem unity.

3. Write an essay for or against giving up one's native language in the process of becoming a U.S. citizen. You might want to include some of Merwin's arguments. Before you begin, make a list of the advantages/disadvantages of speaking only English in public and in private with friends and family. In your essay use examples from selections in this unit.

Grandma's ★ Primo ★

LEROY V. QUINTANA

Leroy Quintana is a Mexican American who currently lives in the Southwest. He writes with humor and affection of the traditions and daily lives of his compatriots.

Grandma had a cousin
who lived in the big city
and looked like a gringo[1]

---

[1] *gringo:* white American, typically one of Anglo-Saxon stock, in Latino slang.

He smoked a big cigar
and spoke English as well   5
as he spoke Spanish

He loved to tell jokes
would always tell them twice—
the first time in Spanish
and the second time in English   10
to impress us

Talking It Through

1. This poem has only twelve lines and is divided into three short stanzas. The first identifies the subject and translates the title—*Primo* is the Spanish word for cousin. It tells us that Grandma's cousin was something of a sophisticate, a fellow who was familiar with urban ways and was not identifiably Latino. Why do you think the poet chose to refer to Grandma's relative as her "primo," using Spanish in the title? What is the effect of the word "gringo" in line three?

2. The second stanza gives three more facts about this individual. What does his "big cigar" imply about him? The bare essentials we need to know are flatly stated, including his mastery of English. What effect does the simplicity of these statements and the even rhythm of the lines create in the first two stanzas?

3. The last stanza contains the punch line that makes the point of the poem. Are the primo's relatives proud of their cousin's linguistic ability? Which language, Spanish or English, does Grandma's cousin think confers greater status? How does the last line make an ironic point?

Writer's Workshop

1. Try to replicate the form of Quintana's poem in one of your own. Describe a family member or friend as simply and succinctly as you can. Think of words to give a portrait of the individual as economically as possible.

   In your first stanza give this person's relationship to the narrator of the poem. Tell something about his/her environment and appearance. In your second stanza give at least two more characteristics by means of simple descriptions. In your final stanza, add a few more facts and include a comment about your subject. Try to make the rhythm work for you.

2. Compare "Learning My Father's Language" with "Grandma's Primo." What does each poet seem to be saying about the experience of acquiring a new language?

AMERICAN DREAM/ AMERICAN REALITY

WITH THE EXCEPTION OF THE AFRICAN SLAVE, WHOSE American reality was the nightmare of servitude and whose dream was of an escape to justice, freedom, or a remembered homeland, emigrés have looked to the United States for the fulfillment of their dreams. These dreams usually involved the anticipation of material success. This was true, as the reader will see, for the resourceful Scottish newsboy Andrew Carnegie, as well as for the enterprising Colon brothers from Puerto Rico who shared a much admired American suit.

Other writers in this section speak of the immigrants' dreams of liberation from constricting social customs or the limitations of their former social class.

But for many of those who arrived with great expectations, the adjustment involved pain, disappointment, prejudice, and even despair. Authors Michael Gold, Upton Sinclair, and Willa Cather, among others in this unit, chronicle the disappointing, often grim realities the new life also entailed.

Prospective
⋆ *Immigrants* ⋆
Please Note

A D R I E N N E   R I C H

*Adrienne Rich, a major American poet who has won the National Book Award for
Poetry, writes here of the symbolic "door" that confronts new immigrants to America.*

Either you will
go through this door
or you will not go through.

If you go through
there is always the risk   5
of remembering your name.

Things look at you doubly
and you must look back
and let them happen.

If you do not go through   10
it is possible
to live worthily

to maintain your attitudes
to hold your position
to die bravely   15

but much will blind you,
much will evade you,
at what cost who knows?

The door itself
makes no promises.   20
It is only a door.

Talking It Through

1. This poem has seven three-line unrhymed stanzas. It uses simple words and just one strong visual image, that of a door. What does this door lead to? What is the risk of the immigrant choosing to "go through"? What would be gained?

2. If the immigrant does not go through the door, what should he or she expect? Does the poet mean that by not going through the immigrant is staying behind in the native country?

3. What "costs" do you foresee could be the result of not choosing to go through the door?

4. Why does Adrienne Rich say "the door itself makes no promises"? What might she mean by this?

Writer's Workshop

1. Use the metaphor of a door in a poem of your own. What will your "door" be the entrance to or exit from? What lies beyond it? Is it associated with a choice you will make or have made?

2. Write an essay with a cautionary tone entitled *Prospective Immigrants Please Note*. What would you select to warn them about or against? What advice would you give today? What should they expect? Decide whether your essay will be serious or humorous and prewrite your ideas accordingly.

The New ★ *Colossus*

★

EMMA LAZARUS

Emma Lazarus, as a young woman, won a prize for her poem commemorating the gift of the Statue of Liberty by France to the United States in 1884. The poem's widespread dissemination and its memorization by thousands of first-generation schoolchildren helped spread the concept of America as a haven for all comers.

Not like the brazen[1] giant of Greek fame,
With conquering limbs astride from land to land;
Here at our sea-washed, sunset gates shall stand
A mighty woman with a torch,[2] whose flame
Is the imprisoned lightning,[3] and her name   5
Mother of Exiles.[4] From her beacon-hand
Glows world-wide welcome; her mild eyes command
The air-bridged harbor that twin cities frame.
"Keep, ancient lands, your storied pomp!"[5] cries she
With silent lips. "Give me your tired, your poor,   10
Your huddled masses yearning to breathe free,
The wretched refuse[6] of your teeming shore.

[1]*brazen:* means bronze, but also bold; "brazen giant" refers to the "Colossus" that was said to bestride the harbor at the island of Rhodes around 280 B.C. It was said to be a gigantic statue of the Greek god Apollo.
[2]*torch:* The Statue of Liberty has a torch in one hand and a book in the other.
[3]*imprisoned lightning:* refers to electricity, then new. Street lights were still being converted to electricity from gaslight in Manhattan at that time.
[4]*exiles:* those forcibly deported from their country.
[5]*pomp:* a showy display of power or wealth.
[6]*wretched refuse:* refers to poor immigrants who left overpopulated lands for America's wide open spaces.

Send these, the homeless, tempest-tost[7] to me,
I lift my lamp beside the golden door!"[8]

Talking It Through

1. Emma Lazarus speaks of the Statue of Liberty as "Mother of Exiles" from whose "beacon-hand/Glows world-wide welcome." This has been for generations of immigrants the embodiment of the American dream. Use examples you have read to demonstrate this ideal view. Was the reality then, or is it now, that welcoming?

2. "Keep, ancient lands, your storied pomp!" What might this exclamation mean?

3. The next imagined words of the statue are perhaps the most famous. Liberty is asking for the poor, the oppressed, the rejects of old-world civilization. Does the United States today follow such a policy of open immigration? Has it in the past?

   Look up a history of immigration laws to determine what the attitude toward newcomers has been from a governmental point of view. Has official policy always been welcoming? Have all ethnic groups been treated the same? Would you make laws to restrict immigration in ways different from the standards used in this poem?

4. "The New Colossus" ends with, "I lift my lamp beside the golden door!" For what is the golden door a metaphor? For which people that you have read about might the golden door metaphor be a reality? For whom would it have been only a dream?

Writer's Workshop

1. This poem starts with a negation, "Not like the brazen giant of Greek fame." Write a poem to make a point by using a series of negative statements, so that your positive position emerges clearly by contrast. Make sure you have strong feelings about your subject so you can write about it convincingly.

[7]*tempest-tost:* refers to storms at sea. A tempest is a severe storm. The portion of the poem within quotation marks is its most famous part and was inscribed on a plaque at the statue's base.

[8]*golden door:* land of opportunity. The Chinese referred to America as the land of "the golden mountain," Eastern European immigrants expected the streets to be "paved with gold." Gold became a symbolic word to express all hopes of success in America.

Alternately, write a poem or story in which an inanimate object (it might be a store window mannequin, a statue in a public park or square) speaks directly to the reader. What will it say? How does it regard the passing scene?

2. In recent years, groups that have felt themselves disenfranchised, such as Native Americans, have tried to gain attention for their position by taking over Liberty Island and its symbolic statue. You may choose to write an imagined report of such a takeover as it might appear in a daily newspaper, or you might write from the point of view of the Statue of Liberty herself as she views change in America.

from The Life
★ *of Gustavus* ★
Vassa

G U S T A V U S   V A S S A
(O L A U D A H   E Q U I A N O)

Gustavus Vassa (known also as Olaudah Equiano) was born the son of an Igbo chieftain in what is now Nigeria. When he was eleven he was kidnapped and sold into slavery, eventually ending up in the hands of white slave traders. He was forced to march hundreds of miles from the interior of Africa to the coast where the ship lay that would transport him to the slave markets of Barbados. Far from home, he found few of his own tribespeople with whom he could even converse. Here he recounts how he was brought on ship, sold in Barbados, and finally brought to Virginia as a slave.

　　Vassa spent only a short time in Virginia when he was sold to an American sea captain. After becoming a skilled seaman, he found ways to earn money and the captain eventually permitted Vassa to buy his own freedom. By the time he wrote his autobiography in 1792, Vassa had become one of the best traveled people of his day.

A SLAVE SHIP

THE FIRST OBJECT THAT SALUTED MY EYES WHEN I ARRIVED ON THE COAST WAS the sea, and a slave ship, which was then riding at anchor, and waiting for its cargo. These filled me with astonishment, that was soon converted into terror, which I am yet at a loss to describe, and much more the then feelings of my mind when I was carried on board. I was immediately handled and tossed up to see if I was sound, by some of the crew; and I was now persuaded that I had got into a world of bad spirits, and that they were going to kill me. Their complexions too, differing so much from ours, their long hair, and the language they spoke, which was very different from any I had ever heard, united to confirm me in this belief.

When I looked round the ship too, and saw a large furnace or copper boiling and a multitude of black people, of every description, chained together, every one of their countenances expressing dejection and sorrow, I no longer doubted of my fate; and, quite overpowered with horror and anguish, I fell motionless on the deck, and fainted. . . .

Soon after this the blacks who brought me on board went off, and left me abandoned to despair. I now saw myself deprived of all chance of returning to my native country, or even the least glimpse of gaining the shore, which I now considered as friendly; and I even wished for my former slavery,[1] in preference to my present situation, which was filled with horrors of every kind, still heightened by my ignorance of what I was to undergo. I was not long suffered to indulge my grief. I was soon put down under the decks, and there I received such a salutation in my nostrils as I had never experienced in my life; so that, with the loathsomeness of the stench, and with my crying together, I became so sick and low that I was not able to eat, nor had I the least desire to taste any thing. I now wished for the last friend, death, to relieve me; but soon, to my grief, two of the white men offered me eatables; and, on my refusing to eat, one of them held me fast by the hands, and laid me across, I think, the windlass,[2] and tied my feet, while the other flogged[3] me severely. I had never experienced any thing of this kind before, and although, not being used to the water, I naturally feared that element the first time I saw it, yet nevertheless, could I have got over the nettings, I would have jumped over the side, but I could not; and besides the crew used to watch us very closely, who were not chained down to the decks, lest we should leap into the water. I have seen some of these

---

[1] *my former slavery:* Vassa was at first a slave of other Africans, in a milder form of slavery.

[2] *windlass:* a crank used to hoist or haul the anchor.

[3] *flogged:* beaten with a strap or whip.

poor African prisoners most severely cut for attempting to do so, and hourly whipped for not eating. This indeed was often the case with myself. In a little time after, amongst the poor chained men, I found some of my own nation, which in a small degree gave ease to my mind. I inquired of these what was to be done with us. They gave me to understand we were to be carried to these white people's country to work for them. I was then a little revived, and thought if it were no worse than working, my situation was not so desperate. But still I feared I should be put to death, the white people looked and acted, as I thought, in so savage a manner. . . .

I could not help expressing my fearful apprehensions[4] to some of my countrymen; I asked them if these people had no country, but lived in this hollow place, the ship. They told me they did not, but came from a distant one. 'Then,' said I, 'how comes it, that in all our country we never heard of them?' They told me, because they lived so very far off. I then asked, where their women were: had they any like themselves. I was told they had. 'And why,' said I, 'do we not see them?' They answered, because they were left behind. I asked how the vessel could go. They told me they could not tell, but that there was cloth put upon the masts by the help of the ropes I saw, and then the vessel went on; and the white men had some spell or magic they put in the water, when they liked, in order to stop the vessel. I was exceedingly amazed at this account, and really thought they were spirits. I therefore wished much to be from amongst them, for I expected they would sacrifice me; but my wishes were in vain, for we were so quartered that it was impossible for any of us to make our escape.

At last, when the ship, in which we were, had got in all her cargo, they made ready with many fearful noises, and we were all put under deck, so that we could not see how they managed the vessel.

But this disappointment was the least of my grief. The stench of the hold, while we were on the coast, was so intolerably loathsome,[5] that it was dangerous to remain there for any time, and some of us had been permitted to stay on the deck for the fresh air; but now that the whole ship's cargo were confined together, it became absolutely pestilential.[6] The closeness of the place, and the heat of the climate, added to the number in the ship, being so crowded that each had scarcely room to turn himself, almost suffocated us. This produced copious[7] perspirations, so that the air soon

[4]*apprehensions:* fears.

[5]*loathsome:* disgusting, detestable.

[6]*pestilential:* like an epidemic disease.

[7]*copious:* plentiful.

became unfit for respiration, from a variety of loathsome smells, and brought on a sickness among the slaves, of which many died, thus falling victims to the improvident avarice,[8] as I may call it, of their purchasers. This deplorable situation was again aggravated by the galling of the chains, now become insupportable; and the filth of necessary tubs, into which the children often fell, and were almost suffocated. The shrieks of the women, and the groans of the dying, rendered it a scene of horror almost inconceivable. Happily, perhaps, for myself, I was soon reduced so low here that it was thought necessary to keep me almost continually on deck; and from my extreme youth, I was not put in fetters. In this situation I expected every hour to share the fate of my companions, some of whom were almost daily brought upon deck at the point of death, and I began to hope that death would soon put an end to my miseries. Often did I think many of the inhabitants of the deep much more happy than myself; I envied them the freedom they enjoyed, and as often wished I could change my condition for theirs. Every circumstance I met with served only to render my state more painful, and heighten my apprehensions and my opinion of the cruelty of the whites. One day they had taken a number of fishes; and when they had killed and satisfied themselves with as many as they thought fit, to our astonishment who were on the deck, rather than give any of them to us to eat, as we expected, they tossed the remaining fish into the sea again, although we begged and prayed for some as well as we could, but in vain; and some of my countrymen, being pressed by hunger, took an opportunity, when they thought no one saw them, of trying to get a little privately; but were discovered, and the attempt procured for them some very severe floggings.

One day, when we had a smooth sea and moderate wind, two of my wearied countrymen, who were chained together, (I was near them at the time) preferring death to such a life of misery, somehow made through the nettings and jumped into the sea: immediately another quite dejected fellow, who on account of his illness was suffered to be out of irons also followed their example; and I believe many more would very soon have done the same, if they had not been prevented by the ship's crew, who were instantly alarmed. Those of us who were the most active were in a moment put down under the deck; and there was such a noise and confusion amongst the people of the ship as I never heard before, to stop her and get the boat out to go after the slaves. However, two of the wretches were drowned; but they got the other, and afterward flogged him unmercifully, for thus attempting to prefer death to slavery. . . .

[8] *improvident avarice:* wasteful greed.

A SLAVE MARKET IN BARBADOS

DURING OUR PASSAGE I FIRST SAW FLYING FISHES, WHICH SURPRISED ME VERY much; they used frequently to fly across the ship, and many of them fell on the deck. I also now first saw the use of the quadrant.[9] I had often with astonishment seen the mariners make observations with it, and I could not think what it meant. They at last took notice of my surprise; and one of them, willing to increase it, as well as to gratify my curiosity, made me one day look through it. The clouds appeared to me to be land, which disappeared as they passed along. This heightened my wonder; and I was now more persuaded than ever that I was in another world, and that every thing about me was magic. At last we came in sight of the island of Barbados, at which the whites on board gave a great shout, and made many signs of joy to us. We did not know what to think of this, but as the vessel drew nearer we plainly saw the harbour, and other ships of different kinds and sizes; and we soon anchored amongst them off Bridge Town. Many merchants and planters now came on board, though it was in the evening. They put us in separate parcels, and examined us attentively. They also made us jump, and pointed to the land, signifying we were to go there. We thought by this we should be beaten by these ugly men, as they appeared to us; and when soon after we were all put down under the deck again, there was much dread and trembling among us, and nothing but bitter cries to be heard all the night from these apprehensions, insomuch that at last the white people got some old slaves from the land to pacify us. They told us we were not to be eaten, but to work, and were soon to go on land, where we should see many of our country people. This report eased us much; and, sure enough, soon after we landed, there came to us Africans of all languages.

We were conducted immediately to the merchant's yard, where we were all pent up together like so many sheep in a fold, without regard to sex or age. As every object was new to me, everything I saw filled me with surprise. What struck me first was that the houses were built with bricks in stories, and were in every other respect different from those I had seen in Africa; but I was still more astonished at seeing people on horseback. I did not know what this could mean; and indeed I thought these people full of nothing but magical arts. . . .

We were not many days in the merchants' custody before we were sold after the usual manner, which is this:—On a signal given, such as the beat

---

[9]*quadrant:* an instrument used by navigators to measure angles.

of a drum, the buyers rush at once into the yard where the slaves are confined, and make choice of that parcel they like best. The noise and clamour with which this is attended, and the eagerness visible in the countenances of the buyers, serve not a little to increase the apprehensions of the terrified Africans, who may well be supposed to consider them the ministers of that destruction to which they think themselves devoted. In this manner, without scruple,[10] are relations and friends separated, most of them never to see each other again. I remember in the vessel in which I was brought over in, in the man's apartment, there were several brothers, who, in the sale, were sold in different lots; and it was very moving on this occasion to see their distress and hear their cries at parting. O, ye nominal Christians! might not an African ask you, "learned you this from your God, who says unto you, Do unto all men as you would men should do unto you? Is it not enough that we are torn from our country and friends, to toil for your luxury and lust of gain? Must every tender feeling be likewise sacrificed to your avarice? Are the dearest friends and relations now rendered more dear by their separation from the rest of their kindred, still to be parted from each other, and thus prevented from cheering the gloom of slavery, with the small comfort of being together, and mingling their sufferings and sorrows? Why are parents to lose their children, brothers their sisters, or husbands their wives? Surely this is a new refinement in cruelty, which, while it has no advantage to atone for it, thus aggravates distress, and adds fresh horrors even to the wretchedness of slavery." . . .

A SLAVE IN VIRGINIA

I NOW TOTALLY LOST THE SMALL REMAINS OF COMFORT I HAD ENJOYED IN conversing with my countrymen; the women, too, who used to wash and take care of me, were all gone different ways, and I never saw one of them afterwards.

I stayed in this island for a few days; I believe it could not be above a fortnight;[11] when I and some few more slaves, who from very much fretting were not saleable among the rest, were shipped off in a sloop for North America. On the passage we were better treated than when coming from Africa, and we had plenty of rice and fat pork. We were landed up a river a good way from the sea, about Virginia county, where we saw few of our

[10]*scruple:* misgiving about something one thinks is wrong.
[11]*fortnight:* two weeks.

native Africans, and not one soul who could talk to me. I was a few weeks weeding grass and gathering stones in a plantation; and at last all my companions were distributed different ways, and only myself was left. I was now exceedingly miserable, and thought myself worse off than any of the rest of my companions; for they could talk to each other, but I had no person to speak to that I could understand. In this state I was constantly grieving and pining, and wishing for death rather than any thing else. While I was in this plantation the gentleman to whom I supposed the estate belonged being unwell, I was one day sent for to his dwelling-house to fan him. When I came into the room where he was, I was very much affrighted at some things I saw, and the more so, as I had seen a black woman slave as I came through the house, who was cooking the dinner, the poor creature was cruelly loaded with various kinds of iron machines; she had one particularly on her head, which locked her mouth so fast that she could scarcely speak, and could not eat or drink. I was much astonished and shocked at this contrivance, which I afterwards learned was called the iron muzzle. Soon after I had a fan put into my hand, to fan the gentleman while he slept; and so I did indeed with great fear. While he was fast asleep I indulged myself a great deal in looking about the room, which to me appeared very fine and curious. The first object that engaged my attention was a watch, which hung on the chimney, and was going. I was quite surprised at the noise it made, and was afraid it would tell the gentleman any thing I might do amiss: and when I immediately after observed a picture hanging in the room, which appeared constantly to look at me, I was still more affrighted, having never seen such things as these before. At one time I thought it was something relative to magic; and not seeing it move, I thought it might be some way the whites had to keep their great men when they died, and offer them libations,[12] as we used to do to our friendly spirits. In this state of anxiety I remained till my master awoke, when I was dismissed out of the room, to my no small satisfaction and relief; for I thought that these people were all made up of wonders. In this place I was called JACOB; but on board the African Snow I was called MICHAEL.

★ ★ ★ ★ ★

Talking It Through

1. In coming to America other immigrant groups endured many hardships in the belief that their lives would be improved. Because of this, newcomers

---

[12]*libations:* a ritual drink offered to a god.

like Michael Pupin and Jamaica Kincaid's Lucy could look upon the unknown with optimism. How does Vassa interpret the unknown? What does he think will happen to him on board the slave ship? Are his fears worse than the reality?

2. Make a list of the physical deprivations endured by the Africans on board the ship and when they are sold in Barbados. Make a list of their psychological hardships. Do you think it a sign of cowardice or strength that some Africans preferred to die rather than endure them? Explain.

3. What do the conditions on the ship reflect about the white's views of the Africans? In what ways is their greed apparent?

4. Why are the Africans forbidden to see how the ship is run? What other precautions are taken on board the ship to prevent the Africans from rebelling or choosing death over slavery? Do you see any inconsistencies in the European view of their African captives?

5. When he reaches Virginia, Vassa does not know the language or customs of his new country. What new things amaze him, and how does he explain them? Why don't we find his situation charming or funny, as we did with the other newcomers? What is the tone of his writing compared to theirs?

Writer's Workshop

1. In many ways the accounts by William Bradford (p. 21) and by Vassa of their arrival in America are mirror images of one another. Both describe sea journeys full of peril. Both describe the terror of the unknown. But the Pilgrims elect to go, while Vassa is forced. The Pilgrims feel themselves fortunate to be "chosen" by God and led to the Promised Land, whereas Vassa is at the mercy of his white captors who force him into slavery.

   In an essay, compare these two accounts. Find as many points of comparison as possible. Try to cover the following topics:
   a. The sea journey itself. How does each writer view the sea? Why?
   b. The role of the community and the role of the individual. In what ways do the Pilgrims gather strength from being part of a community? In what ways has the process of enslavement attempted to destroy African communities?
   c. The tone of the narrators. In what way are both authors writing "for history"? What effect does each hope to have on the reader and what techniques are used to accomplish it?

2. Vassa and other freed or escaped slaves wrote their autobiographies in an attempt to speak for the millions of their brethren still in chains. At the time

that Vassa published his work, both American and British slave trade was flourishing, and in America slavery was spreading west.

Using the information provided by Vassa, write a petition to Congress asking for the abolition of the slave trade and slavery.

a. Open your petition with a polite address to your Congressman.

b. State clearly what it is you are petitioning for.

c. Give your reasons for believing slavery wrong.

d. Support your reasons with facts drawn from Vassa's account.

e. Conclude your petition as persuasively as possible, and sign it.

How I
★ Served My ★
Apprenticeship

ANDREW CARNEGIE

Andrew Carnegie was born in Scotland in 1837. Here he recounts how his parents moved to Pittsburgh when he was a boy, seeking work and a brighter future for their children. Carnegie eventually built his fortune in the steel industry, becoming one of the richest Americans of his day. After retiring in 1901, he devoted his time to spending his money on worthy causes. Among other projects, he founded 2500 public libraries, established schools, and financed the building of Carnegie Hall in New York City. It is as a philanthropist that he is still remembered today.

IT IS A GREAT PLEASURE TO TELL HOW I SERVED MY APPRENTICESHIP[1] AS A business man. But there seems to be a question preceding this: Why did

---

[1]*apprenticeship:* the learning of a craft or trade.

I become a business man? I am sure that I should never have selected a business career if I had been permitted to choose.

The eldest son of parents who were themselves poor, I had, fortunately, to begin to perform some useful work in the world while still very young in order to earn an honest livelihood, and was thus shown even in early boyhood that my duty was to assist my parents and, like them, become as soon as possible a breadwinner in the family. What I could get to do, not what I desired, was the question.

When I was born [1837] my father was a well-to-do master weaver in Dunfermline, Scotland. He owned no less than four damask[2] looms and employed apprentices. This was before the days of steam factories for the manufacture of linen. A few large merchants took orders and employed master weavers such as my father to weave the cloth, the merchants supplying the materials.

As the factory system developed, hand-loom weaving naturally declined, and my father was one of the sufferers by the change. The first serious lesson of my life came to me one day when he had taken in the last of his work to the merchant and returned to our little home greatly distressed because there was no more work for him to do. I was then just about ten years of age, but the lesson burned into my heart, and I resolved then that the wolf of poverty should be driven from our door some day if I could do it.

The question of selling the old looms and starting for the United States came up in the family council, and I heard it discussed from day to day. It was finally resolved to take the plunge and join relatives already in Pittsburgh. I well remember that neither Father nor Mother thought the change would be otherwise than a great sacrifice for them, but that "it would be better for the two boys."

In after life, if you can look back as I do and wonder at the complete surrender of their own desires which parents make for the good of their children, you must reverence their memories with feelings akin to worship.

On arriving in Allegheny City (there were four of us: Father, Mother, my younger brother, and myself), my father entered a cotton factory. I soon followed and served as a "bobbin[3] boy," and this is how I began my preparation for subsequent apprenticeship as a business man. I received one dollar and twenty cents a week and was then just about twelve years old.

I cannot tell you how proud I was when I received my first week's own earnings. One dollar and twenty cents made by myself and given to me

[2]*damask:* a durable fabric woven with an intricate and reversible pattern.

[3]*bobbin:* a spool for thread or yarn.

because I had been of some use in the world! No longer entirely dependent upon my parents, but at last admitted to the family partnership as a contributing member and able to help them! I think this makes a man out of a boy sooner than almost anything else, and a real man, too, if there be any germ of true manhood in him. It is everything to feel that you are useful. . . .

For a lad of twelve to rise and breakfast every morning except the blessed Sunday morning and go into the streets and find his way to the factory and begin to work while it was still dark outside, and not be released until after darkness came again in the evening, forty minutes' interval only being allowed at noon, was a terrible task.

But I was young and had my dreams, and something within always told me that this would not, could not, should not last—I should some day get into a better position. Besides this, I felt myself no longer a mere boy, but quite a little man, and this made me happy.

A change soon came, for a kind old Scotsman, who knew some of our relatives, made bobbins, and took me into his factory before I was thirteen. But here for a time it was even worse than in the cotton factory, because I was set to fire a boiler in the cellar and actually to run the small steam engine which drove the machinery. The firing of the boiler was all right, for fortunately we did not use coal, but the refuse wooden chips; and I always liked to work in wood. But the responsibility of keeping the water right and of running the engine and the danger of my making a mistake and blowing the whole factory to pieces caused too great a strain, and I often awoke and found myself sitting up in bed through the night, trying the steam gauges. But I never told them at home that I was having a hard tussle. No, no! everything must be bright to them.

This was a point of honor, for every member of the family was working hard, except, of course, my little brother, who was then a child, and we were telling each other only all the bright things. Besides this, no man would whine and give up—he would die first.

There was no servant in our family, and several dollars per week were earned by the mother by binding shoes after her daily work was done! Father was also hard at work in the factory. And could I complain?

My kind employer, John Hay—peace to his ashes!—soon relieved me of the undue strain, for he needed some one to make out bills and keep his accounts, and finding that I could write a plain schoolboy hand and could cipher,[4] he made me his only clerk. But still I had to work hard upstairs in the factory, for the clerking took but little time. . . .

I come now to the third step in my apprenticeship, for I had already taken two, as you see—the cotton factory and then the bobbin factory; and with

---

[4]*cipher:* to solve math problems.

the third—the third time is the chance, you know—deliverance came. I obtained a situation as messenger boy in the telegraph office of Pittsburgh when I was fourteen. Here I entered a new world.

Amid books, newspapers, pencils, pens and ink and writing pads, and a clean office, bright windows, and the literary atmosphere, I was the happiest boy alive.

My only dread was that I should some day be dismissed because I did not know the city, for it is necessary that a messenger boy should know all the firms and addresses of men who are in the habit of receiving telegrams. But I was a stranger in Pittsburgh. However, I made up my mind that I would learn to repeat successively each business house in the principal streets and was soon able to shut my eyes and begin at one side of Wood Street and call every firm successively to the top, then pass to the other side and call every firm to the bottom. Before long I was able to do this with the business streets generally. My mind was then at rest upon that point.

Of course every ambitious messenger boy wants to become an operator,[5] and before the operators arrived in the early mornings the boys slipped up to the instruments and practised. This I did and was soon able to talk to the boys in the other offices along the line who were also practising.

One morning I heard Philadelphia calling Pittsburgh and giving the signal, "Death message." Great attention was then paid to "death messages," and I thought I ought to try to take this one. I answered and did so, and went off and delivered it before the operator came. After that the operators sometimes used to ask me to work for them.

Having a sensitive ear for sound, I soon learned to take messages by the ear, which was then very uncommon—I think only two persons in the United States could then do it. Now every operator takes by ear, so easy is it to follow and do what any other boy can—if you only have to. This brought me into notice, and finally I became an operator and received the, to me, enormous recompense of twenty-five dollars per month—three hundred dollars a year!

This was a fortune—the very sum that I had fixed when I was a factory worker as the fortune I wished to possess, because the family could live on three hundred dollars a year and be almost or quite independent. Here it was at last! But I was soon to be in receipt of extra compensation for extra work.

The six newspapers of Pittsburgh received telegraphic news in common. Six copies of each dispatch were made by a gentleman who received six dollars per week for the work, and he offered me a gold dollar every week

---

[5]*operator:* telegraph operator who could use Morse code.

if I would do it, of which I was very glad indeed, because I always liked to work with news and scribble for newspapers.

The reporters came to a room every evening for the news which I had prepared, and this brought me into most pleasant intercourse with these clever fellows, and besides, I got a dollar a week as pocket money, for this was not considered family revenue by me.

I think this last step of doing something beyond one's task is fully entitled to be considered "business." The other revenue, you see, was just salary obtained for regular work; but here was a little business operation upon my own account, and I was very proud indeed of my gold dollar every week.

The Pennsylvania Railroad shortly after this was completed to Pittsburgh, and that genius, Thomas A. Scott, was its superintendent. He often came to the telegraph office to talk to his chief, the general superintendent, at Altoona; and I became known to him in this way.

When that great railway system put up a wire of its own, he asked me to be his clerk and operator; so I left the telegraph office—in which there is great danger that a young man may be permanently buried, as it were—and became connected with the railways.

The new appointment was accompanied by what was to me a tremendous increase of salary. It jumped from twenty-five to thirty-five dollars per month. Mr. Scott was then receiving one hundred and twenty-five dollars per month, and I used to wonder what on earth he could do with so much money.

I remained for thirteen years in the service of the Pennsylvania Railroad Company and was at last superintendent of the Pittsburgh division of the road, successor to Mr. Scott, who had in the meantime risen to the office of vice-president of the company.

One day, Mr. Scott, who was the kindest of men and had taken a great fancy to me, asked if I had or could find five hundred dollars to invest.

Here the business instinct came into play. I felt that as the door was opened for a business investment with my chief, it would be willful flying in the face of Providence if I did not jump at it; so I answered promptly:

"Yes sir; I think I can."

"Very well," he said, "get it; a man has just died who owns ten shares in the Adams Express Company which I want you to buy. It will cost you fifty dollars per share, and I can help you with a little balance if you cannot raise it all."

Here was a queer position. The available assets of the whole family were not five hundred dollars. But there was one member of the family whose ability, pluck and resource never failed us; and I felt sure the money could be raised somehow or other by my mother.

Indeed, had Mr. Scott known our position he would have advanced it himself; but the last thing in the world the proud Scot will do is to reveal his poverty and rely upon others. The family had managed by this time to purchase a small house and pay for it in order to save rent. My recollection is that it was worth eight hundred dollars.

The matter was laid before the council of three that night, and the oracle[6] spoke: "Must be done. Mortgage our house. I will take the steamer in the morning for Ohio and see Uncle and ask him to arrange it. I am sure he can." This was done. Of course her visit was successful—where did she ever fail?

The money was procured, paid over; ten shares of Adams Express Company stock was mine; but no one knew our little home had been mortgaged "to give our boy a start."

Adams Express stock then paid monthly dividends of one per cent, and the first check for five dollars arrived. I can see it now, and I well remember the signature of "J.D. Babcock, Cashier," who wrote a big "John Hancock" hand.

The next day being Sunday, we boys—myself and my ever-constant companions—took our usual Sunday afternoon stroll in the country, and sitting down in the woods, I showed them this check, saying: "Eureka! We have found it."

Here was something new to all of us, for none of us had ever received anything but from toil. A return from capital was something strange and new.

How money could make money, how, without any attention from me, this mysterious golden visitor should come, led to much speculation upon the part of the young fellows; and I was for the first time hailed as a "capitalist."

You see, I was beginning to serve my apprenticeship as a business man in a satisfactory manner.

A very important incident in my life occurred when one day in a train a nice, farmer-looking gentleman approached me, saying that the conductor had told him I was connected with the Pennsylvania Railroad, and he would like to show me something. He pulled from a small green bag the model of the first sleeping car. This was Mr. Woodruff, the inventor.

Its value struck me like a flash. I asked him to come to Altoona the following week, and he did so. Mr. Scott, with his usual quickness, grasped the idea. A contract was made with Mr. Woodruff to put two trial cars on the Pennsylvania Railroad. Before leaving Altoona, Mr. Woodruff came and offered me an interest in the venture, which I promptly accepted. But how I was to make my payments rather troubled me, for the cars were to

[6]*oracle:* a wise person who has powers to see the future.

be paid for in monthly instalments after delivery, and my first monthly payment was to be two hundred and seventeen dollars and a half.

I had not the money, and I did not see any way of getting it. But I finally decided to visit the local banker and ask him for a loan, pledging myself to repay at the rate of fifteen dollars per month. He promptly granted it. Never shall I forget his putting his arm over my shoulder, saying, "Oh, yes, Andy; you are all right!"

I then and there signed my first note. Proud day this, and surely now no one will dispute that I was becoming a business man. I had signed my first note, and most important of all—for any fellow can sign a note—I had found a banker willing to take it as good.

My subsequent payments were made by the receipts from the sleeping cars, and I really made my first considerable sum from this investment in the Woodruff Sleeping Car Company, which was afterward absorbed by Mr. Pullman, a remarkable man whose name is now known over all the world.

Shortly after this I was appointed superintendent of the Pittsburgh division and returned to my dear old home, smoky Pittsburgh. Wooden bridges were then used exclusively upon the railways, and the Pennsylvania Railroad was experimenting with a bridge built of cast iron. I saw that wooden bridges would not do for the future and organized a company in Pittsburgh to build iron bridges.

Here again I had recourse to the bank, because my share of the capital was twelve hundred and fifty dollars, and I had not the money; but the bank lent it to me, and we began the Keystone Bridge Works, which proved a great success. This company built the first great bridge over the Ohio River, three hundred feet span, and has built many of the most important structures since.

This was my beginning in manufacturing, and from that start all our other works have grown, the profits of one building the other. My apprenticeship as a business man soon ended, for I resigned my position as an officer of the Pennsylvania Railroad Company to give exclusive attention to business.

I was no longer merely an official working for others upon a salary, but a full-fledged business man working upon my own account.

And so ends the story of my apprenticeship and graduation as a business man.

★ ★ ★ ★ ★

Talking It Through

1. How does Carnegie set an optimistic tone in the first paragraph? How do we know he will succeed?

2. Why have Carnegie's parents come to America? As a young boy, why does Carnegie remain hopeful and determined, even under terrible hardships?

3. Carnegie writes about the "steps" in his apprenticeship very much as if he were climbing a ladder of success. Make your own chart of Carnegie's progress in the form of a ladder with steps.

   a. At each level, write down notes about his job and age, and the money and status he earned.

   b. Looking back at your chart, what qualities helped Carnegie succeed? What roles did luck, intelligence, and determination play? How did he make use of the new technologies of his age to get ahead? (Note that as a Scottish immigrant Carnegie already knew English, and Scots did not face the prejudice that greeted many other immigrant groups when they arrived.)

4. Carnegie writes that when he was first offered the opportunity to invest money "the door was opened." What is "this mysterious golden visitor" that he writes about later on? How do you think Carnegie would define the American Dream? What are his nightmares along the way?

5. What qualities do you think define a businessman, according to Carnegie? How do you regard businessmen and businesswomen today? Does American society still admire the entrepreneurial spirit, in your opinion? Why or why not?

Writer's Workshop

1. Write a story or short biography of someone who has climbed the "ladder of success." What motivated the person to "reach the top"? What were the steps along the way, and how did the person deal with setbacks in attaining them? Whether you are developing a fictional character, or writing about someone you know, make it interesting by developing your protagonist's personality as he or she strives to win success.

2. Imagine that you knew Andrew Carnegie when he was coming of age in Pittsburgh. You have been asked to describe what you remember of him from the "old days" when you grew up together. Create a fictional character for yourself. You could be a messenger boy who worked with him, or "the girl next door," for example. Describe his personality, what you admired or disliked about him, and create a fictional episode involving the two of you.

3. How did Carnegie achieve such success and prosperity? What rules, either explicitly stated or implicit in his behavior, guide his conduct? Based upon

this excerpt, make up a list of "Steps for Success." These can be rules that Carnegie lived and worked by. Number your Steps for Success and write the list as though it will appear in your local newspaper.

★ *from* **My**
Ántonia ★

W I L L A   C A T H E R

Willa Cather grew up among the Bohemian, German, Russian, Swedish, and Norwegian immigrants who had come to the vast empty landscape of Nebraska in search of a better life, and she based the characters in several of her works, notably O Pioneers! *and* My Ántonia, *on her observations of childhood playmates and neighbors. Cather was a Pulitzer-Prize winner, and in her writing made much use of a world she permanently left behind by 1896, when she moved east to become a magazine editor, a journalist, and a novelist.*

In her novel My Ántonia, *Cather tells the story of a Bohemian immigrant family, the Shimerdas, who have bought for more than its worth the undesirable homestead of a fellow-countryman. Knowing no English, and little of farming (the father was a weaver and craftsman in his native land), they struggle against the forces of nature, their poverty, and their disappointments. Only the elder daughter, Ántonia, who enters the story at the age of fourteen, is undaunted by the circumstances of her harsh surroundings.*

In these chapters, we see the effects of prairie life on some members of the Shimerda family.

THE WEEK FOLLOWING CHRISTMAS BROUGHT IN A THAW, AND BY NEW YEAR'S Day all the world about us was a broth of gray slush, and the guttered slope between the windmill and the barn was running black water. The soft black earth stood out in patches along the roadsides. I resumed all my chores, carried in the cobs and wood and water, and spent the afternoons at the barn, watching Jake shell corn with a hand-sheller.

One morning, during this interval of fine weather, Ántonia and her mother rode over on one of their shaggy old horses to pay us a visit. It was the first time Mrs. Shimerda had been to our house, and she ran about examining our carpets and curtains and furniture, all the while commenting upon them to her daughter in an envious, complaining tone. In the kitchen she caught up an iron pot that stood on the back of the stove and said: "You got many, Shimerdas no got." I thought it weak-minded of grandmother to give the pot to her.

After dinner, when she was helping to wash the dishes, she said, tossing her head: "You got many things for cook. If I got all things like you, I make much better."

She was a conceited, boastful old thing, and even misfortune could not humble her. I was so annoyed that I felt coldly even toward Ántonia and listened unsympathetically when she told me her father was not well.

"My papa sad for the old country. He not look good. He never make music any more. At home he play violin all the time; for weddings and for dance. Here never. When I beg him for play, he shake his head no. Some days he take his violin out of his box and make with his fingers on the strings, like this, but never he make the music. He don't like this kawn-tree."

"People who don't like this country ought to stay at home," I said severely. "We don't make them come here."

"He not want to come, nev-er!" she burst out. "My *mamenka* make him come. All the time she say: 'America big country; much money, much land for my boys, much husband for my girls,' My papa, he cry for leave his old friends what make music with him. He love very much the man what play the long horn like this"—she indicated a slide trombone. "They go to school together and are friends from boys. But my mama, she want Ambrosch for be rich, with many cattle."

"Your mama," I said angrily, "wants other people's things."

"Your grandfather is rich," she retorted fiercely. "Whey he not help my papa? Ambrosch be rich, too, after while, and he pay back. He is very smart boy. For Ambrosch my mama come here."

Ambrosch was considered the important person in the family. Mrs. Shimerda and Ántonia always deferred to him, though he was often surly with them and contemptuous[1] toward his father. Ambrosch and his mother had everything their own way. Though Ántonia loved her father more than she did anyone else, she stood in awe of her elder brother.

After I watched Ántonia and her mother go over the hill on their miserable

---

[1]*contemptuous:* haughty, disdainful.

horse, carrying our iron pot with them, I turned to grandmother, who had taken up her darning, and said I hoped that snooping old woman wouldn't come to see us any more.

Grandmother chuckled and drove her bright needle across a hole in Otto's sock. "She's not old, Jim, though I expect she seems old to you. No, I wouldn't mourn if she never came again. But, you see, a body never knows what traits poverty might bring out in 'em. It makes a woman grasping to see her children want for things. Now read me a chapter in 'The Prince of the House of David.'[2] Let's forget the Bohemians."

We had three weeks of this mild, open weather. The cattle in the corral ate corn almost as fast as the men could shell it for them, and we hoped they would be ready for an early market. One morning the two big bulls, Gladstone and Brigham Young, thought spring had come, and they began to tease and butt at each other across the barbed wire that separated them. Soon they got angry. They bellowed and pawed up the soft earth with their hoofs, rolling their eyes and tossing their heads. Each withdrew to a far corner of his own corral, and then they made for each other at a gallop. Thud, thud, we could hear the impact of their great heads, and their bellowing shook the pans on the kitchen shelves. Had they not been de-horned, they would have torn each other to pieces. Pretty soon the fat steers took it up and began butting and horning each other. Clearly, the affair had to be stopped. We all stood by and watched admiringly while Fuchs rode into the corral with a pitchfork and prodded the bulls again and again, finally driving them apart.

The big storm of the winter began on my eleventh birthday, the 20th of January. When I went down to breakfast that morning, Jake and Otto came in white as snow-men, beating their hands and stamping their feet. They began to laugh boisterously when they saw me, calling:—

"You've got a birthday present this time, Jim, and no mistake. They was a full-grown blizzard ordered for you."

All day the storm went on. The snow did not fall this time, it simply spilled out of heaven, like thousands of feather-beds being emptied. That afternoon the kitchen was a carpenter-shop; the men brought in their tools and made two great wooden shovels with long handles. Neither grand-mother nor I could go out in the storm, so Jake fed the chickens and brought in a pitiful contribution of eggs.

Next day our men had to shovel until noon to reach the barn—and the

---

[2] *The Prince of the House of David:* refers to reading the Bible. The House of David was founded by King David and its account is found in the Book of Samuel. David eventually succeeded Saul and was followed as king by Solomon. The story of David as King of the Israelites continues in the Book of Kings.

snow was still falling! There had not been such a storm in the ten years my grandfather had lived in Nebraska. He said at dinner that we would not try to reach the cattle—they were fat enough to go without their corn for a day or two; but to-morrow we must feed them and thaw out their water-tap so that they could drink. We could not so much as see the corrals, but we knew the steers were over there, huddled together under the north bank. Our ferocious bulls, subdued enough by this time, were probably warming each other's backs. "This'll take the bile out of 'em!" Fuchs remarked gleefully.

At noon that day the hens had not been heard from. After dinner Jake and Otto, their camp clothes now dried on them, stretched their stiff arms and plunged again into the drifts. They made a tunnel under the snow to the henhouse, with walls so solid that grandmother and I could walk back and forth in it. We found the chickens asleep; perhaps they thought night had come to stay. One old rooster was stirring about, pecking at the solid lump of ice in their water-tin. When we flashed the lantern in their eyes, the hens set up a great cackling and flew about clumsily, scattering down-feathers. The mottled, pin-headed guinea-hens, always resentful of captivity, ran screeching out into the tunnel and tried to poke their ugly, painted faces through the snow walls. By five o'clock the chores were done—just when it was time to begin them all over again! That was a strange, unnatural sort of day.

On the morning of the 22d I wakened with a start. Before I opened my eyes, I seemed to know that something had happened. I heard excited voices in the kitchen—grandmother's was so shrill that I knew she must be almost beside herself. I looked forward to any new crisis with delight. What could it be, I wondered, as I hurried into my clothes. Perhaps the barn had burned; perhaps the cattle had frozen to death; perhaps a neighbor was lost in the storm.

Down in the kitchen grandfather was standing before the stove with his hands behind him. Jake and Otto had taken off their boots and were rubbing their woolen socks. Their clothes and boots were steaming, and they both looked exhausted. On the bench behind the stove lay a man, covered up with a blanket. Grandmother motioned me to the dining-room. I obeyed reluctantly. I watched her as she came and went, carrying dishes. Her lips were tightly compressed and she kept whispering to herself: "Oh, dear Saviour!" "Lord, Thou knowest!"

Presently grandfather came in and spoke to me: "Jimmy, we will not have prayers this morning, because we have a great deal to do. Old Mr. Shimerda is dead, and his family are in great distress. Ambrosch came over here in the middle of the night, and Jake and Otto went back with him. The boys have had a hard night, and you must not bother them with questions. That is Ambrosch, asleep on the bench. Come in to breakfast, boys.''

After Jake and Otto had swallowed their first cup of coffee, they began to talk excitedly, disregarding grandmother's warning glances. I held my tongue, but I listened with all my ears.

"No, sir," Fuchs said in answer to a question from grandfather, "nobody heard the gun go off. Ambrosch was out with the ox team, trying to break a road, and the women folks was shut up tight in their cave. When Ambrosch come in it was dark and he didn't see nothing, but the oxen acted kind of queer. One of 'em ripped around and got away from him—bolted clean out of the stable. His hands is blistered where the rope run through. He got a lantern and went back and found the old man, just as we seen him.''

"Poor soul, poor soul!" grandmother groaned. "I'd like to think he never done it. He was always considerate and un-wishful to give trouble. How could he forget himself and bring this on us!"

"I don't think he was out of his head for a minute, Mrs. Burden," Fuchs declared. "He done everything natural. You know he was always sort of fixy, and fixy he was to the last. He shaved after dinner, and washed hisself all over after the girls was done with the dishes. Ántonia heated the water for him. Then he put on a clean shirt and clean socks, and after he was dressed he kissed her and the little one and took his gun and said he was going out to hunt rabbits. He must have gone right down to the barn and done it then. He layed down on that bunk-bed, close to the ox stalls, where he always slept. When we found him, everything was decent except,"— Fuchs wrinkled his brow and hesitated,—"except what he couldn't nowise foresee. His coat was hung on a peg, and his boots was under the bed. He'd took off that silk neckcloth he always wore, and folded it smooth and stuck his pin through it. He turned back his shirt at the neck and rolled up his sleeves.''

"I don't see how he could do it!" grandmother kept saying.

Otto misunderstood her. "Why, mam, it was simple enough; he pulled the trigger with his big toe. He layed over on his side and put the end of the barrel in his mouth, then he drew up one foot and felt for the trigger. He found it all right!"

"Maybe he did" said Jake grimly. "There's something mighty queer about it."

"Now what do you mean, Jake?" grandmother asked sharply.

"Well, mam, I found Krajiek's axe under the manger, and I picks it up and carries it over to the corpse, and I take my oath it just fit the gash in the front of the old man's face. That there Krajiek had been sneakin' around, pale and quiet, and when he seen me examinin' the axe, he begun whimperin', 'My God, man, don't do that!' 'I reckon I'm a-goin' to look into this,' says I. Then he begun to squeal like a rat and run about wringin' his hands. 'They'll hang me!' says he. 'My God, they'll hang me sure!' ''

Fuchs spoke up impatiently. "Krajiek's gone silly, Jake, and so have you. The old man wouldn't have made all them preparations for Krajiek to murder him, would he? It don't hang together. The gun was right beside him when Ambrosch found him."

"Krajiek could 'a' put it there, couldn't he?" Jake demanded.

Grandmother broke in excitedly: "See here, Jake Marpole, don't you go trying to add murder to suicide. We're deep enough in trouble. Otto reads you too many of them detective stories."

"It will be easy to decide all that, Emmaline," said grandfather quietly. "If he shot himself in the way they think, the gash will be torn from the inside outward."

"Just so it is, Mr. Burden," Otto affirmed. "I seen bunches of hair and stuff sticking to the poles and straw along the roof. They was blown up there by gunshot, no question."

Grandmother told grandfather she meant to go over to the Shimerdas with him.

"There is nothing you can do," he said doubtfully. "The body can't be touched until we get the coroner from Black Hawk, and that will be a matter of several days, this weather."

"Well, I can take them some victuals, anyway, and say a word of comfort to them poor little girls. The oldest one was his darling, and was like a right hand to him. He might have thought of her. He's left her alone in a hard world." She glanced distrustfully at Ambrosch, who was now eating his breakfast at the kitchen table.

Fuchs, although he had been up in the cold nearly all night, was going to make the long ride to Black Hawk to fetch the priest and the coroner. On the gray gelding, our best horse, he would try to pick his way across the country with no roads to guide him.

"Don't you worry about me, Mrs. Burden," he said cheerfully, as he put on a second pair of socks. "I've got a good nose for directions, and I never did need much sleep. It's the gray I'm worried about. I'll save him what I can, but it'll strain him, as sure as I'm telling you!"

"This is no time to be over-considerate of animals, Otto; do the best you can for yourself. Stop at the Widow Steaven's for dinner. She's a good woman, and she'll do well by you."

After Fuchs rode away, I was left with Ambrosch. I saw a side of him

I had not seen before. He was deeply, even slavishly, devout. He did not say a word all morning, but sat with his rosary[3] in his hands, praying, now silently, now aloud. He never looked away from his beads, nor lifted his hands except to cross himself. Several times the poor boy fell asleep where he sat, wakened with a start, and began to pray again.

No wagon could be got to the Shimerda's until a road was broken, and that would be a day's job. Grandfather came from the barn on one of our big black horses, and Jake lifted grandmother up behind him. She wore her black hood and was bundled up in shawls. Grandfather tucked his bushy white beard inside his overcoat. They looked very Biblical as they set off, I thought. Jake and Ambrosch followed them, riding the other black and my pony, carrying bundles of clothes that we had got together for Mrs. Shimerda. I watched them go past the pond and over the hill by the drifted cornfield. Then, for the first time, I realized that I was alone in the house.

I felt a considerable extension of power and authority, and was anxious to acquit myself creditably. I carried in cobs and wood from the long cellar, and filled both the stoves. I remembered that in the hurry and excitement of the morning nobody had thought of the chickens, and the eggs had not been gathered. Going out through the tunnel, I gave the hens their corn, emptied the ice from their drinking-pan, and filled it with water. After the cat had had his milk, I could think of nothing else to do, and I sat down to get warm. The quiet was delightful, and the ticking clock was the most pleasant of companions. I got *Robinson Crusoe*[4] and tried to read, but his life on the island seemed dull compared with ours. Presently, as I looked with satisfaction about our comfortable sitting-room, it flashed upon me that if Mr. Shimerda's soul were lingering about in this world at all, it would be here, in our house, which had been more to his liking than any other in the neighborhood. I remembered his contented face when he was with us on Christmas Day. If he could have lived with us, this terrible thing would never have happened.

I knew it was homesickness that had killed Mr. Shimerda, and I wondered whether his released spirit would not eventually find its way back to his own country. I thought of how far it was to Chicago, and then to Virginia, to Baltimore,—and then the great wintry ocean. No, he would not at once set out upon that long journey. Surely, his exhausted spirit, so tired of cold and crowding and the struggle with the ever-falling snow, was resting now in this quiet house.

[3]*Rosary:* string of beads for keeping count of prayers, one said for each bead.
[4]*Robinson Crusoe:* hero of Daniel Defoe's book of that title, who as a shipwrecked sailor ingeniously survives on a desert island. He is alone until he encounters his "Man Friday."

I was not frightened, but I made no noise. I did not wish to disturb him. I went softly down to the kitchen which, tucked away so snugly underground, always seemed to me the heart and center of the house. There, on the bench behind the stove, I thought and thought about Mr. Shimerda. Outside I could hear the wind singing over hundreds of miles of snow. It was as if I had let the old man in out of the tormenting winter, and were sitting there with him. I went over all that Ántonia had ever told me about his life before he came to this country; how he used to play the fiddle at weddings and dances. I thought about the friends he had mourned to leave, the trombone-player, the great forest full of game,—belonging, as Ántonia said, to the "nobles,"— from which she and her mother used to steal wood on moon-light nights. There was a white hart that lived in that forest, and if any one killed it, he would be hanged, she said. Such vivid pictures came to me that they might have been Mr. Shimerda's memories, not yet faded out from the air in which they had haunted him.

It had begun to grow dark when my household returned, and grand-mother was so tired that she went at once to bed. Jake and I got supper, and while we were washing the dishes he told me in loud whispers about the state of things over at the Shimerdas'. Nobody could touch the body until the coroner came. If any one did, something terrible would happen, apparently. The dead man was frozen through, "just as stiff as a dressed turkey you hang out to freeze," Jake said. The horses and oxen would not go into the barn until he was frozen so hard that there was no longer any smell of blood. They were stabled there now, with the dead man, because there was no other place to keep them. A lighted lantern was kept hanging over Mr. Shimerda's head. Ántonia and Ambrosch and the mother took turns going down to pray beside him. The crazy boy went with them, because he did not feel the cold. I believed he felt cold as much as any one else, but he liked to be thought insensible to it. He was always coveting distinction, poor Marek!

Ambrosch, Jake said, showed more human feeling than he would have supposed him capable of; but he was chiefly concerned about getting a priest, and about his father's soul, which he believed was in a place of torment and would remain there until his family and the priest had prayed a great deal for him. "As I understand it," Jake concluded, "it will be a matter of years to pray his soul out of Purgatory,[5] and right now he's in torment."

"I don't believe it," I said stoutly. "I almost know it isn't true." I did

[5]*Purgatory:* intermediate state of suffering and misery where repentant souls are cleansed of sin before admittance to heaven. Catholics believe that such souls can be helped by prayer and charity of the faithful. To commit suicide is a grave sin in the eyes of the church.

not, of course, say that I believed he had been in that very kitchen all afternoon, on his way back to his own country. Nevertheless, after I went to bed, this idea of punishment and Purgatory came back on me crushingly. I remembered the account of Dives[6] in torment, and shuddered. But Mr. Shimerda had not been rich and selfish; he had only been so unhappy that he could not live any longer.

★ ★ ★ ★ ★

Talking It Through

1. On their visit to the prosperous farm of the narrator's grandparents, Mrs. Shimerda and Ántonia speak of the family's dissatisfaction with America. Mrs. Shimerda, particularly, is portrayed here unsympathetically. What picture do we get of her American dream? Is it different from that of other immigrants we have encountered thus far? What does the writer do to make Mrs. Shimerda and the older son, Ambrosch, seem unlikable to the reader? What is the attitude of Ántonia's father toward America?

2. Jim Burden's grandmother says, "It makes a woman grasping to see her children want for things." Explain in your own words what she means by this. Do you agree?

3. The narrator describes a blizzard on the prairie, a steady two-day snowfall. The farmhands have to dig a tunnel under the snow from the farmhouse to the henhouse. How do Cather's descriptions make the storm real for the reader? What effects do the descriptions at the opening and closing of the chapter have on our impressions of the Shimerdas?

4. The selection begins with a dramatic event. The author starts suspensefully, using the interval of the snowstorm as prelude to a crescendo of vividly specific descriptive detail of a violent act. What do we learn of the personal habits and personality of Mr. Shimerda? Otto Fuchs (an Austrian emigré who first was a cowboy, then a farmhand) describes him as "sort of fixy." From the details given, what does he mean by this? How does this description help to establish his character?

5. Jake, one of the hired hands, speaks of Krajiek as Mr. Shimerda's possible killer. This is quickly dismissed by Otto Fuchs. The evidence clearly points to suicide. But there is irony in the brief accusation. Krajiek has sold his

---

[6]*Dives:* name given to the rich man in the New Testament parable (Luke xvi:19–31) who refused Lazarus, the beggar, and found himself in Hell when he died.

worthless farm to the Shimerdas, and then remained on as a farmhand. How is Mr. Shimerda's hopelessness tied to his countryman's behavior? What might Krajiek be feeling?

6. Jim's grandparents, Jake, and Ambrosch ride off through the trackless snow, leaving Jim alone in the house. What does he mean when he says, "I felt a considerable extension of power and authority"? What gives him this feeling? How does he respond to it?

7. Jim says that "homesickness had killed Mr. Shimerda." He chronicles the long trip from the snowbound prairie to the "wintry ocean" which he would then have to cross. Then he suggests that the spirit of his unhappy neighbor has sought rest within the peaceful farmhouse. There follows a lyrical passage of descriptive reminiscence. Reread this for details of the life Mr. Shimerda had left. How do they relate to the nostalgic descriptions of other immigrants about their homelands? Are there good times in your own life which already seem part of the past and which make you wistful? Share with your classmates some of these memories, "not yet faded out from the air."

8. Jim's grandparents return and Jake brings news of the grim reality of life and death at the Shimerdas. What are the effects of these details after the preceding passage? Contrast the descriptions of Mr. Shimerda's life in Bohemia with those of his death in Nebraska. What do you think is the author's purpose here?

   At the end of this selection Jim reflects on his own solitary imaginings, and on the simple truth behind his neighbor's violent act. In your own words, explain why continuing to live might have been a truer "purgatory" to Mr. Shimerda.

Writer's Workshop

1. Willa Cather in these passages treats the winter weather of the Nebraska prairie almost as if it were another character in the story. She describes first the Christmas thaw and then the blizzard and its frozen aftermath. Both heighten the human drama, building suspense and highlighting the moods and feelings of the characters.

   Think about the effects of weather on your own emotions. How does the color of the sky affect your day? Willa Cather talks about the "broth of gray slush," the snow "spilling out of heaven . . . like thousands of featherbeds being emptied," and she describes the rooster "pecking at the solid lump of ice" in the water tin.

   What have you noticed in your environment on a particularly rainy or hot, stifling, day? What changes are there in the behavior of people or animals? Does the tempo of life change with the weather for all of us? Write a description of a particular weather change you remember vividly.

2. Ántonia says, "My papa sad for the old country . . . He don't like this kawn-tree. He never make music any more." Jim's stern rejoinder is, "People who don't like this country ought to stay at home . . . We don't make them come here."

   Reflecting on the opinions expressed above, write an essay to discuss attitudes toward immigrants by the native population. What causes such attitudes, in your opinion? How might they be changed for the better? Use examples from the literature in this book as well as any from current world events you may find relevant. Try to think in terms of developing an official immigration policy that would be positive and helpful in overcoming resentment and misunderstanding.

3. Write a monologue in the voice of Mrs. Shimerda either after her visit to Jim's farm or upon learning from Ambrosch of her husband's death.

★ *from* ***The*** ★
Jungle

U P T O N   S I N C L A I R

The Jungle is an American novel, first published in 1906, that dramatically exposed abuses in the Chicago meat-packing industry in the early years of the twentieth century, when safety and sanitation were ignored for the sake of huge profits. Sinclair's rousing polemic resulted in federal laws that governed the processing of foods, and it succeeded in raising the consciousness of exploited immigrant laborers. A strengthening of employee unions was another outcome of Sinclair's book. In this excerpt Lithuanian immigrants find that the reality of Chicago falls far short of their expectations of America.

IT WAS NEARLY A YEAR AND A HALF AGO THAT JURGIS HAD MET ONA, AT A horse fair a hundred miles from home. Jurgis had never expected to get married—he had laughed at it as a foolish trap for a man to walk into; but here, without ever having spoken a word to her, with no more than the exchange of half a dozen smiles, he found himself, purple in the face with embarrassment and terror, asking her parents to sell her to him for his wife—and offering his father's two horses he had been sent to the fair to sell. But Ona's father proved as a rock—the girl was yet a child, and he was a rich man, and his daughter was not to be had in that way. So Jurgis went home with a heavy heart, and that spring and summer toiled and tried hard to forget. In the fall, after the harvest was over, he saw that it would not do, and tramped the full fortnight's journey that lay between him and Ona.

He found an unexpected state of affairs—for the girl's father had died, and his estate was tied up with creditors; Jurgis's heart leaped as he realized that now the prize was within his reach. There was Elzbieta Lukoszaite, Teta, or Aunt, as they called her, Ona's stepmother, and there were her six children, of all ages. There was also her brother Jonas, a dried-up little man who had worked upon the farm. They were people of great consequence, as it seemed to Jurgis, fresh out of the woods; Ona knew how to read, and knew many other things that he did not know; and now the farm had been sold, and the whole family was adrift—all they owned in the world being about seven hundred rubles, which is half as many dollars. They would have had three times that, but it had gone to court, and the judge had decided against them, and it had cost the balance to get him to change his decision.

Ona might have married and left them, but she would not, for she loved Teta Elzbieta. It was Jonas who suggested that they all go to America, where a friend of his had gotten rich. He would work, for his part, and the women would work, and some of the children, doubtless—they would live somehow. Jurgis, too, had heard of America. That was a country where, they said, a man might earn three rubles a day, and Jurgis figured what three rubles a day would mean, with prices as they were where he lived, and decided forthwith that he would go to America and marry, and be a rich man in the bargain. In that country, rich or poor, a man was free, it was said; he did not have to go into the army, he did not have to pay out his money to rascally officials—he might do as he pleased, and count himself as good as any other man. So America was a place of which lovers and young people dreamed. If one could only manage to get the price of a passage, he could count his troubles at an end.

It was arranged that they should leave the following spring, and meantime Jurgis sold himself to a contractor for a certain time, and tramped nearly four hundred miles from home with a gang of men to work upon a railroad in Smolensk. This was a fearful experience, with filth and bad food and cruelty and overwork, but Jurgis stood it and came out in fine trim, and with eighty rubles sewed up in his coat. He did not drink or fight, because he was thinking all the time of Ona, and for the rest, he was a quiet, steady man, who did what he was told to, did not lose his temper often, and when he did lose it made the offender anxious that he should not lose it again. When they paid him off he dodged the company gamblers and dramshops, and so they tried to kill him; but he escaped, and tramped it home, working at odd jobs, and sleeping always with one eye open.

So in the summer time they had all set out for America. At the last moment there joined them Marija Berczynskas, who was a cousin of Ona's. Marija was an orphan, and had worked since childhood for a rich farmer at Vilna, who beat her regularly. It was only at the age of twenty that it had occurred to Marija to try her strength, when she had risen up and nearly murdered the man, and then come away.

There were twelve in all in the party, five adults and six children—and Ona, who was a little of both. They had a hard time on the passage; there was an agent who helped them, but he proved a scoundrel, and got them into a trap with some officials, and cost them a good deal of their precious money, which they clung to with such horrible fear. This happened to them again in New York—for, of course, they knew nothing about the country, and had no one to tell them, and it was easy for a man in a blue uniform to lead them away, and to take them to a hotel and keep them there, and make them pay enormous charges to get away. The law says that the rate card shall be on the door of a hotel, but it does not say that it shall be in Lithuanian.

It was in the stockyards that Jonas's friend had gotten rich, and so to Chicago the party was bound. They knew that one word, Chicago—and that was all they needed to know, at least until they reached the city. Then, tumbled out of the cars without ceremony, they were no better off than before; they stood staring down the vista of Dearborn Street, with its big black buildings towering in the distance, unable to realize that they had arrived, and why, when they said "Chicago," people no longer pointed in some direction, but instead looked perplexed, or laughed, or went on without paying any attention. They were pitiable in their helplessness; above all things they stood in deadly terror of any sort of person in official uniform, and so whenever they saw a policeman they would cross the street and hurry by. For the whole of the first day they wandered about in the midst of deafening confusion, utterly lost; and it was only at night that, cowering in the doorway of a house, they were finally discovered and taken by a policeman to the station. In the morning an interpreter was found, and they were taken and put upon a car, and taught a new word—"stockyards." Their delight at discovering that they were to get out of this adventure without losing another share of their possessions, it would not be possible to describe.

They sat and stared out of the window. They were on a street which seemed to run on forever, mile after mile—thirty-four of them, if they had known it—and each side of it one uninterrupted row of wretched little two-story frame buildings. Down every side street they could see, it was the same—never a hill and never a hollow, but always the same endless vista of ugly and dirty little wooden buildings. Here and there would be a bridge crossing a filthy creek, with hard-baked mud shores and dingy sheds and docks along it; here and there would be a railroad crossing, with a tangle of switches, and locomotives puffing, and rattling freight cars filing by; here and there would be a great factory, a dingy building with innumerable windows in it, and immense volumes of smoke pouring from the chimneys, darkening the air above and making filthy the earth beneath. But after each of these interruptions, the desolate procession would begin again—the procession of dreary little buildings.

A full hour before the party reached the city they had begun to note the perplexing changes in the atmosphere. It grew darker all the time, and upon the earth the grass seemed to grow less green. Every minute, as the train sped on, the colors of things became dingier; the fields were grown parched and yellow, the landscape hideous and bare. And along with the thickening smoke they began to notice another circumstance, a strange, pungent odor. They were not sure that it was unpleasant, this odor; some might have called it sickening, but their taste in odors was not developed, and they were only sure that it was curious. Now, sitting in the trolley car, they realized that they were on their way to the home of it—that they had travelled all the way from Lithuania to it. It was now no longer something far off and faint, that you caught in whiffs; you could literally taste it, as well as smell it—you could take hold of it, almost, and examine it at your leisure. They were divided in their opinions about it. It was an elemental odor, raw and crude; it was rich, almost rancid, sensual, and strong. There were some who drank it in as if it were an intoxicant; there were others who put their handkerchiefs to their faces. The new emigrants were still tasting it, lost in wonder, when suddenly the car came to a halt, and the door was flung open, and a voice shouted—"Stockyards!"

They were left standing upon the corner, staring; down a side street there were two rows of brick houses, and between them a vista: half a dozen chimneys, tall as the tallest buildings, touching the very sky—and leaping from them half a dozen columns of smoke, thick, oily, and black as night. It might have come from the center of the world, this smoke, where the fires of the ages still smoulder. It came as if self-impelled, driving all before it, a perpetual explosion. It was inexhaustible; one stared, waiting to see it stop, but still the great streams rolled out. They spread in vast clouds overhead, writhing, curling; then, uniting in one giant river, they streamed away down the sky, stretching a black pall as far as the eye could reach.

Then the party became aware of another strange thing. This, too, like the odor, was a thing elemental; it was a sound, a sound made up of ten thousand little sounds. You scarcely noticed it at first—it sunk into your consciousness, a vague disturbance, a trouble. It was like the murmuring of the bees in the spring, the whisperings of the forest; it suggested endless activity, the rumblings of a world in motion. It was only by an effort that one could realize that it was made by animals, that it was the distant lowing of ten thousand cattle, the distant grunting of ten thousand swine.

They would have liked to follow it up, but, alas, they had no time for adventures just then. The policeman on the corner was beginning to watch them, and so, as usual, they started up the street. Scarcely had they gone a block, however, before Jonas was heard to give a cry, and began pointing excitedly across the street. Before they could gather the meaning of his breathless ejaculations he had bounded away, and they saw him enter a shop, over which was a sign: J. SZEDVILAS, DELICATESSEN. When he came out again it was in company with a very stout gentleman in shirt sleeves and an apron, clasping Jonas by both hands and laughing hilariously. Then Teta Elzbieta recollected suddenly that Szedvilas had been the name of the mythical friend who had made his fortune in America. To find that he had been making it in the delicatessen business was an extraordinary piece of good fortune at this juncture; though it was well on in the morning, they had not breakfasted, and the children were beginning to whimper.

Thus was the happy ending of a woeful voyage. The two families literally fell upon each other's necks—for it had been years since Jokubas Szedvilas had met a man from his part of Lithuania. Before half the day they were lifelong friends. Jokubas understood all the pitfalls of this new world, and could explain all of its mysteries; he could tell them the things they ought to have done in the different emergencies—and what was still more to the point, he could tell them what to do now. He would take them to poni Aniele, who kept a boarding house the other side of the yards; old Mrs. Jukniene, he explained, had not what one would call choice accommodations, but they might do for the moment. To this Teta Elzbieta hastened to respond that nothing could be too cheap to suit them just then, for they were quite terrified over the sums they had had to expend. A very few days of practical experience in this land of high wages had been sufficient to make clear to them the cruel fact that it was also a land of high prices, and that in it the poor man was almost as poor as in any other corner of the earth; and so there vanished in a night all the wonderful dreams of wealth that had been haunting Jurgis. What had made the discovery all the more painful was that they were spending, at American prices, money which they had earned at home rates of wages—and so were really being cheated by the world! The last two days they had all but starved themselves—it made them quite sick to pay the prices that the railroad people asked them for food.

Yet, when they saw the home of the Widow Jukniene they could not but recoil, even so. In all their journey they had seen nothing so bad as this. Poni Aniele had a four-room flat in one of that wilderness of two-story frame tenements that lie "back of the yards." There were four such flats in each building, and each of the four was a "boarding house" for the occupancy of foreigners—Lithuanians, Poles, Slovaks, or Bohemians. Some of these places were kept by private persons, some were co-operative. There would be an average of half a dozen boarders to each room—sometimes there were thirteen or fourteen to one room, fifty or sixty to a flat. Each one of the occupants furnished his own accommodations—that is, a mattress and some bedding. The mattresses would be spread upon the floor in rows—and there would be nothing else in the place except a stove. It was by no means unusual for two men to own the same mattress in common, one working by day and using it by night, and the other working at night and using it in the daytime. Very frequently a lodging-house keeper would rent the same beds to double shifts of men.

Mrs. Jukniene was a wizened up little woman, with a wrinkled face. Her home was unthinkably filthy; you could not enter by the front door at all, owing to the mattresses, and when you tried to go up the backstairs you found that she had walled up most of the porch with old boards to make a place to keep her chickens. It was a standing jest of the boarders that Aniele cleaned house by letting the chickens loose in the rooms. Undoubtedly this did keep down the vermin, but it seemed probable, in view of all the circumstances, that the old lady regarded it rather as feeding the chickens than as cleaning the rooms. The truth was that she had definitely given up the idea of cleaning anything, under pressure of an attack of rheumatism, which had kept her doubled up in one corner of her room for over a week, during which time eleven of her boarders, heavily in her debt, had concluded to try their chances of employment in Kansas City. This was July, and the fields were green. One never saw the fields, nor any green thing whatever in Packingtown; but one could go out on the road and "hobo it," as the men phrased it, and see the country, and have a long rest, and an easy time riding on the freight cars.

Such was the home to which the new arrivals were welcomed. There was nothing better to be had—they might not do so well by looking further, for

Mrs. Jukniene had at least kept one room for herself and her three little children, and now offered to share this with the women and the girls of the party. They could get bedding at a second-hand store, she explained, and they would not need any, while the weather was so hot—doubtless they would all sleep on the sidewalk such nights as this, as did nearly all of her guests. "Tomorrow," Jurgis said, when they were left alone, "tomorrow I will get a job, and perhaps Jonas will get one also; and then we can get a place of our own."

Later that afternoon he and Ona went out to take a walk and look about them, to see more of this district which was to be their home. In back of the yards the dreary two-story frame houses were scattered farther apart, and there were great spaces bare—that seemingly had been overlooked by the great sore of a city as it spread itself over the surface of the prairie. These bare places were grown up with dingy, yellow weeds, hiding innumerable tomato cans; innumerable children playing upon them, chasing one another here and there, screaming and fighting. The most uncanny thing about this neighborhood was the number of the children; you thought there must be a school just out, and it was only after long acquaintance that you were able to realize that there was no school, but that these were the children of the neighborhood—that there were so many children to the block in Packingtown that nowhere on its streets could a horse and buggy move faster than a walk!

It could not move faster anyhow, on account of the state of the streets. Those through which Jurgis and Ona were walking resembled streets less than they did a miniature topographical map. The roadway was commonly several feet lower than the level of the houses, which were sometimes joined by high boardwalks; there were no pavements—there were mountains and valleys and rivers, gullies and ditches, and great hollows full of stinking green water. In these pools the children played, and rolled about in the mud of the streets; here and there one noticed them digging in it, after trophies which they had stumbled on. One wondered about this, as also about the swarms of flies which hung about the scene, literally blackening the air, and the strange, fetid odor which assailed one's nostrils, a ghastly odor, of all the dead things of the universe. It impelled the visitor to questions—and then the residents would explain, quietly, that all this was "made" land, and that it had been "made" by using it as a dumping ground for the city garbage. After a few years the unpleasant effect of this would pass away, it was said; but meantime, in hot weather—and especially when it rained— the flies were apt to be annoying. Was it not unhealthful? the stranger would ask, and the residents would answer, "Perhaps; but there is no telling."

A little way further on, and Jurgis and Ona, staring open-eyed and wondering, came to the place where this "made" ground was in process of making. Here was a great hole, perhaps two city blocks square, and with long files of garbage wagons creeping into it. The place had an odor for which there are no polite words, and it was sprinkled over with children, who raked in it from dawn till dark. Sometimes visitors from the packing houses would wander out to see this "dump," and they would stand by and debate as to whether the children were eating the food they got, or merely collecting it for the chickens at home. Apparently none of them ever went down to find out.

Beyond this dump there stood a great brickyard, with smoking chimneys. First they took out the soil to make bricks, and then they filled it up again with garbage, which seemed to Jurgis and Ona a felicitous arrangement, characteristic of an enterprising country like America. A little way beyond was another great hole, which they had emptied and not yet filled up. This held water, and all summer it stood there, with the nearby soil draining into it, festering and stewing in the sun; and then, when winter came, somebody cut the ice on it, and sold it to the people of the city. This, too, seemed to the newcomers an economical arrangement; for they did not read the newspapers, and their heads were not full of troublesome thoughts about "germs."

They stood there while the sun went down upon this scene, and the sky in the west turned blood red, and the tops of the houses shone like fire. Jurgis and Ona were not thinking of the sunset, however—their backs were turned to it, and all their thoughts were of Packingtown, which they could see so plainly in the distance. The line of the buildings stood clear-cut and black against the sky; here and there out of the mass rose the great chimneys, with the river of smoke streaming away to the end of the world. It was a study in colors now, this smoke; in the sunset light it was black and brown and gray and purple. All the sordid suggestions of the place were gone— in the twilight it was a vision of power. To the two who stood watching while the darkness swallowed it up, it seemed a dream of wonder, with its tale of human energy, of things being done, of employment for thousands upon thousands of men, of opportunity and freedom, of life and love and joy. When they came away, arm in arm, Jurgis was saying, "Tomorrow I shall go there and get a job!"

★ ★ ★ ★ ★

Talking It Through

1. Jurgis, Ona, and their respective families come from Lithuania where they have been peasant farmers, he from a six-acre tract in the midst of the

Imperial Forest. City life, even village life, is remote to his experience. Yet both have heard of America and its legendary promise of wealth. What reasons does Jurgis have for wanting to emigrate? How does this compare with Michael Pupin's and George Papashvily's version of the American dream? What do they hope to avoid or escape from? What do they look forward to?

2. How does Jurgis earn money for his trip to America? What is different about his circumstances compared to Pupin's? Find where Smolensk is on a map of Europe. For what is it noted? Use an encyclopedia to find what its important industries were or are.

3. Do the Lithuanian emigrés find their initial experience of America welcoming? What, in fact, happens to them?

4. When the party finally arrives in Chicago, how are they treated? Why are they so fearful of people in uniforms? Note that "stockyards" is the new word they learn as they head out of downtown Chicago. Discuss the feelings they might have, knowing no English and finding no one who spoke Lithuanian. Compare their vulnerability with that of the Rodriguez family and with the father in "My Father's Language." Who is the most exposed? What is so different about their experiences? Do you think contemporary immigrants would have similar difficulties? Would it depend on their countries of origin? Give your reasons.

5. Sinclair's description of a train trip to the outskirts of Chicago is particularly graphic. He enables us to experience the feelings of the Lithuanian travelers. Note again the use of the word "stockyards." What effect does this have? What descriptions does Sinclair use? What is implied?

6. A striking coincidence occurs: They come upon the shop of Jokubas Szedvilas, their "rich" compatriot. What irony does Sinclair emphasize here? Szedvilas takes them in hand; he "understood all the pitfalls of this new world, and could explain all of its mysteries." In previous selections is there a person who fills the same role for other immigrants? Are their functions comparable?

7. What is the sobering reality Jurgis discovers about life in America? Does the land of high wages come up to expectation? Explain. Would the promise of Emma Lazarus's poem sustain an immigrant exposed to the conditions of Mrs. Jukniene's boarding house? Note that even today, illegal immigrants willingly submit to extraordinarily severe conditions in order to earn wages to send to their relatives abroad and to save for the future.

8. This chapter ends not with the stench of the garbage dump nor with the squalor of the "Packingtown" slums, but with a sunset that, even when

polluted by the belching smokestacks, seems splendid to Ona and Jurgis. What do they see in this landscape? What are their expectations? Do Upton Sinclair's descriptions make their dreams seem possible? Discuss.

Writer's Workshop

1. Sinclair very effectively uses sensory descriptions to create a mood, to develop suspense, and to convey his own attitude toward what he sees as exploitation of vulnerable immigrant workers.

   Write a description of a locale with which you are familiar in such a way as to influence the reader's opinion of it. Decide first what you want that opinion to be. Then select the details of your description to suit your purpose. Remember, particular words can influence our perceptions positively or negatively. For example: the odor of chocolate can be "delicious" or "cloying"; the inside of a fast-food restaurant can seem efficient, friendly, welcoming, or mechanical, blandly impersonal, rushed. Be sure you know well the place you choose to describe, and then see how words can manipulate feelings.

2. Compare the "greenhorn" experiences of Gustavus Vassa with that of Jurgis, the Lithuanian. Both arrive in America knowing no English. How are they both vulnerable to the manipulations of others? What is the greatest difference in their circumstances? Consider in your piece whether poverty is a form of servitude. Discuss how the circumstances of both men affect their dignity and aspirations.

3. Write Ona's story of emigration. Note that in Lithuania her family had been prosperous, above Jurgis's in wealth and position. (Jurgis notes that Ona could read, a fact that impresses him.) Consider how her father's death changes Ona's fortunes. What would her expectations be? How would she perceive the surroundings in Chicago, in Packingtown? What should she hope for Jurgis?

How to Rent
an Apartment
★ # Without ★
Money

J E S U S   C O L O N

Jesus Colon came to the United States in the first wave of immigrants from the
island of Puerto Rico. He writes of his young manhood experiences both before and
after the arrival of his family. He also explains the ways in which ingenuity
helped poor dream-seekers to survive.

A GOOD WAY TO FIND OUT IF A PUERTO RICAN HAS BEEN IN NEW YORK OVER
forty years is by asking him if he knew Markofsky. Markofsky had a coat
and suit store somewhere on Second Avenue near 106th Street. The store
looked like a tunnel with racks of suits and coats dangling from the walls.
This tunnel of suits and coats had a little space in the back with a desk from
which Markofsky waded out to greet you as you came in.

Old man Markofsky was quite a guy among the Puerto Ricans of those
days. He was your clothier on the long, long instalment plan. His name
and his store was even mentioned in one of the most popular dance pieces
of those days.

Markofsky was small, a little over five feet. His pace was deliberate, his
steps were short. He walked a little bent to the front. He had a sort of dignity
and confidence in his walk. His face always wore a sad smile over which
he superimposed a cigar. If you observed him well, he seemed like a biblical
patriarch[1] who liked to be eternally smoking a cigar.

[1]*patriarch:* the father and ruler or founder of a family or tribe; in the Bible, Abraham,
   Isaac, Jacob, and his sons were patriarchs.

As soon as anybody came from Puerto Rico—especially during the winter—you would take him to Markofsky. Markofsky would take care of outfitting him with a winter suit and a heavy coat to repel the winter cold. Then the newcomer was set to go out and look for a job. All you had to do was to put two dollars on top of Markofsky's old desk and you walked out with an overcoat. Your credit would be good if you came with two dollars every week for a certain number of weeks. If you kept it up steadily and did not miss any weekly payments, I know you could even "touch"[2] Markofsky sometimes for a five "until Saturday," when you received that urgent letter from Puerto Rico asking for a little extra money that week for some emergency.

My brother and I had reached the "touching" stage with old benign[3] Markofsky.

We had to have an apartment. Our family was coming from Puerto Rico and we did not even have the money to pay the first month's rent or to buy a bed or a couch, to say nothing of tables and chairs. So we went to Markofsky. Instead of asking for a five "until Saturday," we asked to see the new suits that were just coming in. The jackets of the suits had belts with very wide shiny buckles. The suits looked very sporty and fashionable and they cost quite a bit of money.

The suits fitted in perfectly with our plans. The more they cost, the better. Markofsky gave us two identical suits with the usual small down payment.

From the store we went directly to a pawn shop[4] a few blocks away. We pawned the two suits that we just bought. With the money we got from the pawn shop we paid the first month's rent on an apartment on 143rd Street between Lenox and Seventh. In those days the few Puerto Ricans around lived in the heart of the Negro neighborhood together with the Negro people in the same buildings; many times as roomers in their homes. Rents were not so high thirty-five years ago.

That very afternoon we got the keys to the apartment—a "railroad" flat.[5] My brother and I felt great.

Night came. We went to the home where we were rooming. Took our two suitcases, said goodbye and thanks and went to our long empty apartment. My brother went into the parlor, laid himself on the floor and with

---

[2]*touch:* (slang) to ask for or get by asking a loan or gift of money from someone.

[3]*benign:* good-natured, kindly.

[4]*pawn shop:* a place where money is loaned at a specified rate of interest on personal property left as security.

[5]*railroad flat:* a long and narrow apartment, usually without windows in the middle room or rooms. These were built as cheap tenements in poorer sections of cities and housed many families crowded into small apartments in multistoried dwellings.

his suitcase as his pillow went to sleep as if he were in the Waldorf Astoria.[6] I did likewise, lying down beside him with my own suitcase as my pillow. After a few minutes we were both sound asleep. Many a night we had to sleep like that.

The family came: mother, father, sisters, brothers, cousins, and just friends, who, because of living with us so many years, had become part of the family. An old Puerto Rican custom. Many times we asked mother about someone who had been living with us for years. "In what way is Jose related to us?" And my mother, after a lot of genealogical hemming and hawing in which the more she explained the more she got involved and confused, would end with a desperate whimsical gesture: "He is just part of the family." And there it ended.

We moved to Brooklyn. Every year either my brother or myself went over to the pawn shop in New York and renewed the tickets for the suits, paying the interest and letting it ride.

One year we were in the chips and instead of renewing the pawn shop tickets we actually took out the two suits. I was saying to myself: "Now I have a new suit with which I can go out to dance the Charleston this coming Saturday night."

But we had not counted on one thing—time. When my brother and I unpacked the "new" suits that we had hardly seen, the color was something between one shade and another, but nothing definite. The lack of air in the closeness of the pawn shop vaults had played havoc with the material and the texture. After we took off the multiple tickets sewed to the pants and jackets, we started for the first time to thoroughly examine the cut and style of the two suits and compare them with what the young sports were wearing those days. The buckles and belts on the jackets looked like something out of a pageant[7] of the medieval[8] ages. When we finally put the suits on and looked at ourselves in the mirror we certainly felt as if we were seeing ourselves in one of those distorted freak mirrors in which you laugh at your own figure when you go to Coney Island.

We had certainly changed in a few years. We were fatter and even taller. The pants were too short. The coat sleeves reached just below the elbows. In short, we looked too ridiculous for words. We laughed very loudly at ourselves until tears came out of our eyes.

We should cry all right. That cheap first apartment we rented in New

---

[6]*Waldorf Astoria:* a luxurious hotel on Park Avenue in New York City.

[7]*pageant:* a spectacular parade or outdoor drama. Originally, a scene in a medieval mystery play.

[8]*medieval:* characteristic of the Middle Ages, especially the time period from about 800 to the 1400s. Colon thinks the buckles on his belted suit resemble medieval costumes.

York came to be one for which we actually paid the highest first month's rent in our lives.

★ ★ ★ ★ ★

Talking It Through

1. The opening paragraphs of this selection, which is really a long personal essay, set the time and place of Colon's memoir and begin to delineate the appearance and character of the clothier, Markofsky. What descriptions of Markofsky serve to establish the author's attitude toward this man? Note how examples are used to actively engage the reader.

2. What is the urgency of the Colon brothers' decision to buy two expensive, fashionable suits? How does the high price of the suits fit in with their plans?

3. How can you tell how Colon and his brother feel about the apartment they have found? Whom will it accommodate? Why?

4. A passage of time is indicated in this account. How long a period do you think it might be? What clues are there in the text to indicate this?

5. In the last two paragraphs of this chapter Colon reveals that he is no longer a greenhorn. How does he do this? What does he mean when he says, "That cheap first apartment . . . came to be one for which we actually paid the highest first month's rent in our lives"?

Writer's Workshop

1. The personal essay is a form used by many writers. It often incorporates narrative and description and usually conveys the writer's strong point of view about events that may or may not deal directly with his own life.

   Analyze Colon's thesis or point of view here. Then write a personal essay, which, like this selection, ends with an opinion statement reflecting on the incident you have described. Your essay may be about a memorable person in your life, a first encounter, or a time when you were placed in a position of responsibility toward others, such as peers, family, or adults in a work or school situation.

2. Write the scene when the Colon family arrives at the apartment on 143rd Street. How will the brothers greet them? How will they show the new immigrants that they are wise in the ways of the big city? How will they

help their family members adjust to the climate, the bustle, the need for livelihood? Will the family be excited, disillusioned, or optimistic? Base your piece on the tone of the reading selection.

⋆ *Bananas* ⋆

M I C H A E L   G O L D

In his autobiographical novel Jews Without Money, *Michael Gold describes growing up in poverty on the Lower East Side of New York City at the turn of the century. Here he recalls how his proud father, an immigrant from Romania, is reduced to peddling bananas.*

THE NEIGHBORS WERE TALKING ABOUT US. THEY WERE WORRYING. IN THE tenement each woman knew what was cooking for supper in her neighbor's pot. Each knew the cares, too, that darkened a neighbor's heart.

One night a neighbor called. He kissed the *mezzuzah*[1] over the door, and wiped his feet on the burlap rags. Then he timidly entered our kitchen like an intruder.

"Good evening, Mr. Lipzin," said my mother. "Please sit down."

"Good evening," he stammered, seating himself. "It was raining to-day, and I did not sell many bananas, so I brought you some. Maybe your children like bananas."

He handed my mother a bunch of bananas, and she took them, saying: "Thanks, Mr. Lipzin."

The pot-bellied little peddler shyly fingered his beard. He had come for a purpose, but was too embarrassed to speak. Sweat appeared on his red, fat, honest face, which wind and sun had tanned. He scratched his head, and stared at us in a painful silence. Minutes passed.

"How is your health, Mr. Lipzin?" my mother asked.

---

[1] *mezzuzah:* a small case attached to the wall of a Jewish home in which there is a portion of Torah.

"I am stronger, thanks be to God," he said bashfully. "It was only the rheumatism again."

"That is good, And how is your new baby, Mr. Lipzin?"

"God be thanked, she is strong like a tiger," he said.

He fell dumb again. He tapped his knees with his fingers, and his shoulders twitched. He was known as a silent man in the tenement; in the ten years we lived there this was the first time he had called on us.

My father fidgeted uneasily. He was about to say something to break the spell cast by the tongue-tied peddler, when Mr. Lipzin became articulate. "Excuse me, but my wife nagged me into coming here," he stammered. "She is worrying about you. Excuse me, but they say you have been out of work a long time and can find nothing to do, Mr. Gold."

"Yes, Mr. Lipzin, why should one conceal it?" said my father. "Life is dark for us now."

"*Nu,*"[2] said the little peddler, as he wiped his forehead, "so that is why my wife nagged me to see you. If there is nothing else, one can at least make a kind of living with bananas. I have peddled them, with God's help, for many years. It is a hard life, but one manages to live.

"Yes," he went on, in a mournful, hesitant sing-song, "for a few dollars one buys a stock of bananas from the wholesalers on Attorney Street. Then one rents a pushcart for ten cents a day from the pushcart stables on Orchard Street. Then one finds a street corner and stands there and the people come and buy the bananas."

"So well?" my father demanded, a hostile glare in his eyes.

The little peddler saw this, and was frightened again into incoherence.

"Excuse me, one makes a living, with God's help," he managed to say.

My father stood up and folded his arms haughtily.

"And you are suggesting, Mr. Lipzin, that I, too, should go out peddling bananas?" he asked.

The peddler sweated like a runner with embarrassment. He stood up and edged toward the door to make his escape.

"No, no, God forbid," he stammered. "Excuse me, it was my wife who nagged me to come here. No, no, Mr. Gold! Good evening to you all; may God be with you!"

He went out, mopping his fiery face with a bandanna. My father stared after him, his arms still folded in that fierce, defiant attitude.

"What a gall![3] What meddling neighbors we have! To come and tell me that I ought to peddle these accursed bananas! After my fifteen years in America, as if I were a greenhorn! I, who once owned a suspender shop,

[2]*nu:* a sigh-like expression.

[3]*gall:* rude boldness.

and was a foreman of house painters! What do you think of such gall, Katie?''

"I don't know,'' said my mother quietly. "It is not disgraceful to make an honest living by peddling.''

"You agree with him?'' my father cried.

"No,'' said my mother, "but Lipzen is a good man. He came here to help you, and you insulted him.''

"So you do agree with him!'' my father stormed. He stamped indignantly into the bedroom, where he flung himself on the bed and smoked his pipe viciously. My mother sighed, then she and my brother and I ate some of the bananas.

My proud father. He raved, cursed, worried; he held long passionate conversations with my mother.

"Must I peddle bananas, Katie? I can't do it; the disgrace would kill me!''

"Don't do it,'' my mother would say gently. "We can live without it.''

"But where will I find work?'' he would cry. "The city is locked against me! I am a man in a trap!''

"Something will happen. God has not forgotten us,'' said my mother.

"I will kill myself! I can't stand it! I will take the gas pipe to my nose! I refuse to be a peddler!''

"Hush, the children will hear you,'' said my mother.

I could hear them thrashing it out at night in the bedroom. They talked about it at the supper table, or sat by the stove in the gloomy winter afternoons, talking, talking. My father was obsessed with the thought of bananas. They became a symbol to him of defeat, of utter hopelessness. And when my mother assured him he need not become a peddler, he would turn on her and argue that it was the one way out. He was in a curious fever of mixed emotions.

Two weeks after Mr. Lipzin's visit he was in the street with a pushcart, peddling the accursed bananas.

He came back the first night, and gave my mother a dollar bill and some silver. His face was gray; he looked older by ten years; a man who had touched bottom. My mother tried to comfort him, but for days he was silent as one who has been crushed by a calamity. Hope died in him; months passed, a year passed; he was still peddling bananas.

I remember meeting him one evening with his pushcart. I had managed to sell all my papers and was coming home in the snow. It was that strange, portentous[4] hour in downtown New York when the workers are pouring

---

[4]*portentous:* ominous.

homeward in the twilight. I marched among thousands of tired men and women whom the factory whistles had unyoked. They flowed in rivers through the clothing factory districts, then down along the avenues to the East Side.

I met my father near Cooper Union. I recognized him, a hunched, frozen figure in an old overcoat standing by a banana cart. He looked so lonely, the tears came to my eyes. Then he saw me, and his face lit with his sad, beautiful smile—Charlie Chaplin's smile.

"Ach, it's Mikey," he said. "So you have sold your papers! Come and eat a banana."

He offered me one. I refused it. I was eleven years old, but poisoned with a morbid proletarian sense of responsibility. I felt it crucial that my father *sell* his bananas, not give them away. He thought I was shy, and coaxed and joked with me, and made me eat the banana. It smelled of wet straw and snow.

"You haven't sold many bananas to-day, pop," I said anxiously.

He shrugged his shoulders.

"What can I do? No one seems to want them."

It was true. The work crowds pushed home morosely over the pavements. The rusty sky darkened over New York buildings, the tall street lamps were lit, innumerable trucks, street cars and elevated trains clattered by. Nobody and nothing in the great city stopped for my father's bananas.

"I ought to yell," said my father dolefully. "I ought to make a big noise like other peddlers, but it makes my throat sore. Anyway, I'm ashamed of yelling, it makes me feel like a fool."

I had eaten one of his bananas. My sick conscience told me that I ought to pay for it somehow. I must remain here and help my father.

"I'll yell for you, pop," I volunteered.

"Ach, no," he said, "go home; you have worked enough to-day. Just tell momma I'll be late."

But I yelled and yelled. My father, standing by, spoke occasional words of praise, and said I was a wonderful yeller. Nobody else paid attention. The workers drifted past us wearily, endlessly; a defeated army wrapped in dreams of home. Elevated trains crashed; the Cooper Union clock burned above us; the sky grew black, the wind poured, the slush burned through our shoes. There were thousands of strange, silent figures pouring over the sidewalks in snow. None of them stopped to buy bananas. I yelled and yelled, nobody listened.

My father tried to stop me at last. "*Nu*," he said smiling to console me, "that was wonderful yelling, Mikey. But it's plain we are unlucky to-day! Let's go home."

I was frantic, and almost in tears. I insisted on keeping up my desperate yells. But at last my father persuaded me to leave with him. It was after nightfall. We covered the bananas with an oilcloth and started for the pushcart stable. Down Second Avenue we plodded side by side. For many blocks my father was thoughtful. Then he shook his head and sighed:

"So you see how it is, Mikey. Even at banana peddling I am a failure. What can be wrong? The bananas are good, your yelling was good, the prices are good. Yes, it is plain; I am a man without luck."

He paused to light his pipe, while I pushed the cart for him. Then he took the handles again and continued his meditations.

"Look at me," he said. "Twenty years in America, and poorer than when I came. A suspender shop I had, and it was stolen from me by a villain. A house painter foreman I became, and fell off a scaffold. Now bananas I sell, and even at that I am a failure. It is all luck." He sighed and puffed at his pipe.

"Ach, Gott, what a rich country America is! What an easy place to make one's fortune! Look at all the rich Jews! Why has it been so easy for them, so hard for me? I am just a poor little Jew without money."

"Poppa, lots of Jews have no money," I said to comfort him.

"I know it, my son," he said, "but don't be one of them. It's better to be dead in this country than not to have money. Promise me you'll be rich when you grow up, Mikey!"

"Yes, poppa."

"Ach," he said fondly, "this is my one hope now! This is all that makes me happy! I am a greenhorn, but you are an American! You will have it easier than I; you will have luck in America!"

"Yes, poppa," I said trying to smile with him. But I felt older than he; I could not share his naïve optimism; my heart sank as I remembered the past and thought of the future.

<u>★ ★ ★ ★ ★</u>

Talking It Through

1. Why has Mr. Lipzin made his visit? How do we know that it is an unusual and painful visit for Mr. Lipzin to make? Look especially at the ways Gold describes Lipzin during the conversation, in addition to what Lipzin says.

2. Why is selling bananas a symbol of defeat for the father? How long has he been in America? What other jobs has he had? Why does he consider the suggestion that he peddle them an insult, "as if I were a greenhorn?"

3. In what ways are mother and son sensitive to the needs of the father? What do they do or say to help him cope with his situation?

4. Why do you think the father feels, "It's better to be dead in this country than not to have money"? Do you agree with him?

5. Because the father has been defeated, he turns to the son to fulfill the American dream. Do you think that Mikey will be another Andrew Carnegie? Why or why not? How does Gold's final description of the city—its streets, crowds, weather—all contribute toward the son's pessimistic view of his own future? Explain.

Writer's Workshop

1. In 1901 Jacob Riis published a book of photographs and commentary called, *How the Other Half Lives.* In this book he documented living conditions on the Lower East Side in the hope of calling attention to the plight of the city's poor. Find a photograph of this time period of a peddler, a child, a tenement dweller. Using the empathy and understanding you have gained, write a descriptive piece about the person in the picture.

2. The Industrial Revolution created the factories and cities into which immigrants poured as workers at the turn-of-the-century. The newcomers, often arriving from rural communities, had to adjust to the city.

   In an essay, compare the descriptions of city life in the writings of Sinclair, Carnegie, and Gold. Compare each author's view of the urban world and how he uses it to convey images of the "American Dream" versus the "American Reality." For Carnegie the Industrial Revolution provided new opportunities. He used his job as a messenger boy to advance himself into the new world of telegraphs, railroads, and steel. For Gold's father and for Jurgis, the city spells despair.

The Grand Gennaro

★   ★

GARIBALDI M. LAPOLLA

Garibaldi M. Lapolla was two years old when his parents came to America from southern Italy. He is the author of several novels depicting the social conditions of Italian-American life in New York City. During his lifetime he was an educator. He also authored textbooks and cookbooks and edited a poetry anthology with Mark Van Doren. This story is the first chapter of his novel The Grand Gennaro. *Set in the 1890s, it describes city life in the peak years of immigration for many ethnic groups.*

1

THE SINGULARLY NARROW HOUSE, THREE STORIES HIGH, IN WHICH THE destinies of the Accuci, the Dauri, and the Monterano families became hopelessly entangled, still throws its late afternoon shadow into the East River. The red bricks are dirtier, the fire-escapes rustier, the narrow stoop is worn down, the narrow grass-plots are bare. It wears the bitter, humorous air of an old relation, once rich, now fallen in with the indigent[1] members of the family assembled at a reunion in which beer and pretzels have taken the place of champagne and fancy sandwiches. All about it dingy tenement houses, tumble-down frame houses, loft-buildings with broken window-panes, long rows of shacks that house the accumulations of hundreds of rag-pickers combine in a dismal demonstration of poverty. Only when the moonlight is clear and widespread, but not intense enough to reveal the numerous details of degradation, does a varnish fall upon the scene, and then the East River becomes a charmed expanse, its islands gem-like intaglios,[2] and all the houses on the street that fronts it subdued into an intricate maze of phantoms. Guitar players are moved to strum sentimental Old World airs, and the children dance on the sidewalks.

---

[1]*indigent:* poor.
[2]*intaglios:* a design or figure cut below the surface of a gem.

In the decade beginning with 1880 the East River front in Harlem was a quiet near-suburban locality, prized for residences by German and Irish immigrants long enough in the country to have established prosperous businesses. A solid German butcher with dubious notions of architecture had bought himself a plot not too far from the river to afford himself the luxury of a view and had erected upon it an odd oblong of a house, and just below the cornice had had the name PARTERRE[3] inscribed in huge brownstone letters.

In it three Italian families, all from different sections of Italy, were to meet, mingle, and separate, each bearing in charred burdens of memory the shock of their encounter.

The depression that really had its beginnings in 1890 but delayed the full force of its fury until 1893, had registered in Europe before it had become fully admitted into the United States. A stream of immigration began to pour into New York City. Especially from the southern portions of Italy great masses of people, for all the world like an ancient migration, braved the terrors of slow, weather-beaten steamers, and, once landed in New York, pooled into scattered communities throughout Manhattan. They accepted any place for a dwelling.

Harlem had already begun to show signs of a too great mellowness. The families that had built themselves rows upon rows of brownstones or spacious frame dwellings set far back from the street behind bush-shaded lawns had already raised their children to manhood. The children had gone off to the modernized apartments of gray stone overlooking the Hudson. The old people found themselves in possession of homes which had achieved through the years only the sadness of places that had once rung with numerous activities. Cherry wood interiors fell into disrepair, mahogany-banistered stairways creaked and lost newel[4] or spindle,[5] and the black-and-white mantelpieces gaped open where they had once been rigidly cemented.

They are all gone, these houses, now—all but a few which some of the second generation Italians, following obscure artistic impulses, have attempted to restore. Into them rushed the peasants that had left their impoverished farms in Calabria or Sicily, in the Apuglie, or in Basilicata. Where one family had lived, now five or six struggled for a bit of space for a bed and a chance at the only sink or water closet.[6]

In the back-yards, goats disported; in the front-yards, shacks mushroomed—old boards covered with rusty tin, plastered with Sunday supple-

---

[3]*parterre:* a garden designed in a formal pattern.
[4]*newel:* the post at the top or bottom of a staircase.
[5]*spindle:* rod.
[6]*water closet:* toilet.

ments. In the streets swarmed tribes of children, bare-footed and scantily clad, forever unwashed but always screeching with glee.

2

Gennaro Accuci actually found a place in this confusion, and sent for his family. But he did not send for his family before he had succeeded in what he called, and all his fellow immigrants called, "making America." "Making good" is an approximation, but without body and associations. Something both finer and coarser clings to the expression. There is a suggestion of envy on the part of the user and also of contempt. For it means that a nobody, a mere clodhopper, a good-for-nothing on the other side, had contrived by hook or crook in this new, strange country, with its queer ways and its lack of distinctions, to amass enough money to strut about and proclaim himself the equal of those who had been his superiors in the old country. And if one said of himself that he had made America, he said it with an air of rough boasting, implying "I told you so" or "Look at me." Although he knew that his spectators would be inclined to despise him for the word, he threw out his chest. And yet there were comfort and solidity, the double fruit of egotism, in its use, and he used it, even roared it out, and laughed.

Gennaro Accuci had made America, and he was not the type to soft-pedal the expression. He pounded his sturdy small chest with his rough-knuckled small hand, having first thrust his heavy short-stemmed pipe between his teeth, and declared mightily, as best he could between closed lips, "I, I made America, and made it quick." And then, removing his pipe and allowing a slight interval to elapse, he would laugh and exclaim with a toss of the head that made his matted black curls move perceptibly, "And what's more, without kow-towing[7] to anybody, see, no, by Saint Jerome, not a bit. I kept my earrings in my ears where my father pierced them through and I'll keep them unless the President in Washington sends me a telegram."

Seven years before, without so much as a by-your-leave to priest or mayor, to both of whom he owed money, he had slipped out of his mountain village and taken ship at Reggio for New York. He had not even told his plans to his wife. She was left with two boys, ten and two years old, and a girl of three weeks—others had mercifully died in between. She would manage somehow to keep up the farm, already overburdened with mortgages and taxes, and stave off starvation from herself and the children. The

[7]*kow-towing:* bowing down.

night before he had boarded *La Sicilia* he had gone to confession. But before going to confession he had knelt at the feet of Sant' Elena in the old church near the docks and, pounding his breast very hard, but only once, he cried in prayer:

"I am leaving behind those I love, especially my oldest Domenico who should grow up and clear the farm of taxes and what I owe on it. It's the wars that eat up our substance. And I am leaving behind those to whom I owe money, but they shall never get it back from me. They take advantage of the poor, and they have the soldiers now everywhere and we cannot run off into the mountains with our women and raid the towns and hold the big folk for ransom and so regain what they steal from us. I shall keep it all even when I make it to pay back, for such a day will come in America where I shall pray to you and keep your statue in a niche day and night with a lamp beneath. And especially I pray you, now that you know, to keep my son Domenico and make him strong and capable with his hands to be a help and an honor to me, and to be good to my wife and the other two children, Emilio the black-haired one, and Elena, named after you. And I promise you now to go to confession and lay bare my heart and do proper penance for my misdeeds, but do you speak for me before the Most High, our God and our Savior, and I shall be good in your eyes and pray to you and keep a lamp burning night and day under your statue, Sant' Elena, the blessed one."

Then he rose and looked about the church for the confessional. He had a mind to pull his pipe out of his pocket but contented himself with stroking his mustache with the back of his hand and stumping determinedly into the booth. He smiled as he came out, looked about him with the air of one who has completed a given task to his satisfaction, and thrusting his pipe into his mouth hurried out of the church.

Gennaro had never gone to school—in the village of Capomonte there were no schools—and the village priest had never got round to instructing him either in the writing of his name or the doing of simple sums on paper. Don Vito was much too old and there were so many children and the farms were none too close, and besides, what did it matter? One need not write his name before entering heaven. So Gennaro at the age of thirty-two had not learned to write or read, but he knew what was what and he made sure that his passport was in good order.

He took out the complicated folds of paper on five portions of which was his photograph, and he knew where to look for the x's that marked his name, and he recognized also the picture of the new king, Humbert, and the seal of the Italian realm. He had paid enough for the wax that went to affix the green ribbon on to the paper. Thankful that all was in order, he kissed the booklet fervently before returning it to his pocket, removed his hat as he passed the church, and hurried to the steamer.

3

Once in New York, he had found his way among the Calabresi already settled in Harlem. Most of them had gone into the small business of pushing a cart with an assortment of bells strung aloft and obtaining for nothing or a few pennies old clothes and rags. They lived like gypsies—in the basements of tenement houses disgracefully overcrowded, in old stores, in shacks in the backyards, some in improvised shanties knocked together out of old lumber and tar-paper and erected against the walls of houses adjacent to empty lots. Their dirty, bare-legged children overran the cobbled streets like the goats their families kept; the older ones made a business of petty thieving from the nearby wholesale markets, or collected, like their fathers but in less formal ways, old tins and coppers and lengths of lead-pipes, all of which they sold to junkshops that lined the avenue.

Gennaro saw his chance at once. Rocco Pagliamini had been a childhood friend. But in his youth, not being like Gennaro the youngest son, he went off to do his stint in the army and, leaving the army, had come right on to New York. He already had a flourishing junk business. The store stood on the corner where the horse cars went by and the wagons passed on their way to the markets and the ferry to Long Island. It was not an uncommon sight to see a huge flat-bottomed van with slats for sides back up against Rocco's store and take on dozens and dozens of bales of rags, all laboriously packed tight and neatly roped in rectangular nets.

Pagliamini was big-chested, and swelling biceps made his arms look gigantic for a short man, especially with his thin, almost girlish, legs. For years now he had packed the bales himself, shoving them about, turning them upside down, stamping them down in the home-made bins with his heavy-weighted tamping irons, and the muscles of his upper structures had bulged and hardened and grown taut. His face alone, above his short sinewy neck, remained soft and laughing. He laughed frequently, for everything was funny to him, even when he managed to allow the tamping-iron to glance off his toes. He laughed if the horses pulled away just after the man had succeeded in lifting a troublesome bale on to the very top of the load and had not tied it down and the bale came tumbling back on them. He laughed in a thin girlish voice and called on the saints to witness how merry it all was. And he laughed when he saw Gennaro Accuci standing in front of his store, big as life.

"*Gennaru bellu, figliu du sacramentu di Gesu!* In America! Why didn't you send us that much of a line (he showed a width of finger) to let us know, hey, you old shaved-off goat?''

They kissed on both cheeks, and since they had been childhood friends they laughed together and then they wept.

''And my mother?''

''Ah, the old thing,'' answered Gennaro, ''still hobbles to church. The priest still lords it over the village.''

''And how is he, the old . . .?''

''Nothing against the old fellow, Rocco, by your leave,'' and putting his mouth to his friend's ear he whispered roguishly, ''I owe him a thousand scuti—that's why I'm here.''

Rocco laughed. ''We've got to have a feast and talk over old times. And what will you be doing here in America?''

''Making America.''

''Hear that? Hear that?'' Rocco cried to all his workmen who, barefooted, shirtless, stood around enjoying the meeting between the old friends. ''Going to make America at once! You got to sweat, my son; you got to starve; you got to turn your own relatives away starving. For instance, will you take off your coat now and pitch in among those filthy, dusty, worm-eaten rags and let the dirt get mixed up with your spittle and your sweat and laugh anyhow?''

''I'm ready.''

''Not like picking the big fat grapes off the vines.''

The workmen laughed.

''Not like packing down the figs.''

More laughter.

''Not like sticking the old pig after the harvest and salting down the hams and having a great feast to celebrate it all.''

''I'm ready.''

He was as good as his word and began at once. And that night Rocco invited all the *paesani*[8] that could be mustered together and, clearing away one of the back-yards, put up improvised tables on barrel ends and set up a keg of beer in a corner of it, and the beer flowed, and the talk flowed, and when Gennaro had drunk enough beer he got up and said boastfully, pounding his chest once with his closed fist, ''I'm going to make America, and make it quick.''

He worked hard in the rag-and-junk shop. The store was in reality a huge, spacious one, but the bins all along the walls and the piles of old lead and copper, pewter cans and spoons, the bales of rags, cluttered it all up, shut out the light and filled it with clouds of lint and flecks of metal small

---

[8]*paesani:* friends.

enough to float in the heavy air. The men coughed constantly between shouts and oaths and laughter at coarse jokes.

4

Gennaro watched his chance. He saw boys bringing in copper bottoms, lead-pipes, old pewter pots. He saw boys bringing in old pieces of plate, scraps of gold—tiny scraps, but gold—copper nails, zinc tubs battered down into lumps. He saw that these things brought in most money. He saw, too, that there were rags *and* rags. He learned soon to pick out the silks and grade them, pick out the linens and grade them, the percales, the cambrics, the broadcloths.[9] He did it so well, Rocco made him chief-assorter and raised his pay. He put the money he got into an old earthen pot, and he buried the pot, peasant-like, in a corner of the back-yard and dug it up only at night. He got permission to make a bunk for himself in the junk-shop and sleep there. Rocco told him he was crazy. It was hell to sleep in that place, hot and crawly with bugs, and the air was filled with lint and dust of the metals. But Gennaro knew his own mind.

He was thinking of Domenico, his oldest son almost going on eleven now, and Emilio the curly-haired one, the little girl, and of his wife, too, with her heavy bosoms and her big eyes that just looked at one wonderingly but filled with trust and affection. This was a dog's life, working for Rocco, working for anybody, fumbling through old rags, cutting one's fingers on tin and scraps of iron. What could he do on a dollar a day? He ate twenty cents of it and saved the eighty. What was that? That wouldn't make America. So he watched the boys coming in with old copper bottoms and pieces of lead-pipe. He took one aside, a slinking, thin lad with slit-like eyes that always looked frightened.

"One cent more a pound for the copper—half of the copper; the other half, the old price. But don't tell nobody."

Gennaro handled the pushcart ragmen the same way. He found ways of hiding the half he bought for himself. He succeeded in getting most of the boys to come after hours, late in the evening. It was then he sorted out his own purchases. He was honest enough in this for a while.

But it was slow work "making America," even in this way. So he threw one rag in every hundred into a pile meant for himself. These he bundled up into bags, but he soon found himself with too many bags, and so he built himself a shed in an empty lot and stored them there. The slit-eyed lad

[9]*percales, cambrics, broadcloths:* kinds of cloth.

assisting, he carted over the stuff in the dead of night. One night in the week the boy piled up the stuff in an old push-cart and pushed it down to an appointed street far away from Rocco. There Gennaro met the youngster and they pushed the cart all the way down to Allen Street and sold the junk to the big Jewish dealers, and then pushed the empty cart all the way back, returning in the small hours of the morning, dead tired.

Rocco found out, and confronted Gennaro. They were alone in the store. The men had left for the day. It was the summer after the one when Gennaro had arrived, and extremely hot. The lint, the flying dirt, the close-packed bales, the piles of metal made the heat into a glue-like cloud that smelled throughout the store, stuck to the eyes of the men, gummed up their bare, sweated biceps, pasted strings of dirt along the neck-muscles.

"What's this I hear, *porcu diavolu?*" Rocco began without preliminaries.

"You hear right."

That was all he said. Gennaro had struck Rocco over the jaw with the back of his fist, swinging his right arm from the left shoulder with terrific speed. Then he calmly stuck his pipe into his mouth and lit it, confident that he had knocked his man unconscious. He had. He waited for Rocco to come to, mopping his face, pulling up his trousers and tightening his belt. When he felt Rocco make the first stir, he planted his foot upon the man's chest and held the body down.

"Let me breathe."

After an interval Gennaro removed his foot, watching warily for the next move. But he knew that Rocco was too good-natured and trusting to carry a knife and must be much too weak to offer further resistance.

"Not a word, Rocco," he said curtly, puffing calmly on his pipe. "I'll give you up all I made, but I want half a share in the business."

"I should have known," Rocco mumbled. "You did the same when we were kids."

At this point the slit-eyed partner of Gennaro's schemes appeared out of a pile of rags.

"One more word, Rocco, and if that ain't yes. . . . What's the use? I'm telling you, you can't make America just working. It's too long to wait. Only bosses get along, like you, like Struzzo round the block owns all those houses. I'm not going to keep on working for others all my life. I got enough now to start my own business, but I'll join up with you and we'll go halves."

The slit-eyed boy gasped and then laughed. Gennaro struck him a blow with the flat of his hand and the boy fell down whimpering.

"All right," said Rocco.

"We go and sign. Come on."

They signed up in the café on the corner opposite, a big barn of a store with sawdust over the floor and three-legged tables smeared with the remains of spilled coffee, sugar and syrups. Cakes dipped in colored sugars, gummed together by the heat, were piled up in the windows. The place was hung with thick, acrid smoke. Gennaro and Rocco, looking groggy and uncertain on his feet, took seats at a table.

"Two coffees and some rum," Gennaro ordered.

In a minute a thin dapper young man in a double-breasted coat, with pants fitting close over his ankles, swung into the door behind a light bamboo cane that seemed to be pulling him along. Bronzed, with a sharp acuiline nose and thick eyebrows set in a narrow forehead, he looked Arabian.

"You're both here, then?" he asked jauntily of Gennaro and Rocco. "That's fine. I have the papers and we shall lose no time."

Salvatore Cicco passed for a lawyer, although he was employed only as a runner for a firm of lawyers. He plied a brisk business in Harlem, drawing contracts, business arrangements, leases, getting the ignorant out of jail for a consideration, fixing up trials even for the guilty, with such a string of successes to his credit that the community looked upon him as having some intimate connection with the law-making powers of the country.

He spread out the papers and they all signed, Gennaro with a cross, Rocco laboriously tracing huge letters across the page. He had learned to spell out his name in the army. After he had completed his difficult task, he looked up, and for the first time since the encounter in his junk-shop he could look Gennaro squarely in the face and laugh.

"Well, you have made America, and made it quick. You were born an American."

Salvatore Cicco extended a bony hand to both.

"Luck."

"Drinks to everybody," shouted Gennaro.

Everybody got a drink, and everybody drank, and that's how Gennaro made America, or really just began to make it. Gennaro did not sleep in the shop that night but insisted without hesitation or fear of contradiction that he would share Rocco's room. It was merely a matter of picking up an old cot at another of the junkies, throwing a mattress on it and placing the thing in any available space in Rocco's hired room.

★ ★ ★ ★ ★

Talking It Through

1. How does Lapolla use the "singularly narrow house" as a symbol of immigrant life in America? What is the neighborhood surrounding it like? Why has it fallen into such disrepair, and how does it exemplify the desire to "move up and out" of so many immigrants? Give some examples of how you think Lapolla paints this scene effectively.

2. What can we infer about the life in Italy that Gennaro has left behind? Why do the men working in the junkyard seem to prefer their sordid work and surroundings to picking grapes in the Italian countryside?

3. Why does Gennaro choose to sleep, as well as work, in the junkyard? How do you feel about the way he goes about "making America" even at the expense of using Rocco? What motivates Gennaro to behave as he does? Do you admire him or dislike him?

4. In what ways are Rocco and Gennaro similar and dissimilar? Why do you think the author spends so much time describing the physical attributes of these men? How does the author use Rocco's laughter, or Gennaro's pipe-smoking as trademarks of their personalities?

5. What does it mean in this story to "make America"? Why does Rocco say to Gennaro, the newly arrived immigrant, "You were born an American"?

Writer's Workshop

1. In an essay discuss Gennaro's boast, "I made America, and made it quick." Compare his success to the success or failure of another immigrant in "American Dream/American Reality." Focus on the personalities of the characters you compare. What motivates them to succeed? To what extent do they pursue personal success at the expense of others?

2. Describe a building or neighborhood so as to endow it with personality and character traits, as Lapolla does as he begins his story. How do the buildings reflect the inhabitants, or the history of prior use? You may wish to make a mental sketch of a neighborhood near you before you write. Alternatively, look at some of the urban scenes painted by John Sloane, Edward Hopper, or George Bellows. These American painters worked in the early decades of the twentieth century and tried to capture urban life at this time.

Jimmy and Death

K A T E   S I M O N

Kate Simon made her name as a travel writer, publishing a series of sensitively written guidebooks to places from Mexico to Italy. In later life she turned to autobiography, recounting her own childhood and coming of age in the Bronx, a borough of New York City, the first home of many immigrant groups to this day. Here she writes about her brother's best friend and how his death affected all the children of the neighborhood.

JIMMY PETRIDES, MY BROTHER'S BEST FRIEND FROM THE TIME WE MOVED TO Lafontaine Avenue when both boys were about five, was lank and had a neat face, as if someone had made a careful drawing of it before he was born; the lines of his thin eyebrows and thin nose straight, the lower line of his eyes straight, and the arches above as complete and round as the pretty hollow at the back of his neck. Like all the other boys he leaped and bellowed in the street but he was quiet and shy when he came to our house on rainy or cold days to make trains of boxes or spools and to match baseball cards with my brother. Although they lived in our house, two stories below us, we knew very little of his family. His father was one of the many anonymous men in caps with paper bags under their arms who rushed to the El[1] in the morning and came back more slowly at night. Jimmy had a younger sister whom he began to take to school when he was about eight, a dark-gold little girl who clutched his hand and wouldn't talk to anyone else. Once home from school, she stayed in the house; we rarely saw her on the street even as she grew older. Mrs. Petrides was also rarely visible and wonderful when she was, a silent solitary thing like a tree alone in a field. There may have been other Greek families on the block but not in

---

[1] *the El:* the elevated railway. In the Bronx, subways were too difficult and costly to build, so when the boom in cheaply constructed low-cost apartments occurred in the 1920s and '30s, bringing tens of thousands of working class immigrants to that section of New York, the El became their lifeline to jobs elsewhere in the city.

our immediate houses, and she had very few English words to exchange with her neighbors. Nevertheless, families in immigrant neighborhoods being inevitably interdependent, for shopping advice, for medical information, for the care of each other's children and the exchange of kitchen delicacies, Mrs. Petrides was offered strudel[2] by Mrs. Nagy, the *Ungarische dripke*[3] who was the best baker on the block. Big, clumsy Mrs. Kaplan, the loudest behemoth of the house, took her a length of *kishka* (stuffed intestine), her specialty, which Jimmy told us they couldn't eat; all that rubbery stuff. My mother's contribution was to ask Jimmy if his mother would like to go to the English classes with her, explaining that they were held during afternoon school hours and she would be back before three o'clock. He said, "She won't, she's too ashamed," the word for embarrassed or shy. There must have been a number of women like Mrs. Petrides on the block, who had no one to speak with when the husband and children were away, no one to ask where she could buy feta cheese[4] or Greek oil. Tall and slender, with Jimmy's long eyebrows and straight nose, her sandy hair in a long full knot at the back of her head, her high-arched eyes fixed straight ahead, she looked like a lady on the front of a storybook ship, as strong and as lonely.

My mother and the other women said that if Mrs. Petrides had taken them into her house to see Jimmy when he got sick—it didn't need words— or had asked the De Santis boys to take him to Fordham Hospital, Jimmy might not have died. We never found out the cause of his death; children were told about the deaths of the old but never of children, a knowledge too dreadful to speak. The first intimations of Jimmy's illness came from my brother, who was hanging around one rainy October day being mean and restless. He got in my mother's way as she was trying to boil diapers in the steaming cauldron on the stove; he woke our little sister, who had been sick and was napping; he hid my brand-new pencil with the removable cap eraser. My mother suggested he go down to play in Jimmy's house or ask him to come up. He said Jimmy was sick, he hadn't gone to school that day. The next day and the next when he was asked if Jimmy had been in school he again answered, "No," and although the weather had cleared, he refused to go down into the street. He pushed spools and boxes around for a while, read for a while, colored a picture with the baby for a while, but mostly he hung around, like a tired little old man.

The whole house was quiet. The women didn't talk much; only Tobie Herman clattered noisily up and down the stairs. My mother must have known that Jimmy was dying, but I knew nothing until my brother burst

---

[2]*strudel:* pastry consisting of layers of paper-thin dough enclosing a fruit filling.

[3]*Ungarische dripke:* Yiddish; derogatory term for Hungarian.

[4]*feta cheese:* hard curd cheese used in Greek cookery.

into the house crying as neither my father with his beatings nor I with my fierce teasing could make him cry. His face was broken, tears pouring down his sweater, his fists clenched and shaking as if he were fighting, his feet stamping. When we calmed him a little, though he still shuddered and wept, he told us that Mr. Petrides, home from the factory that day, came over to him and said that Jimmy was dead, that we would never see him again. "What does he mean, *never*? That I won't ever see Jimmy again? What does he mean?" and his heels stamped the floor and his fist punched the air again and the terrible crying started again. I wanted to console him, not quite knowing what to say, saying something while my mother held him on her lap, a big boy of nine who allowed the indignity because he was in terrible trouble.

That evening when my father came home he was still shuddering, lying on our bed with the baby, who offered him her doll and conversation. He didn't respond, which made her cry. That night he didn't eat, and he slept deeply, shuddering every once in a while. Like the street, school was hushed the next morning. The news of Jimmy's death, carried in whispers through the auditorium, in the playground, on the stairs, in toilets, was a funerary garland[5] that wrapped itself around the whole red brick building. Street life stopped: no ball, no marbles, no ropes lashing at the sidewalk, no stickball, no fights, no singing on the stoop.[6] The day of the funeral must have been Saturday, there was no school. We returned books to the library and picked out others early and quickly, then went home to clean up and wait, not knowing quite what we were waiting for. We had seen funerals in the movies, in the news, but they were of grand and old people, not of a boy, not on our street. It was a cool sunny day, the big garbage cans and the metal roof of the De Santis garage shining bright and hard. As we sat on the stoop we heard stirrings on the inside stairs. The inner door opened and two men came down into the small hall where the letter boxes were, carrying a long black box. My brother gasped and I dragged him down the block, looking back to see what was happening. After the box came Mr. Petrides in a black coat and Mrs. Petrides with a black veil over her head and falling down her black coat. Behind them a few more people in black, one of the women holding by the hand the little Petrides girl whose head, too, was covered with a black scarf. The box was carried slowly down the stoop stairs, into the gutter, and then, followed by the family, headed toward 180th Street. Telling my brother that funerals were quiet so he shouldn't make noise, I ran ahead to look at Mrs. Petrides from the sidewalk. She

[5]*funerary garland:* commemorative wreath of flowers used as a memorial.
[6]*stoop:* platform with steps leading from a house, originally a Dutch style.

wasn't crying; she had died, too, with only the clear drawing of her features left on dull white paper.

As the family walked slowly, following the black box, held high by the four black arms like burned tree branches, the children began to trail after, led off by the two youngest De Santis boys, both in their early teens, and then the other Italian children, who seemed to know about funerals: Maria Silvestri and her brother Louis, Caroline and Petey Santini, the Bianchi kids. My brother ran into the gutter[7] to join Petey, and I followed him, hesitating for a moment, to walk with Caroline. Awkwardly, hesitantly, the Jewish kids watching from the sidewalk began to walk with us, some of them kids who might later be hit for joining a goyish[8] funeral. The two Ruthies came and Helen, Rachel, and Hannah, Sidney and Milton, the Sammies, the Izzys. My brother began to cry, quietly, and I went to him while Caroline took Petey, whose face had begun to quiver. More crying around me, behind me, growing louder and louder, coming out of twisted eyes, leaking into open mouths. (Those weeping faces combine inextricably in my memory with the image of the mourning cherubim of Giotto,[9] wailing as they hover over the body of Christ.)

I couldn't understand why they were all crying. My brother, yes, Jimmy had always been his very best friend and he liked him more than anyone else in the world, more than our mother. The other boys had liked him too, an easy, gentle boy who yielded to them rather than fight. But why were the girls crying over a Greek boy they had hardly ever played with? What did they know about death that I didn't? What were they seeing? What were they feeling? Like them, I knew dead people were put in a hole in the ground and covered with earth. Were they crying because the earth might choke him, because he might open his eyes in the dark, alone, screaming, and no one to hear him? Maybe then he would really, truly die. Was that what they meant by "frightened to death"? As a Christian boy he should become an angel. Was there a saw in the coffin to cut through the black wood and a shovel to dig away the dirt? And once out, how long would he have to stand in the dark alone before God sent the blond lady with the naked baby[10] down through the windy night clouds to carry him back up with her?

[7]*gutter:* the street beyond the sidewalk, usually used by cars.

[8]*goyish:* Yiddish for gentile, non-Jewish.

[9]*cherubim of Giotto:* angels depicted as babies, usually unclothed, by a master artist of the early Italian renaissance who lived in Florence at the beginning of the fifteenth century.

[10]*blond lady with the naked baby:* the Virgin Mary and the Infant Jesus. The author, herself Jewish, would have seen them depicted in religious art reproductions.

Seeing sick Jimmy standing alone, waiting—for how long?—to be rescued from the dark made me cry as fully, with my whole body, as I couldn't on Third Avenue in the dark, when I was five. Maybe my brother was crying the same memory: in a dark, unknown place, lost, unprotected. We were crying for the same reason that we hid our heads in the movies when a child wandered alone, that we quickly skipped pages when a book threatened to tell about an abandoned child. (Maybe we were also crying, like the women who went to the movies "to enjoy a good cry," for the relief not too often permitted us.)

By the time we reached 180th Street, my mother had caught up with us. Taking us each by the hand, she said she didn't think they would let us into the Greek church and certainly not into the cemetery; come home, stop crying. We ate, we slept, we went to school, we asked no questions. One of the block chroniclers said the Petrides family had gone back to Greece, another said they moved downtown near cousins who had a stable. We were no longer interested in the family—the godlike child's gesture of quickly dissolving away anything that wasn't immediately attached to our ears, our eyes, our greeds, our envies. Our fears hung on for a while. No one mentioned Jimmy. His name was a black omen, a sign that children could die, and as fast as we could, we obliterated his name, too.

★ ★ ★ ★ ★

Talking It Through

1. Kate Simon begins this memoir with a description of Jimmy Petrides and his family. Reread the opening paragraph (it extends over a page) to note how Simon develops our empathy for these people. We quickly get a picture of their appearance, their circumstances, their closeness. What do they have in common with their neighbors in the Bronx apartment house?

   Here we get a picture of "the rainbow" Langston Hughes speaks of in his poem "Little Song" (see p. 325) and of "the tired and poor" who have passed through Lazarus' "golden door." Pick out examples to share with your classmates where Simon has tellingly sketched entire lives in a few words.

2. In the second paragraph of the story Simon informs us that Jimmy has died. She moves swiftly here to the central fact of her chapter, Jimmy and Death. Although we already know that Jimmy died, she builds suspense nonetheless as we see Kate's brother restlessly pushing around "the spools and boxes" that serve the boys as toys, and moping around "like a tired old man," waiting for his friend to recover and play with him.

In the third paragraph, we have her brother's dramatic confrontation with the reality and finality of death. "What does he mean *never*?" he rages at the prospect of never seeing his friend again. Does Simon's account seem true to life? Cite other particulars from this paragraph that you feel build its emotional impact on the reader.

3. With great economy Kate Simon fills in our picture of school and play for the immigrant youngsters. What is usual? What changes with the news of Jimmy's death? Why does the author say Mrs. Petrides "had died too"? How does Simon convey the mixture of awe and fear at the sight of the coffin and mourners?

4. In the next paragraph, Simon lists the names of the neighborhood children who follow the Petrides family to the funeral service. What is the effect of this? How does this paragraph tie in with other selections in this section of the text?

5. The end of this passage is less about Jimmy Petrides and more about universal childhood experiences and fears. What does Simon speculate about? Do you think her descriptions are effective in describing death in terms of claustrophobic terror?

6. The Simon children's mother brings Kate and her brother home. Normalcy returns, but "No one mentioned Jimmy. His name was a black omen, a sign that children could die . . ." How does Simon's childhood memory convey the American dream as well as the American reality?

Writer's Workshop

1. An obituary is a biographical article written in a newspaper to announce an individual's death and to sum up his or her life. Write an obituary for Jimmy Petrides. Feel free to imagine his life before and after his family emigrated from Greece to America. Include information about his parents and younger sister. You might want to read the obituary page of your daily newspaper first to acquaint yourself with the style and format.

2. Write the story from the point of view of Mrs. Petrides. What does this silent, composed woman think about? Is she frustrated at not being able to communicate with her neighbors? Why doesn't she ask for their help when her son becomes ill? What might have happened to her and her family after the funeral, and after they leave the Bronx apartment in which they had been living? From the clues given in the narrative describing Mrs. Petrides and her family, try to build a character and a life.

3. Write a personal essay dealing with the subject of death. You may draw

on personal experience, or what you have seen or heard in newspapers or on television about times when tragedy strikes a family, particularly when death is not expected.

I Learned ★ *to Sew* ★

MITSUYE YAMADA

In this poem a Japanese woman tells her grandchild how she came to America as a picture bride. Mitsuye Yamada, the author of Desert Run: Poems and Stories, *has retired from teaching at Cypress College in California.*

How can I say this?
My child
My life is nothing
There is nothing to tell

My family in Japan was too poor   5
to send me to school
I learned to sew
always I worked to help my family
when I was seventeen years old
and no one made marriage offer   10
a friend in our village who was going
to Hawaii a picture bride[1]
said to me
Come with me.

[1]*picture bride:* a bride who has never seen the man she is to marry. He has received her photograph, and agreed to marry her.

I did not want to   15
my parents did not want me to
my picture was sent to a stranger anyway
a young man's photograph and letter came
I was already seventeen years old
I went to the island of Hawaii to marry   20
this photograph.

This man came to the boat
he was too shy to talk to me
the Immigration man said to him
Here   25
sign here for her
He walked away
The Immigration man came to me
Don't you have relatives in Hawaii?

I said   30
Yes I have that man who will marry me
He said
Go back to Japan on the next boat
I said
I will wait here for my man   35
The immigration man said
No
your man is not coming back
he told me he does not want you
he said you are too ugly for him   40
why don't you go back to Japan
on the next boat?
I said
No
I am not going back   45
I am staying here

    Just
    A minute
    My child
    Put that pen down   50
    Do not write this
    I never told this to anybody
    Not even to my oldest son, your father

I now tell this story
To you first time in sixty years   55

I sat at Immigration for a long time
people came and people went
I stayed
I could not see the sky
I could not see the sun   60
outside the window
I saw a seaweed forest
the crickets made scraping sounds
the geckos[2] went tuk tuk tuk
sometimes a gecko would come into my room   65
but I was not afraid to talk to it
it came and it went as it pleased.

I was thinking about Urashima Taro[3]
you know the story?
Urashima disappeared into the sea   70
lived in the undersea world
married a beautiful princess
returned to his village
a very old man
I was thinking   75
I will leave this place
only when I am an old lady.

Pretty soon the Immigration man came to me
We found your cousin
In two weeks a cousin I met once   80
in Japan came for me
I stayed with him and his wife until
my cousin found a job for me
I worked doing housework
I did this for one year.   85

My cousin found a husband for me
he was a merchant
we had a small store

[2]*gecko:* a type of lizard.
[3]*Urashima Taro:* a figure in Japanese folklore.

and sold dry goods
my husband died after three sons   90
your father, my oldest son, was six years old
I could not keep the store
I could not read
I could not write
the only thing I knew how to do was sew.   95

I took the cloth from our store
sewed pants and undergarments
put the garments on a wooden cart
ombu the baby on my back
we went from plantation to plantation   100
sold my garments to the workers
I was their only store
sewed more garments at night
I did this for five years.

Your father grew up to love study and books   105
my friends called him the professor
he was then eleven years old
I said to him you need a father
He said I want to go to college
I said to him I will marry any man you say   110
I will marry any man
who will send you to college.

One day he came home and said
I went to a matchmaker[4] and
found a husband for you   115
he will marry a widow with three sons
will send them to college
he is a plantation foreman.

I married this man.

By and by my oldest son went away   120
to college in Honolulu
but my husband's boss told him
I need workers

---

[4]*matchmaker:* someone who makes arranged marriages.

your three sons must work
on my plantation like the others.   125
My husband said
No
He kept his word to my oldest son
and lost his job.

After that we had many hard times   130
I am nothing
know nothing
I only know how to sew
I now sew for my children and grandchildren
I turn to the sun every day of my life   135
pray to Amaterasu Omikami[5]
for the health and
education of my children
for me that is enough

My child   140
Write this
There   take your pen
There   write it
Say that I am not going back
I am staying here   145

Talking It Through

1. This poem is written as a monologue, a long speech given by one person.
   In the poem we hear a woman's voice as she describes her life to her
   grandchild. How is the poem structured? What stanzas are indented, and
   why? In what way does each stanza represent a segment of the narrator's
   life? Make a brief chronology of the events she describes.

2. What do we find out in the second stanza about the narrator's life in Japan?
   Why is she uneducated? Why does she learn to sew? What values do you
   think she holds important?

3. At what points has the narrator done what is expected of her, or what
   others have told her to do? At what points has she taken charge of her life
   and determined her own fate? What has been her "dream"? How is it the

[5]*Amaterasu Omikami:* a god in Japanese mythology.

same as other immigrants you have read about; how is it different? Has she attained it? Explain.

4. In what ways is the narrator's language like the everyday talk of a simple woman? In what way is it poetry? Look carefully at how the lines are arranged and how certain words repeat.

5. Taking the expression "I learned to sew" as a metaphor, what has the narrator learned to do in her life? Why is sewing a symbol of it?

6. The narrator tells her grandchild, "My life is nothing . . ." "I am nothing/ know nothing . . ." Do you believe she truly sees herself this way? Has seeing herself this way advanced or impeded her life, in your opinion? Do you agree with her that her life is nothing or do you see her life as heroic? Explain.

Writer's Workshop

1. Although the grandchild in this poem never speaks a word, it is easy to imagine the kinds of questions he or she might ask while listening to the grandmother. Write an interview of the grandmother, with the grandchild posing questions and the grandmother answering them. What would arouse the child's curiosity? How would the grandmother respond, based on what we have learned about her personality in the poem?

2. Write a story from the grandchild's point of view. How has the child seen the grandmother in the past? Create an event which has prompted the grandmother to tell the child the story of her life. ("I never told this to anybody/not even to my oldest son . . ." she confesses.) What impact does the new information have on the child's relationship to the grandparent? Does the child see him- or herself differently, after hearing the story?

3. Write a poem that is a narrative monologue in which one person tells another a story. For example, write a poetic monologue in which Michael Gold's father tells his son the story of his life.

Tears of
Autumn

★ ★

Y O S H I K O   U C H I D A

Yoshiko Uchida was a Japanese American who wrote of the discrimination and injustice faced by Japanese Americans during World War II. She also retold folk tales from her heritage. This story begins on shipboard as a young woman contemplates her decision to wed sight-unseen a Japanese emigré who has preceded her to America. The bridegroom has left Japan to seek his future in Oakland, California, where he is a shopkeeper. The bride-to-be hopes to escape a constricting life in her homeland. The only romance in this venture lies in Hana Omiya's hopes for the future.

HANA OMIYA STOOD AT THE RAILING OF THE SMALL SHIP THAT SHUDDERED toward America in a turbulent November sea. She shivered as she pulled the folds of her silk kimono close to her throat and tightened the wool shawl about her shoulders.

She was thin and small, her dark eyes shadowed in her pale face, her black hair piled high in a pompadour that seemed too heavy for so slight a woman. She clung to the moist rail and breathed the damp salt air deep into her lungs. Her body seemed leaden and lifeless, as though it were simply the vehicle transporting her soul to a strange new life, and she longed with childlike intensity to be home again in Oka Village.

She longed to see the bright persimmon dotting the barren trees beside the thatched roofs, to see the fields of golden rice stretching to the mountains where only last fall she had gathered plum white mushrooms, and to see once more the maple trees lacing their flaming colors through the green pine. If only she could see a familiar face, eat a meal without retching, walk on solid ground, and stretch out at night on a *tatami* mat instead of in a hard narrow bunk. She thought now of seeking the warm shelter of her bunk but could not bear to face the relentless smell of fish that penetrated the lower decks.

Why did I ever leave Japan? she wondered bitterly. Why did I ever listen to my uncle? And yet she knew it was she herself who had begun the chain of events that placed her on this heaving ship. It was she who had first planted in her uncle's mind the thought that she would make a good wife for Taro Takeda, the lonely man who had gone to America to make his fortune in Oakland, California.

It all began one day when her uncle had come to visit her mother.

"I must find a nice young bride," he had said, startling Hana with this blunt talk of marriage in her presence. She blushed and was ready to leave the room when her uncle quickly added, "My good friend Takeda has a son in America. I must find someone willing to travel to that far land."

This last remark was intended to indicate to Hana and her mother that he didn't consider this a suitable prospect for Hana, who was the youngest daughter of what once had been a fine family. Her father, until his death fifteen years ago, had been the largest landholder of the village and one of its last samurai. They had once had many servants and field hands, but now all that was changed. Their money was gone. Hana's three older sisters had made good marriages, and the eldest remained in their home with her husband to carry on the Omiya name and perpetuate the homestead. Her other sisters had married merchants in Osaka and Nagoya and were living comfortably.

Now that Hana was twenty-one, finding a proper husband for her had taken on an urgency that produced an embarrassing secretive air over the entire matter. Usually, her mother didn't speak of it until they were lying side by side on their quilts at night. Then, under the protective cover of darkness, she would suggest one name and then another, hoping that Hana would indicate an interest in one of them.

Her uncle spoke freely of Taro Takeda only because he was so sure Hana would never consider him. "He is a conscientious, hardworking man who has been in the United States for almost ten years. He is thirty-one, operates a small shop, and rents some rooms above the shop where he lives." Her uncle rubbed his chin thoughtfully. "He could provide well for a wife," he added.

"Ah," Hana's mother said softly.

"You say he is successful in this business?" Hana's sister inquired.

"His father tells me he sells many things in his shop—clothing, stockings, needles, thread, and buttons—such things as that. He also sells bean paste, pickled radish, bean cake, and soy sauce. A wife of his would not go cold or hungry."

They all nodded, each of them picturing this merchant in varying degrees of success and affluence. There were many Japanese emigrating to America these days, and Hana had heard of the picture brides who went with nothing more than an exchange of photographs to bind them to a strange man.

"Taro San is lonely," her uncle continued. "I want to find for him a fine young woman who is strong and brave enough to cross the ocean alone."

"It would certainly be a different kind of life," Hana's sister ventured, and for a moment, Hana thought she glimpsed a longing ordinarily concealed behind her quiet, obedient face. In that same instant, Hana knew she wanted more for herself than her sisters had in their proper, arranged, and loveless marriages. She wanted to escape the smothering strictures of life in her village. She certainly was not going to marry a farmer and spend her life working beside him planting, weeding, and harvesting in the rice paddies until her back became bent from too many years of stooping and her skin was turned to brown leather by the sun and wind. Neither did she particularly relish the idea of marrying a merchant in a big city as her two sisters had done. Since her mother objected to her going to Tokyo to seek employment as a teacher, perhaps she would consent to a flight to America for what seemed a proper and respectable marriage.

Almost before she realized what she was doing, she spoke to her uncle. "Oji San, perhaps I should go to America to make this lonely man a good wife."

"You, Hana Chan?" Her uncle observed her with startled curiosity. "You would go all alone to a foreign land so far away from your mother and family?"

"I would not allow it." Her mother spoke fiercely. Hana was her youngest and she had lavished upon her the attention and latitude that often befall the last child. How could she permit her to travel so far, even to marry the son of Takeda who was known to her brother?

But now, a notion that had seemed quite impossible a moment before was lodged in his receptive mind, and Hana's uncle grasped it with the pleasure that comes from an unexpected discovery.

"You know," he said looking at Hana, "it might be a very good life in America."

Hana felt a faint fluttering in her heart. Perhaps this lonely man in America was her means of escaping both the village and the encirclement of her family.

Her uncle spoke with increasing enthusiasm of sending Hana to become Taro's wife. And the husband of Hana's sister, who was head of their household, spoke with equal eagerness. Although he never said so, Hana guessed he would be pleased to be rid of her, the spirited younger sister who stirred up his placid life with what he considered radical ideas about life and the role of women. He often claimed that Hana had too much schooling for a girl. She had graduated from Women's High School in Kyoto, which gave her five more years of schooling than her older sister.

"It has addled her brain—all that learning from those books," he said when he tired of arguing with Hana.

A man's word carried much weight for Hana's mother. Pressed by the two men, she consulted her other daughters and their husbands. She discussed the matter carefully with her brother and asked the village priest. Finally, she agreed to an exchange of family histories and an investigation was begun into Taro Takeda's family, his education, and his health, so they would be assured there was no insanity or tuberculosis or police records concealed in his family's past. Soon Hana's uncle was devoting his energies entirely to serving as go-between for Hana's mother and Taro Takeda's father.

When at last an agreement to the marriage was almost reached, Taro wrote his first letter to Hana. It was brief and proper and gave no more clue to his character than the stiff formal portrait taken at his graduation from middle school. Hana's uncle had given her the picture with apologies from his parents, because it was the only photo they had of him and it was not a flattering likeness.

Hana hid the letter and photograph in the sleeve of her kimono and took them to the outhouse to study in private. Squinting in the dim light and trying to ignore the foul odor, she read and reread Taro's letter, trying to find the real man somewhere in the sparse unbending prose.

By the time he sent her money for her steamship tickets, she had received ten more letters, but none revealed much more of the man than the first. In none did he disclose his loneliness or his need, but Hana understood this. In fact, she would have recoiled from a man who bared his intimate thoughts to her so soon. After all, they would have a lifetime together to get to know one another.

So it was that Hana had left her family and sailed alone to America with a small hope trembling inside of her. Tomorrow, at last, the ship would dock in San Francisco and she would meet face to face the man she was soon to marry. Hana was overcome with excitement at the thought of being in America, and terrified of the meeting about to take place. What would she say to Taro Takeda when they first met, and for all the days and years after?

Hana wondered about the flat above the shop. Perhaps it would be luxuriously furnished with the finest of brocades and lacquers, and perhaps there would be a servant, although he had not mentioned it. She worried whether she would be able to manage on the meager English she had learned at Women's High School. The overwhelming anxiety for the day to come and the violent rolling of the ship were more than Hana could bear. Shuddering in the face of the wind, she leaned over the railing and became violently and wretchedly ill.

By five the next morning, Hana was up and dressed in her finest purple silk kimono and coat. She could not eat the bean soup and rice that appeared for breakfast and took only a few bits of the yellow pickled radish. Her bags, which had scarcely been touched since she boarded the ship, were easily packed, for all they contained were her kimonos and some of her favorite books. The large willow basket, tightly secured by a rope, remained under the bunk, untouched since her uncle had placed it there.

She had not befriended the other women in her cabin, for they had lain in their bunks for most of the voyage, too sick to be company to anyone. Each morning Hana had fled the closeness of the sleeping quarters and spent most of the day huddled in a corner of the deck, listening to the lonely songs of some Russians also travelling to an alien land.

As the ship approached land, Hana hurried up to the deck to look out at the gray expanse of ocean and sky, eager for a first glimpse of her new homeland.

"We won't be docking until almost noon," one of the deckhands told her.

Hana nodded, "I can wait," she answered, but the last hours seemed the longest.

When she set foot on American soil at last, it was not in the city of San Francisco as she had expected, but on Angel Island, where all third-class passengers were taken. She spent two miserable days and nights waiting, as the immigrants wee questioned by officials, examined for trachoma and tuberculosis, and tested for hookworm by a woman who collected their stools on tin pie plates. Hana was relieved she could produce her own, not having to borrow a little from someone else, as some of the women had to do. It was a bewildering, degrading beginning, and Hana was sick with anxiety, wondering if she would ever be released.

On the third day, a Japanese messenger from San Francisco appeared with a letter for her from Taro. He had written it the day of her arrival, but it had not reached her for two days.

Taro welcomed her to America, and told her that the bearer of the letter would inform Taro when she was to be released so he could be at the pier to meet her.

The letter eased her anxiety for a while, but as as soon as she was released and boarded the launch for San Francisco, new fears rose up to smother her with a feeling almost of dread.

The early morning mist had become a light chilling rain, and on the pier black umbrellas bobbed here and there, making the task of recognition even harder. Hanna searched desperately for a face that resembled the photo she had studied so long and hard. Suppose he didn't come. What would she do then?

Hana took a deep breath, lifted her head and walked slowly from the launch. The moment she was on the pier, a man in a black coat, wearing a derby and carrying an umbrella, came quickly to her side. He was of slight build, not much taller than she, and his face was sallow and pale. He bowed stiffly and murmured, "You have had a long trip, Miss Omiya. I hope you are well."

Hana caught her breath. "You are Takeda San?" she asked.

He removed his hat and Hana was further startled to see that he was already turning bald.

"You are Takeda San?" she asked again. He looked older than thirty-one.

"I am afraid I no longer resemble the early photo my parents gave you. I am sorry."

Hana had not meant to begin like this. It was not going well.

"No, no," she said quickly. "It is just that I . . . that is, I am terribly nervous . . ." Hana stopped abruptly, too flustered to go on.

"I understand," Taro said gently. "You will feel better when you meet my friends and have some tea. Mr. and Mrs. Toda are expecting you in Oakland. You will be staying with them until . . ." He couldn't bring himself to mention the marriage just yet and Hana was grateful he hadn't.

He quickly made arrangements to have her baggage sent to Oakland then led her carefully along the rain-slick pier toward the streetcar that would take them to the ferry.

Hana shuddered at the sight of another boat, and as they climbed to its upper deck she felt a queasy tightening of her stomach.

"I hope it will not rock too much," she said anxiously. "Is it many hours to your city?"

Taro laughed for the first time since their meeting, revealing the gold fillings of his teeth. "Oakland is just across the bay," he explained. "We will be there in twenty minutes."

Raising a hand to cover her mouth, Hana laughed with him and suddenly felt better. I am in America now, she thought, and this is the man I came to marry. Then she sat down carefully beside Taro, so no part of their clothing touched.

★ ★ ★ ★ ★

Talking It Through

1. This story begins with a flashback, a cinematic technique which establishes a setting and a time frame in the present and then allows us to go back in

time to see what has brought the characters to their current circumstances. The device is used here to tell us what Hana Omiya's life was like in Japan and how she came to be traveling across the Pacific to become the wife of a man she has never met.

Tell why and how the circumstances of Hana's life in Japan have motivated her decision. Are her reasons for embarking on this adventure prompted more by family pressures or by cultural ones? What in Hana's own character brings her to make this momentous decision?

What aspects of life in Japan does Hana remember fondly while she is enroute to Oakland? What similarities and differences do you see in her circumstances and those of the grandmother in Mitsuye Yamada's poem?

2. What insights does the author provide about attitudes toward men and women in Japan? Find specific examples to illustrate these. Do you think Hana expects something different in America?

3. The suspense in the story builds. Finally Hana arrives at Angel Island for immigration processing, certainly a humbling and depersonalizing experience as described here. Compare this account with earlier ones about encounters with immigration officials. Is there a difference in tone or point of view? Discuss.

At last, Hana boards the launch for San Francisco, What now smothers her with "a feeling almost of dread"? Do you consider her fears justified? Explain.

4. When Hana Omiya first meets Taro Takeda, how does she react? How different is the reality from her dream? In what ways has the author foreshadowed the tone of this meeting?

Does this marriage seem to offer more than that of the grandmother who was a picture bride in"I Learned to Sew"? Do these women have anything in common?

5. When Taro laughs for the first time, Hana's mood changes. What accounts for this? On what note does the story end?

6. Why do you think Yoshiko Uchida ends with Hana sitting beside her future husband "so no part of their clothing touched"?

Writer's Workshop

1. What would you choose to tell about yourself to a prospective but unknown marriage partner? How frank or accurate would you be about your circumstances, character, or appearance? What would you omit? Write a letter to a "picture" bride or groom. Imagine that a go-between has con-

tacted you. Alternately, write an advertisement for yourself. Such ads still appear for marriage partners in many parts of the world. Then write the reply you receive from an imagined respondent.

2. Write an essay to compare Hana Omiya and the grandmother in "I Learned to Sew." What are their respective reasons for leaving Japan? What impels each woman to risk such an uncertain future? What constitutes the dream for each? What is the reality? How do they adjust? How do dream and reality overlap in each case?

★ # *Choosing a Dream* ★

MARIO PUZO

Mario Puzo is best known as the author of The Godfather. *Here he describes growing up in the Italian ghetto of ''Hell's Kitchen'' in New York City. Childhood provided him with time to dream, and America provided the opportunity to pursue the dream he chose.*

As a child and in my adolescence, living in the heart of New York's Neopolitan ghetto, I never heard an Italian singing. None of the grown-ups I knew were charming or loving or understanding. Rather they seemed coarse, vulgar, and insulting. And so later in my life when I was exposed to all the clichés of lovable Italians, singing Italians, happy-go-lucky Italians, I wonder where the hell the moviemakers and storywriters got all their ideas from.

At a very early age I decided to escape these uncongenial[1] folk by becoming an artist, a writer. It seemed then an impossible dream. My father and

---

[1]*uncongenial:* unsympathetic, disagreeable.

mother were illiterate, as were their parents before them. But practising my art I tried to view the adults with a more charitable eye and so came to the conclusion that their only fault lay in their being foreigners; I was an American. This didn't really help because I was only half right. I was the foreigner. They were already more "American" that I could ever become.

But it did seem then that the Italian immigrants, all the fathers and mothers that I knew, were a grim lot; always shouting, always angry, quicker to quarrel than embrace. I did not understand that their lives were a long labor to earn their daily bread and that physical fatigue does not sweeten human natures.

And so even as a very small child I dreaded growing up to be like the adults around me. I heard them saying too many cruel things about their dearest friends, saw too many of their false embraces with those they had just maligned,[2] observed with horror their paranoiac[3] anger at some small slight or a fancied injury to their pride. They were, always, too unforgiving. In short, they did not have the careless magnanimity[4] of children.

In my youth I was contemptuous of my elders, including a few under thirty. I thought my contempt special to their circumstances. Later when I wrote about these illiterate men and women, when I thought I understood them, I felt a condescending pity. After all, they had suffered, they had labored all the days of their lives. They had never tasted luxury, knew little more economic security than those ancient Roman slaves who might have been their ancestors. And alas, I thought, with new-found artistic insight, they were cut off from their children because of the strange American tongue, alien to them, native to their sons and daughters.

Already an artist but not yet a husband or father, I pondered omnisciently on their tragedy, again thinking it special circumstance rather than a constant in the human condition. I did not yet understand why these men and women were willing to settle for less than they deserved in life and think that "less" quite a bargain. I did not understand that they simply could not afford to dream, I myself had a hundred dreams from which to choose. For I was already sure that I would make my escape, that I was one of the chosen. I would be rich, famous, happy. I would master my destiny.

And so it was perhaps natural that as a child, with my father gone, my mother the family chief, I, like all the children in all the ghettos of America, became locked in a bitter struggle with the adults responsible for me. It was inevitable that my mother and I became enemies.

[2]*maligned:* spoken ill of.
[3]*paranoiac:* overly suspicious.
[4]*magnanimity:* generosity in overlooking insult or injury.

As a child I had the usual dreams. I wanted to be handsome, specifically as cowboy stars in movies were handsome. I wanted to be a killer hero in a world-wide war. Or if no wars came along (our teachers told us another was impossible), I wanted at the very least to be a footloose adventurer. Then I branched out and thought of being a great artist, and then, getting ever more sophisticated, a great criminal.

My mother, however, wanted me to be a railroad clerk. And that was her *highest* ambition; she would have settled for less. At the age of sixteen when I let everybody know that I was going to be a great writer, my friends and family took the news quite calmly, my mother included. She did not become angry. She quite simply assumed that I had gone off my nut. She was illiterate and her peasant life in Italy made her believe that only a son of the nobility could possibly be a writer. Artistic beauty after all could spring only from the seedbed of fine clothes, fine food, luxurious living. So then how was it possible for a son of hers to be an artist? She was not too convinced she was wrong even after my first two books were published many years later. It was only after the commercial success of my third novel that she gave me the title of poet.

My family and I grew up together on Tenth Avenue, between Thirtieth and Thirty-first streets, part of the area called Hell's Kitchen. This particular neighborhood could have been a movie set for one of the Dead End Kid flicks or for the social drama of the East Side in which John Garfield played the hero. Our tenements were the western wall of the city. Beneath our windows were the vast black iron gardens of the New York Central Railroad, absolutely blooming with stinking boxcars freshly unloaded of cattle and pigs for the city slaughterhouse. Steers sometimes escaped and loped through the heart of the neighborhood followed by astonished young boys who had never seen a live cow.

The railroad yards stretched down to the Hudson River, beyond whose garbagey waters rose the rocky Palisades of New Jersey. There were railroad tracks running downtown on Tenth Avenue itself to another freight station called St. Johns Park. Because of this, because these trains cut off one side of the street from the other, there was a wooden bridge over Tenth Avenue, a romantic looking bridge despite the fact that no sparkling water, no silver flying fish darted beneath it; only heavy dray carts drawn by tired horses, some flat-boarded trucks, tin lizzie automobiles and, of course, long strings of freight cars drawn by black, ugly engines.

What was really great, truly magical, was sitting on the bridge, feet dangling down, and letting the engine under you blow up clouds of steam that made you disappear, then reappear all damp and smelling of fresh ironing. When I was seven years old I fell in love for the first time with the tough little girl who held my hand and disappeared with me in that magical cloud of steam. This experience was probably more traumatic and damaging to my later relationships with women than one of those ugly childhood adventures Freudian novelists use to explain why their hero has gone bad.

My father supported his wife and seven children by working as a track man laborer for the New York Central Railroad. My oldest brother worked for the railroad as a brakeman, another brother was a railroad shipping clerk in the freight office. Eventually I spent some of the worst months of my life as the railroad's worst messenger boy.

My oldest sister was just as unhappy as a dressmaker in the garment industry. She wanted to be a school teacher. At one time or another my other two brothers also worked for the railroad—it got all six males in the family. The two girls and my mother escaped, though my mother felt it her duty to send all our bosses a gallon of homemade wine on Christmas. But everybody hated their jobs except my oldest brother who had a night shift and spent most of his working hours sleeping in freight cars. My father finally got fired because the foreman told him to get a bucket of water for the crew and not to take all day. My father took the bucket and disappeared forever.

Nearly all the Italian men living on Tenth Avenue supported their large families by working on the railroad. Their children also earned pocket money by stealing ice from the refrigerator cars in summer and coal from the open stoking cars in the winter. Sometimes an older lad would break the seal of a freight car and take a look inside. But this usually brought down the "Bulls," the special railroad police. And usually the freight was "heavy" stuff, too much work to cart away and sell, something like fresh produce or boxes of cheap candy that nobody would buy.

The older boys, the ones just approaching voting age, made their easy money by hijacking silk trucks that loaded up at the garment factory on Thirty-first Street. They would then sell the expensive dresses door to door, at bargain prices no discount house could match. From this some graduated into organized crime, whose talent scouts alertly tapped young boys versed in strongarm. Yet despite all this, most of the kids grew up honest, content with fifty bucks a week as truck drivers, deliverymen, and white-collar clerks in the civil service.

I had every desire to go wrong but I never had a chance. The Italian family structure was too formidable.

I never came home to an empty house; there was always the smell of supper cooking. My mother was always there to greet me, sometimes with a policeman's club in her hand (nobody ever knew how she acquired it). But she was always there, or her authorized deputy, my older sister, who preferred throwing empty milk bottles at the heads of her little brothers when they got bad marks on their report cards. During the great Depression of the 1930s, though we were the poorest of the poor, I never remember not dining well. Many years later as a guest of a millionaire's club, I realized that our poor family on home relief ate better than some of the richest people in America.

My mother would never dream of using anything but the finest imported olive oil, the best Italian cheeses. My father had access to the fruits coming off ships, the produce from railroad cars, all before it went through the stale process of middlemen; and my mother, like most Italian women, was a fine cook in the peasant style. . . .

My direct ancestors for a thousand years have most probably been illiterate. Italy, the golden land, so loving to vacationing Englishmen, so majestic in its language and cultural treasures (they call it, I think, the cradle of civilization), has never cared for its poor people. My father and mother were both illiterates. Both grew up on rocky, hilly farms in the countryside adjoining Naples. My mother remembers never being able to taste the ham from the pig they slaughtered every year. It brought too high a price in the marketplace and cash was needed. My mother was also told the family could not afford the traditional family gift of linens when she married and it was this that decided her to emigrate to America to marry her first husband, a man she barely knew. When he died in a tragic work accident on the docks, she married my father, who assumed responsibility for a widow and her four children perhaps out of ignorance, perhaps out of compassion, perhaps out of love. Nobody ever knew. He was a mystery, a Southern Italian with blue eyes who departed from the family scene three children later when I was twelve. But he cursed Italy even more than my mother did. Then again, he wasn't too pleased with America either. My mother never heard of Michelangelo; the great deeds of the Caesars had not yet reached her ears. She never heard the great music of her native land. She could not sign her name.

And so it was hard for my mother to believe that her son could become an artist. After all, her one dream in coming to America had been to earn her daily bread, a wild dream in itself. And looking back she was dead right. Her son an artist? To this day she shakes her head. I shake mine with her.

$$\bigstar \bigstar \bigstar \bigstar \bigstar$$

Talking It Through

1. Puzo starts off his autobiographical essay with a strong paragraph designed to capture our interest. How does he gain our attention and make us want to read further about his life?

2. Why does Puzo say that adults "could not afford to dream"? As a child, what were some of the dreams he had for the future? Which dream did he choose? Why do you think he chose it?

3. What did his mother want him to be and why? What made her think it was impossible for a child of hers to become an artist?

4. The railroad cut through the heart of the section of New York City where Puzo grew up. Around it, Italian immigrants organized their lives. Explain the adult view of the railroads—the reality of work and ugliness. Who in this family worked on the railroads? What were they transporting to the city? Then explain Puzo's view of this as a child. How did it bring romance and excitement to his world? Focus especially on some of the images he uses to describe it. How is Puzo, the child, already an artist in his perceptions?

5. Puzo organizes his reminiscences around several key stereotypes, which he then attempts to break down. Among these are the typical image of the "lovable Italian," the "suffering immigrant," Italy as a "golden land," his mother's view of "the artist." Discuss each stereotype. How does it threaten real understanding, especially between mother and son. How does Puzo break through the stereotype? What do you think Puzo is searching for, as a writer?

6. Do you think that becoming an artist is a typical American dream, or an unusual one? Do you think America values its artists as much as its business people? If you were an artist, would you rather live in America than elsewhere, and if so, why? How have artists contributed to the "American dream," in your opinion?

Writer's Workshop

1. As a writer, Puzo realizes that he must look beyond stereotypes of people to find the more complex reality. At first he writes that he was "contemptuous of my elders" and viewed his mother as an enemy. But with greater compassion, he came to understand and appreciate her and her values. In a story or autobiographical essay, write about a person who is at first viewed as a stereotype, but who becomes a person with whom we can empathize as we learn more about his or her life.

2. Puzo writes that, "I myself had a hundred dreams from which to choose." In a poem or essay, tell us about your childhood dreams of the future. In your writing, try to draw on some of the imagery discussed in "American Dream/American Reality." (Dreamers also have nightmares.) Do you envi-

sion a ladder of success? Are there doors to open? Is there a "golden visitor"? Let your imagination and memory roam for a while, before you try to write.

★ *Prelude* ★

A L B E R T   H A L P E R

Halper's story is about a Jewish family living in Chicago in 1938, as Hitler comes to power in Europe. As the Silversteins struggle to earn a living selling newspapers, they realize that even in America they are not safe from the terrifying effects of prejudice.

I WAS COMING HOME FROM SCHOOL, CARRYING MY BOOKS BY A STRAP, WHEN I passed Gavin's poolroom and saw the big guys hanging around. They were standing in front near the windows, looking across the street. Gavin's has a kind of thick window curtain up to eye level, so all I saw was their heads. The guys were looking at Mrs. Oliver, who lately has started to get talked about. Standing in her window across the street, Mrs. Oliver was doing her nails. Her nice red hair was hanging loose down her back. She certainly is a nice-looking woman. She comes to my father's newspaper stand on the corner and buys five or six movie magazines a week, also the afternoon papers. Once she felt me under the chin, and laughed. My father laughed, too, stamping about in his old worn leather jacket to keep warm. My old man stamps a lot because he has leg pains and he's always complaining about a heavy cold in his head.

When I passed the poolroom one or two guys came out. "Hey, Ike, how's your good-looking sister?" they called, but I didn't turn around. The guys are eighteen or nineteen and haven't ever had a job in their life. "What they need is work," my father is always saying when they bother him too much. "They're not bad; they get that way because there's nothing to do," and he tries to explain the meanness of their ways. But I can't see it like my father. I hate those fellas and I hope every one of them dies under a truck. Every time I come home from school past Lake Street they jab me, and every time my sister Syl comes along they say things. So when one of them, Fred Gooley, calls, "Hey, Ike, how's your sister?" I don't answer. Besides, Ike isn't my name anyway. It's Harry.

I passed along the sidewalk, keeping close to the curb. Someone threw half an apple but it went over my head. When I went a little farther someone threw a stone. It hit me in the back of the leg and stung me but it didn't hurt much. I kept a little toward the middle of the sidewalk because I saw a woman coming the other way and I knew they wouldn't throw.

When I reached the corner under the Elevated[1] two big news trucks were standing with their motors going, giving my father the latest editions. The drivers threw the papers onto the sidewalk with a nice easy roll so the papers wouldn't get hurt. The papers are bound with the heavy yellow cord which my father saves and sells to the junkyard when he fills up a bag. "All right, Silverstein," a driver called out. "We'll give you a five-star at six," and both trucks drove off.

The drivers are nice fellas and when they take back the old papers they like to kid my old man. They say, "Hey, you old banker, when are you gonna retire?" or, "Let's roll him, boys, he's got bags of gold in his socks." Of course they know my old man isn't wealthy and that the bags in the inside of the newsstand hold only copper pennies. But they like to kid him and they know he likes it. Sometimes the guys from Gavin's pitch in, but the truck drivers would flatten them if they ever got rough with my old man.

I came up to the newsstand and put my school books inside. "Well, Pa," I said, "you can go to Florida now." So my Pa went to "Florida," that is, a chair near the radiator that Nick Pappas lets him use in his restaurant. He has to use Nick's place because our own flat is too far away, almost a quarter-mile off.

While my father was in Nick's place another truck came to a stop. They dropped off a big load of early sport editions and yelled, "Hey, there, Harry, how's the old man?" I checked off the papers, yelling back, "He's okay, he's in Nick's." Then the truck drove away and the two helpers waved.

I stood around, putting the papers on the stand and making a few sales. The first ten minutes after coming home from school and taking care of the newsstand always excites me. Maybe it's the traffic. The trucks and cars pound along like anything and of course there's the Elevated right up above you which thunders to beat the band. We have our newsstand right up against a big El post and the stand is a kind of cabin which you enter from

[1]*Elevated:* the elevated trains which ran on tracks above street level.

the side. But we hardly use it, only in the late morning and around two P.M., when business isn't very rushing. Customers like to see you stand outside over the papers ready for business and not hidden inside where they can't get a look at you at all. Besides, you have to poke your head out and stretch your arm to get the pennies, and kids can swipe magazines from the sides, if you don't watch. So we most always stand outside the newsstand, my father, and me, and my sister. Anyhow, I like it. I like everything about selling papers for my father. The fresh air gets me and I like to talk to customers and see the rush when people are let out from work. And the way the news trucks bring all the new editions so we can see the latest headlines, like a bank got held up on the South Side on Sixty-third Street, or the Cubs are winning their tenth straight and have a good chance to cop the pennant, is exciting.

The only thing I don't like is those guys from Gavin's. But since my father went to the police station to complain they don't come around so often. My father went to the station a month ago and said the gang was bothering him, and Mr. Fenway, he's the desk sergeant there, said, "Don't worry any more about it, Mr. Silverstein, we'll take care of it. You're a respectable citizen and taxpayer and you're entitled to protection. We'll take care of it." And the next day they sent over a patrolman who stood around almost two hours. The gang from Gavin's saw him and started to go away, but the cop hollered, "Now listen, don't bother this old fella. If you bother him any I'll have to run some of you in."

And then one of the guys recognized that the cop was Butch, Fred Gooley's cousin. "Listen who's talkin'," he yells back. "Hey, Fred, they got your cousin Butch takin' care of the Yid."[2] They said a lot of other things until the cop got mad and started after them. They ran faster than lightning, separating into alleys. The cop came back empty-handed and said to my father, "It'll blow over, Mr. Silverstein; they won't give you any more trouble." Then he went up the street, turning into Steuben's bar.

Well, all this happened three or four weeks ago and so far the gang has let us alone. They stopped pulling my sixteen-year-old sister by her sweater and when they pass the stand going home to supper all they give us is dirty looks. During the last three or four days, however, they passed by and kinda muttered, calling my father a communist banker and me and my sister reds. My father says they really don't mean it, it's the hard times and bad feelings, and they got to put the blame on somebody, so they put the blame on us. It's certain speeches on the radio and the pieces in some of the papers, my father told us. "Something is happening to some of the people and we got to watch our step," he says.

[2] *Yid:* a derogatory slang expression for Jew.

I am standing there hearing the traffic and thinking it over when my little fat old man comes out from Nick's looking like he liked the warm air in Nick's place. My old man's cheeks looked rosy, but his cheeks are that way from high blood pressure and not from good health. "Well, colonel," he says smiling, "I am back on the job." So we stand around, the two of us, taking care of the trade. I hand out change snappy and say thank you after each sale. My old man starts to stamp around in a little while and, though he says nothing, I know he's got pains in his legs again. I look at the weather forecast in all the papers and some of them say flurries of snow and the rest of them say just snow. "Well, Pa," I tell my old man, "maybe I can go skating tomorrow if it gets cold again."

Then I see my sister coming from high school carrying her briefcase and heading this way. Why the heck doesn't she cross over so she won't have to pass the poolroom, I say to myself; why don't she walk on the other side of the street? But that's not like Sylvia; she's a girl with a hot temper, and when she thinks she is right you can't tell her a thing. I knew she wouldn't cross the street and then cross back, because according to her, why, that's giving in. That's telling those hoodlums that you're afraid of their guts. So she doesn't cross over but walks straight on. When she comes by the pool hall two guys come out and say something to her. She just holds herself tight and goes right on past them both. When she finally comes up she gives me a poke in the side. "Hello, you mickey mouse, what mark did you get in your algebra exam?" I told her I got A, but the truth is I got a C.

"I'll check up on you later," she says to me. "Pa, if he's lying to us we'll fine him ten years!"

My father started to smile and said, "No, Harry is a good boy, two years is enough."

So we stand around kidding and pretty soon, because the wind is coming so sharp up the street, my old man has to "go to Florida" for a while once more. He went into Nick's for some "sunshine," he said, but me and Syl could tell he had the pains again. Anyway, when he was gone we didn't say anything for a while. Then Hartman's furniture factory, which lately has been checking out early, let out and we were busy making sales to the men. They came up the sidewalk, a couple of hundred, all anxious to get home, so we had to work snappy. But Syl is a fast worker, faster than me, and we took care of the rush all right. Then we stood waiting for the next rush from the Hillman's cocoa factory up the block to start.

We were standing around when something hit me in the head, a half of a rotten apple. It hurt a little. I turned quick, but didn't see anybody, but Syl started yelling. She was pointing to a big El post across the street behind which a guy was hiding.

"Come on, show your face," my sister was saying. "Come on, you hero, show your yellow face!'' But the guy sneaked away, keeping the post between. Syl turned to me and her face was boiling. ''The rats! It's not enough with all the trouble in Europe; they have to start it here.''

Just then our old man came out of Nick's and when he saw Syl's face he asked what was the matter.

''Nothing,'' she says. ''Nothing, I'm just thinking.''

But my old man saw the half of a rotten apple on the sidewalk, and at first he didn't say anything but I could see he was worried. ''We just have to stand it,'' he said, like he was speaking to himself, ''we just have to stand it. If we give up the newstand where else can we go?''

''Why do we have to stand it?'' I exploded, almost yelling. ''Why do we—''

But Mrs. Oliver just then came up to the stand, so I had to wait on her. Besides, she's a good customer and there's more profit on two or three magazines than from a dozen papers.

''I'll have a copy of *Film Fan*, a copy of *Breezy Stories* and a copy of *Movie Stars on Parade*,'' she says. I go and reach for the copies.

''Harry is a nice boy,'' Mrs. Oliver told my father, patting my arm. ''I'm very fond of him.''

''Yes, he's not bad,'' my father answered smiling. ''Only he has a hot temper once in a while.''

But who wouldn't have one, that's what I wanted to say! Who wouldn't? Here we stand around minding our own business and the guys won't let us alone. I tell you sometimes it almost drives me crazy. We don't hurt anybody and we're trying to make a living, but they're always picking on us and won't let us alone. It's been going on for a couple of years now, and though my old man says it'll pass with the hard times, I know he's worried because he doesn't believe what he says. He reads the papers as soon as he gets them from the delivery trucks and lately the news about Europe is all headlines and I can see that it makes him sick. My old man has a soft heart and every time he sees in the papers that something bad in Europe has happened again he seems to grow older and he stands near the papers kind of small and all alone. I tell you, sometimes it almost drives me crazy. My old man should be down in Florida, where he can get healthy, not in Nick Pappas' ''Florida,'' but down in real Florida where you have to go by train. That's where he should be. Then maybe his legs would be all right and he wouldn't have that funny color in his cheeks. Since our mother died last year it seems the doctor's treatments don't make him any better, and he has to skip a treatment once in a while because he says it costs too much. But when he stands there with a customer chuckling you think he's healthy and hasn't got any worries and you feel maybe he has a couple thousand in the bank.

And another thing, what did he mean when he said something two days ago when the fellas from Gavin's passed by and threw a stone at the stand? What did he mean, that's what I want to know. Gooley had a paper rolled up with some headlines about Europe on it and he wiggled it at us and my father looked scared. When they were gone my father said something to me, which I had been thinking and thinking about. My Pa said we got to watch our step extra careful now because there's no other place besides this country where we can go. We've always been picked on, he said, but we're up against the last wall now, he told me, and we got to be calm because if they start going after us here there's no other place where we can go. I been thinking and thinking about that, especially the part about the wall. When he said that, his voice sounded funny and I felt like our newsstand was a kind of island and if that went we'd be under the waves.

"Harry, what are you thinking of?" Mrs. Oliver asked me. "Don't I get any change?" She was laughing.

And then I came down from the clouds and found she had given me two quarters. I gave her a nickel change. She laughed again. "When he looks moody and kind of sore like that, Mr. Silverstein, I think he's cute."

My old man crinkled up his eyes and smiled. "Who can say, Mrs. Oliver. He should only grow up to be a nice young man and a good citizen and a credit to his country. That's all I want."

"I'm sure Harry will." Mrs. Oliver answered, then talked to Syl a while and admired Syl's new sweater and was about to go away. But another half of a rotten apple came over and splashed against the stand. Some of it splashed against my old man's coat sleeve. Mrs. Oliver turned around and got mad.

"Now you boys leave Mr. Silverstein alone! You've been pestering him long enough! He's a good American citizen who doesn't hurt anybody! You leave him alone!"

"Yah!" yelled Gooley, who ducked behind an El post with two other guys. "Yah! Sez you!"

"You leave him alone!" hollered Mrs. Oliver.

"Aw, go peddle your papers," Gooley answered. "Go run up a rope."

"Don't pay any attention to them," Syl told Mrs. Oliver. "They think they're heroes, but to most people they're just yellow rats."

I could tell by my old man's eyes that he was nervous and wanted to smooth things over, but Syl didn't give him a chance. When she gets started and knows she's in the right not even the Governor of the State could make her keep quiet.

"Don't pay any attention to them," she said in a cutting voice while my old man looked anxious. "When men hide behind Elevated posts and throw rotten apples at women you know they're not men but just things that wear pants. In Europe they put brown shirts[3] on them and call them saviors of civilization. Here they haven't got the shirts yet and hang around poolrooms.''

Every word cut like a knife and the guys ducked away. If I or my father would have said it we would have been nailed with some rotten fruit, but the way Syl has of getting back at those guys makes them feel like yellow dogs. I guess that's why they respect her even though they hate her, and I guess that's why Gooley and one or two of his friends are always trying to get next to her and date her up.

Mrs. Oliver took Syl's side and was about to say something more when Hillman's cocoa factory up the block let out and the men started coming up the street. The 4:45 rush was on and we didn't have time for anything, so Mrs. Oliver left, saying she'd be back when the blue-streak edition of the *News* would arrive. Me and Syl were busy handing out the papers and making change and our Pa helped us while the men took their papers and hurried for the El. It started to get darker and colder and the traffic grew heavier along the street.

Then the *Times* truck, which was a little late, roared up and dropped a load we were waiting for. I cut the strings and stacked the papers and when my father came over and read the first page he suddenly looked scared. In his eyes there was that hunted look I had noticed a couple of days ago. I started to look at the first page of the paper while my old man didn't say a word. Nick came to the window and lit his new neon light and waved to us. Then the light started flashing on and off, flashing on the new headlines. It was all about Austria[4] and how people were fleeing toward the borders and trying to get out of the country before it was too late. My old man grew sick and looked kind of funny and just stood there. Sylvia, who is active in the high-school social science club, began to read the *Times* out loud and started analyzing the news to us; but our Pa didn't need her analysis and kept standing there kind of small with that hunted look on his face. He looked sick all right. It almost drove me crazy.

"For Pete's sake," I yelled at Syl. "Shut up, shut up!''

Then she saw our Pa's face, looked at me, and didn't say anything more.

In a little while it was after five and Syl had to go home and make supper. "I'll be back in an hour," she told me. "Than Pa can go home and rest a bit and me and you can take care of the stand." I said all right.

After she was gone it seemed kind of lonesome. I couldn't stop thinking about what my father had said about this being our last wall. It got me

---

[3]*brown shirts:* Hitler's storm troopers; Nazis.

[4]*Austria:* On the eve of World War II, German troops marched triumphantly into Austria and annexed it.

feeling funny and I didn't want to read the papers any more. I stood there feeling queer, like me and my old man were standing on a little island and the waves were coming up. There was still a lot of traffic and a few people came up for papers, but from my old man's face I could tell he felt the same as me.

But pretty soon some more editions began coming and we had to check and stack them up. More men came out from factories on Walnut Street and we were busy making sales. It got colder than ever and my old man began to stamp again. "Go into Nick's, Pa," I told him. "I can handle it out here." But he wouldn't do it because just then another factory let out and we were swamped for a while. "Hi, there Silverstein," some of the men called to him, "what's the latest news, you king of the press?" They took the papers, kidding him, and hurried up the stairs to the Elevated, reading all about Austria and going home to eat. My father kept staring at the headlines and couldn't take his eyes off the print where it said that soldiers were pouring across the border and mobs were robbing people they hated and spitting on them and making them go down on their hands and knees to scrub the streets. My old man's eyes grew small, like he had the toothache and he shook his head like he was sick. "Pa, go into Nick's," I told him. He just stood there, sick over what he read.

Then the guys from Gavin's poolroom began passing the stand on their way home to supper after a day of just killing time. At first they looked as if they wouldn't bother us. One or two of them said something mean to us, but my old man and me didn't answer. If you don't answer hoodlums, my father once told me, sometimes they let you alone.

But then it started. The guys who passed by came back and one of them said: "Let's have a little fun with the Yids." That's how it began. A couple of them took some magazines from the rack and said they wanted to buy a copy and started reading.

In a flash I realized it was all planned out. My father looked kind of worried but stood quiet. There were about eight or nine of them, all big boys around eighteen and nineteen, and for the first time I got scared. It was just after six o'clock and they had picked a time when the newspaper trucks had delivered the five-star and when all the factories had let out their help and there weren't many people about. Finally one of them smiled at Gooley and said, "Well, this physical culture magazine is mighty instructive, but don't you think we ought to have some of the exercises demonstrated?" Gooley said, "Sure, why not?"

So the first fella pointed to some pictures in the magazine and wanted me to squat on the sidewalk and do the first exercise. I wouldn't do it. My father put his hand on the fella's arm and said, "Please, please." But the guy pushed my father's hand away.

"We're interested in your son, not you. Go on, squat."

"I won't," I told him.

"Go on," he said. "Do the first exercise so that the boys can learn how to keep fit."

"I won't," I said.

"Go on," he said, "do it."

"I won't."

Then he came over to me smiling, but his face looked nasty. "Do it. Do it if you know what's good for you."

"Please, boys," said my Pa. "Please go home and eat and don't make trouble. I don't want to have to call a policeman—"

But before I knew it someone got behind me and tripped me so that I fell on one knee. Then another of them pushed me, trying to make me squat. I shoved someone and then someone hit me, and then I heard someone trying to make them stop. While they held me down on the sidewalk I wiggled and looked up. Mrs. Oliver, who had come for the blue-flash edition, was bawling them out.

"You let him alone! You tramps, you hoodlums, you let him alone!" She came over and tried to help me, but they pushed her away. Then Mrs. Oliver began to yell as two guys twisted my arm and told me to squat.

By this time a few people were passing and Mrs. Oliver called at them to interfere. But the gang were big fellows and there were eight or nine of them, and the people were afraid.

Then while they had me down on the sidewalk Syl came running up the street. When she saw what was happening she began kicking them and yelling and trying to make them let me up. But they didn't pay any attention to her, merely pushing her away.

"Please," my Pa kept saying. "Please let him up; he didn't hurt you. I don't want to have to call the police—"

Then Syl turned to the people who were watching and yelled at them. "Why don't you help us? What are you standing there for?" But none of them moved. Then Syl began to scream:

"Listen, why don't you help us? Why don't you make them stop picking on us? We're human beings the same as you!"

But the people just stood there afraid to do a thing. Then while a few guys held me, Gooley and about four others went for the stand, turning it over and mussing and stamping on all the newspapers they could find. Syl started to scratch them, so they hit her, then I broke away to help her, and then they started socking me too. My father tried to reach me, but three guys kept him away. Four guys got me down and started kicking me and all the time my father was begging them to let me up and Syl was screaming at the people to help. And while I was down, my face was squeezed against some papers on the sidewalk telling about Austria and I guess I went nuts while they kept hitting me, and I kept seeing the headlines against my nose.

Then someone yelled, "Jiggers, the cops!" and they got off of me right away. Nick had looked out the window and had called the station, and the guys let me up and beat it away fast.

But when the cops came it was too late; the stand was a wreck. The newspapers and magazines were all over the sidewalk and the rack that holds the *Argosy* and *Western Aces* was all twisted up. My Pa, who looked sicker than ever, stood there crying and pretty soon I began to bawl. People were standing looking at us like we were some kind of fish, and I just couldn't help it, I started to bawl.

Then the cops came through the crowd and began asking questions right and left. In the end they wanted to take us to the station to enter a complaint, but Syl wouldn't go. She looked at the crowd watching and she said, "What's the use? All those people standing around and none of them would help!" They were standing all the way to the second El post, and when the cops asked for witnesses none of them except Mrs. Oliver offered to give their names. Then Syl looked at Pa and me and saw our faces and turned to the crowd and began to scream.

"In another few years, you wait! Some of you are working people and they'll be marching through the streets and going after you too! They pick on us Jews because we're weak and haven't any country; but after they get us down they'll go after you! And it'll be your fault; you're all cowards, you're afraid to fight back!"

"Listen," one of the cops told my sister, "are you coming to the station or not? We can't hang around here all evening."

Then Syl broke down and began to bawl as hard as me. "Oh, leave us alone," she told them and began wailing her heart out. "Leave us alone. What good would it do?"

By this time the crowd was bigger, so the cops started telling people to break it up and move on. Nick came out and took my father by the arm into the lunchroom for a drink of hot tea. The people went away slowly and then, as the crowd began to dwindle, it started to snow. When she saw that, Syl started bawling harder than ever and turned her face to me. But I was down on my hands and knees with Mrs. Oliver, trying to save some of the magazines. There was no use going after the newspapers, which were smeared up, torn, and dirty from the gang's feet. But I though I could save a few, so I picked a couple of them up.

"Oh, leave them be," Syl wept at me. "Leave them be, leave them be!"

Talking It Through

1. A good short-story writer must condense a great deal of material into very little space. There is little time to develop characters, setting, and plot; every sentence counts. Look over Halper's first paragraph carefully. What information does he give us which will later have significance in the story?

2. The setting of this story is central to the lives of the main characters, and to the action. If the story were made into a play, what would the stage look like? Make your own sketch of the set, paying careful attention to details. Be sure to include the newsstand, the Elevated, Gavin's, "Florida," Mrs. Oliver's, the various factories mentioned, and whatever else you feel would be essential. How would you show the time of the year, time of day? Why are they significant in setting the tone of the story?

3. Make a list of the characters in the story, and discuss them. What do we know about the Silverstein family? Who are their friends in the neighborhood? What do we know about the gang, and their motives for tormenting the Silversteins?

4. When the gang starts to attack, Harry says, "In a flash I realized it was all planned out." What does he mean by that? How has the gang been emboldened by the latest news from Europe?

5. Each member of the Silverstein family reacts to the gang differently. What is the father's strategy, and why? How does Harry behave? What is Sylvia's tactic and do you think it works? Do you agree with her when she says to the crowd, " . . . it'll be your fault; you're all cowards, you're afraid to fight back"?

6. America has often been seen as a refuge from persecution and prejudice. "There's no other place besides this country where we can go," says Mr. Silverstein. Harry says, ". . . I felt like our newsstand was a kind of island . . ." How does the newsstand function as a symbol in this story? How do events at the newsstand parallel what is happening in Europe? Why do you think the author has given this story the title, "Prelude"?

Writer's Workshop

1. Transform "Prelude" into a one-act play. You have already designed your "set." Now make your cast of characters. In a play, everything must be told through dialogue. Halper uses a good deal of dialogue, but a great deal is told through narration, including flashback. For example, we learn

through flashback that Mrs. Silverstein died a year ago and that Mr. Silverstein went to the police a month earlier. What else do we know through narration that you will have to put into dialogue? For example, how will the audience know what is happening in the news as the story unfolds? As you plan your play, think carefully about how the characters interact with one another, and how you will portray these relationships on stage. How will you build suspense, leading to the climax?

2. Halper in his story makes great use of foreshadowing. He drops clues and hints about what is to come, heightening suspense and our sense of anticipation. For example, the news from Europe foreshadows action in the story. In this particular story, foreshadowing is not only a technique, but a theme. A "prelude" is itself an introduction to what comes next. Thus the present foreshadows what Halper perceives will be the future.

In an essay, discuss Halper's use of foreshadowing in this story. Give examples of how he uses it to enhance both suspense and his meaning.

3. Many authors in "American Dream/American Reality" have discussed the importance of the family in the lives of immigrants. The Silversteins try to support one another through hard times. In an essay, compare and contrast the Silversteins to another family you have read about. You may wish to compare them to the Golds in "Bananas," to the Carnegies, to the Puzos, or to the picture bride's family in "I learned to Sew." What is the relationship between children and parents? How do family members support or fail to support one another as they strive to attain their dreams?

★ *I Have a Dream* ★

M A R T I N   L U T H E R   K I N G ,   J R.

King delivered this speech at the height of the Civil Rights Movement, in 1963. More than two hundred thousand people came from all over America to attend the rally in Washington, D. C., which was televised to the entire nation.

King forcefully reminds us that he is speaking in front of a symbolic place—the Lincoln Memorial—at a historic moment, one hundred years after Lincoln signed the Emancipation Proclamation.

Although African-Americans did not bring the dream with them, they have extended the meaning of the dream for all of us.

I AM HAPPY TO JOIN WITH YOU TODAY IN WHAT WILL GO DOWN IN HISTORY as the greatest demonstration for freedom in the history of our nation.

Fivescore[1] years ago, a great American, in whose symbolic shadow we stand today, signed the Emancipation Proclamation.[2] This momentous decree came as a great beacon light of hope to millions of negro slaves who had been seared in the flames of withering injustice. It came as a joyous daybreak to end the long night of their captivity.

But one hundred years later, the Negro still is not free; one hundred years later, the life of the Negro is still sadly crippled by the manacles[3] of segregation and the chains of discrimination; one hundred years later, the Negro lives on a lonely island of poverty in the midst of a vast ocean of material prosperity; one hundred years later, the Negro is still languished in the corners of American society and finds himself in exile in his own land.

So we've come here today to dramatize a shameful condition. In a sense we've come to our nation's capital to cash a check. When the architects of our republic wrote the magnificent words of the Constitution and the Declaration of Independence, they were signing a promissory note[4] to which every American was to fall heir. This note was the promise that all men, yes, black men as well as white men, would be guaranteed the unalienable rights of life, liberty, and the pursuit of happiness.

It is obvious today that America has defaulted on this promissory note in so far as her citizens of color are concerned. Instead of honoring this sacred obligation, America has given the Negro people a bad check; a check which has come back marked "insufficient funds." We refuse to believe that there are insufficient funds in the great vaults of opportunity of this nation. And so we've come to cash this check, a check that will give us upon demand the riches of freedom and the security of justice.

We have also come to this hallowed[5] spot to remind America of the fierce urgency of now. This is no time to engage in the luxury of cooling off or to take the tranquilizing drug of gradualism. Now is the time to make real the promises of democracy; now is the time to rise from the dark and desolate valley of segregation to the sunlit path of racial justice; now is the time to lift our nation from the quicksands of racial injustice to the solid

---

[1]*fivescore:* one hundred. Lincoln began his Gettysburg Address with "Four score and seven years ago our fathers . . ."

[2]*Emancipation Proclamation:* the document signed by Lincoln in 1863 freeing the slaves in the Confederacy.

[3]*manacles:* handcuffs.

[4]*promissory note:* a written promise to pay a certain sum of money.

[5]*hallowed:* holy. Lincoln used the term "this hallowed ground" in his Gettysburg Address.

rock of brotherhood; now is the time to make justice a reality for all God's children. It would be fatal for the nation to overlook the urgency of the moment. This sweltering summer of the Negro's legitimate discontent will not pass until there is an invigorating autumn of freedom and equality.

Nineteen sixty-three is not an end, but a beginning. And those who hope that the Negro needed to blow off steam and will now be content, will have a rude awakening if the nation returns to business as usual.

There will be neither rest nor tranquility in America until the Negro is granted his citizenship rights. The whirlwinds of revolt will continue to shake the foundations of our nation until the bright day of justice emerges.

But there is something that I must say to my people who stand on the warm threshold which leads into the palace of justice. In the process of gaining our rightful place we must not be guilty of wrongful deeds.

Let us not seek to satisfy our thirst for freedom by drinking from the cup of bitterness and hatred. We must forever conduct our struggle on the high plane of dignity and discipline. We must not allow our creative protest to degenerate into physical violence. Again and again we must rise to the majestic heights of meeting physical force with soul force.

The marvelous new militancy which has engulfed the Negro community must not lead us to a distrust of all white people, for many of our white brothers, as evidenced by their presence here today, have come to realize that their destiny is tied up with our destiny and they have come to realize that their freedom is inextricably bound to our freedom. This offense we share mounted to storm the battlements of injustice must be carried forth by a biracial army. We cannot walk alone.

And as we walk, we must take the pledge that we shall always march ahead. We cannot turn back. There are those who are asking the devotees of civil rights, "When will you be satisfied?" We can never be satisfied as long as the Negro is the victim of the unspeakable horrors of police brutality.

We can never be satisfied as long as our bodies, heavy with fatigue of travel, cannot gain lodging in the motels of the highways and the hotels of the cities. We cannot be satisfied as long as the Negro's basic mobility is from a smaller ghetto to a larger one.

We can never be satisfied as long as our children are stripped of their selfhood and robbed of their dignity by signs stating "for whites only." We cannot be satisfied as long as a Negro in Mississippi cannot vote and a Negro in New York believes he has nothing for which to vote. No, we are not satisfied, and we will not be satisfied until justice rolls down like waters and righteousness like a mighty stream.

I am not unmindful that some of you have come here out of excessive trials and tribulation. Some of you have come fresh from narrow jail cells. Some of you have come from areas where your quest for freedom left you battered by the storms of persecution and staggered by the winds of police brutality. You have been the veterans of creative suffering. Continue to work with the faith that unearned suffering is redemptive.

Go back to Mississippi; go back to Alabama; go back to South Carolina; go back to Georgia; go back to Louisiana; go back to the slums and ghettos of the northern cities, knowing that somehow this situation can, and will be changed. Let us not wallow in the valley of despair.

So I say to you, my friends, that even though we must face the difficulties of today and tomorrow, I still have a dream. It is a dream deeply rooted in the American dream that one day this nation will rise up and live out the true meaning of its creed—we hold these truths to be self-evident, that all men are created equal.

I have a dream that one day on the red hills of Georgia, sons of former slaves and sons of former slave-owners will be able to sit down together at the table of brotherhood.

I have a dream that one day, even the state of Mississippi, a state sweltering with the heat of injustice, sweltering with the heat of oppression, will be transformed into an oasis of freedom and justice.

I have a dream my four little children will one day live in a nation where they will not be judged by the color of their skin but by content of their character. I have a dream today!

I have a dream that one day, down in Alabama, with its vicious racists, with its governor having his lips dripping with the words of interposition and nullification,[6] that one day, right there in Alabama, little black boys and black girls will be able to join hands with little white boys and white girls as sisters and brothers. I have a dream today!

I have a dream that one day every valley shall be exalted, every hill and mountain shall be made low, the rough places shall be made plain, and the crooked places shall be made straight and the glory of the Lord will be revealed and all flesh shall see it together.

This is our hope. This is the faith that I go back to the South with.

With this faith we will be able to hear out of the mountain of despair a stone of hope. With this faith we will be able to transform the jangling discords of our nation into a beautiful symphony of brotherhood.

With this faith we will be able to work together, to pray together, to struggle together, to go to jail together, to stand up for freedom together, knowing that we will be free one day. This will be the day when all of God's children will be able to sing with new meaning—"my country 'tis of thee; sweet land of liberty; of thee I sing; land where my fathers died, land of

---

[6]*interposition and nullification:* doctrines that put state's rights above Federal law.

the pilgrim's pride; from every mountain side, let freedom ring"—and if America is to be a great nation, this must become true.

So let freedom ring from the prodigious hilltops of New Hampshire.

Let freedom ring from the mighty mountains of New York.

Let freedom ring from the heightening Alleghenies of Pennsylvania.

Let freedom ring from the snow-capped Rockies of Colorado.

Let freedom ring from the curvaceous slopes of California.

But not only that.

Let freedom ring from Stone Mountain of Georgia.

Let freedom ring from Lookout Mountain of Tennessee.

Let freedom ring from every hill and molehill of Mississippi, from every mountainside, let freedom ring.

And when we allow freedom to ring, when we let it ring from every village and hamlet, from every state and city, we will be able to speed up that day when all of God's children—black men and white men, Jews and Gentiles, Catholics and Protestants—will be able to join hands and to sing in the words of the old Negro spiritual, "Free at last, free at last; thank God Almighty, we are free at last."

★ ★ ★ ★ ★

Talking It Through

1. In his opening three paragraphs, King explains "why we have come here today." What are the reasons? How does he use light as a metaphor for freedom in his early paragraphs, and throughout his speech? Why does he refer to "manacles" and "chains"?

2. You have noted how in "People of the Beginnings" Chiefs Seattle and Speckled Snake used repetition in their speeches. Why do you think King repeats "one hundred years ago" in his opening paragraphs? What other key phrases repeat in his speech, and to what effect?

3. In his fourth paragraph King develops an extended metaphor of the "promissory note." Why has he chosen this metaphor, and how does he develop it? What do you think he means by the "riches of freedom"?

4. In his opening paragraphs, King addresses the entire nation. But beginning with, "But there is something that I must say to my people . . ." he addresses African Americans. What are his messages to them? What metaphors does he use to express them?

5. King warns, "Let us not wallow in the valley of despair." In many images throughout the speech, King associates height with hope and freedom. How does he do this, especially at the climactic end? What is his final vision?

Writer's Workshop

1. Both Chief Seattle and Martin Luther King, Jr., writing about America over a hundred years apart, had impassioned visions of its future. Compare and contrast these two speeches, focusing on the speakers' oratory, rhetoric, and message. How do both writers emphasize the brotherhood of man?

2. Using the format of the repeated phrase, "I have a dream," write your own dream for America today.

3. Choose one pair of images that King uses in his speech, such as light and darkness, depths and heights, and write an essay about it. Show how his use of these opposing images enhances his meaning. If possible, compare his use of these images to passages of the Bible, or the works of another author.

THE WORLD LEFT BEHIND

★ ★ ★ ★ ★
★ ★ ★ ★ ★
★ ★ ★ ★ ★
★ ★ ★ ★ ★
★ ★ ★ ★ ★
★ ★ ★ ★ ★

HAVING ARRIVED IN A NEW LAND, MASTERED A NEW language, and struggled to attain a dream in a new world, the immigrant is yet reminded of the past. The process of recollection, the reasons for remembering, and the expression of those memories are as various as are the writers, the countries from which they came, and their reasons for coming.

We begin "The World Left Behind" with an African-American folktale, "The Ibo Landing Story." Forcibly deprived of their homeland, and forbidden by law to learn to read or write, slaves turned toward an oral tradition to preserve their heritage. In this story, memory brings feelings of empowerment.

For some political exiles and refugees, like Joseph Brodsky and the Rocas in Zaldívar's story, the pain of memory lies in the relatives left behind, sometimes forever. Both Eva Hoffman and Xin Zhang left their native lands reluctantly as children. Their recollections preserve the child's idyllic world view, as both country and childhood are left behind simultaneously. Whether recalled with pleasure or pain, the memories of a different self in a different world remain.

The Ibo
★ Landing Story ★

FRANKIE AND DOUG QUIMBY
as told to
MARIAN E. BARNES

The Sea Islands off the Georgia and Carolina coasts were famous during the time of slavery for the quality of their cotton. More recently there have been other reasons for the islands' renown. Such islands as St. Simon's, St. Helena, and Cumberland have preserved by their isolation much authentic African American culture. Descendants of West African people such as the Gullahs (a corruption of Angola) have handed down stories, words from original tribal languages, and beliefs and traditions that echo their original roots. Increasingly folklorists and musicologists have visited these places seeking links to the African homelands.

There are many variants of the brief but stirring resistance story retold here of the Ibo landing, as well as of its accompanying song.

DURING THE TIME OF SLAVERY THEY WOULD LOAD AND UNLOAD SLAVES AT Dunbar Creek, on the north end of St. Simon's Island on the east coast of Georgia. On one particular trip a ship went to Africa to get more people to bring them here to America to sell them for slaves.

While the slave traders were in Africa, they went by the Ibo tribe, and they found eighteen grown people. They fooled them. They told them, "We want you to go to America to work."

When these people got to St. Simon's Island, they found out that they had been tricked and they were going to be sold as slaves. Then all eighteen of these people agreed together. They all said, "No! Rather than be a slave here in America, we would rather be dead."

They linked themselves together with chains and they said a prayer. They said, "Water brought us here, and water is going to carry us away." Then they backed themselves out into Dunbar Creek and drowned themselves.

As they were going down, they were singing a song in their African language. We continue to sing that same song today using English words.

Today, Dunbar Creek on St. Simon's Island is a historical spot visited by throngs of people who have heard the story. Some visitors who have gone to Dunbar Creek on nights when the moon shines a certain way say they have heard the muffled sounds of voices talking, people wailing, and chains clinking.

"The Ibo Landing Song"

> Oh freedom, oh freedom, oh freedom over me
> And before I'd be a slave I'll be buried in my grave
> And go home to my Lord and be free.
>
> No more crying, no more crying, no more crying will there be
> And before I'd be a slave I'll be buried in my grave   5
> And go home to my Lord and be free.
> No more groaning, no more dying will there be
> And before I'd be a slave I'll be buried in my grave
> And go home to my Lord and be free.
> Oh freedom, oh freedom, oh freedom over me   10
> And before I'd be a slave I'll be buried in my grave
> And go home to my Lord and be free.

Talking It Through

1. Locate on a map of the southern United States the coastal islands off Georgia such as St. Simon's. A folklorist, poet, and photographer, Carrie Mae Weems, has recently documented the heritage of these unwilling "Ebo" immigrants in both poetry and photographs. An excellent documentary on Gullah life was presented by PBS, and a film, "Daughters of the Dust" has won wide acclaim.

   This simple and powerful story serves to dramatize the meaning of resistance. What is your opinion of the Ibos' choice of death over slavery? The captives say, "Water brought us here and water is going to carry us away." What other ways did enslaved people have to resist their captors? Compare the treatment here of the Ibos' decision with that described by Gustavus Vassa in his account of the voyage from Africa. They may be the "Igbo" spoken of by Vassa.

   With your classmates prepare a debate on the pros and cons of the Ibos' choice. Try to find arguments both for and against the value of their drastic act. The Ibos' story has survived over many generations of slaves and former slaves in America. How does their act serve to inspire?

2. You may already know some version of the "Ibo Landing Song" which begins, "Oh, freedom." Discuss the kind of freedom the lyrics imply. What other kinds of freedom are available to people who are subjected to oppression?

    Notice the cumulative nature of the lyrics: "No more crying . . . No more groaning . . . No more dying . . ." Death is seen here as a release from bondage. Compare this piece with the passage on Mr. Shimerda's suicide in *My Ántonia.*

3. There is an element of the supernatural in the story recounted here. What is it? What do you think accounts for it? How does it enhance the narrative? How does it relate to the song that follows?

Writer's Workshop

1. Retell the Ibo Landing story by embellishing it and adding imaginative details. Give some of the eighteen captives individual characters and identities. How might they have arrived at their unanimous decision? Use dialogue. Try to give your reader insight into the thoughts and feelings of the slaves. Will you have your ship arrive in America by day or by night? What sights or sounds would be heard? For background, read some accounts of the Middle Passage, and find out what you can about the Sea Islands: their geography, history, and present status.

    The Ibo are a cultural group which currently survives in Nigeria and parts of modern Ghana. Find out what you can about them. They have recently been a refugee people within Western Africa. Look for articles in *The Reader's Guide to Periodical Literature.*

2. Write an essay comparing the ideas expressed in "The Ibo Landing Song" with those in Emma Lazarus's poem about the Statue of Liberty. How do their ideas about freedom differ?

3. Imagine you are a storyteller. Use the continuous present tense to tell the story of how on a moonlit night you hear the sounds and see the Ibo captives perform their act of defiance.

Nothing in Our Hands But Age

★ ★

R A Q U E L   P U I G   Z A L D Í V A R

*In this short story Raquel Puig Zaldívar writes compassionately of an elderly
Cuban couple whose hopes of starting over in America include their dream of being
joined here by their daughter. Like her narrator here, Ms. Zaldívar teaches as well
as writes.*

"AND SINCE I HAVE REALIZED THAT MANY PEOPLE GO THROUGH LIFE WITHOUT
thinking, my most important goal in this course will be to teach you to
think, and, hopefully, help you make a habit of it." I paused to catch my
breath and the door behind me clacked to announce the arrival of a new
student. The first day of classes it is very difficult to gather all of them at
the same time. They cruise in and out of several wrong rooms before they
finally reach the proper destination. I was quiet without looking back. As
usually, I expected the student to sit down before continuing my lecture.
The door did not clack back right away and I had to turn around.

A heavy set, dark-haired woman was holding the door open, waiting for
someone else to come in. She had an over-sized flowery plastic bag hanging
from her arm and a fairly large brown paper bundle firmly grasped with
her hand. At this point the whole class was interested in who or what was
finally going to enter. The door, with a personality of its own, struggled with
the woman's arm, but she was victorious. A frail-looking man, dragging his
feet, entered and glanced at us triumphantly a little out of breath. The
woman let go of the door and approached me energetically. The man I
suspected to be her husband trailed along with much effort, unable to keep
up. "Alicia Pérez de Roca"; she pronounced every syllable carefully and
pointed to herself as she opened her enormous eyes even wider. "Antonio
Roca," she said pointing to her husband who had not quite reached us.

The group was starting to get restless. Some were speaking to their friends
and others were just staring at the newcomers and laughing. I glared at
them and for once it worked. They straightened up and looked respectful
once more. Then I turned my attention to the couple:

"Mrs. Roca," I began.

"Pérez de Roca," she interrupted; "Alicia Pérez de Roca, Antonio Roca," she added pointing to her husband.

"All right, Mrs. Pérez de Roca, please sit down and I will speak to you again after class." I tried my best to be calm.

It took them five more minutes to settle down. I was able to add a few comments about the grading system and the books that were required for the course, but it was time to leave before I realized it.

"If you have any questions please come to my office. If not, I'll see you Thursday. Have a nice day."

One by one the students gathered their belongings and emptied the room, all of them except the Roca couple, who were standing up and slowly making it to the front. I was waiting for them and felt an unexpected gush of tenderness. Alicia was not very tall, somewhat wide around the hips and the bustline. She was probably past sixty but had a very white, clear complexion on which the years had not cared to leave too many traces. Antonio could have been approximately ten years her senior. He was obviously weak but did not lack enthusiasm. His small eyes glowed with excitement; they were younger than the rest of him and very ill-matched with the multiple folds surrounding his eyes and lips and the wart that sat ungraciously on his nose.

Their attire was spotless, old but well-preserved. It had been ironed and starched with careful, experienced hands. She wore a long black skirt with a pleat in the back. Her white blouse was completely embroidered in the front with what had been colorful threads, the type of work that was imported years ago from the Canary Islands. He wore a firmly starched *guayabera* with long sleeves, four pockets and tiny pleats, the kind Cubans used to wear on grand occasions. There was no doubt in my mind that they were my countrymen.

"You see, professor," she automatically emphasized her *r*'s, "wee come from Cuba and my hoosband was a pharmacist and I was a doctor of pheelosophee and we come to the Junited States of America to find freedom and the social worker tell us we can come to the school for the, the, revalidation of our title. . . ." she looked uncertain.

"Degree," I corrected; "you want to study to revalidate your degrees to continue in your professions." Smiling she nodded profusely; Antonio followed doubtful. "Do you wish to speak Spanish? I'm Cuban, too. I can understand."

"Oh no," she shook her head back and held the heavy plastic bag with both her hands in front of her stomach. "Wee want to comprehend English better, wee have to revalidate in English. This is pheelosophee, correct?"

"Yes."

"My hoosband and me have mooch experience of many years with pheelosophee, we love it very mooch and we want to do good in yourr class."

"Do you know the titles of the books?" I asked.

"Mmmmmm, wee were not able to grasp those names. The vision I don't have it very well and you speek too fast. Wee may come to yourr offiz, yes?"

"Of course, come right up and I'll give you all the details."

I smiled and left the room ahead of them. Where did these people get their energy? They apparently were honest about the whole thing and were seriously considering a new beginning at a point when most individuals are realizing they have to face the end. I wondered how they would pass my course, but decided not to worry about it so soon.

My office was locked. I opened the door, turned on the lights and barely had time to sit down when they appeared at the threshold and asked permission to come in.

"Of course, come right in and sit down," I said as cheerfully as I knew how. They accepted my invitation and looked at me with all their attention.

"Mrs. Roca."

"Pérez de Roca. You know, professor, in Cuba the married ladies keep the father's name. That for me is Pérez."

"Mrs. Pérez de Roca and Mr. Roca, this is a course divided in two parts; philosophy and drama."

"Excellent, excellent," said Antonio and smiled.

"It is not an easy course," I stressed; "you will have to read a lot."

"No problem, we have a good bilingual dictionary," she said.

"There will be weekly quizzes." Mrs. Pérez de Roca wrote everything I said in her new notebook. They could not be dissuaded.

"Alicia, ¿no se te parece a la niña?" The old man's expression became very soft and he looked at me insistently. I understood him perfectly, but:

"My hoosband says you are alike that our daughter." I smiled at him; he was obviously pleased.

"Is your daughter here?" I asked not knowing what else to say.

"In Cuba, in Cuba." Antonio understood for the first time.

"Wee come to the school for her. She come here very soon and then she is goin to need our help."

"When did you see her last?"

"Oh, fifteen years ago, but now she is goin to come very, very soon."

Weeks later Alicia barely passed the first test and Antonio failed miserably but neither of them became discouraged. It was close to impossible for them to understand the lectures. The terminology was difficult and I know I went too fast for them. I realized, however, that they enjoyed the small group sessions the most. Once a week the students were supposed to meet with me in groups of no more than twelve to discuss the assignments. It was here where Alicia gave all her comments and Antonio listened attentively. Most of the students didn't mind them, but others expressed their disgust very openly, and disagreed with them constantly.

"I don't think men need goals," said Matt discussing a passage from *Siddhartha.* "Why can't we just live and take things as they come, and not worry? We spend too much time planning for the future and forget our present."

"I disagree," answered Alicia. Her husband nodded faithfully in the back. "When I was a young woman I wanted to care for my family the best way and wanted to teech history. I had a goal and that made me continue in life and do thins and brin out a family and be happy."

"But what for? We all can do something but without living only for that," insisted the younger man. "In our society we waste our lives in futile things."

"Futile?" asked Alicia. A student who sat next to her translated the word into Spanish.

"Well, maybe goals should be there, we must have one, but we shouldn't devote all our lives to them. Don't you think, Mrs. Morales?" asked another student.

"I don't want to influence your opinions. I know what I believe in, but I want you to do your own thinking."

"Futile not!" refuted Mrs. Pérez de Roca with conviction. "No goals and when you arrive to be as old as me, you see yourr life behind you and you don't have . . . Mmmmm . . . How is it that you say? Anythin to show."

"Is that so?" said Matt sarcastically; "then what do you have to show? If your goals had worked you wouldn't be here. Your circumstances have put you here, goals or no goals. Goals, what they do is chain you, don't let you be free."

"Goals do not chain, they direct," Alicia turned very solemn.

"Well," I interrupted; "we're beginning to talk in circles and besides our time is up. Read the next ten pages for Monday and have a nice day."

The students left immediately. Alicia and Antonio stayed behind as usual. They took a little longer standing up and picking up their belongings. I felt a bit attached to these two souls. They came from the country to which I belong, but of which I have no memory. Sometimes they came to my office and talked to me about the street vendors, the *guajiros* or peasants and the tall palm trees, always in "carrreful" English. More than one time their tales made me smile.

"Do not worry about the commentaries this children make. Wee are not offended. Wee know wee are too old but wee talk because wee have somethin to . . . Mmmmmm!!. . . . How do you say? Compart?"

"Share," I corrected.

"Correct, "share." Wee share, they share too. This new method of teachin is very new and it function well. When I was a teacher I only taught from the outside. You teech from the inside also."

While the woman talked, Antonio looked at me with affection. Often, as I left, I heard him discuss with his wife how much I resembled their daughter.

"Where do you live, Alicia?" I asked one morning.

"In the block of apartments in Seventh and Thirteen. Nice place but no good to stay there all the day. Very sad, many old people with no family. Wee are not sad," she explained. "Wee have our daughter. She is far away but she is close here." She indicated her heart and nodded resolutely opening her eyes and smiling.

"Did she arrive yet?"

"No, not yet, but she is comin soon. Wee don't see her since fifteen years ago. She cannot write often. It's a little problem. But when she come, we're going to help an awful mooch."

"An awful lot, Alicia."

"Da's correct," she stopped as if looking for the right words. "You know, wee already bought for her all for the house. All new thins. Wee save and wee buy little by little. Pillows and mantels . . ."

"Tablecloths."

"Correct! and dishes and towels. Everysin, her father and me buy it for her. When she comes."

"Is she married?" I asked.

"No, she had all prepared. You know," she smacked her lips in a sorrowful gesture; "but she was prisioned, you know, to the . . . Mmmmm . . . How do you say it?"

"Jail?"

"Dat is it, to the jail. She is forty years old now. It happened fifteen years ago on March. But she is getting out on dis year. Then she is comin to us. She is our family, you know? Nobody else," she shook her head.

They weren't as disturbed by their jailed daughter as I was. The idea was already part of them and nothing mattered but the fact that she would be free again next March. Fifteen years! My body went cold with the thought.

Humanities 202 continued as usual. The Rocas were never absent. They knew they were slow settling down and they made it a point to arrive early. When I got to class they were usually excited, with new questions and comments to make. The course was more than halfway through when we began discussing *Macbeth*.

"Well, class, how could you describe the character of Macbeth?"

"Imaginative," said Justo.

"Courageous," answered another student.

"Ambitious," exclaimed Alicia.

"What was it that he most desired?"

"Power," explained Justo.

"Why do you suppose he wanted power?" Sometimes it was very hard to make the students talk.

"He wanted to control others and make them do what he wanted," said the young man.

"He was willing to go to any extreme to achieve this," added another one.

"He assessinated the king and his friend B . . . B . . . Bbb . . ."

"Banquo," I said, helping Alicia. She nodded. "Does he represent men of his time or mankind as a whole?"

"Menkind," Alicia was quick to reply. "Dere are," she rolled her *r*'s mercilessly, "men in our world today dat are equal to Macbeth. For example, you know in Cuba know, wee have a man in the power dat kills many people to be powerfool and dominate the whole nation." I knew the subject matter was getting touchy but it was my policy to accept any comments students made and I had to listen and pray the situation wouldn't get out of hand.

"It's not at all the same," answered Jenny; "Macbeth did it to satisfy his own desire. In Cuba it's being done for a purpose, to help the poor." I wished I could have stopped them but I couldn't. That would have been going against my own rules. I remained quiet.

"No, Jenny, you are mistaken," said another one. "Killing and destruction are wrong. We mustn't consider the purpose for which those things are committed."

"You know, people, what I consider is valuable?" Justo was wondering out loud. "My freedom to express any disagreement, man." Several classmates assented.

"Well, that's necessary," Jenny was quick to reply; "but that's allowed in Cuba today, any fool knows that."

"I am not in accordance." This time Alicia stood up as she always did when she was going to say something she considered important. "Nobody can express his opinions in my country today."

"Oh, there she goes again!" I heard someone whisper in boredom. Alicia paid no heed. She wasn't excited; her voice was soft, her words paused. Only a competent observer could have noticed she trembled a little. Antonio usually sat motionless behind her. He knew enough English to realize that things were getting rough for his wife.

"You know, Miss, I know a young woman who was only a little bit older dat you and very pretty also,'' she smiled and nodded; ''and she has espent many years in a prision for the only mistake dat she did not want to teech the wrong way to little childrens.''

''Ah!'' Jenny exclaimed with exaggerated disgust. ''We have learned enough in this class to know that words like 'wrong' are relative.'' Alicia simply ignored her.

''She went to the country, you know, with the farmers, to teech dem the grammar and the aritmetic and the oder sings importants. She did not desire to teech Communist doctrine.'' The class became very quiet. ''She said dis to her chief and asked to leave the country and she was incarcelated, in prision, you know? For fifteen years.''

''Well, that's all a nice tale, a story,'' answered Jenny stubbornly; ''but they are always things that people make up. Rumors. How do you know they are true?'' The whole class, including me, was paying close attention to the discussion. We followed with our heads the words that, like arrows, went from one end of the room to the other.

''Dat is not correct. Dis is not a rumor. It is a true story.'' Alicia's words were paused.

''That's what they always say,'' rebutted Jenny.

''I know dis is true,'' the old woman's tone was forgiving, not defiant. ''You see, I am espeakin about my daughter.''

Everyone was still. Any movement would have wounded the woman's solemn declaration. Moments later other students began trying to enter the room for their next class and we had to leave. Nobody, however, even bothered to speak.

Cuba was never again discussed in that class. We finished with Shakespeare, with Ibsen, with Bernard Shaw, but Cuba was never again touched. Justo, Jenny and the others were sensitive enough to imagine the burden the old couple bore. They stopped raising their eyebrows and sighing hard enough to be noticed every time Alicia spoke. A certain respect grew out of that experience and even though the discussions continued and the disagreements were frequent, the atmosphere of the class was less tight, more pleasant.

Mrs. Pérez de Roca passed the course with few problems. Her test grades were very humble, but throughout the discussions she showed me that she read the material. Her husband Antonio didn't make it. I wondered what tests, group discussions and classes like mine were supposed to mean when a man like Antonio Roca, a college graduate, a man who had supported his family with dignity so many years, did not manage to pass it. I blamed his age but quickly dismissed from my mind the ''F'' I entered in the gradebook.

When the last class was over, they came to my office one morning.

"Mrs. Morales, wee want to show our appreciacion for yourr pacience and help." She sounded as if she had memorized the lines the night before. "Yesterday I ovened some pastries."

"Baked," I said.

"Correct; baked some *guayaba* pastries for you and your family. Wee learned very mooch in yourr class. Our grades are not so good but wee learned English, and wee learned what young people sink today and many, many sings, Mrs. Morales. Wee are grateful." Antonio assented and handed me the homemade pastries wrapped in wax paper.

"We want to ask one last question."

"By all means, Alicia, and please don't say the last, I hope you come back and visit me very often." Both of them smiled.

"Our friend told us dat somesin very useful for a teacher is a en-cy-clo-pe-dia. It is somesin good to have in the home and check a correct date or find out somesin important. Is that correct?"

"Of course! An encyclopedia is something very useful to own, even if you are not a teacher. The information is right there all the time."

"Exactly like ourr friend says. You know, wee want to buy one for ourr daughter which is comin very soon. You know, it is already April so she must be gettin everysin ready now. Wee sent her all the money and everysin wiz an agency and she is going to need a en-cy-clo-pe-dia. Correct? When she wants to be a teacher again."

"It is a very good idea." I looked at both of them and thought there was something beautiful in their hopeful, wrinkled stares.

We shook hands and they left. Alicia, as usual, walking ahead with her determined attitude, her very clean embroidered old blouse, and Antonio trailing not too close behind with his spotless *guayabera* and shiny laced shoes.

At the beginning of the fall term it was Jenny who telephoned me one morning and said Antonio had died.

"I heard it over the radio, the Spanish radio station announces such things," she said.

"I know. When did you hear it?"

"Oh, it was last week but I couldn't call you then. You weren't in school and I didn't know your home number. Know what?"

"What is it, Jenny?"

"I'd sure like to go and visit Alicia. Do you know where she lives?"

"She said once that she lived in those government projects on Seventh and Thirteenth. Yes, it must be there."

"Wanna come and look for her?"

"Sure!" I was happy to see the young girl taking an interest.

"Pick you up at lunch time tomorrow?"

"At twelve thirty," I answered.

Alicia opened the door the following afternoon looking the same as always. Her big eyes, less energetic perhaps, were grateful yet silent. She stepped aside; wiping her hands in her apron, she asked us in. It was a very small efficiency apartment with the kitchen and the bedroom separated from the main living area by tall wooden superimposed walls. The tiny coffee table was monopolized by a picture of a young woman—"their daughter," I thought—with lively dark eyes looking far away. In one of the corners of the picture, Alicia secured to the frame an instant shot of Antonio sitting in a rocking chair, wearing a *guayabera*.

There was a map of Cuba hanging from a wall and on top of the sewing machine a statue of Our Lady of Charity, Cuba's patron saint, with lit candles in front of it. By far the most spectacular piece in the room was a very simple bookcase with the complete set of the *Encyclopaedia Britannica*.

"Sit down, pliz. Sank you vey mooch for comin, Jenny," she looked at her. "Mrs. Morales," she said facing me, "it is very sad for me, therefore do not say you are sorry. It is all right, Antonio was an old man."

"You are not alone, Alicia. You are an energetic woman. You have a lot to give and you can still help other people," Jenny said.

"You are not alone. Your daughter will be coming soon and she will need you to help her begin. Life is very important you know." Everything I said was unfit and I was concerned.

"Correct. Wee know all about estarting all over. You know when Antonio married me I was a telephone operator and he was a estudent. Wee lived in a esmall room. Oh yes, esmaller dan dis. I helped him become a pharmacist and when he was finished I began estudyin at the University to become a professor. Of history," she didn't look at us, she stared at her lap. "It was a very hard task. He worked and saved penny after penny. I finished when ourr daughter was born. Wee had an apartment at that time. It was in La Vibora. Do you know La Vibora? Nice place. Wee were happy. When my daughter went to eschool, I too worked teachin history of Cuba. Many years pass and den wee had enough money to buy a pharmacy. Antonio was a good man. He was happy with the new pharmacy."

I was wondering why she didn't cry. She stared at her black skirt but not a drop fell.

"Wee were honest people, dat is why wee could not understand dat the government came and dey took the pharmacy, and two houses wee had bought for, you know, how is it dat you say? gainin money I sink. It was so eslow, when wee woke up one day it was the law dat wee couldn't have nosing. Only ourr careers, ourr titles, degree like you say, Mrs. Morales. Wee were there because ourr daughter, you know, she like the system and she was happy dat the rich was sharing with the poor and . . . Well she was ourr daughter and wee love her very mooch and wee want to be wiz her. Den she left for the country and she saw what she did not like and complained and when the chiefs did not hear her complaints she was a counter-revolutionary. She was put in prision, for fifteen years, in a prision with oders bad womans and little food and all dirty. . . . One friend tol us to come to the Junited States and save all the money we can get to send ourr daughter the passage—she meant the ticket—when she was out of the prision. Ourr daughter said yes, one day when wee saw her. Wee were old, the government did not want us, we lef. Here wee estart, like when wee were young, nosing in our hand, but wee had the age, very important and very bad. You know, Mrs. Morales. I tol you when I was yourr estudent.''

"You are really praiseworthy, Alicia, both you and your husband. You still have such energy, desire to become a better person." I wanted to sound convincing because I meant what I said. "Forget the past, forget . . ." I knew I was telling her to forget her whole life and I felt ridiculous. ". . . what you lost. Think ahead, think of how you will help your daughter, you are the only thing she has here. Don't lose your spirit, your vitality."

"You see, it is difficult to be the same. One month ago, a woman prisoner dat was inside with my daughter. She has liberty now, she wrote and she tells us that ourr daughter is no longer alive." Alicia looked at us, put her hand on the encyclopedia and tightened her lips.

★ ★ ★ ★ ★

Talking It Through

1. The narrator in the philosophy class attended by Mr. and Mrs. Roca empathizes with her Cuban countrymen. It is soon established that their young teacher bears a resemblance to the daughter left behind fifteen years earlier, a coincidence which further helps to bridge the age and language barriers.

    Notice how Raquel Puig Zaldívar wins our sympathy as well for this older, displaced couple. How are they described? What do they look like? How are they dressed? How much harder is it for them to become "Americanized" than other students in the class? Compare them with Richard Rodriguez's parents (p.68). What is especially different about their circumstances? Are the Rocas emigrés or exiles?

2. Mrs. Pérez de Roca comments on "this new method of teachin." She adds, "When I was a teacher I only taught from the outside. You teech from the inside also." What, in your opinion, is the difference between the two methods? How does the teacher in the story accomplish this?

3. We learn that the absent daughter has been in a Cuban jail for the past

fifteen years, but that the Rocas still anticipate her release and emigration to the U.S. In a discussion of Shakespeare's *Macbeth*, Alicia, who is far more forthcoming in English than her husband, compares the Scottish thane to Fidel Castro, saying that both men seek power and attempt to dominate others. Other students object to the comparison, on the grounds that their motivations to power are different.

Do you think the purpose or motive for a repressive or violent act can justify it, as the student Jenny does? Or do you agree with the unnamed student who challenges her? Why or why not? What dramatic purpose in the story is served by their differences?

4. Finally, Alicia tells the other students the story behind her daughter's imprisonment. It silences the class, and Cuba is never again discussed by the group. After this episode, their younger classmates no longer ridicule the Rocas. Mrs. Roca subsequently earns a passing grade for the class, but her husband does not. How does the story of their daughter function within the story of the Rocas' participation in the philosophy class? Is the author's choice of the literature discussed important? Explain.

How does the author depict Mr. Roca? What emotions are we meant to feel for him? How does he compare with Richard Rodriquez's father (p.68) and with Michael Gold's father in "Bananas" (p.132)?

5. In gratitude the Rocas bring their teacher some Cuban pastries and ask her advice about purchasing an encyclopedia for their daughter's use in America. What does the encyclopedia symbolize?

6. The story ends with Jenny and the narrator, whom we learn is "Mrs. Morales," paying a condolence call on Alicia Pérez de Roca. They have heard on a Spanish-language radio station that her husband has died. In the last lines of the piece we learn that the Rocas' daughter has also died. She will never leave prison and join her mother in the U.S. The encyclopedia will never be used. Discuss the irony in this story. Also discuss whether or not the author has foreshadowed the ending earlier in the piece. Look back, as well, for the ways in which Ms. Puig Zaldívar conveys the quality of immigrant speech throughout this piece, expressing the awkwardness with humor at times, but always without ridicule. Find examples to read aloud. Explain how this gentle humor helps to relieve the starkness of this story. What emotions are played upon by the author? How would you define the theme?

Writer's Workshop

1. Write a monologue as if you were Antonio Roca. Tell your story as fully as possible from the time of your marriage until you fail the philosophy course

you have taken with your wife in the U.S. Look back at the story and outline your autobiography as given in the text before you begin. Establish rough dates so that the time frame in your piece is accurate and not anachronistic. You might also want to know when the Cuban revolution took place, and what the early days of the Castro regime were like. Note that Antonio Roca would be a little over seventy years old when the story begins.

2. Much of this story is told through conversation. As with all written dialogue, the author is selective. We hear only what she wishes to report. Write a conversation between the Rocas as they review one of their classes at home. Have them speak in English. What will Mrs. Pérez de Roca have to explain to her husband? What will he be most interested in talking about? If you need to, for the purposes of your piece, review either *Macbeth*, or look up an account of Hermann Hesse's novel, *Siddhartha*.

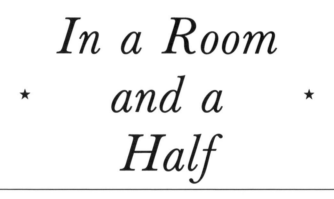

In a Room ★ *and a* ★ *Half*

J O S E P H   B R O D S K Y

Joseph Brodsky, who won the Nobel Prize for Literature in 1987, was exiled from the Soviet Union in 1972. He currently lives and works in the United States, where he has also served as this country's poet laureate. He has written in both Russian and English and frequently translates his own poetry from his native language. In this excerpt from his book of autobiographic essays, Less Than One, *he remembers life at home with his parents.*

THE ROOM AND A HALF (IF SUCH A SPACE UNIT MAKES ANY SENSE IN ENGLISH) in which the three of us lived had a parquet floor, and my mother strongly objected to the men in her family, me in particular, walking around with our socks on. She insisted on us wearing shoes or slippers at all times. Admonishing me about this matter, she would evoke an old Russian superstition; it is an ill omen, she would say, it may bode a death in the family.

Of course, it might be that she simply regarded this habit as uncivilized, as plain bad manners. Men's feet smell, and that was the pre-deodorant era. Yet I thought that, indeed, one could easily slip and fall on a polished parquet, especially if one wore woolen socks. And that if one were old and frail, the consequences could be disastrous. The parquet's affinity with wood, earth, etc., thus extended in my mind to any ground under the feet of our close and distant relatives who lived in the same town. No matter what the distance, it was the same ground. Even living on the other side of the river, where I would subsequently rent an apartment or a room of my own, didn't constitute an excuse, for there were too many rivers and canals in that town. And although some of them were deep enough for the passage of seagoing ships, death, I thought, would find them shallow, or else, in its standard underground fashion, it could creep across under their bottoms.

Now my mother and my father are dead. I stand on the Atlantic seaboard: there is a great deal of water separating me from two surviving aunts and my cousins: a real chasm, big enough to confuse even death. Now I can walk around in my socks to my heart's content, for I have no relatives on this continent. The only death in the family I can now incur is presumably my own, although that would mean mixing up transmitter with receiver. The odds of that merger are small, and that's what distinguishes electronics from superstition. Still, if I don't tread these broad Canadian-maple floorboards in my socks, it's neither because of this certitude nor out of an instinct for self-preservation, but because my mother wouldn't approve of it. I guess I want to keep things the way they were in our family, now that I am what's left of it.

2

There were three of us in that room and a half of ours: my father, my mother, and I. A family, a typical Russian family of the time. The time was after the war, and very few people could afford more than one child. Some of them couldn't even afford to have the father alive or present: great terror and war took their toll in big cities, in my hometown especially. So we should have considered ourselves lucky, especially since we were Jews. All three of us survived the war (and I say "all three" because I, too, was born before it, in 1940); my parents, however, survived the thirties also.

I guess they considered themselves lucky, although they never said as much. In general, they were not terribly self-aware, except when they grew old and malaises began to beset them. Even then, they wouldn't talk about themselves and death in that way that terrifies a listener or prods him to compassion. They would simply grumble, or complain addresslessly about their aches, or discuss at length some medicine or other. The closest my mother would ever come to uttering something of the sort would be while pointing at an extremely delicate set of china, saying: This will become yours when you get married or when . . . and she would interrupt herself. And, once, I remember her on the phone talking to some distant friend of hers who I was told was ill: I remember my mother emerging from the telephone booth on the street, where I was waiting for her, with a somewhat unfamiliar look in her so familiar eyes, behind her tortoiseshell-rimmed glasses. I leaned toward her (I was already a good deal taller) and asked what the woman had said, and my mother replied, staring aimlessly ahead: "She knows that she is dying and was crying into the phone."

They took everything as a matter of course: the system, their powerlessness, their poverty, their wayward son. They simply tried to make the best of everything: to keep food on the table—and whatever that food was, to turn it into morsels; to make ends meet—and although we always lived from payday to payday, to stash away a few rubles for the kid's movies, museum trips, books, dainties. What dishes, utensils, clothes, linen we had were always clean, polished, ironed, patched, starched. The tablecloth was always spotless and crisp, the lampshade above it dusted, the parquet shining and swept.

The amazing thing is that they were never bored. Tired, yes, but not bored. Most of their time at home, they were on their feet: cooking, washing, circulating between the communal kitchen of our apartment and our room and a half, fiddling with this or that item of the household. When they were seated, it was of course for meals, but mainly I remember my mother in a chair, bent over her manual-cum-pedal Singer sewing machine, fixing our clothes, turning old shirt collars inside out, repairing or readjusting old coats. As for my father, his only time in a chair was when he was reading the paper, or else at his desk. Sometimes in the evening they would watch a movie or a concert on our 1952 TV set. Then they would also be seated . . . This way, seated in a chair in the empty room and a half, a neighbor found my father dead a year ago.

3

He had outlived his wife by thirteen months. Out of seventy-eight years of her life and eighty of his, I've spent only thirty-two years with them. I know

almost nothing about how they met, about their courtship; I don't even
know in what year they were married. Nor do I know the way they lived
the last eleven or twelve years of their lives, the years without me. Since
I am never to learn it, I'd better assume that the routine was the usual, that
perhaps they were even better off without me: in terms both of money and
of not having to worry about my being rearrested.

Except that I couldn't help them in their old age; except that I wasn't
there when they were dying. I am saying this not so much out of a sense
of guilt as because of the rather egotistical desire of a child to follow his
parents through all the stages of their life; for every child, one way or
another, repeats his parents' progress. I could argue that, after all, one
wants to learn from one's parents about one's own future, one's own aging;
one wants to learn from them also the ultimate lesson: how to die. Even
if one doesn't want any of these, one knows that one learns from them,
however unwittingly. "Shall I look this way when I am old, too? Is this
cardiac—or any other—problem hereditary?"

I don't and I never will know how they felt during those last years of their
life. How many times they were scared, how many times they felt prepared
to die, how they felt then, reprieved, how they would resume hoping that
the three of us would get together again. "Son," my mother would say over
the telephone, "the only thing I want from this life is to see you again.
That's the only thing that keeps me going." And a minute later: "What
wee you doing five minutes ago, before you called?" "Actually, I was doing
the dishes." "Oh, that's very good. It's a very good thing to do: the dishes.
Sometimes it's awfully therapeutic."

4

Our room and a half was part of a huge enfilade,[1] one-third of a block in
length, on the northern side of a six-story building that faced three streets
and a square at the same time. The building was one of those tremendous
cakes in so-called Moorish style that in Northern Europe marked the turn
of the century. Erected in 1903, the year of my father's birth, it was the
architectural sensation of the St. Petersburg of that period, and Akhmatova[2]
once told me that her parents took her in a carriage to see this wonder. On
its western side, facing one of the most famous avenues of Russian literature,

---

[1]*enfilade*: technically, a placement of troops in a column, here used to convey the precise
   row of apartment buildings.
[2]*Akhmatova*: Russian poetess.

Liteiny Prospect, *Alexander Blok*[3] had an apartment at one time. As for our enfilade, it was occupied by the couple that dominated the pre-revolutionary Russian literary scene as well as the intellectual climate of Russian emigration in Paris later on, in the twenties and thirties: by Dmitry Merezhkovsky and Zinaida Gippius. And it was from our room and a half's balcony that the larva-like Zinka shouted abuse to the revolutionary sailors.

After the Revolution, in accordance with the policy of "densening up" the *bourgeoisie*,[4] the enfilade was cut up into pieces, with one family per room. Walls were erected between the rooms—at first of plywood. Subsequently, over the years, boards, brick, and stucco would promote these partitions to the status of architectural norm. If there is an infinite aspect to space, it is not its expansion but its reduction. If only because the reduction of space, oddly enough, is always more coherent. It's better structured and has more names: a cell, a closet, a grave. Expanses have only a broad gesture.

In the U.S.S.R., the living quarters' minimum per person is 9 square meters. We should have considered ourselves lucky, because due to the oddity of our portion of the enfilade, the three of us wound up with a total of 40 meters. That excess had to do also with the fact that we had obtained this place as the result of my parents' giving up the two separate rooms in different parts of town in which they had lived before they got married. This concept of exchange—or, better still, swap (because of the finality of such exchange)—is something there is no way to convey to an outsider, to a foreigner. Property laws are arcane[5] everywhere, but some of them are more arcane than others, especially when your landlord is the state. Money has nothing to do with it, for instance, since in a totalitarian state income brackets are of no great variety—in other words, every person is as poor as the next. You don't buy your living quarters: at best, you are entitled to the square equivalent of what you had before. If there are two of you, and you decide to live together, you are therefore entitled to an equivalent of the square sum total of your previous residencies. And it is the clerks in the borough property office who decide what you are going to get. Bribery is of no use, since the hierarchy of those clerks is, in its own turn, terribly arcane and their initial impulse is to give you less. The swaps take years, and your only ally is fatigue; i.e., you may hope to wear them down by refusing to move into something quantitatively inferior to what you previously had. Apart from pure arithmetic, what goes into their decision is

---

[3]*Alexander Blok*: Russian revolutionary poet.

[4]*bourgeoisie*: middle class, between aristocrats and workers, in Marxist doctrine between capitalists and proletariat.

[5]*arcane*: hidden or secret.

a vast variety of assumptions never articulated in law, about your age, nationality, race, occupation, the age and sex of your child, social and territorial origins, not to mention the personal impression you make, etc. Only the clerks know what is available, only they judge the equivalence and can give or take a few square meters here and there. And what a difference those few square meters make! They can accommodate a bookshelf, or, better yet, a desk.

5

Apart from an excess of thirteen square meters, we were terribly lucky because the communal apartment we had moved into was very small. That is, the part of the enfilade that constituted it contained six rooms partitioned in such a way that they gave home to only four families. Including ourselves, only eleven people lived there. As communal apartments go, the dwellers can easily amount to a hundred. The average, though, is somewhere between twenty-five and fifty. Ours was almost tiny.

Of course, we all shared one toilet, one bathroom, and one kitchen. But the kitchen was fairly spacious, the toilet very decent and cozy. As for the bathroom, Russian hygienic habits are such that eleven people would seldom overlap when either taking a bath or doing their basic laundry. The latter hung in the two corridors that connected the rooms to the kitchen, and one knew the underwear of one's neighbors by heart.

The neighbors were good neighbors, both as individuals and because all of them were working and thus absent for the better part of the day. Save one, they didn't inform to the police; that was a good percentage for a communal apartment. But even she, a squat, waistless woman, a surgeon in the nearby polyclinic, would occasionally give you medical advice, take your place in the queue for some scarce food item, keep an eye on your boiling soup. How does that line in Frost's "The Star-Splitter"[6] go? "For to be social is to be forgiving"?

For all the despicable aspects of this mode of existence, a communal apartment has perhaps its redeeming side as well. It bares life to its basics: it strips off any illusions about human nature. By the volume of the fart, you can tell who occupies the toilet, you know what he/she had for supper as well as for breakfast. You know the sounds they make in bed and when the women have their periods. It's often you in whom your neighbor confides his or her grief, and it is he or she who calls for an ambulance should

[6]*Frost's "The Star-Splitter"*: reference to New England poet Robert Frost.

you have an angina attack or something worse. It is he or she who one day may find you dead in a chair, if you live alone, or vice versa.

What barbs or medical and culinary advice, what tips about goods suddenly available in this or that store are traded in the communal kitchen in the evening when the wives cook their meals! This is where one learns life's essentials: by the rim of one's ear, with the corner of one's eye. What silent dramas unfurl there when somebody is all of a sudden not on speaking terms with someone else! What a school of mimics it is! What depths of emotion can be conveyed by a stiff, resentful vertebra or by a frozen profile! What smells, aromas, and odors float in the air around a hundred-watt yellow tear hanging on a plait-like tangled electric cord. There is something tribal about this dimly lit cave, something primordial—evolutionary, if you will; and the pots and pans hang over the gas stoves like would-be tom-toms.

6

I recall these not out of nostalgia but because this was where my mother spent one-fourth of her life. Family people seldom eat out; in Russia almost never. I don't recall either her or my father across the table in a restaurant, or for that matter in a cafeteria. She was the best cook I ever knew, with the exception, perhaps, of Chester Kallman; but then he had more ingredients. I recall her most frequently in the kitchen, in her apron, face reddened and eyeglasses a bit steamy, shooing me away from the stove as I try to fish this or that item from the burner. Her upper lip glistens with sweat; her short, cropped, dyed-red but otherwise gray hair curls disorderly. "Go away!" she exclaims. "What impatience!" I won't hear that anymore.

Nor shall I see the door opening (How did she do it with both her hands holding a casserole or two big pans? By lowering them onto the latch and applying their weight to it?) and her sailing in with our dinner/supper/tea/dessert. My father would be reading the paper, I would not move from my book unless told to do so, and she knew that any help she could expect from us would be delayed and clumsy anyway. The men in her family *knew* more about courtesy than they themselves could master. Even when they were hungry. "Are you reading your Dos Passos[7] again?" she would remark, setting the table. "Who is going to read Turgenev?"[8] "What do you expect from him?" my father would echo, folding the paper. "Loafer is the word."

---

[7]*Dos Passos*: John Dos Passos (1898–1970) American novelist who traveled widely; author of *Manhattan Transfer, U.S.A.*

[8]*Turgenev*: Ivan Turgenev, nineteenth-century Russian novelist.

7

How is it possible that I see myself in this scene? And yet, I do; as clearly as I see them. Again, it is not nostalgia for my youth, for the old country. No, it is more likely that, now that they are dead, I see their life as it was then; and then their life included me. This is what they would remember about me as well, unless they now have the gift of omniscience[9] and observe me at present, sitting in the kitchen of the apartment that I rent from my school, writing this in a language they didn't understand, although now they should be *pan-glot*.[10] This is their only chance to see me and America. This is the only way for me to see them and our room.

★ ★ ★ ★ ★

Talking It Through

1. In the first section of his memoir, Joseph Brodsky tells why he still doesn't walk about his apartment in his socks. Why do you think he begins with this homey recollection? What does it mean to him? Are there such prohibitions and/or superstitions in your own personal history? If so, share and compare their meaning to you with that of Brodsky.

2. Brodsky looks back as an adult in America at his youth in Russia with his parents. What is his attitude toward them? What does he regret?
   Brodsky describes his parents' lives as being made up of minutiae—small, day-to-day events of little consequence. Yet he manages to evoke powerful feelings despite the simplicity of the events described. Choose passages which you think are particularly striking. How does the structure of Section 2 help to achieve its impact on the reader?

3. In the third section we learn that the author has not seen his parents for eleven or twelve years, that they might have been "better off" without him and would not have had to worry about his being "rearrested." Indirectly we learn of the author's exile. How would you feel if you could *never* go home again? How different or similar is Brodsky's forcible exile from the voluntary exile of other immigrants about whom you have read in this collection? What does the author miss the most?

4. Brodsky describes the family apartment. Discuss the pros and cons enumerated by the author of communal living at such close quarters. How different

[9]*omniscience*: the state of knowing all things, of having infinite knowledge.

[10]*pan-glot: pan-* a combining form meaning all, every, universal; *glot*–a combining form meaning knowledge of or communication in language.

is this from your own dwelling arrangements? What would you have in common with Soviet citizen life as described here? What similarities are there to life in the Bronx apartment house as described by Kate Simon (p.148)?

5. What would enable Brodsky's parents to see him "and America"? Does he mean to be taken seriously? How do we know? He has previously described his mother's cooking and serving meals to him and his father. What symbolic meaning is intended by the passage about the preparation of food? Brodsky tells us this family portrait is not merely nostalgia. What is the difference between nostalgia and the feeling the author wishes to convey?

Writer's Workshop

1. Brodsky writes this family portrait out of small ordinary details and the commonplace events of daily life. Write a family portrait of your own. Begin as Brodsky does with the actual space; then describe the people who inhabit it; the day-to-day routines; the intimate sounds and smells and sights usually unremarked or taken for granted; and end with the overall significance to you of what you have described. What is your place in this household? Are you caught up in it, on the threshold, or a distant observer?

2. Thomas Wolfe wrote a popular novel in the 1940s entitled *You Can't Go Home Again.* Decide whether or not this statement is true (for Brodsky, or anyone) and write an essay to back up your point of view using examples from this text.

3. Do you think Emma Lazarus is correct in calling the Statue of Liberty "Mother of Exiles"? Write a poem or description of your own from the viewpoint of one "exiled" from his or her native land, either by forcible expulsion or self-imposed abandonment. What is permanently lost to you? One suggestion is to write each stanza in the voice of a different "exile."

Unspoken World

HELEN   RUGGIERI

Helen Ruggieri's parents and sister came to the United States in 1927 from northern Scotland before her birth. Ruggieri was born in America and became the first in her family to receive a college education. She writes that "On a trip to where my parents were born in rural Scotland, I suddenly imagined a whole other life I might have lived, another person I might have been." She is a writer who currently teaches at the University of Pittsburgh in Bradford, Pennsylvania.

I sometimes think about
the colder, smaller life
I might have lived

a far latitude
a distant occupation   5
another language

how I might have stopped
in the middle of a task
forgetting what it was

I had been reaching for   10
how the eyes of an extinct
animal would shadow me

hungry, amber and full of
more dead worlds than the
plains have grass   15

and outside that dark
window flightless birds
would mimic languages

I never learned and
mock in plangorous[1] bleats   20
poems I never wrote

Talking It Through

1. This poem is composed of seven stanzas of three lines each. Looking at the first two stanzas, what about the poet's life would have been different had she lived in her parents' homeland? What key words indicate that her life would have been less fulfilling?

2. Why do you think the poet imagines herself in her parents' homeland, "forgetting what it was/I had been reaching for"? Discuss the different ways in which we "reach" for things in life.

3. The poet imagines how in Scotland "the eyes of an extinct/animal would shadow me/hungry . . ." Discuss the metaphor of the extinct animal. What features does it have? What might it represent?

4. Discuss the image of the "flightless birds." Birds usually sing or chirp, but in an ominous nightmare image these birds "bleat." In what ways do they mock the poet?

5. Why do you think the poet chose "Unspoken World" as the title for this poem?

6. In your opinion, can an immigrant, or the child of an immigrant, ever leave the old world completely behind? Explain.

Writer's Workshop

1. Use the theme of "the life I might have lived" to write a personal essay or story. Review some of the immigrants' lives in *In A New Land.* Each one left behind a life he or she might have lived. Write a story from that immigrant's point of view imagining the "world left behind." Or, write about a "what if . . ." concerning a turning point in your own life—whether you left behind a country, a school, a friend.

[1]*plangorous:* lamenting, wailing.

2. Poets use the placement of each word in a line or stanza to enhance its meaning. Sometimes Ruggieri contains one idea within one stanza. Sometimes she begins a thought that she completes after jumping into the next stanza. For example, she completes line 9 ("forgetting what it was") in line 10 ("I had been reaching for") of the next stanza. As readers, we have to reach to the next stanza.

   Take Ruggieri's words, but create your own poem with lines and stanzas of different lengths. Think about what you wish to emphasize. Then write a brief essay analyzing Ruggieri's choices and explaining your own.

3. Ruggieri's poem is given to us in very dreamlike "unspoken" images. The Surrealist painters of the early twentieth century painted very incongruous dreamlike images which you might want to look at. Draw your own picture of Ruggieri's poem, being careful to include every image ("that dark window," the poet "reaching," the "extinct animal . . . amber eyes" etc.). After you complete your drawing write a description of the mood you wished to convey, and how you did it.

The Tropics in New York

★ ★

CLAUDE MCKAY

Claude McKay (1890-1948) was a well-known poet and writer of the Harlem Renaissance. He grew up in Jamaica, where his land-owning father grew large tracts of cocoa, bananas, sugarcane, and coffee. He came to the United States in 1912. In this poem he is reminded of his homeland as he passes a shop window full of tropical fruits.

Bananas ripe and green, and ginger-root,
Cocoa in pods and alligator pears,[1]
And tangerines and mangoes and grapefruit,
Fit for the highest prize at parish[2] fairs,

Set in the window, bringing memories   5
Of fruit-trees laden by low-singing rills,[3]
And dewy dawns, and mystical blue skies
In benediction[4] over nun-like hills.

My eyes grew dim, and I could no more gaze;
A wave of longing through my body swept,   10
And, hungry for the old, familiar ways,
I turned aside and bowed my head and wept.

Talking It Through

1. How does the poet capture our attention with just the names of fruits? What is special or different about each one he names? What colors, or what images of the tropics do they evoke?

2. What does McKay mean when he says, "Fit for the highest prize at parish fairs . . ."?

3. In stanza two, what memories of his homeland do the fruits evoke? Where does McKay use religious imagery and why do you think he does so?

4. What is the poet's reaction to his memories in the last stanza? What physical reactions does he describe? What spiritual reactions does he describe? How is "hungry" used in both ways?

5. This poem rhymes and has a measured number of syllables in each line. Which words rhyme? How many syllables are there in each line of the poem? What effect do you think this has on the poem?

Writer's Workshop

1. Write a poem or short story about a sudden encounter with homesickness. In what way is the feeling both emotional and physical? What evoked it?

[1]*alligator pears*: avocados.

[2]*parish*: church district.

[3]*rill*: a little brook.

[4]*benediction*: prayer or blessing.

What does the person remember about his or her "home" whether it be a family, or another country? What effect does the reminiscence have?

2. Foods can have a powerful, emotional effect on people. In an essay, explore a food or meal you love, and tell why. Does it have any family or ethnic significance to you? Is it associated with a holiday or special event? Do any particular memories surround it? Use as many descriptive words and images as you can to evoke your feelings and associations with this food.

3. Collect a group of items that reminds you of the locale in which you grew up. (These could come from a different country, or be typically American.) Arrange them in a "still life" to be painted in words. Describe the objects you have chosen, their "flavor," and why they remind you of home.

My Father Sits in the Dark

★ ★

J E R O M E   W E I D M A N

Jerome Weidman was born in New York City in 1913. He was the author of many plays and novels, including I Can Get It For You Wholesale. *In this story a boy wonders why his immigrant father sits up alone, at all hours of the night.*

MY FATHER HAS A PECULIAR HABIT. HE IS FOND OF SITTING IN THE DARK, alone. Sometimes I come home very late. The house is dark. I let myself in quietly because I do not want to disturb my mother. She is a light sleeper. I tiptoe into my room and undress in the dark. I go to the kitchen for a drink of water. My bare feet make no noise. I step into the room and almost trip over my father. He is sitting in a kitchen chair, in his pajamas, smoking his pipe.

"Hello, Pop," I say.

"Hello, Son."

"Why don't you go to bed, Pa?"

But he remains there. Long after I am asleep I feel sure that he is still sitting there, smoking.

Many times I am reading in my room. I hear my mother get the house ready for the night. I hear my kid brother go to bed. I hear my sister come in. I hear her do things with jars and combs until she, too, is quiet. I know she has gone to sleep. In a little while I hear my mother say good night to my father. I continue to read. Soon I become thirsty. (I drink a lot of water.) I go to the kitchen for a drink. Again I almost stumble across my father. Many times it startles me. I forget about him. And there he is—smoking, sitting, thinking.

"Why don't you go to bed, Pop?"

"I will, son."

But he doesn't. He just sits there and smokes and thinks. It worries me. I can't understand it. What can he be thinking about? Once I asked him.

"What are you thinking about, Pa?"

"Nothing," he said.

Once I left him there and went to bed. I awoke several hours later. I was thirsty. I went to the kitchen. There he was. His pipe was out. But he sat there, staring into a corner of the kitchen. After a moment I became accustomed to the darkness. I took my drink. He still sat and stared. His eyes did not blink. I thought he was not even aware of me. I was afraid.

"Why don't you go to bed, Pop?"

"I will, son," he said. "Don't wait up for me."

"But," I said, "you've been sitting here for hours. What's wrong? What are you thinking about?"

"Nothing, son," he said. "Nothing. It's just restful. That's all."

The way he said it was convincing. He did not seem worried. His voice was even and pleasant. It always is. But I could not understand it. How could it be restful to sit alone in an uncomfortable chair far into the night, in darkness?

What can it be?

I review all the possibilities. It can't be money. I know that. We haven't much, but when he is worried about money he makes no secret of it. It can't be his health. He is not reticent about that either. It can't be the health of anyone in the family. We are a bit short on money, but we are long on health. (Knock wood, my mother would say.) What can it be? I am afraid I do not know. But that does not stop me from worrying.

Maybe he is thinking of his brothers in the old country. Or of his mother and two step-mothers. Or of his father. But they are all dead. And he would not brood about them like that. I say brood, but it is not really true. He does not brood. He does not even seem to be thinking. He looks too peaceful, too, well not contented, just too peaceful, to be brooding. Perhaps it is as he says. Perhaps it is restful. But it does not seem possible. It worries me.

If I only knew what he thinks about. If I only knew that he thinks at all. I might not be able to help him. He might not even need help. It may be as he says. It may be restful. But at least I would not worry about it.

Why does he just sit there, in the dark? Is his mind failing? No, it can't be. He is only fifty-three. And he is just as keen-witted as ever. In fact, he is the same in every respect. He still likes beet soup. He still reads the second section of the *Times* first. He still wears wing collars. He still believes that Debs[1] could have saved the country and that T.R. was a tool of the moneyed interests. He is the same in every way. He does not even look older than he did five years ago. Everybody remarks about that. Well-preserved, they say. But he sits in the dark, alone, smoking, staring straight ahead of him, unblinking, into the small hours of the night.

If it is as he says, if it is restful, I will let it go at that. But suppose it is not. Suppose it is something I cannot fathom. Perhaps he needs help. Why doesn't he speak? Why doesn't he frown or laugh or cry? Why doesn't he do something? Why does he just sit there?

Finally I become angry. Maybe it is just my unsatisfied curiosity. Maybe I *am* a bit worried. Anyway, I become angry.

"Is something wrong, Pop?"

"Nothing son. Nothing at all."

But this time I am determined not to be put off. I am angry.

"Then why do you sit here all alone, thinking, till late?"

"It's restful, son. I like it."

I am getting nowhere. Tomorrow he will be sitting there again. I will be puzzled. I will be worried. I will not stop now. I am angry.

"Well what do you *think* about, Pa? Why do you just sit here? What's worrying you? What do you think about?"

"Nothing's worrying me, son. I'm all right. It's just restful. That's all. Go to bed, son."

My anger has left me. But the feeling of worry is still there. I must get an answer. It seems so silly. Why doesn't he tell me? I have a funny feeling that unless I get an answer I will go crazy. I am insistent.

"But what do you *think* about, Pa? What is it?"

"Nothing, son. Just things in general. Nothing special. Just things."

I can get no answer.

It is very late. The street is quiet and the house is dark. I climb the steps softly, skipping the ones that creak. I let myself in with my key and tiptoe

---

[1]*Debs . . . T.R.*: Eugene Victor Debs, a socialist candidate for the presidency, and Teddy Roosevelt, president from 1901–1909.

into my room. I remove my clothes and remember that I am thirsty. In my bare feet I walk to the kitchen. Before I reach it I know he is there.

I can see the deeper darkness of his hunched shape. He is sitting in the same chair, his elbows on his knees, his cold pipe in his teeth, his unblinking eyes staring straight ahead. He does not seem to know I am there. He did not hear me come in. I stand quietly in the doorway and watch him.

Everything is quiet, but the night is full of little sounds. As I stand there motionless I begin to notice them. The ticking of the alarm clock on the icebox. The low hum of an automobile passing many blocks away. The swish of papers moved along the street by the breeze. A whispering rise and fall of sound, like low breathing. It is strangely pleasant.

The dryness in my throat reminds me. I step briskly into the kitchen. "Hello, Pop," I say.

"Hello, son," he says. His voice is low and dream-like. He does not change his position or shift his gaze.

I cannot find the faucet. The dim shadow of light that comes through the window from the street lamp only makes the room seem darker, I reach for the short chain in the center of the room. I snap on the light.

He straightens up with a jerk, as though he has been struck. "What's the matter, Pop?" I ask.

"Nothing," he says. "I don't like the light."

"What's the matter with the light?" I say. "What's wrong?"

"Nothing," he says. "I don't like the light."

I snap the light off. I drink my water slowly. I must take it easy, I say to myself. I must get to the bottom of this.

"Why don't you go to bed? Why do you sit here so late in the dark?"

"It's nice," he says. "I can't get used to lights. We didn't have lights when I was a boy in Europe."

My heart skips a beat and I catch my breath happily. I begin to think I understand. I remember the stories of his boyhood in Austria. I see the wide-beamed *kretchma*,[2] with my grandfather behind the bar. It is late, the customers are gone, and he is dozing. I see the bed of glowing coals, the last of the roaring fire. The room is already dark, and growing darker. I see a small boy, crouched on a pile of twigs at one side of the huge fireplace, his starry gaze fixed on the dull remains of the dead flames. The boy is my father.

I remember the pleasure of those few moments while I stood quietly in the doorway watching him.

"You mean there's nothing wrong? You just sit in the dark because you like it, Pop?" I find it hard to keep my voice from rising in a happy shout.

[2]*kretchma*: tavern.

"Sure," he says. "I can't think with the light on."

I set my glass down and turn to go back to my room. "Good night, Pop," I say.

"Good night," he says.

Then I remember. I turn back. "What do you think about, Pop?" I ask.

His voice seems to come from far away. It is quiet and even again. "Nothing," he says softly. "Nothing special."

★ ★ ★ ★ ★

Talking It Through

1. How does the son become aware of his father's habit of sitting up late in the dark? What is unusual about the father's manner as he sits there? Why does it disturb the son, even though the father says convincingly, "It's just restful"?

2. What emotions does the father's habit evoke in the son, and why? What does he imagine is keeping the father awake? Why does he dismiss those reasons?

3. The last scene in the story differs in many ways from the earlier ones. Rather than tripping over his father in the kitchen, "Before I reach it I know he is there." What else does the son see and hear that he has ignored before? What does he mean when he says, "I can see the deeper darkness . . ."?

4. Why does the son "snap on the light" that night? How does it differ from his former behavior? In what way is it also a symbolic act, and how does it "shed light" on the father's reasons for sitting in the dark?

5. What is the significance of the son's vision of his father as a little boy in Austria? How does this vision finally breach the divide between the immigrant father and his son?

6. At the end of the story the son asks again what the father thinks about and he answers, "Nothing . . . Nothing special." What do you think he means by this? What do you think he thinks about?

Writer's Workshop

1. Images of light and dark have special significance in this story. We usually associate light with being able to "see" the truth, with being "enlightened." The son feels for most of the story that he is "in the dark" about

why his father sits up late. Reread the story carefully, noting how Weidman uses images of light and dark to enhance his meaning. Then write an essay in which you discuss the symbolism of light and dark in the story.

2. Most of this story is written in the present tense, even though it takes place in the past. Review the story, carefully noting which passages are in past and present tense. Why would Weidman choose to describe a recurring habit (sitting in the dark) in the present tense? In what way does Weidman's use of tenses enhance our understanding that, for the father, the past lives?

3. Write a poetic monologue of the father's thoughts as he sits in the dark. What sounds, sights, smells would you include?

⋆ *A Moving Day* ⋆

S U S A N   N U N E S

In this story the narrator searches for the meaning of her Japanese ancestry as her mother, who is moving, must decide which of her treasured items to save, and which to give away. Susan Nunes grew up in Honolulu, the daughter of a Japanese mother and Portuguese father.

ACROSS THE STREET, THE BULLDOZER ROARS TO LIFE. DISTRACTED, MY MOTHER looks up from the pile of embroidered linen that she has been sorting. She is seventy, tiny and fragile, the flesh burned off her shrinking frame. Her hair is grey now—she has never dyed it—and she wears it cut no-nonsense short with the nape shaved. She still has a beautiful neck, in another life, perfect for a kimono. She has taken a liking to jeans, cotton smocks, baggy sweaters, and running shoes. When I was a child she wouldn't leave the house without nylons.

Her hands, large-jointed with arthritis, return with a vengeance to the pile of linen. I have been wary of her energy. Now she is making two stacks, the larger one for us, the smaller for her to keep. There is a finality in the way she places things in the larger pile, as if to say that's *it*. For her, it's all over but this last accounting. She does not look forward to what is coming. Strangers. Schedules. The regulated activities of those considered too old to regulate themselves. But at least, at the *very* least, she'll not be a burden. She sorts through the possessions of a lifetime, she and her three daughters. It's time she passed most of this on. Dreams are lumber. She can't *wait* to be rid of them.

My two sisters and I present a contrast. There is nothing purposeful or systematic about the way we move. In fact, we don't know where we're going. We know there is a message in all this activity, but we don't know what it is. Still, we search for it in the odd carton, between layers of tissue paper and silk. We open drawers, peer into the recesses of cupboards, rummage through the depths of closets. We lift, untuck, unwrap, and set aside. The message is there, we know. But what is it? Perhaps if we knew, then we wouldn't have to puzzle out our mother's righteous determination to shed the past.

There is a photograph of my mother taken on the porch of my grandparents' house when she was in her twenties. She is wearing a floral print dress with a square, lace-edged collar and a graceful skirt that shows off her slim body. Her shoulder length hair has been permed. It is dark and thick and worn parted on the side to fall over her right cheek. She is very fair; "one pound powder," her friends called her. She is smiling almost reluctantly, as if she meant to appear serious but the photographer has said something amusing. One arm rests lightly on the railing, the other, which is at her side, holds a handkerchief. They were her special pleasures, handkerchiefs of hand-embroidered linen as fine as ricepaper. Most were gifts (she used to say that when she was a girl, people gave one another little things—a handkerchief, a pincushion, pencils, hair ribbons), and she washed and starched them by hand, ironed them, taking care with the rolled hems, and stored them in a silk bag from Japan.

There is something expectant in her stance, as if she were waiting for something to happen. She says, your father took this photograph in 1940, before we were married. She lowers her voice confidentially and adds, now he cannot remember taking it. My father sits on the balcony, an open book on his lap, peacefully smoking his pipe. The bulldozer tears into the foundations of the Kitamura house.

What about this? My youngest sister has found a fishing boat carved of tortoise shell.

Hold it in your hand and look at it. Every plank on the hull is visible. Run your fingers along the sides, you can feel the joints. The two masts, about six inches high, are from the darkest part of the shell. I broke one of the sails many years ago. The remaining one is quite remarkable, so thin that the light comes through it in places. It is delicately ribbed to give the effect of canvas pushed gently by the wind.

My mother reaches for a sheet of tissue paper and takes the boat from my sister. She says, it was a gift from Mr. Oizumi. He bought it from an artisan in Kamakura. ,

Stories cling to the thing, haunt it like unrestful spirits. They are part of the object. They have been there since we were children. In 1932, Mr. Oizumi visits Japan. He crosses the Pacific by steamer, and when he arrives he is hosted by relatives eager to hear of his good fortune. But Mr. Oizumi soon tires of their questions. He wants to see what has become of the country. It will be arranged, he is told. Mr. Oizumi is a meticulous man. Maps are his passion. A trail of neat X's marks the steps of his journey. On his map of China, he notes each military outpost in Manchuria and appends a brief description of what he sees. Notes invade the margins, march over the blank spaces. The characters are written in a beautiful hand, precise, disciplined, orderly. Eventually, their trail leads to the back of the map. After Pearl Harbor, however, Mr. Oizumi is forced to burn his entire collection. The U.S. Army has decreed that enemy aliens caught with seditious[1] material will be arrested. He does it secretly in the shed behind his home, his wife standing guard. They scatter the ashes in the garden among the pumpkin vines.

My grandfather's library does not escape the flames either. After the Army requisitions the Japanese school for wartime headquarters, they give my mother's parents twenty-four hours to vacate the premises, including the boarding house where they lived with about twenty students from the plantation camps outside Hilo. There is no time to save the books. Her father decides to nail wooden planks over the shelves that line the classrooms. After the Army moves in, they rip open the planks, confiscate the books, and store them in the basement of the post office. Later, the authorities burn everything. Histories, children's stories, primers, biographies, language texts, everything, even a set of Encyclopaedia Brittanica. My grandfather is shipped to Oahu and imprisoned on Sand Island. A few months later, he is released after three prominent Caucasians vouch for his character. It is a humiliation he doesn't speak of, ever.

All of this was part of the boat. After I broke the sail, she gathered the pieces and said, I'm not sure we can fix this. It was not a toy. Why can't you leave my things alone?

For years the broken boat sat on our bookshelf, a reminder of the brutality of the next generation.

Now she wants to give everything away. We have to beg her to keep things. Dishes from Japan, lacquerware, photographs, embroidery, letters.

---

[1]*seditious*: rebellious.

She says, I have no room. You take them, here, *take* them. Take them or I'll get rid of them.

They're piled around her, they fill storage chests, they fall out of open drawers and cupboards. She only wants to keep a few things—her books, some photographs, three carved wooden figures from Korea that belonged to her father, a few of her mother's dishes, perhaps one futon.

My sister holds a porcelain teapot by its bamboo handle. Four white cranes edged in black and gold fly around it. She asks, Mama, can't you hang on to this? If you keep it, I can borrow it later.

My mother shakes her head. She is adamant. And what would I do with it? I don't want any of this. Really.

My sister turns to me. She sighs. The situation is hopeless. You take it, she says. It'll only get broken at my place. The kids.

It had begun slowly, this shedding of the past, a plate here, a dish there, a handkerchief, a doily, a teacup, a few photographs, one of grandfather's block prints. Nothing big. But then the odd gesture became a pattern; it got so we never left the house empty-handed. At first we were amused. After all, when we were children she had to fend us off her things. Threaten. We were always at them. She had made each one so ripe with memories that we found them impossible to resist. We snuck them outside, showed them to our friends, told and retold the stories. They bear the scars of all this handling, even her most personal possessions. A chip here, a crack there. Casualties. Like the music box her brother brought home from Italy after the war. It played a Brahms lullaby. First we broke the spring, then we lost the winding key, and for years it sat mutely on her dresser.

She would say again and again, it's impossible to keep anything nice with you children. And we'd retreat, wounded, for a while. The problem with children is they can wipe out your history. It's a miracle that anything survives this onslaught.

There's a photograph of my mother standing on the pier in Honolulu in 1932, the year she left Hawaii to attend the University of California. She's loaded to the ears with leis. She's wearing a fedora pulled smartly to the side. She's not smiling. Of my mother's two years there, my grandmother recalled that she received good grades and never wore a kimono again. My second cousin, with whom my mother stayed when she first arrived, said she was surprisingly sophisticated—she liked hats. My mother said that she was homesick. Her favorite class was biology and she entertained thoughts of becoming a scientist. Her father, however, wanted her to become a teacher, and his wishes prevailed, even though he would not have forced them upon her. She was a dutiful daughter.

During her second year, she lived near campus with a mathematics professor and his wife. In exchange for room and board she cleaned house, ironed, and helped prepare meals. One of the things that survives from this period is a black composition book entitled, *Recipes of California.* As a child, I read it like a book of mysteries for clues to a life both alien and familiar. Some entries she had copied by hand; others she cut out of magazines and pasted on the page, sometimes with a picture or drawing. The margins contained her cryptic comments: "Saturday bridge club," "From Mary G. Do not give away," underlined, "chopped suet by hand, wretched task, bed at 2 a.m., exhausted." I remember looking up "artichoke" in the dictionary and asking Mr. Okinaga, the vegetable vendor, if he had any edible thistles. I never ate one until I was twenty.

That book holds part of the answer to why our family rituals didn't fit the norm of either our relatives or the larger community in which we grew up. At home, we ate in fear of the glass of spilled milk, the stray elbow on the table, the boarding house reach. At my grandparents', we slurped our chasuke. We wore tailored dresses, white cotton pinafores, and Buster Brown shoes with white socks; however, what we longed for were the lacy dresses in the National Dollar Store that the Puerto Rican girls wore to church on Sunday. For six years, I marched to Japanese language school after my regular classes; however, we only spoke English at home. We talked too loudly and all at once, which mortified my mother, but she was always complaining about Japanese indirectness. I know that she smarted under a system in which the older son is the center of the familial universe, but at thirteen I had a fit of jealous rage over her fawning attention to our only male cousin.

My sister has found a photograph of my mother, a round faced and serious twelve or thirteen, dressed in kimono and seated, on her knees, on the tatami[2] floor. She is playing the koto.[3] According to my mother, girls were expected to learn this difficult stringed instrument because it was thought to teach discipline. Of course, everything Japanese was a lesson in discipline—flower arranging, caligraphy, judo, brush painting, embroidery, everything. One summer my sister and I had to take ikebana, the art of flower arrangement, at Grandfather's school. The course was taught by Mrs. Oshima, a diminutive, softspoken, terrifying woman, and my supplies were provided by my grandmother, whose tastes ran to the oversized. I remember little of that class and its principles. What I remember most clearly is having to walk home carrying one of our creations, which, more often than not, towered above our heads.

[2]*tatami*: traditional Japanese mats.

[3]*koto*: traditional Japanese stringed instrument.

How do we choose among what we experience, what we are taught, what we run into by chance, or what is forced upon us? What is the principle of selection? My sisters and I are not bound by any of our mother's obligations, nor do we follow the rituals that seemed so important. My sister once asked, do you realize that when she's gone that's *it*? She was talking about how to make sushi, but it was a profound question nonetheless.

I remember, after we moved to Honolulu and my mother stopped teaching and began working long hours in administration, she was less vigilant about the many little things that once consumed her attention. While we didn't exactly slide into savagery, we economized in more ways than one. She would often say, there's simply no time anymore to do things right.

I didn't understand then why she looked so sad, but somehow I knew the comment applied to us.

So how do I put her wish, whatever it was, into perspective? It is hidden in layers of silk, sheathed in the folds of an old kimono that no one knows how to wear any more. I don't understand why we carry out this fruitless search. Whatever it is we are looking for, we're not going to find it. My sister tries to lift a box filled with record albums, old seventy-eights, gives up, and sets it down again. My mother says, there are people who collect these things. Imagine.

Right, just imagine.

I think about my mother bathing me and singing, ''The snow is snowing, the wind is blowing, but I will weather the storm.'' And I think of her story of the village boy carried by the Tengu on a fantastic flight over the cities of Japan, but who chooses in the end to return to the unchanging world of his village. So much for questions which have no answers, why we look among objects for meanings which have somehow escaped us in the growing up and growing old.

However, my mother is a determined woman. She will take nothing with her if she can help it. It is all ours. And on the balcony my father knocks the ashes of his pipe into a porcelain ashtray, and the bulldozer is finally silent.

★ ★ ★ ★ ★

Talking It Through

1. Describe the narrator's mother, her attitude and activities as she packs her belongings. Why is she making ''two stacks, the larger one for us, the smaller for her to keep''? Why do you think she is so determined to discard or give away so many of her treasures from Japan? Do you dislike the mother's attitude? Do you think she is wise or cruel, or just practical?

2. In the story, three photographs of the mother are described, each going further back in time. What do these photos reveal about her? What has been her attitude about preserving her Japanese heritage, and passing it along to her daughters?

3. During World War II, Japanese Americans were rounded up, their property confiscated, and they were forced into isolated "relocation camps," and internment camps surrounded by barbed wire in total disregard for their rights as citizens. Only recently has the U.S. government apologized and made reparations. What happened to the narrator's family during World War II, and how did it affect them?

4. What other factors are described which threatened the ability of this family to preserve its heritage? How does the broken boat symbolize some of them?

5. Why is this "moving day" so significant in the narrator's life? What has she come to realize?

Writer's Workshop

1. Objects can hold great symbolic and personal meaning in our lives. Which do we remember, which do we save, and why? Choose an object which holds special memories for you. Perhaps it is something from your childhood, or a gift which means a lot to you. Bring your object to school and exchange objects for a class period with a friend. Write a description of the object given to you, while your friend describes yours.

   Next, write about your own memento. How did you get it? What small details about it are significant to you? What events do you associate it with? If possible, recount some stories about it, as Susan Nunes does about the broken boat.

   After you and your partner are finished, share with the class your two descriptions of the same object. How do they differ? How has the more personal description made the object symbolic?

2. In an essay compare the parent-child relationship in "My Father Sits in the Dark" and "A Moving Day." How has the parent's former life in another country influenced his or her relationship with the child? How is the past being remembered by the parent ? Are their memories being passed on to the next generation or left behind? How do the parents communicate with the children, and how do the children attempt to understand?

★   *from* **Lost in Translation**   ★

E V A   H O F F M A N

Eva Hoffman was born in Cracow, Poland. In 1959, at the age of thirteen, she left the beloved country of her childhood as an emigré to Canada. Educated at Rice University in Texas, and later at Harvard, she has written, taught literature, and been an editor of The New York Times Book Review. *In this brief excerpt she writes passionately about being torn away from the world she has known and loved.*

IT IS APRIL 1959, I'M STANDING AT THE RAILING OF THE *BATORY'S* UPPER deck, and I feel that my life is ending. I'm looking out at the crowd that has gathered on the shore to see the ship's departure from Gdynia—a crowd that, all of a sudden, is irrevocably[1] on the other side—and I want to break out, run back, run toward the familiar excitement, the waving hands, the exclamations. We can't be leaving all this behind—but we are. I am thirteen years old, and we are emigrating. It's a notion of such crushing, definitive finality that to me it might as well mean the end of the world.

My sister, four years younger than I, is clutching my hand wordlessly; she hardly understands where we are, or what is happening to us. My parents are highly agitated; they had just been put through a body search by the customs police, probably as the farewell gesture of anti-Jewish harassment. Still, the officials weren't clever enough, or suspicious enough, to check my sister and me—lucky for us, since we are both carrying some silverware we were not allowed to take out of Poland in large pockets sewn onto our skirts especially for this purpose, and hidden under capacious sweaters.

When the brass band on the shore strikes up the jaunty mazurka[2] rhythms of the Polish anthem, I am pierced by a youthful sorrow so powerful that

---

[1] *irrevocably*: in a way that cannot be altered or changed.
[2] *mazurka*: a lively Polish dance like the polka.

I suddenly stop crying and try to hold still against the pain. I desperately want time to stop, to hold the ship still with the force of my will. I am suffering my first, severe attack of nostalgia, or *tesknota*—a word that adds to nostalgia the tonalities of sadness and longing. It is a feeling whose shades and degrees I'm destined to know intimately, but at this hovering moment, it comes upon me like a visitation from a whole new geography of emotions, an annunciation of how much an absence can hurt. Or a premonition of absence, because at this divide, I'm filled to the brim with what I'm about to lose—images of Cracow, which I loved as one loves a person, of the sun-baked villages where we had taken summer vacations, of the hours I spent poring over passages of music with my piano teacher, of conversations and escapades with friends. Looking ahead, I come across an enormous, cold blankness—a darkening, an erasure, of the imagination, as if a camera eye has snapped shut, or as if a heavy curtain has been pulled over the future. Of the place where we're going—Canada—I know nothing. There are vague outlines of half a continent, a sense of vast spaces and little habitation. When my parents were hiding in a branch-covered forest bunker during the war, my father had a book with him called *Canada Fragrant with Resin*[3] which, in his horrible confinement, spoke to him of majestic wilderness, of animals roaming without being pursued, of freedom. That is partly why we are going there, rather than to Israel, where most of our Jewish friends have gone. But to me, the word "Canada" has ominous echoes of the "Sahara." No, my mind rejects the idea of being taken there, I don't want to be pried out of my childhood, my pleasures, my safety, my hopes for becoming a pianist. The *Batory* pulls away, the foghorn emits its lowing, shofar[4] sound, but my being is engaged in a stubborn refusal to move. My parents put their hands on my shoulders consolingly; for a moment, they allow themselves to acknowledge that there's pain in this departure, much as they wanted it.

Many years later, at a stylish party in New York, I met a woman who told me that she had had an enchanted childhood. Her father was a highly positioned diplomat in an Asian country, and she had lived surrounded by sumptuous elegance, the courtesy of servants, and the delicate advances of older men. No wonder, she said, that when this part of her life came to an end, at age thirteen, she felt she had been exiled from paradise, and had been searching for it ever since.

No wonder. But the wonder is what you can make a paradise out of. I told her that I grew up in a lumpen apartment in Cracow, squeezed into

[3]*resin*: a gummy sap of a pine tree.
[4]*shofar*: a ram's horn, first used as a signaling trumpet, now used on Jewish High Holy Days to announce the New Year. It sounds to Hoffman like a boat's foghorn.

three rudimentary rooms with four other people, surrounded by squabbles, dark political rumblings, memories of wartime suffering, and daily struggle for existence. And yet, when it came time to leave, I too, felt I was being pushed out of the happy, safe enclosures of Eden.

★ ★ ★ ★ ★

Talking It Through

1. In this beginning passage of her book *Lost in Translation*, Eva Hoffman writes dramatically of her uprooting. There is great compression in her account. Look for the many places in these few paragraphs which sum up a whole history. Locate references to Eva's earlier life and that of her parents. What impressions do they give you of the Poland they are leaving? Also, what literary techniques does the author use to convey the immediacy of an experience long past?

2. Hoffman speaks of a pain so strong that she wants "to hold the ship still with the force of my will." She is suffering her first "severe attack of nostalgia." For whom else in this text is the looking backward, the sense of loss, very great? Do you think Hoffman's *tesknota* is so profound because of the age at which her displacement occurs? Compare her reactions with those of the student pieces you will read later in this chapter.

3. The author writes as an adult of her departure from her native land as an adolescent. She lets you know that she now lives a life of sophistication in New York, and yet she cannot forget this vivid memory of being "pushed out of the happy, safe enclosures of Eden." Discuss the irony she includes as part of the final paragraph of this excerpt. Contrast this view of one's homeland with the other Biblical view presented in many of these excerpts: that of America as "Promised Land."

Writer's Workshop

1. How does the age at which one emigrates affect one's life? Is childhood an "age of innocence" that makes the experiences of daily life somehow magical or special despite one's circumstances? Write an essay discussing these issues. Cite examples from this book to strengthen your arguments. Use your own experiences as well.

2. Use the format of Eva Hoffman's autobiographical memoir to write a memoir of your own. Write as she does in the present tense, the active voice,

the first person. Start with the outstanding memory or experience. Where are you? How old? Who else is present at the time? In succeeding paragraphs explain how you feel, what the moment means to you when it occurs. Use your final paragraphs to review the event from the present.

3. Try rewriting Hoffman's opening to her book in the third person, from a journalist's point of view. You are a reporter present as the *Batory* is leaving Gdynia, Poland, and you are telling the story of a family leaving their homeland. Why are they going? What "color" will you add to your account? What background? What quotes will you use in your piece? Think about these questions, then do some prewriting to organize your article before you start your "lead."

School Life in China

★ ★

XIN ZHANG

Xin Zhang's recollections of her homeland first appeared in a 1988 collection of student autobiographies written by newly arrived immigrants at Newcomer High School, in San Francisco. Myron Berkman, their teacher, worked with students over a three-to-four-week period as their autobiographies went through several drafts. They also received help from peer editors at University High.

Mr. Berkman writes that the students ". . . had studied little, if any, English in their countries. I have kept the writing in its original text wherever possible . . . so the writing will remain authentic."

China is one of the most famous and biggest countries in the world. Nangchang is one of the famous historical cities in China. My childhood was spent there. It was both happy and sad. There were singing, laughter, and there were tears too. It will always remain in my memory.

I began elementary school when I was six years old. My school was old. Although there were only five hundred students there, it was a beautiful school. It was built in a quiet place and there were no factories. The two sides of the school were surrounded by a small hill. The hill was always green because there was a pine forest. The pines were green in all four seasons. When Spring came, the azaleas bloomed, over the hill and dale, red as fire. They rocked back and forth with the soft wind, just like a flickering flame. The green trees, blue sky, and white clouds, together with red flowers, set each other off beautifully. When Winter came, all the leaves of the tree fell, but the pines were still so green, against the strong cold wind. They were like brave soldiers.

Oh! It was snowing! The whole world was covered by a silvery jacket. The pines were more beautiful, as pure as jade, and as clean as ice, like slim and graceful girls. The other side of the school was surrounded by camellias. The flowers were white as snow, their delicate fragrance spread through the soft wind. It seemed like wonderland.

The outside of school was beautiful, however the inside was beautiful too. My old school had two buildings; one was used for teaching, and the other was teachers' offices. In front of the buildings there were two flower-beds. Around the flower-beds were bushes. At the bottoms was a grassy lawn. Some small wild flowers grew on it. They were blue, red, yellow, white and orange . . . so many trees surrounded the school. As I said, pines, Chinese parasols, maples . . . when it was summer the sun showed through dense leaves. Under the trees it was very cold. It was a good place for studying.

In elementary school, my first year in Kindergarten, most of the teachers taught us singing, dancing, or drawing. Sometimes I studied how to read and write numbers. We often went out on field trips. The destinations were small hill or grassy lawns. We stayed in line and sang songs with smiles on our faces. When we got to our destinations, like birds we flied out in all directions. The boys fought and rolled on the grassy lawn. Some boys and girls played "hide and seek." In Spring, I would collect wild flowers with my friends. Sometimes we made small garlands to put on our necks. In Fall we would collect wild fruit which we could eat, and it tasted delicious. Oh! It was time to each lunch. You see there were so much food on the ground; cake, steamed bread , steamed buns, cookies, chicken, eggs, apples, bananas, oranges . . . and we all shared it with each other.

When I was seven years old I was in Grade One. I studied Math, Chinese, Art, P.E., and Music. My favorite subject was Chinese. My hobby was reading. But to read you had to know a lot of words. So I liked to study Chinese because I would learn many words to read.

My Chinese teacher was Mrs. Guo. She was a very good teacher. Her teaching was very patient. If you couldn't understand one word after two or three times, she could teach you ten times, or even more. Some mischievous students under other teachers were not good, but they became good students in her hands. Mrs. Guo was my favorite teacher. She taught me from Grade One until I graduated from elementary school. She taught not only in class, but after class also. She taught us how to play games good for the mind and the body. One of the interesting games we played after class was "Eagle catch the chicken." Children got in line and a leader stood in front of the line. He had to stretch his arm to protect his members. Another person who stood outside of the line tried to catch someone who was in line. This game could test your reactions. After class, many students played this game on the playground. But I didn't like it. I liked to sit and watch.

In Grade Two I studied two more subjects; Chinese Geography and Chinese History. Art, Music, PE classes became less important. I also began to write compositions. Usually I spent two periods to finish it in school. I got higher grades than my friends.

In Grade Five, it was the last year of elementary school. I only studied Chinese and Math. I only had to pass these two subjects. Then I could graduate from school. At that time, one of my compositions was called, "My Father." It was published under Mrs. Guo's help. My family was happy with me. I keep the publication in my drawer even now. After big exams I passed Chinese and Math. I smoothly graduated from elementary school.

During my five elementary years, I not only gained a lot of knowledge but I also made a lot of friends. Three girls were my close friends. We knew each other from Grade Two. They were named Ming, Bin, and Jun. Ming was a happy girl. I still hear her sounds of laughter everyday. She never seemed to be sad. Bin was also a humorous girl. Wherever she was, there was laughter. Jun was a simple and honest girl. She usually made funny mistakes. How about me? Yes, I was a quiet girl. Although each of us had different personalities, we got on well with each other. Of course we had arguments. We often sat on a grassy lawn near our school. We discussed lessons and spoke glowingly of our ideals and dreams.

I began to go to middle school when I was twelve years old. My middle school was a major school. It had two-story buildings for teaching, and a four-story building for teachers. There were five thousand students. In front of the offices there was a big garden. A tree grew up in the center. It was surrounded by many beautiful flowers and bushes. A big playground was in front of all these buildings.

In Grade Six, I studied Chinese, Algebra, English, Art, P.E., Geography, History, and Music. I studied in a normal classroom everyday. Chinese was still my favorite subject, but I became interested in English. After classes, I usually talked with my classmates and rarely went out to play.

But I had a big surprise. We were put together again. Ming, Bin, Jun, and me. Sunday we often went to the grassy lawn which was on way to the elementary school. We often went there. We recalled our childhood.

Everyday we went to school together. On the way to school was a wild pear tree. In the Spring it spread its white flowers like snow on our bodies. In the Summer the tree provided a large green shade for us. Our laughter was mixed into the green shade.

In Grade 7 I studied two more subjects, Geometry and Physics. It was my last year of studying in China. In the summer holiday I went to the capital of China, Peking, with my family. We needed to get an entry visa to go to the U.S. After getting the visa, I visited many scenic spots; The Forbidden City, Summer Palace, the Great Wall, and Peihai Park. The most tiring place to climb up was the Great Wall. The tired climb still remain in mind.

After we came back to Nangchang, one day I asked my mother. "Why are we going to the U.S.?" She said, "Your grandfather is in the U.S., you already know. Now he is old. He needs us to take care of him."

October 24, 1985, was my last day in Nangchang. In the morning I went to school and joined a farewell party that my classmates made for me. At the party I sang two songs—"Leave Each Other," and "Meet You." At the end they said, "Don't forget us. Remember, in the distant East, your friends miss you each day and night."

On the way home, Ming, Bin, Jun, and me were silent. We just walked and walked and walked. . . . It seemed like God sent a ghost. We got to the grassy area before we knew it. We visited our old haunts. The past, like an old man, appeared in my mind. I don't know who made the first sobbing, but soon we all were crying. It was so sad. There was no other sounds. Only the birds were singing.

In the afternoon I said goodbye to my maternal grandmother, aunt, teachers, friends, and the house that I lived in for eleven long years. When we got to Shanghai by train, my aunt was there.

December 11, 1985, was my last day in China, At noon, my aunt cooked a big lunch for our farewell. We took some pictures. At two o'clock in the afternoon, I was at the Honggiao International Airport. We would take the 2:14 plane to the U.S. My aunt said, "Try hard to study and work. I'm waiting for you good news."

When I got on the plane, I looked back at the charm and beauty of my country through the window. I said in my heart, 'Good-bye grandmother, aunt, teachers, friends. Good-bye mountains, rivers, fields. Wait for me! I will come back. Please believe me. I will come back. Wait for me!' The tears dropped slowly from my eyes, falling down my face.

Talking It Through

1. How does Xin Zhang feel about China? What images of China remain most vividly in your mind from reading her account? How does this contrast with other images or stereotypes you may have had about growing up in China?

2. The beauty of her natural surroundings seems to be very important to Xin Zhang. She makes her descriptions vivid by using metaphors and similes, by depicting colors and physical sensations. "When Spring came, the azaleas bloomed, over the hill and dale, red as fire. They rocked back and forth with the soft wind, just like a flickering flame." Find some other similes and metaphors in her writing, and discuss why you like them.

3. What can we tell about Xin Zhang's personality and interests from her autobiography? How is she like her friends, and how is she different? How does her life at school change as she grows older?

4. How does Xin Zhang convey her sorrow at leaving China? What about her leavetaking seems saddest to you?

5. What authors in "The World Left Behind" remember their homelands with equal longing? What do you think might determine how an immigrant remembers the past?

Writer's Workshop

1. Xin Zhang leads us into her childhood world gradually. It is almost as if she takes us on an airplane trip. First we see all of China, then her home city. Next we see the general landscape around her school. Finally we enter the buildings and her particular life there.

   Write a description in which you zoom into the world where you spent your childhood, moving from the place in which you live(d) down to the particulars of your house and school. Think about how where you grew up affected you. Write about how it felt to leave, if you did, or imagine how it would feel to leave, if you are still there.

2. Eva Hoffman writes, "I don't want to be pried out of my childhood, my pleasures, my safety, my hopes . . . I felt I was being pushed out of the happy, safe enclosures of Eden." Compare her description of leaving Poland to Xin Zhang's leaving China. Both left their native countries when they were young girls, although Hoffman writes about it many years later, from an adult's perspective.

3. If one of Xin Zhang's friends could write her a letter, what would it say?

Imagine how the friend would feel, what she would include about life in China based on what Xin Zhang herself has written. What stereotypes of life in America might this friend have? Write such a letter, addressed to Xin Zhang in San Francisco.

★  ★

A Childhood in Cambodia

SOKKA LIM

Sokka Lim writes as a high-school student at Newcomer High about his life in war-torn Cambodia under the Khmer Rouge, his experiences at a refugee camp in Thailand, and his arrival in America in 1984.

In 1973 my family moved from Phnom Penh to Battambang, a city which is near Thailand. My family moved to Battambang because there was a war between Vietnam and Cambodia. They fought for land and for power. My family travelled from Phnom Penh to Battambang by train. We travelled by train because that way we saved more money. Buses and planes cost a lot of money.

I started school when I was five years old. When I went to school I had to wear a uniform. The boys wore shorts and short sleeve shirts. The girls wore short blue skirts and a special kind of short-sleeve blouse. I studied for only one year. When I started school I was too young to remember anything.

Two months after my first year in school, there was a big war between Cambodia and the Khmer Rouge. Khmer Rouge was Pol Pot. Cambodia eventually lost the war. The Khmer Rouge were the Communist Party, and they took power and they decided to turn Cambodia upside-down. When they got into Phnom Penh and Battambang, they told all the people to quickly get out of the cities. They wanted the people to go to the countryside. Teachers, doctors, and soldiers, everyone was killed when the Khmer Rouge came to Cambodia.

My family and my relatives moved to the countryside. The Khmer Rouge told the people to move out of the cities in 24 hours, so everyone moved. If we didn't do what they said, they would kill us, so we had to obey them. When my relatives and I got to the countryside, we had to find a place to live. One month passed by. The Khmer Rouge started to tell people to go to work. They told my father to go to work at a farm. They didn't let my father come home at all. He had to eat and sleep at the farm. Not only father, but a lot of people had to go together. The farm was very far away from my home. My father had to work from 6:00 A.M. to 12:00 P.M. in the afternoon, before he had lunch. After lunch he started to work again from 12:30 to 5:30. At 5:40 he had dinner. As the movie, "Killing Field" showed, it was not enough to eat.

The first year there was a lot of food for the people to eat, but the year after, food became scarcer and scarcer. My father couldn't get enough food to eat. My father got hungry so he came home. If the Khmer Rouge saw him, they would kill him. He came at night so the Khmer Rouge couldn't see him. When he got home, he found something to trade with our neighbors. My father had gold, and our neighbor had rice. So my father had to exchange it for rice. Rice we could eat, but gold we couldn't eat at all. People who traded rice for gold had houses full of rice. They ate when they wanted to eat. People who didn't have rice, ate everything. They ate mice, snakes, and frogs. Whatever animals could eat, we could eat too! We also ate parts of the banana tree.

At home if the Khmer Rouge saw smoke, they would take us to Angka. The first and second time, they told us to stop doing that thing. If we got caught twice, they would give us lectures. But on the third time, they would kill us.

At night when we were asleep spies came under the house to investigate. If we talked at night, they will take us to Angka too. When we talk, we had to talk softly. In the house if we have something to eat they will come and take it. People who had something to eat hid it underground. When they wanted to eat, they went and take it. Sometimes they looked in the ground to find what we hid.

The Khmer Rouge hated the Vietnamese very much. Before 1975, the Khmer Rouge were having a war with the Vietnamese. When the Vietnamese caught Khmer Rouge soldiers they killed them all. Now, Khmer Rouge desired to kill all the Vietnamese. If they knew you were Vietnamese, they take you away, and you never come back home. Most of the Vietnamese in Cambodia were killed by Khmer Rouge. When the Khmer Rouge came to take prisoners, they came by boat. When they took the prisoner back to the boat, sometimes they killed him and threw the body in the river. When the river flooded many bodies floated on the river.

The Khmer Rouge said my mother was Vietnamese because she couldn't speak Cambodian clearly. The Khmer Rouge made my mother work hard too. But my mother didn't work at the farm. She worked in the village. Her job was growing vegetables by the river. Married women stayed in the village. Single women work at the farm like the men. When they worked so hard and didn't have enough food to eat, their knees were bigger than their heads. I saw many people whose knees were bigger than their heads. When they were tired, sometimes they couldn't walk. Many people died in their sleep.

The Khmer Rouge told me to go to work like my father. They didn't let me come home at all. I had to live on the farm. I ate and slept at the farm. A lot of us young boys went together. I went to work when I was ten years old. The place that I worked was very far away from my home. I walked to work. It took about 6 hours. Everyday I had to work from 7:30 to 11:30. At 11:50 I had lunch. After lunch I had one hour to rest. When I had free time, I went to fish. When I caught fish, I cooked it at the place I caught it. Sometimes I ate dried salted fish without cooking because I was very hungry. After I rested I started to work again from 1:30 P.M. to 5:30. At 5:45 I had dinner. Dinner and lunch were the same. Do you know what I had for lunch and dinner? I had rice soup. I had rice soup just like Dith Pran had in "The Killing Fields." The dish of rice soup had only one spoonful of rice. In the dish there was only water. Everyday I had only rice soup, just like my father had.

My job was to cut down the small trees and grass. When I worked there wasn't enough food for me to eat. I became sick. At night when I slept, I slept on the ground because I didn't know how to make a bed. When I slept, I always thought about my mother. I didn't want to go away from my mother. I missed my mother so much that I came home. If the Khmer Rouge saw me, they would take me back and make me work 7 hours. But I made it. I got home. I didn't have any food to eat so I had to go and steal. In front of my home there were many banana trees. Some of them had fruit. I stole only the fruit. When I stole, I cut the whole tree. I stole only in the night. If I stole in the day, and the Khmer Rouge would see me, they would kill me. So, I had to steal at night.

My family had a lot of strife. My sister didn't go to work because she was too small. She couldn't work. Everyday she just sat and waited for lunch. Sometimes I sneaked out. When my sister went to eat lunch, I would go with them too. If I didn't cheat, I would die. So I had to sneak away to eat.

In 1979, Vietnam invaded Cambodia and ousted Pol Pot and the Khmer Rouge. Two million people out of a total of 7 million Cambodians were killed between 1975 and 1979. After the war broke out, my family came to live in my old house again in Battambang. I didn't know it was my house because it was destroyed by bombs. When I looked inside my house, I saw everything was different. My father and my relatives started to build it again. While my father and my relatives started to build it, we had to spend some money to buy wood and bricks. When the house was finished, there were three families living together. My uncle's family and my aunt's family lived together with us.

My father started to work. His job was to repair bicycles. My father fixed the bicycle by trading for gold and rice. In 1979 Cambodia used only bicycles.

On September 15, 1979, my family and my relatives moved from Battambang to another city. This city was close to Thailand. My family lived in this city for about one month and then we decided to go to Thailand. We wanted to leave Cambodia because we didn't like the Communists and we wanted to have a better future.

One night my relatives told my father to get everything ready because we would leave soon. My father told me and my sister not to tell anyone about it. If we told anybody, they would tell the Vietnamese soldiers who would take us to jail. We had to leave at night without anyone knowing. When my family and my relatives left Cambodia, we divided into four groups because we couldn't go together. This way the Vietnamese soldiers wouldn't find out. It took about two hours to wait for everyone. We had to meet together in the jungle. On the way, I was very tired and thirsty. There wasn't enough water to drink. The trip is long and dangerous. I had to walk for 3 days from Cambodia to Thailand. My feet were blistered. Because I had blisters on my feet, I couldn't walk fast. I had to walk very slowly. When I got to Thailand the Thai soldiers took my family and my relatives to Khao I Dang Refugee Camp.

I got to Khao I Dang Refugee Camp on November 29, 1979. The United Nations gave food, dishes, spoons, pillows, pans, and bamboo to make our houses.

My sister and I started school again. My school was near the mountain. At school I studied Math and Reading. I didn't have any best friend or a favorite teacher at all. Everyday I went to school from 7:30 to 11 o'clock. I studied for 3 years in Khao I Dang camp. In the camp people couldn't go anywhere. The gates surrounded the camp. And the Thai soldiers guarded the gate everyday. If people went to buy something in the Thai village, and the Thai soldiers saw you, they would take you to jail.

We lived in Khao I Dang camp for three years. On September 28, 1983, my family and my relatives came to America. Before we came to America, we had to go to interview with the U.S. government. The first interview we had with J.V.A., we had to interview twice. If you said the right answers you could go to the Immigration. (I.N.S.) And if you said the right answers again, you can come to America. When my family left the camp, there were many neighbors who helped my family take things to the bus station. Before we came to America, my family had to go to Cholburi, Thailand. After that I went to the Philippines. We flew from Cholburi to Philippines by airplane. When I got on the airplane for the Philippines I'm very sad. Because I missed my beautiful country and I didn't think I would come back again. We stayed in Bataan Refugee Camp for about five months. We stayed there and studied English everyday. In the afternoon I usually went to the stream to swim with my uncle. On February 18, 1984, my family came to America.

★ ★ ★ ★ ★

Talking It Through

1. Sokka Lim's account of his family's hardships under the Khmer Rouge differs from many in this volume in that it is told without embellishment in the English at Lim's command at the time of the writing. In this way it differs from other more literary accounts in the text. What is the effect of style on a story? Do you think this piece would be more compelling if the author had at hand the vocabulary of a writer like Joseph Brodsky or Eva Hoffman? What are the advantages of this unadorned narrative ? Do you wish the author had been able to be more descriptive in English?

2. The format of this piece is strictly chronological. If you were revising Sokka Lim's account of his childhood, where would you begin? Would you use a "flashback" technique? How could this piece have been more suspenseful? Make an outline of the way you would organize the material and discuss the reasons for your choice with your classmates.

3. In his story Sokka Lim refers twice to another account of an experience similar to his, Dith Pran's story of "The Killing Fields" as told by former *New York Times* corespondent Sydney Schanberg, which was later made into a motion picture. If possible, read Schanberg's book *The Death and Life of Dith Pran*, which was published by Penguin in 1985. Compare Lim's bald statement "it was not enough to eat" and "I had rice soup just like Dith Pran had" with the descriptions of deprivation as recounted by Schanberg, a veteran reporter. Note, however, the power of Sokka Lim's matter-of-fact description of people working so hard "their knees were bigger than their heads."

4. At the end of his account, the author describes his family's escape to Thailand, where they spend three years behind the barriers of a refugee camp; their interview with U.S. immigration authorities where "if you said the right answers you can come to America"; their flight for the Philippines, another waiting period, then finally arrival in America. Enroute to the Philippines he says, "I am very sad . . . I missed my beautiful country and I didn't think I would come back again." After his experiences in Cambodia as a child, does this nostalgia seem surprising? How would you account for it? Look for points of similarity between Sokka Lim's and other immigrants' experiences of the legal and emotional aspects of embarking on a new life.

Writer's Workshop

1. Write Sokka Lim's thoughts as he waits in the Thai refugee camp for the trip to America.

2. Begin with a different starting point and add imaginative details of your own to make Sokka Lim's story more vivid. You may consult periodicals and books about the period in the library to add authenticity to your account. This is a method used by many fiction writers to lend authenticity to their work. Try also for a believable emotional tone to your piece.

3. Write a character sketch of either of Sokka Lim's parents. How does their dilemma seem to them? How is it different from that experienced by their son? See if you can get inside the skin of an older person whose power and responsibility as head of a family has been destroyed. You may write *as* or *about* the character you choose.

Memories
★ of Korea ★

PIERS KIM BOLNICK

Piers Kim Bolnick wrote these passages of his autobiography in 1990 when he was an eighth grader at the Village Community School in New York City. Bolnick uses writing as a way to preserve his memories, which are especially elusive and dear to him; he was a very young orphan when he came to America and was adopted by his parents.

"THEY'RE PROBABLY NOT TRUE OR PARTLY TRUE OR MAYBE THEY'RE NOT EVEN memories at all."

"Who knows?" "Him?" "Not me."

I would often question myself like this asking if what I remember of my past life is really true or just some memories of something else, like a conversation or a scene from a television movie. Maybe they are memories based on a picture and I just think they're memories, when really I just don't remember it deep down inside of me.

Many of the memories I write about in this autobiography are most likely to have been true events that happened in my childhood life. I cannot be absolutely positive that they are one hundred percent true, for no one knew much about me before I was adopted. But most likely they are true, thanks to my mother who took me into her care and helped me to keep many of these memories within me.

One night Halmuny[1] and I were robbed. I remember clearly that there were three men dressed in what kind of looked like Ninja suits, now that I think about it. Each one had on black cloth masks that covered everything except their eyes. It is hard to remember but only, or at least I think only, two of them had guns.

They had come bursting in through the door and immediately started to

---

[1]*Halmuny*: The Korean word for grandmother. Bolnick does not know whether Halmuny was his real grandmother, or a foster parent.

shout at us to sit against the wall. They tied Halmuny up but left me untied. I guess I was too young then to know that I was being robbed. I just stood there like a statue and watched while one of the men stood guard with a gun pointed at Halmuny and me. I don't remember what Halmuny's reactions were but I think she was calmly crying, too shocked or scared to do anything else but that.

The other two men went about searching the house. I have no idea what they were searching for but whatever it was they never found, for as fast as they had come they left. The only clue that something had happened was that Halmuny was still tied.

When the men left she told me to untie her, so I did and as soon as I did she ran into one of the two rooms we had in the house to check on the two babies that had been sleeping. They were fine and still sleeping, undisturbed by the men.

Later in my life I was told that these men were probably some members of the Shoguns, the Secret Service Police.

I don't remember being taken to the orphanage, or what my feelings were when I left Halmuny, or what they were when at the orphanage, but I do remember the orphanage.

One of the things I remember about the orphanage is the lunch room. It was small and very crowded. The lunch tables were yellowish with benches attached to them. These tables could be folded to make more room. The room itself was yellowish-white with wooden floor boards. It always had a constant smell of food being cooked. It wasn't a bad smell like some lunch rooms that I have been in, but in a way fishy, and salty as if we were eating near a seaport. There was a big rectangular hole that allowed you to see into the kitchen and also where you got your food.

Another memory that I have of the orphanage is of the room that I had slept in. This room could fit five to six kids in it comfortably but crowded. My room had a T.V. The walls had yellowish-white paper patterns on them and the floor had a big carpet. Outside of the orphanage there were slides. These slides were very long with wooden frames. The whole area was covered with trees that kept the playground shaded and cool.

The funny thing is that I cannot remember any of my friends from the orphanage. Now, when I look at pictures of them I sometimes wish that I still knew them. I think how neat it would have been to know them and to, if possible, write to them. I don't even remember any of the people who worked at the orphanage.

While I was living with Halmuny in Korea, I didn't have many friends, or at least I don't remember them. But of those that I had they were all considerably older than I. They were American soldiers probably between the ages of 29 and 35.

They worked as officers for a little army base that was near my house. I would sometimes go and lean against the fence of the base and watch the activities that went on in there. I remember that one time some of the soldiers took me into the base and showed me around. They even let me go into one of the tanks there. There were so many lights blinking on and off, and scanners, dials, knobs and buttons. I didn't know that a tank had so many things inside of it. It was as if it were a Christmas tree, with lights shining in a dimly lit room.

Another time, the army officers took me to the ocean. I had never been to the beach before and I remember this best, that it was one of those times I had fun. It's not that I didn't have happy times or fun before. It's just that I didn't play around much because Halmuny wouldn't let me out because she was too busy to watch me and take me places. The beach had a lot of big rocks in which you could climb. I would go and climb the biggest and tallest of these rocks. We must have stayed till sundown because the one image that I always see whenever I think about it, is of me standing on the tall groups of rocks with the sky a reddish orange and three soldiers near me with lighted cigarettes, a weird smell of tobacco and sea salt in the wind. The waves make a swishing sound as the tide comes in for the day and the sea gulls cry for food and there is the distant sound of a boat's horn.

I was not the only one living with Halmuny. There was an older boy there, too, named Kiongie, and two babies. I don't remember anything about Kiongie. I don't know who he really was in relation to me. He might have been Halmuny's son or nephew. Maybe he was of no relation to her. Anyhow, I called him my older brother although I never really saw him much or I would have remembered him. As for the two babies I don't know or remember anything about them either. I did see them a lot for they stayed in a crib in a separate room.

Halmuny's house was small. I can't remember what it looked like inside, but outside the ground was made of concrete. There were four doors. One led to my house, another to my neighbor's and the last to our storage room where we kept extra food and pots.

Next to the neighbor's door there was a wooden barrel with a hose sticking out of it. The barrel held fresh water. I would, when I had nothing to do, come out of my house in my green-with-white-sides rubber shoes, and turn the hose on and squirt water into them. I loved the sloshiness and the noise it made when you walked in them. That is what I did for fun instead of going to play with other kids. I do remember going to the lake once by myself. The lake was not clean and it was very rocky and muddy. There were some people sitting in the sun or swimming, but I would just sit on a rock and throw sticks in the water.

Halmuny was a calm, tired-looking old woman. She had wrinkles but not many. By looking at her you would get the impression that she was in her fifties, but inside she was more like a mid-forty year old.

She was a gentle, caring person who tried her best to make do with what little she had and to make me and the two other babies happy.

I guess you could say that Halmuny and I were pretty close, or at least I was with her, or else I wouldn't have remembered her so much.

. . . Halmuny takes me to a small building where I get my picture taken for adoption and other records . . . she drives me to the airport . . . I'm put on the airplane . . . Kiongie is behind me on the plane . . . I'm scared and tired . . . the plane takes off . . .

That's how I imagine my coming to America, and that's also I think how it really was. After being put in the orphanage someone wanted to adopt a little Korean boy and so I was the picked candidate. I vaguely remember having pictures taken of me and Halmuny. I'm not sure what the actual purpose of these pictures were, but I like to think that they were for me to keep as a memory of Halmuny and my childhood days in Korea. These photos were probably given to Halmuny, too, to remember me.

I remember being taken to the airport. It must have been cold out because I was wearing a sweater. It was a brown sweater. Actually it was tan with a cartoon of a dog on it. I had on brown corduroys and I think brownish-white shoes.

I was on a dirty bus that was very crowded with people and luggage. It was stuffy and the whole bus smelled of sweat as if everybody on the bus had gone on a three mile race and then come on the bus without taking a shower or bath. I would imagine that all these people on the bus were immigrants going to America except that I didn't know that I was going to America. There were a lot of old people on the bus but some were young. The old people especially were making a lot of noise. They were talking loudly and laughing and yelling at each other to shut up. There must have been sick people on the bus, too, because there was a lot of coughing, and moans of pain.

I don't remember the bus ever stopping at the airport, because the last thing I remember is being on the airplane. I must have fallen asleep on the bus and not wakened up until I was up in the air and already far from home.

Kiongie was on the airplane, too, because he was also being adopted, but by people who were from New Jersey as I found out later. I don't remember the plane ride much either except that I was in a way scared. But I kept that to myself for I do remember that I was totally silent during the whole trip. I remember sitting in the window seat and looking out the window and seeing the clouds floating by me in what seemed to be ever slow motion, like a clock ticking away . . . tick . . . tak . . . tick . . . tak . . . I would watch the clouds floating and changing shape, like wooden boats in a still lake, suddenly a big boat taking over a small boat. I would hope to see some sign of the blue sky. Seeing the blue of the sky was a rare sight to see and it made me happy. I guess that's why to this day, blue is my favorite color and also why I love window seats. I still love looking up at the sky at daytime and seeing the blueness of the sky. . . .

Coming to my new home from the airport was scary. I remember that I had just gotten off the airplane from Korea and I was tired. I was then led by somebody to be greeted by three people. These strange people were making noises at me and, not knowing what they were saying in English, I was more scared. The airport was cold and all I wanted to do was go home and sleep. The person who was making the most noise (my mother) picked me up and gave me a hug while the other two (my sister and father) patted me on the back. The youngest one (my sister) gave me a yellow stuffed dog.

. . . After I drank a Coke I was carried outside and put into a car. The car ride wasn't that bad. I was given a bag of wind-up planes which I gladly took. I sat in the back seat of the car and played with the planes while everyone else watched me with loving, smiling faces.

When we got to my new home in America (in Greenwich Village, New York), I was attacked by their dog, Benji. He came charging after me, barking and jumping on me. Of course, I had seen dogs before, but being in a strange new place made me more scared. I was chased into the house and around a small table, screaming until finally someone caught hold of him and put him in another room.

After I was calm and had stopped crying I looked around the house. I came to the table that I had been chased around and studied a glass tank that had fish in it. I had never seen fish of these kinds before and they fascinated me. I started tapping at the glass with my finger and whistling at them. I don't know why I did it, because it had no effect.

A while after I came to America my mom and I would often sit and talk about Korea. I was still young, maybe 5 or 5-1/2 years old at the most. We would talk about what I remembered of Korea. I still didn't know that she was to be my mother for the rest of my life. I thought that I was just visiting this person and soon I would be going back to Halmuny. But I never did go back to my grandmother. All I have of her (Halmuny) is her picture and my memories of her. I guess to compensate for not seeing Halmuny I would often play a game with my mother.

The game went like this. I would pretend that I was traveling from Halmuny to my mother. My mother would pretend to be both Halmuny and herself. Sometimes I would pretend Halmuny had made something for mom or that I would bring the two babies from Korea to my mom. My mom didn't mind playing these games with me. When we played she would have a tape recorder and a pencil and pad. With these she would record things that I said about Korea. She says that these are for future references.

. . . When I think about the past I think how much I have missed it, and loved it, but had I stayed in Korea how much more miserable I would have been. My mother says that if I had stayed in Korea, I would probably be working in a rice field, which is what most poor people do in Korea. So adoption was the best thing for me, because now I have a future and I can do anything I want to for a job, or at least try.

★ ★ ★ ★ ★

Talking It Through

1. Why is it so hard for Piers Bolnick to be certain that his memories are "true"? Do you think that very early childhood memories are always hard to recall? If so, what makes them so elusive? What makes Bolnick's especially so?

2. Piers Bolnick writes how he remembers certain things about his life in Korea and does not remember others. As he writes, he is trying to understand the mysteries of how his own memory functions.

   Read again several of his memories of Korea (the robbers, visit to the beach with the soldiers, depictions of the orphanage, Halmuny and her house). Why do you think he thinks he has held on to each memory? What about his writing (specific details, images) convinces you that the memory is or is not "deep down" true?

3. Piers Bolnick's trip to America is a transition between two worlds. How does he lead us into his memories of it? How does he reconstruct what must have happened, even if he is not sure that it actually happened that way? What do you think the color blue represents to him? What colors are important to you, and why?

4. Describe Bolnick's new family. What about his descriptions lets us know they are welcoming and loving?

5. What is the game Piers and his mother play? Why is it important? How does Pier's mother help him preserve his memories of Korea, and how does he feel about her role?

Writer's Workshop

1. As an experiment, sit down for half an hour and write about whatever very early memories come into your mind. Try to capture the images, sensations,

and emotions which have made the memories vivid to you. Do not try to write in chronological order. Rather, see where each memory leads you next, as Piers Bolnick does in his early memories. Experiment by writing some of these memories in past tense, others in present tense. What effect does each tense have on the narration?

2. Compare the way the three student writers in *In A New Land*, Xin Zhang, Sokka Lim, and Piers Kim Bolnick, have written about their memories of their original country. How do you think the act of writing functions for each one in preserving the past?

TRANSPLANTINGS

A GARDEN TRANSPLANT IS DELICATE. IT NEEDS RICH SOIL IN which to flourish, the nurture of careful planting to keep its roots intact, and sufficient attention to enable it to grow sturdily and steadily into bloom. And when an organ is transplanted, there is always the possibility of rejection to be guarded against and overcome.

The selections in this section deal with the efforts of first-generation Americans and their descendants, who seek to make themselves a secure place, in Gish Jen's words, "In the American Society." Some do this easily and eagerly. For some, looking forward incorporates all that has come before. For others the process is not without pain. For all the characters encountered in these pages, self-acceptance is at the heart of a successful transplanting to the new land.

The Negro ★ *Speaks of* ★ *Rivers*

LANGSTON HUGHES

In this poem the poet Langston Hughes traces the Negroes' heritage as it is transported and transplanted throughout time and place. Humankind originated in Africa, and the great early civilizations of Mesopotamia and Egypt originated in the Euphrates and Nile river valleys.

I've known rivers:
I've known rivers ancient as the world and older than
      the flow of human blood in human veins.

My soul has grown deep like the rivers.

I bathed in the Euphrates when dawns were young.   5
I built my hut near the Congo and it lulled me to sleep.
I looked upon the Nile and raised the pyramids above it.
I heard the singing of the Mississippi when Abe Lincoln
      went down to New Orleans, and I've seen its muddy
      bosom turn all golden in the sunset.   10

I've known rivers:
Ancient, dusky[1] rivers.

My soul has grown deep like the rivers.

---

[1]*dusky:* dark, shadowy.

Talking It Through

1. Who is the speaker in this poem? Why do you think Hughes entitled it "*The* Negro Speaks of Rivers" rather than "A Negro . . ."? How would the poem be different had Hughes written, as Chief Seattle did, about "my people"?

2. In what ways could you compare rivers to human veins? What do rivers symbolize in this poem?

3. Each line in the second stanza begins with "I" and then a verb: I bathed . . . , I built . . . , I looked . . . , I heard." What is the effect of this introduction to each line? What does each river bring to the speaker's experience, and to the history of civilization?

4. Hughes is speaking of the Negro's experience in America when he writes "I heard the singing of the Mississippi . . ." What do you think he feels has been the effect of America on the Negro? In your opinion, is Hughes writing as an African, an American, an African-American? Explain.

5. What do you think Hughes means by, "My soul has grown deep like the rivers"? What different meanings can "soul" have? Can you think of any which have been contributed to our culture by the African-American experience?

Writer's Workshop

1. In "The Negro Speaks of Rivers" the speaker represents all Negroes throughout time. Write a poem in which you assume the identity of a people, or a particular group. For example, write a poem with a title like "The New Yorker Speaks of Buildings" or "The Sophomore Speaks of Homework."

2. In an essay, discuss Hughes's use of repetition. Which lines and words repeat, and why? What is the effect of this repetition, and how does it enhance his meaning?

For My Great-Grandfather: A Message Long Overdue

★   ★

MAXINE KUMIN

Maxine Kumin has written novels and poetry, for which she was awarded a Pulitzer Prize. Many of her poems have appeared first in magazines such as the New Yorker. In this work, from her 1970 collection The Nightmare Factory, *Kumin writes about her great-grandfather, Rosenberg the Tailor.*

You with the beard as red as Barbarossa's[1]
uncut from its first sprouting to the hour
they tucked it in your belt and closed your eyes,
you with the bright brass water pipe, a surefire
playing under the neighbors' children's noses   5
for you to puff and them to idolize

—the pipe you'd packed up out of somewhere
in Bohemia, along with the praying shawl[2]
and the pair of little leather praying boxes—[3]
Great-Grandfather, old blue-eyed fox of foxes,   10
I have three pages of you. That is all.

---

[1]*Barbarossa:* Frederick I of Germany, called Barbarossa for his red beard.
[2]*praying shawl:* tallith; fringed garment worn by Jews at prayer.
[3]*praying boxes:* phylacteries; boxes containing prayers, strapped on by orthodox Jews for certain prayers.

1895. A three-page letter
from Newport News, Virginia, written
on your bleached out bills of sale under the stern
heading: ROSENBERG THE TAILOR, DEBTOR,   15
A FULL LINE OF GOODS OF ALL THE LATEST IN
SUITING AND PANTS. My mother has just been born.

You write to thank your daughter for the picture
of that sixth grandchild. There are six more to come.
"My heart's tenderest tendrils" is your style.   20
"God bless you even as He blessed Jacob." Meanwhile
you stitch the year away in Christendom.

Meanwhile it seems you've lost your wife, remarried
a girl your daughter's age and caused distress.
"It was a cold relentless hand of Death   25
that scattered us abroad," you write, "robbing us
of Wife and Mother." Grieving for that one buried
you send new wedding pictures now herewith
and close with *mazel* and *brocha*,[4] words that bless.

The second bride lived on in one long study   30
of pleats and puckers to the age of ninety-two,
smoked cigarettes, crocheted and spoke of you
to keep our kinship threaded up and tidy.

Was that the message—the erratic ways[5]
the little lore that has been handed on   35
suffers, but sticks it out in the translation?
I tell you to my children, who forget,
are brimful of themselves, and anyway
might have preferred a farmer or a sailor,
but you and I are buttoned, flap to pocket.   40
Welcome, ancestor, Rosenberg the Tailor!
I choose to be a lifetime in your debt.

[4]*mazel and brocha:* Yiddish words for luck and blessing.
[5]*erratic:* irregular, eccentric.

Talking It Through

1. In this poem, Maxine Kumin addresses her deceased great-grandfather who came to America at the end of the nineteenth century from "somewhere in Bohemia" (now part of Czechoslovakia). She says, "I have three pages of you. That is all."

   Many descendants of immigrants have little more than such meager "heirlooms." However in his three-page letter, great-grandfather Rosenberg manages to tell where he has relocated, gives his occupation, and economic and marital status. Furthermore, the poet senses his personality through his epistolary style.

   How does Ms. Kumin let us know how close she feels to her great-grandfather? How does she depict and characterize this relative she has never actually known? How might she have learned the other information imparted in the first two stanzas?

2. In the next-to-last stanza the poet describes the great-grandfather's second wife. Kumin says his widow kept "our kinship threaded up and tidy." How was this accomplished? Why is the metaphor used by the poet an apt one?

3. What does the poet mean when she says "the little lore that has been handed on/suffers but sticks it out in the translation"? By whom? For whom?

4. "I tell you to my children," continues Kumin. Do Kumin's children value these stories about their family's history? Explain. Note how the poet continues her earlier metaphor with "you and I are buttoned, flap to pocket." Why do you think Kumin feels indebted to Rosenberg the Tailor? Why does she see herself so closely bound to him? What universal truth is there to this poem?

Writer's Workshop

1. A frequently used poetic device is to apostrophize, or to directly address, a person (or thing), whether absent or present, usually in an exclamatory tone.

   Choose a subject of your own to speak directly to in this way. Then write two or more stanzas talking to your subject as if you were actually in the subject's presence. End as Maxine Kumin does with some words of greeting to show your regard for or feelings toward whomever or whatever is being addressed in your poem. Kumin's line is, "Welcome, ancestor, Rosenberg the Tailor!"

2. The title of this chapter is "Transplantings." In what ways does the poem

"For My Great-Grandfather: A Message Long Overdue" relate to this theme? What does one have to worry about when transplanting a living organism, whether in the plant or the animal kingdom?

Write an essay explaining whether or not in the case of Kumin's subject the transplant was a success.

Rules of the Game

★ ★

A M Y   T A N

Amy Tan was born in 1952 in California, shortly after her parents emigrated to America. In "Rules of the Game," which is from the best-selling novel The Joy Luck Club, *Tan focuses on the relationship between a Chinese immigrant mother and her daughter. In the first half of the story Mrs. Jong teaches Waverly the strength and wisdom of Chinese ways and encourages her to adapt them to the "new American rules."*

I WAS SIX WHEN MY MOTHER TAUGHT ME THE ART OF INVISIBLE STRENGTH. IT was a strategy for winning arguments, respect from others, and eventually, though neither of us knew it at the time, chess games.

"Bite back your tongue," scolded my mother when I cried loudly, yanking her hand toward the store that sold bags of salted plums. At home, she said, "Wise guy, he not go against wind. In Chinese we say, Come from South, blow with wind—poom!—North will follow. Strongest wind cannot be seen."

The next week I bit back my tongue as we entered the store with the forbidden candies. When my mother finished her shopping, she quietly plucked a small bag of plums from the rack and put it on the counter with the rest of the items.

My mother imparted her daily truths so she could help my older brothers and me rise above our circumstances. We lived in San Francisco's Chinatown. Like most of the other Chinese children who played in the back alleys of restaurants and curio shops, I didn't think we were poor. My bowl was always full, three five-course meals every day, beginning with a soup full of mysterious things I didn't want to know the names of.

We lived on Waverly Place, in a warm, clean, two-bedroom flat that sat above a small Chinese bakery specializing in steamed pastries and dim sum. In the early morning, when the alley was still quiet, I could smell fragrant red beans as they were cooked down to a pastry sweetness. By daybreak, our flat was heavy with the odor of fried sesame balls and sweet curried chicken crescents. From my bed, I would listen as my father got ready for work, then locked the door behind him, one-two-three clicks.

At the end of our two-block alley was a small sandlot playground with swings and slides well-shined down the middle with use. The play area was bordered by wood-slat benches where old-country people sat cracking roasted watermelon seeds with their golden teeth and scattering the husks to an impatient gathering of gurgling pigeons. The best playground, however, was the dark alley itself. It was crammed with daily mysteries and adventures. My brothers and I would peer into the medicinal herb shop, watching old Li dole out onto a stiff sheet of white paper the right amount of insect shells, saffron-colored seeds, and pungent leaves for his ailing customers. It was said that he once cured a woman dying of an ancestral curse that had eluded the best of American doctors. Next to the pharmacy was a printer who specialized in gold-embossed wedding invitations and festive red banners.

Farther down the street was Ping Yuen Fish Market. The front window displayed a tank crowded with doomed fish and turtles struggling to gain footing on the slimy green-tiled sides. A hand-written sign informed tourists, "Within this store, is all for food, not for pet." Inside, the butchers with their blood-stained white smocks deftly gutted the fish while customers cried out their orders and shouted, "Give me your freshest," to which the butchers always protested, "All are freshest." On less crowded market days, we would inspect the crates of live frogs and crabs which we were warned not to poke, boxes of dried cuttlefish, and row upon row of iced prawns, squid, and slippery fish. The sanddabs made me shiver each time; their eyes lay on one flattened side and reminded me of my mother's story of a careless girl who ran into a crowded street and was crushed by a cab. "Was smash flat," reported my mother.

At the corner of the alley was Hong Sing's, a four-table cafe with a recessed stairwell in front that led to a door marked "Tradesmen." My brothers and I believed the bad people emerged from this door at night.

Tourists never went to Hong Sing's, since the menu was printed only in Chinese. A Caucasian man with a big camera once posed me and my playmates in front of the restaurant. He had us move to the side of the picture window so the photo would capture the roasted duck with its head dangling from a juice-covered rope. After he took the picture, I told him he should go into Hong Sing's and eat dinner. When he smiled and asked me what they served, I shouted, "Guts and duck's feet and octopus gizzards!" Then I ran off with my friends, shrieking with laughter as we scampered across the alley and hid in the entryway grotto of the China Gem Company, my heart pounding with hope that he would chase us.

My mother named me after the street that we lived on: Waverly Place Jong, my official name for important American documents. But my family called me Meimei, "Little Sister." I was the youngest, the only daughter. Each morning before school, my mother would twist and yank on my thick black hair until she had formed two tightly wound pigtails. One day, as she struggled to weave a hard-toothed comb through my disobedient hair, I had a sly thought.

I asked her, "Ma, what is Chinese torture?" My mother shook her head. A bobby pin was wedged between her lips. She wetted her palm and smoothed the hair above my ear, then pushed the pin in so that it nicked sharply against my scalp.

"Who say this word?" she asked without a trace of knowing how wicked I was being. I shrugged my shoulders and said, "Some boy in my class said Chinese people do Chinese torture."

"Chinese people do many things," she said simply. "Chinese people do business, do medicine, do painting. Not lazy like American people. We do torture. Best torture."

My older brother Vincent was the one who actually got the chess set. We had gone to the annual Christmas party held at the First Chinese Baptist Church at the end of the alley. The missionary ladies had put together a Santa bag of gifts donated by members of another church. None of the gifts had names on them. There were separate sacks for boys and girls of different ages.

One of the Chinese parishioners had donned a Santa Claus costume and a stiff paper beard with cotton balls glued to it. I think the only children who thought he was the real thing were too young to know that Santa Claus was not Chinese. When my turn came up, the Santa man asked me how old I was. I thought it was a trick question: I was seven according to the American formula and eight by the Chinese calendar. I said I was born on March 17, 1951. That seemed to satisfy him. He then solemnly asked if I had been a very, very good girl this year and did I believe in Jesus Christ and obey my parents. I knew the only answer to that. I nodded back with equal solemnity.

Having watched the other children opening their gifts, I already knew that the big gifts were not necessarily the nicest ones. One girl my age got a large coloring book of biblical characters, while a less greedy girl who selected a smaller box received a glass vial of lavender toilet water. The sound of the box was also important. A ten-year-old boy had chosen a box that jangled when he shook it. It was a tin globe of the world with a slit for inserting money. He must have thought it was full of dimes and nickels, because when he saw that it had just ten pennies, his face fell with such undisguised disappointment that his mother slapped the side of his head and led him out of the church hall, apologizing to the crowd for her son who had such bad manners he couldn't appreciate such a fine gift.

As I peered into the sack, I quickly fingered the remaining presents, testing their weight, imagining what they contained. I chose a heavy, compact one that was wrapped in shiny silver foil and a red satin ribbon. It was a twelve-pack of Life Savers and I spent the rest of the party arranging and rearranging the candy tubes in the order of my favorites. My brother Winston chose wisely as well. His present turned out to be a box of intricate plastic parts; the instructions on the box proclaimed that when they were properly assembled he would have an authentic miniature replica of a World War II submarine.

Vincent got the chess set, which would have been a very decent present to get at a church Christmas party, except it was obviously used and, as we discovered later, it was missing a black pawn and a white knight. My mother graciously thanked the unknown benefactor,[1] saying, "Too good. Cost too much." At which point, an old lady with fine white, wispy hair nodded toward our family and said with a whistling whisper, "Merry, merry Christmas."

When we got home, my mother told Vincent to throw the chess set away. "She not want it. We not want it," she said, tossing her head stiffly to the side with a tight, proud smile. My brothers had deaf ears. They were already lining up the chess pieces and reading from the dog-eared instruction book.

I watched Vincent and Winston play during Christmas week. The chess board seemed to hold elaborate secrets waiting to be untangled. The chessmen were more powerful than Old Li's magic herbs that cured ancestral curses. And my brothers wore such serious faces that I was sure something was at stake that was greater than avoiding the tradesmen's door to Hong Sing's.

"Let me! Let me!" I begged between games when one brother or the

[1]*benefactor:* patron, person who gives financial help.

other would sit back with a deep sigh of relief and victory, the other annoyed, unable to let go of the outcome. Vincent at first refused to let me play, but when I offered my Life Savers as replacements for the buttons that filled in for the missing pieces, he relented. He chose the flavors: wild cherry for the black pawn and peppermint for the white knight. Winner could eat both.

As our mother sprinkled flour and rolled out small doughy circles for the steamed dumplings that would be our dinner that night, Vincent explained the rules, pointing to each piece. "You have sixteen pieces and so do I. One king and queen, two bishops, two knights, two castles, and eight pawns. The pawns can only move forward one step, except on the first move. Then they can move two. But they can only take men by moving crossways like this, except in the beginning, when you can move ahead and take another pawn."

"Why" I asked as I moved my pawn. "Why can't they move more steps?"

"Because they're pawns," he said.

"But why do they go crossways to take other men. Why aren't there any women and children?"

"Why is the sky blue? Why must you always ask stupid questions?" asked Vincent. "This is a game. These are the rules. I didn't make them up. See. Here. In the book." He jabbed a page with a pawn in his hand. "Pawn. P-A-W-N. Pawn. Read it yourself."

My mother patted the flour off her hands. "Let me see book," she said quietly. She scanned the pages quickly, not reading the foreign English symbols, seeming to search deliberately for nothing in particular.

"This American rules," she concluded at last. "Every time people come out from foreign country, must know rules. You not know, judge say, Too bad, go back. They not telling you why so you can use their way go forward. They say, Don't know why, you find out yourself. But they knowing all the time. Better you take it, find out why yourself." She tossed her head back with a satisfied smile.

I found out about all the whys later. I read the rules and looked up all the big words in a dictionary. I borrowed books from the Chinatown library. I studied each chess piece, trying to absorb the power each contained.

I learned about opening moves and why it's important to control the center early on; the shortest distance between two points is straight down the middle. I learned about the middle game and why tactics between two adversaries[2] are like clashing ideas; the one who plays better has the clearest plans for both attacking and getting out of traps. I learned why it is essential

---

[2]*adversaries:* opponents.

in the endgame to have foresight, a mathematical understanding of all possible moves, and patience; all weaknesses and advantages become evident to a strong adversary and are obscured to a tiring opponent. I discovered that for the whole game one must gather invisible strengths and see the endgame before the game begins.

I also found out why I should never reveal "why" to others. A little knowledge withheld is a great advantage one should store for future use. That is the power of chess. It is a game of secrets in which one must show and never tell.

I loved the secrets I found within the sixty-four black and white squares. I carefully drew a handmade chessboard and pinned it to the wall next to my bed, where at night I would stare for hours at imaginary battles. Soon I no longer lost any games or Life Savers, but I lost my adversaries. Winston and Vincent decided they were more interested in roaming the streets after school in their Hopalong Cassidy cowboy hats.

On a cold spring afternoon, while walking home from school, I detoured through the playground at the end of our alley. I saw a group of old men, two seated across a folding table playing a game of chess, others smoking pipes, eating peanuts, and watching. I ran home and grabbed Vincent's chess set, which was bound in a cardboard box with rubber bands. I also carefully selected two prized rolls of Life Savers. I came back to the park and approached a man who was observing the game.

"Want to play?" I asked him. His face widened with surprise and he grinned as he looked at the box under my arm.

"Little sister, been a long time since I play with dolls," he said, smiling benevolently. I quickly put the box down next to him on the bench and displayed my retort.

Lau Po, as he allowed me to call him, turned out to be a much better player than my brothers. I lost many games and many Life Savers. But over the weeks, with each diminishing roll of candies, I added new secrets. Lau Po gave me the names. The Double Attack from the East and West Shores. Throwing Stones on the Drowning Man. The Sudden Meeting of the Clan. The Surprise from the Sleeping Guard. The Humble Servant Who Kills the King. Sand in the Eyes of Advancing Forces. A Double Killing Without Blood.

There were also the fine points of chess etiquette. Keep captured men in neat rows, as well-tended prisoners. Never announce "Check" with vanity, lest someone with an unseen sword slit your throat. Never hurl pieces into the sandbox after you have lost a game, because then you must find them again, by yourself, after apologizing to all around you. By the end of the summer, Lau Po had taught me all he knew, and I had become a better chess player.

A small weekend crowd of Chinese people and tourists would gather as I played and defeated my opponents one by one. My mother would join the crowds during these outdoor exhibition games. She sat proudly on the bench, telling my admirers with proper Chinese humility, "Is luck."

A man who watched me play in the park suggested that my mother allow me to play in local chess tournaments. My mother smiled graciously, an answer that meant nothing. I desperately wanted to go, but I bit back my tongue. I knew she would not let me play among strangers. So as we walked home I said in a small voice that I didn't want to play in the local tournament. They would have American rules. If I lost, I would bring shame on my family.

"Is shame you fall down nobody push you," said my mother.

During my first tournament, my mother sat with me in the front row as I waited for my turn. I frequently bounced my legs to unstick them from the cold metal seat of the folding chair. When my name was called, I leapt up. My mother unwrapped something in her lap. It was her *chang,* a small tablet of red jade which held the sun's fire. "Is luck," she whispered, and tucked it into my dress pocket. I turned to my opponent, a fifteen-year-old boy from Oakland. He looked at me, wrinkling his nose.

As I began to play, the boy disappeared, the color ran out of the room, and I saw only my white pieces and his black ones waiting on the other side. A light wind began blowing past my ears. It whispered secrets only I could hear.

"Blow from the South," it murmured. "The wind leaves no trail." I saw a clear path, the traps to avoid. The crowd rustled. "Shhh! Shh!" said the corners of the room. The wind blew stronger. "Throw sand from the East to distract him." The knight came forward ready for the sacrifice. The wind hissed, louder and louder. "Blow, blow, blow. He cannot see. He is blind now. Make him lean away from the wind so he is easier to knock down."

"Check," I said, as the wind roared with laughter. The wind died down to little puffs, my own breath.

My mother placed my first trophy next to a new plastic chess set that the neighborhood Tao society had given to me. As she wiped each piece with a soft cloth, she said, "Next time win more, lose less."

"Ma, it's not how many pieces you lose," I said. "Sometimes you need to lose pieces to get ahead."

"Better to lose less, see if you really need."

At the next tournament, I won again, but it was my mother who wore the triumphant grin.

"Lost eight piece this time. Last time was eleven. What I tell you? Better off lose less!" I was annoyed, but I couldn't say anything.

I attended more tournaments, each one farther away from home. I won all games, in all divisions. The Chinese bakery downstairs from our flat displayed my growing collection of trophies in its window, amidst the dust-covered cakes that were never picked up. The day after I won an important regional tournament, the window encased a fresh sheet cake with whipped-cream frosting and red script saying, "Congratulations, Waverly Jong, Chinatown Chess Champion." Soon after that, a flower shop, headstone engraver, and funeral parlor offered to sponsor me in national tournaments. That's when my mother decided I no longer had to do the dishes. Winston and Vincent had to do my chores.

"Why does she get to play and we do all the work," complained Vincent.

"Is new American rules," said my mother. "Meimei play, squeeze all her brains out for win chess. You play, worth squeeze towel."

By my ninth birthday, I was a national chess champion. I was still some 429 points away from grand-master status, but I was touted as the Great American Hope, a child prodigy and a girl to boot. They ran a photo of me in *Life* magazine next to a quote in which Bobby Fischer said, "There will never be a woman grand master." "Your move, Bobby," said the caption.

The day they took the magazine picture I wore neatly plaited braids clipped with plastic barrettes trimmed with rhinestones. I was playing in a large high school auditorium that echoed with phlegmy coughs and the squeaky rubber knobs of chair legs sliding across freshly waxed wooden floors. Seated across from me was an American man, about the same age as Lau Po, maybe fifty. I remember that his sweaty brow seemed to weep at my every move. He wore a dark, malodorous suit. One of his pockets was stuffed with a great white kerchief on which he wiped his palm before sweeping his hand over the chosen chess piece with great flourish.

In my crisp pink-and-white dress with scratchy lace at the neck, one of two my mother had sewn for these special occasions, I would clasp my hands under my chin, the delicate points of my elbows poised lightly on the table in the manner my mother had shown me for posing for the press. I would swing my patent leather shoes back and forth like an impatient child riding on a school bus. Then I would pause, suck in my lips, twirl my chosen piece in midair as if undecided, and then firmly plant it in its new threatening place, with a triumphant smile thrown back at my opponent for good measure.

I no longer played in the alley of Waverly Place. I never visited the playground where the pigeons and old men gathered. I went to school, then directly home to learn new chess secrets, cleverly concealed advantages, more escape routes.

But I found it difficult to concentrate at home. My mother had a habit of standing over me while I plotted out my games. I think she thought of herself as my protective ally. Her lips would be sealed tight, and after each move I made, a soft "Hmmmmph" would escape from her nose.

"Ma, I can't practice when you stand there like that," I said one day. She retreated to the kitchen and made loud noises with the pots and pans. When the crashing stopped, I could see out of the corner of my eye that she was standing in the doorway. "Hmmmph!" Only this one came out of her tight throat.

My parents made many concessions to allow me to practice. One time I complained that the bedroom I shared was so noisy that I couldn't think. Thereafter, my brothers slept in a bed in the living room facing the street. I said I couldn't finish my rice; my head didn't work right when my stomach was too full. I left the table with half-finished bowls and nobody complained. But there was one duty I couldn't avoid. I had to accompany my mother on Saturday market days when I had no tournament to play. My mother would proudly walk with me, visiting many shops, buying very little. "This my daugher Wave-ly Jong," she said to whoever looked her way.

One day, after we left a shop I said under my breath, "I wish you wouldn't do that, telling everybody I'm your daughter." My mother stopped walking. Crowds of people with heavy bags pushed past us on the sidewalk, bumping into first one shoulder, then another.

"Aiii-ya. So shame be with mother?" She grasped my hand even tighter as she glared at me.

I looked down. "It's not that, it's just so obvious. It's just so embarrassing."

"Embarrass you be my daughter?" Her voice was cracking with anger.

"That's not what I meant. That's not what I said."

"What you say?"

I knew it was a mistake to say anything more, but I heard my voice speaking. "Why do you have to use me to show off? If you want to show off, then why don't you learn to play chess."

My mother's eyes turned into dangerous black slits. She had no words for me, just sharp silence.

I felt the wind rushing around my hot ears. I jerked my hand out of my mother's tight grasp and spun around, knocking into an old woman. Her bag of groceries spilled to the ground.

"Aii-ya! Stupid girl!" my mother and the woman cried. Oranges and tin cans careened down the sidewalk. As my mother stopped to help the old woman pick up the escaping food, I took off.

I raced down the street, dashing between people, not looking back as my mother screamed shrilly, "Meimei! Meimei!" I fled down an alley, past dark curtained shops and merchants washing the grime off their windows. I sped into the sunlight, into a large street crowded with tourists examining trinkets and souvenirs. I ducked into another dark alley, down another street, up another alley. I ran until it hurt and I realized I had nowhere to go, that I was not running from anything. The alleys contained no escape routes.

My breath came out like angry smoke. It was cold. I sat down on an upturned plastic pail next to a stack of empty boxes, cupping my chin with my hands, thinking hard. I imagined my mother, first walking briskly down one street or another looking for me, then giving up and returning home to await my arrival. After two hours, I stood up on creaking legs and slowly walked home.

The alley was quiet and I could see the yellow lights shining from our flat like two tiger's eyes in the night. I climbed the sixteen steps to the door, advancing quietly up each so as not to make any warning sounds. I turned the knob; the door was locked. I heard a chair moving, quick steps, the locks turning—click! click! click!—and then the door opened.

"About time you got home," said Vincent. "Boy, are you in trouble."

He slid back to the dinner table. On a platter were the remains of a large fish, its fleshy head still connected to bones swimming upstream in vain escape. Standing there waiting for my punishment, I heard my mother speak in a dry voice.

"We not concerning this girl. This girl not have concerning for us."

Nobody looked at me. Bone chopsticks clinked against the insides of bowls being emptied into hungry mouths.

I walked into my room, closed the door, and lay down on my bed. The room was dark, the ceiling filled with shadows from the dinnertime lights of neighboring flats.

In my head, I saw a chessboard with sixty-four black and white squares. Opposite me was my opponent, two angry black slits. She wore a triumphant smile. "Strongest wind cannot be seen," she said.

Her black men advanced across the plane, slowly marching to each successive level as a single unit. My white pieces screamed as they scurried and fell off the board one by one. As her men drew closer to my edge, I felt myself growing light. I rose up into the air and flew out the window. Higher and higher, above the alley, over the tops of tiled roofs, where I was gathered up by the wind and pushed up toward the night sky until everything below me disappeared and I was alone.

I closed my eyes and pondered my next move.

Talking It Through

1. What elements of life in China are carried over in San Francisco's Chinatown? In what ways does Waverly's neighborhood define who she is?

2. How does Waverly's mother teach her that "the strongest wind cannot be seen" (or, "the art of invisible strength")? How does she teach Waverly to "bite back her tongue"? When does Waverly apply the rules, and what are the consequences? Does she *always* apply them; does her mother?

3. What does the discussion of "Chinese torture" reveal about Waverly's mother? What is Waverly's motive in bringing up the subject?

4. Mrs. Jong looks at the book that came with the chess set and says, "This American rules. Every time people come out from foreign country, must know rules." What does she mean by this and her follow-up comments? In your opinion, what are the "American rules"? Give some examples, if possible, either from your own experience as an immigrant or from those of someone you know who is.

5. When Waverly improves her chess game by playing with Lau Po, what do the names of the moves reveal? Take one of the names and translate it into your own words. How important are traditions from the past in our day-to-day lives?

6. In your opinion, is Mrs. Jong too pushy and proud by the end of the story? Is Waverly right to rebuke her mother, or just plain ungrateful? When, if ever, is a parent justified in taking credit for a child's accomplishments? If you were Waverly, what would your next move be?

7. How does Amy Tan relate the end of the story to the opening lines? What symbols does she use to enhance the theme?

Writer's Workshop

1. Amy Tan uses descriptions of the Jong's neighborhood to give a sense of foreignness within the American locale. Is there a section or a place within your community that could be described to give a similar exotic flavor? Tan also uses Mrs. Jong's not-quite-colloquial English to develop the contrast between first and second generation Americans. This requires careful attention to the order of words in sentences and a keen ear and memory.

   Describe a locale you know well that gives you a sense of another

culture. Include details of the sounds, sights, and aromas of the neighborhood and use dialogue to bring it to life.

2. When Waverly Jong enters the world of competitive chess, her mental
   attitude plays a large part in her achievements. Have you ever felt the
   pressure of competition? (It might be a sports event, a performance or
   recital, an academic test, or an instance of sibling rivalry.) Have you ever
   been coached to perform in public? Describe your feelings at the time, and
   the outcome of events.

3. An important theme in "Rules of the Game" is pride. Mrs. Jong teaches
   Waverly to be proud of her Chinese heritage and the community takes
   pride in Waverly's accomplishments. Yet Mrs. Jong also believes in
   "proper Chinese humility" and tells a crowd watching Waverly play that
   her success is due to luck.

   Write a well-organized essay in which you discuss the theme of pride
   in this story. When does pride pay off? When, if ever, do the characters
   become too proud? Use specific examples from the story to support your
   thesis.

★ *from* **I Remember Mama** ★

J O H N   V A N   D R U T E N

"I Remember Mama" is about a family living in San Francisco in 1910.
Katrin, the eldest daughter, is both the narrator of the play, and a character in it.
As it opens she reads from her memoirs of her family: "Papa and Mama had
both been born in Norway, but they came to San Francisco because Mama's sisters
were here. All of us were born here. Nels, the oldest and the only boy—my sister
Christine—and the littlest sister, Dagmar." As she describes scenes, she steps
back in time and onto the stage to play her younger self.

John Van Druten wrote the play in 1944, based on the stories of Kathryn
Forbes, and it has since become a classic of the American stage.

From Act II

SCENE: *Opening,* KATRIN *at her desk.*

KATRIN (*reading*): "It wasn't very often that I could get Mama to talk—about herself, or her life in the old country or what she felt about things. You had to catch her unawares, or when she had nothing to do, which was very, very seldom. I don't think I can ever remember seeing Mama unoccupied." (*Laying down the manuscript and looking out front.*) I do remember one occasion, though. It was the day before Dagmar came home from the hospital. And as we left, Mama suggested treating me to an ice cream soda. (*She rises, gets her hat from beside her—a schoolgirl hat—puts it on and crosses while she speaks the next lines.*) She had never done such a thing before and I remember how proud it made me feel—just to sit and talk to her quietly like a grown-up person. It was a kind of special *treat*—a moment in my life that I'll always remember—quite apart from the soda, which was *wonderful.* (MAMA *has come from between the curtains, and starts down the steps.*)

MAMA: Katrin, you like we go next door, and I treat you to an ice-cream soda?

KATRIN (*young now, and overcome*): Mama—do you mean it?

MAMA: Sure. We celebrate. We celebrate that Dagmar is well, and coming home again. (*They cross to the turntable, which represents a drugstore, with a table and two chairs at which they seat themselves.* MAMA *is at the left of table.*) What you like to have, Katrin?

KATRIN (*with desperate earnestness*): I think a chocolate . . . no, a strawberry . . . no, a chocolate soda.

MAMA (*smiling*): You are sure?

KATRIN (*gravely*): I think so. But, Mama, can we *afford* it?

MAMA: I think this once we can afford it.

(*The* SODA CLERK *appears.*)

SODA CLERK: What's it going to be, ladies?

MAMA: A chocolate ice-cream soda, please—and a cup of coffee.

(*The* SODA CLERK *goes.*)

KATRIN: Mama, he called us "ladies"! (MAMA *smiles.*) Why aren't you having a soda, too?

MAMA: Better I like coffee.

Katrin: When can I drink coffee?

Mama: When you are grown up.

Katrin: When I'm eighteen?

Mama: Maybe before that.

Katrin: When I graduate?

Mama: Maybe. I don't know. Comes the day you are grown up, Papa and I will know.

Katrin: Is coffee really nicer than a soda?

Mama: When you are grown up, it is.

Katrin: Did you used to like sodas better . . . before you were grown up?

Mama: We didn't have sodas before I was grown up. It was in the old country.

Katrin (incredulous): You mean they don't have sodas in Norway?

Mama: Now, maybe. Now I think they have many things from America. But not when I was little girl.

(The Soda Clerk brings the soda and the coffee.)

Soda Clerk: There you are, folks. (He sets them down and departs.)

Katrin (after a good pull at the soda): Mama, do you ever want to go back to the old country?

Mama: I like to go back once to look, maybe. To see the mountains and the fjords.[1] I like to show them once to you all. When Dagmar is big, maybe we all go back once . . . one summer . . . like tourists. But that is how it would be. I would be tourist there now. There is no one I would know any more. And maybe we see the little house where Papa and I live when we first marry. And . . . (her eyes grow misty and reminiscent) something else I would look at.

Katrin: What is that? (Mama does not answer.) What would you look at, Mama?

Mama: Katrin, you do not know you have brother? Besides Nels?

Katrin: No! A brother? In Norway? Mama . . .

Mama: He is my first baby. I am eighteen when he is born.

---

[1]fjords: Norway's beautiful sea inlets, bordered by steep cliffs.

Katrin: Is he there now?

Mama (*simply*): He is dead.

Katrin (*disappointed*): Oh, I thought you meant . . . I thought you meant a real brother. A long-lost one, like in stories. When did he die?

Mama: When he is two years old. It is his grave I would like to see again. (*She is suddenly near tears, biting her lip and stirring her coffee violently, spilling some. She gets her handkerchief from her pocketbook, dabs at her skirt, then briefly at her nose, then she returns the handkerchief and turns to* Katrin *again. Matter-of-factly.*) Is good, your ice-cream soda?

Katrin (*more interested now in* Mama *than in it*): Yes. Mama . . . have you had a very hard life?

Mama (*surprised*): Hard? No. No life is easy all the time. It is not meant to be. (*She pours the spilled coffee back from the saucer into her cup.*)

Katrin: But . . . rich people . . . aren't *their* lives easy?

Mama: I don't know, Katrin. I have never known rich people. But I see them sometimes in stores and in the streets, and they do not *look* as if they were easy.

Katrin: Wouldn't you like to be rich?

Mama: I would like to be rich the way I would like to be ten feet high. Would be good for some things—bad for others.

Katrin: But didn't you come to American to *get* rich?

Mama (*shocked*): No. We come to America because they are all here—all the others. Is good for families to be together.

Katrin: And did you like it right away?

Mama: Right away. When we get off the ferry boat and I see San Francisco and all the family, I say: "Is like Norway," only it is better than Norway. And then you are all born here, and I become American citizen. But not to get rich.

Katrin: I want to be rich. Rich and famous. I'd buy you your warm coat. When are you going to get that coat, Mama?

Mama: Soon now, maybe—when we pay doctor, and Mr. Hyde pay his rent. I think now I *must* ask him. I ask him tomorrow, after Dagmar comes home.

Katrin: When I'm rich and famous, I'll buy you lovely clothes. White satin gowns with long trains to them. And jewelry. I'll buy you a pearl necklace.

MAMA: We talk too much! (*She signs to the* SODA CLERK.) Come, finish your soda. We must go home. (*The* SODA CLERK *comes.*) How much it is, please?

SODA CLERK: Fifteen cents.

MAMA: Here are two dimes. You keep the nickel. And thank you. Was good coffee. (*They start out and up the steps toward the curtains.*)

(PAPA *puts down the morning paper he is reading and takes the evening one from* NELS.)

PAPA (*at table*): Is there any news?

NELS: No. (*He takes out a package of cigarettes with elaborate unconcern.* MAMA *watches with disapproval. Then, as he is about to light his cigarette, he stops, remembering something.*) Oh, I forgot. There's a letter for Katrin. I picked it up on the mat as I came in. (*Going to back door and calling.*) Katrin! Katrin! There's a letter for you.

KATRIN (*answering from off stage*): Coming!

MAMA (*at table*): Nels, you know who the letter is from?

NELS: Why, no, Mama. (*Hands it to her.*) It looks like her own handwriting.

MAMA (*gravely inspecting it*): Is bad.

PAPA: Why is bad?

MAMA: She get too many like that. I think they are stories she send to the magazines.

DAGMAR (*closing her book loudly, rising*): Well, I'll go and see if I have any puppies yet. (*Crosses below the table and then turns.*). Mama, I've just decided something.

MAMA: What have you decided?

DAGMAR: If Nels is going to be a doctor, when I grow up, I'm going to be a—(*looking at the book title, and stumbling over the word*)—vet-vet-veterinarian.

MAMA: And what is that?

DAGMAR: A doctor for animals.

MAMA: Is good. Is good.

DAGMAR: There are far more animals in the world than there are human beings, and far more human doctors than animal ones. It isn't fair. (*She goes to the pantry door.*) I suppose we couldn't have a horse, could we? (*This only produces a concerted laugh from the family. She turns, sadly.*) No. . . . I was afraid we couldn't. (*She goes into the pantry.*)

(KATRIN *comes in. She wears a slightly more adult dress than before. Her hair is up and she looks about eighteen.*)

KATRIN: Where's the letter?

MAMA (*handing it to her*): Here.

(KATRIN *takes it, nervously. She looks at the envelope, and her face falls. She opens it, pulls out a manuscript and a rejection slip, looks at it a moment, and then replaces both in the envelope. The others watch her covertly.*[2] *Then she looks up, with determination.*)

KATRIN (*above table*): Mama . . . Papa . . . I want to say something.

PAPA: What is it?

KATRIN: I'm not going to go to college.

PAPA: Why not?

KATRIN: Because it would be a waste of time and money. The only point in my going to college was to be a writer. Well, I'm not going to be one, so . . .

MAMA: Katrin, is it your letter that makes you say this? It is a story come back again?

KATRIN: Again is right. This is the tenth time. I made this one a test. It's the best I've ever written or ever shall write. I know that. Well, it's no good.

NELS: What kind of a story is it?

KATRIN: Oh . . . it's a story about a painter, who's a genius, and he goes blind.

NELS: Sounds like *The Light That Failed.*

KATRIN: Well, what's wrong with that?

NELS (*quickly*): Nothing. Nothing!

KATRIN (*moving down*): Besides, it's not like that. My painter gets better. He has an operation and recovers his sight, and paints better than ever before.

MAMA: Is good.

---

[2]*covertly:* secretly.

Katrin (*bitterly unhappy*): No, it isn't. It's rotten. But it's the best I can do.

Mama: You have asked your teachers about this?

Katrin: Teachers don't know anything about writing. They just know about literature.

Mama: If there was someone we could ask . . . for advice . . . to tell us . . . tell us if your stories are good.

Katrin: Yes. Well, there isn't. And they're *not*.

Papa (*looking at the evening paper*): There is something here in the paper about a lady writer. I just noticed the headline. Wait. (*He looks back for it and reads.*) "Woman writer tells key to literary success."

Katrin: Who?

Papa: A lady called Florence Dana Moorhead. It gives her picture. A fat lady. You have heard of her?

Katrin: Yes, of course. Everyone has. She's terribly successful. She's here on a lecture tour.

Mama: What does she say is the secret?

Papa: You read it, Katrin. (*He hands her the paper.*)

Katrin (*grabbing the first part*): "Florence Dana Moorhead, celebrated novelist and short story writer . . . blah-blah-blah . . . interviewed today in her suite at the Fairmont . . . blah-blah-blah . . . pronounced sincerity the essential quality for success as a writer." (*Throwing aside the paper.*) A lot of help that is.

Mama: Katrin, this lady . . . maybe if you sent her your stories, *she* could tell you what is wrong with them?

Katrin (*wearily*): Oh, Mama, don't be silly.

Mama: Why is silly?

Katrin (*behind table*): Well, in the first place because she's a very important person . . . a celebrity . . . and she'd never read them. And in the second, because . . . you seem to think writing's like . . . well, like cooking, or something. That all you have to have is the recipe. It takes a lot more than that. You have to have a gift for it.

Mama: You have to have a gift for cooking, too. But there are things you can learn, if you have the gift.

Katrin: Well, that's the whole point. I haven't. I *know* . . . now, So, if you've finished with the morning paper, Papa, I'll take the want ad section, and see if I can find myself a job. (*She takes the morning paper and goes out.*)

MAMA: Is bad. Nels, what you think?

NELS: I don't know, Mama. Her stories seem all right to me, but I don't know.

MAMA: It would be good to know. Nels, this lady in the paper . . . what else does she say?

NELS (*taking up the paper*): Not much. The rest seems to be about *her* and her home. Let's see. . . . (*He reads—walking down.*) "Apart from literature, Mrs. Moorhead's main interest in life is gastronomy."[3]

MAMA: The stars?

NELS: No—eating. "A brilliant cook herself, she says that she would as soon turn out a good soufflé as a short story, or find a new recipe as she would a first edition."

MAMA (*reaching for the paper*): I see her picture? (*She looks at it.*) Is kind face. (*Pause while she reads a moment. Then she looks up and asks.*) What is first edition?

(*Blackout. Lights up on turntable, representing the lobby of the Fairmont Hotel. A couch against a column with a palm behind it. An orchestra plays softly in the background.* MAMA *is discovered seated on the couch, waiting patiently. She wears a hat and a suit, and clutches a newspaper and bundle of manuscripts. A couple of guests come through the curtains and cross, disappearing into the wings.* MAMA *watches them. Then* FLORENCE DANA MOORHEAD *enters through the curtains. She is a stout, dressy, good-natured, middle-aged woman. A* BELLBOY *comes from the right, paging her.*)

BELLBOY: Miss Moorhead?

F. D. MOORHEAD: Yes?

BELLBOY: Telegram.

F. D. MOORHEAD: Oh, . . . Thank you, (*She tips him, and he goes.* MAMA *rises and moves toward her.*)

MAMA: Please . . . Please . . . Miss Moorhead . . . Miss Moorhead.

F. D. MOORHEAD (*looking up from her telegram, on the steps*): Were you calling me?

MAMA: Yes. You are . . . Miss Florence Dana Moorhead?

[3]*gastronomy:* the art or science of good eating.

F. D. Moorhead: Yes.

Mama: Please . . . might I speak to you for a moment?

F. D. Moorhead: Yes—what's it about?

Mama: I read in the paper what you say about writing.

F. D. Moorhead (*with a vague social smile*): Oh, yes?

Mama: My daughter, Katrin, wants to be writer.

F. D. Moorhead (*who has heard that one before*): Oh, really? (*She glances at her watch on her bosom.*)

Mama: I bring her stories.

F. D. Moorhead: Look, I'm afraid I'm in rather a hurry. I'm leaving San Francisco this evening . . .

Mama: I wait two hours here for you to come in. Please, if I may talk to you for one, two minutes. That is all.

F. D. Moorhead (*kindly*): Of course, but I think I'd better tell you that if you want me to read your daughter's stories, it's no use. I'm very sorry, but I've had to make a rule never to read anyone's unpublished material.

Mama (*nods—then after a pause*): It said in the paper you like to collect recipes . . . for eating.

F. D. Moorhead: Yes, I do. I've written several books on cooking.

Mama: I, too, am interested in gastronomy. I am good cook. Norwegian. I make good Norwegian dishes. Lutefisk. And Kjötboller. That is meat balls with cream sauce.

F. D. Moorhead: Yes, I know. I've eaten them in Christiania.

Mama: I have a special recipe for Kjötboller . . . my mother give me. She was best cook I ever knew. Never have I told this recipe, not even to my own sisters, because they are not good cooks.

F. D. Moorhead (*amused*): Oh?

Mama: But . . . if you let me talk to you . . . I give it to you. I promise it is good recipe.

F. D. Moorhead (*vastly tickled now*): Well that seems fair enough. Let's sit down. (*They move to the couch and sit.*) Now, your daughter wants to write, you say? How old is she?

Mama: She is eighteen. Just.

F. D. Moorhead: *Does* she write, or does she just . . . *want* to write?

Mama: Oh, she write all the time. Maybe she should not be author, but it is hard to give up something that has meant so much.

F. D. Moorhead: I agree, but . . .

Mama: I bring her stories. I bring twelve.

F. D. Moorhead (*aghast*): Twelve!

Mama: But if you could read maybe just one . . . To know if someone is good cook, you do not need to eat a whole dinner.

F. D. Moorhead: You're very persuasive. How is it your daughter did not come herself?

Mama: She was too unhappy. And too scared . . . of you. Because you are celebrity. But I see your picture in the paper. . .

F. D. Moorhead: That frightful picture!

Mama: Is the picture of woman who like to eat good. . . .

F. D. Moorhead (*with a rueful smile*): It certainly is. Now, tell me about the Kjötboller.

Mama: When you make the meat balls you drop them in boiling stock. Not water. That is one of the secrets.

F. D. Moorhead: Ah!

Mama: And the cream sauce. That is another secret. It is half *sour* cream, added at the last.

F. D. Moorhead: That sounds marvelous.

Mama: You must grind the meat six times. I could write it out for you. And . . . (*tentatively*) while I write, you could read?

F. D. Moorhead (*with a laugh*): All right. You win. Come upstairs to my apartment. (*She rises.*)

Mama: Is kind of you. (*They start out.*) Maybe if you would read *two* stories, I could write the recipe for Lutefisk as well. You know Lutefisk . . . ?

(*They have disappeared into the wings, and the turntable revolves out.* Katrin *is at her desk.*)

Katrin: When Mama came back, I was sitting with my diary, which I called my Journal now, writing a Tragic Farewell to my Art. It was very seldom that Mama came to the attic, thinking that a writer needed privacy, and I was surprised to see her standing in the doorway. (*She looks up.* Mama *is standing on the steps.*) Mama!

Mama: You are busy, Katrin?

Katrin (*jumping up*): No, of course not. Come in.

Mama (*coming down*): I like to talk to you.

Katrin: Yes, of course.

Mama (*seating herself at the desk*): You are writing?

Katrin (*on the steps*): No. I told you, that's all over.

Mama: That is what I want to talk to you about.

Katrin: It's all right, Mama. Really, it's all right. I was planning to tear up all my stories this afternoon, only I couldn't find half of them.

Mama: They are here.

Katrin: Did *you* take them? What for?

Mama: Katrin, I have been to see Miss Moorhead.

Katrin: Who's Miss . . . ? You don't mean Florence Dana Moorhead? (Mama *nods.*) You don't mean . . . (*She comes down to her.*) Mama, you don't mean you took her my stories?

Mama: She read five of them. I was two hours with her. We have glass of sherry. Two glass of sherry.

Katrin: What . . . did she say about them?

Mama (*quietly*): She say they are not good.

Katrin (*turning away*): Well, I knew that. It was hardly worth your going to all that trouble just to be told that.

Mama: She say more. Will you listen, Katrin?

Katrin (*trying to be gracious*): Sure. Sure. I'll listen.

Mama: I will try and remember. She say you write now only because of what you have read in other books, and that no one can write good until they have felt what they write about. That for years she write bad stories about people in the olden times, until one day she remember something that happen in her own town . . . something that only she could know and understand . . . and she feels she must tell it . . . and that is how she write her first good story. She say you must write more of things you know.

Katrin: That's what my teacher always told me at school.

MAMA: Maybe your teacher was right. I do not know if I explain good what Miss Moorhead means, but while she talks I think I understand. Your story about the painter who is blind . . . that is because . . . forgive me if I speak plain, my Katrin, but it is important to you . . . because you are the dramatic one, as Papa has said . . . and you think it would feel good to be a painter and be blind and not complain. But never have you imagined how it would really be. Is true?

KATRIN (*subdued*): Yes, I . . . guess it's true.

MAMA: But she say you are to go on writing. That you have the gift. (KATRIN *turns back to her, suddenly aglow.*) And that when you have written story that is real and true . . . then you send it to someone whose name she give me. (*She fumbles for a piece of paper.*) It is her . . . agent . . . and say she recommend you. Here. No, that is recipe she give me for goulash as her grandmother make it . . . here . . . (*She hands over the paper.*) It helps, Katrin, what I have told you?

KATRIN (*subdued again*): Yes, I . . . I guess it helps. Some. But what have *I* got to write about? I haven't seen anything, or been anywhere.

MAMA: Could you write about San Francisco, maybe? Is fine city. Miss Moorhead write about her home town.

KATRIN: Yes, I know. But you've got to have a central character or something. She writes about her grandfather . . . he was a wonderful old man.

MAMA: Could you maybe write about Papa?

KATRIN: Papa?

MAMA: Papa is fine man. Is wonderful man.

KATRIN: Yes, I know, but . . .

MAMA (*rising*): I must go fix supper. Is late. Papa will be home. (*She goes up the steps to the curtains, and then turns back.*) I like you should write about Papa. (*She goes inside.*)

KATRIN (*going back to her seat behind the desk*): Papa. Yes, but what's he ever done? What's ever happened to him? What's ever happened to *any* of us? Except always being poor and having illness, like the time when Dagmar went to hospital and Mama . . . (*The idea hits her like a flash.*) Oh . . . . Oh . . . . (*Pause—then she becomes the* KATRIN *of today.*) And that was how it was born . . . suddenly in a flash . . . the story of "Mama and the Hospital" . . . the first of all the stories. I wrote it . . . oh, quite soon after that. I didn't tell Mama or any of them. But I sent it to Miss Moorhead's agent. It was a long time before I heard anything . . . and then one evening the letter came. (*She takes an envelope from the desk in front of her.*) For a moment I couldn't believe it. Then I went rushing into the kitchen, shouting . . . (*She rises from the desk, taking some papers with her, and rushes upstage, crying, "Mama, Mama." The curtains have parted on the kitchen—and the family tableau—* MAMA, PAPA, CHRISTINE, *and* NELS. DAGMAR *is not present.* KATRIN *comes rushing in, up the steps. The turntable revolves out as soon as she has left it.*) Mama . . . Mama . . . I've sold a story!

MAMA (*at table*): A story?

KATRIN: Yes, I got a letter from the agent . . . with a check for . . . (*gasping*) five hundred dollars!

NELS (*on the chest*): No kidding? (*He rises.*)

MAMA: Katrin . . . is true?

KATRIN: Here it is. Here's the letter. Maybe I haven't read it right. (*She hands the letter.* PAPA *and* MAMA *huddle and gloat over it.*)

CHRISTINE (*behind Mama's chair*): What will you *do* with five hundred dollars?

KATRIN: I don't know. I'll buy Mama her warm coat, I know that.

CHRISTINE: Coats don't cost five hundred dollars.

KATRIN: I know. We'll put the rest in the Bank.

NELS (*kidding*): Quick. Before they change their mind, and stop the check.

KATRIN: Will you, Mama? Will you take it to the Bank downtown tomorrow? (MAMA *looks vague.*). What is it?

MAMA: I do not know how.

NELS: Just give it to the man and tell him to put it in your account, like you always do.

(MAMA *looks up at* PAPA.)

PAPA: You tell them . . . now.

CHRISTINE: Tell us what?

MAMA (*desperately*): Is no bank account! (*She rises, feeling hemmed in by them— sits on bench.*) Never in my life have I been inside a bank.

CHRISTINE: But you always told us . . .

KATRIN: Mama, you've always said . . .

MAMA: I know. But was not true. I tell a lie.

KATRIN: But why, Mama? Why did you pretend?

MAMA: Is not good for little ones to be afraid . . . to not feel secure. (*Rising again.*) But now . . . with five hundred dollar . . . I think I can tell.

KATRIN (*going to her, emotionally*): Mama!

MAMA (*stopping her, quickly*): You read us the story. You have it there?

KATRIN: Yes.

MAMA: Then read.

KATRIN: Now?

MAMA: Yes. No—wait. Dagmar must hear. (*She opens pantry door and calls.*) Dagmar.

DAGMAR (*off*): Yes, Mama?

MAMA (*calling*): Come here, I want you.

DAGMAR (*off*): What is it?

MAMA: I want you. No, you leave the rabbits! (*She comes back.*) What is it called . . . the story?

KATRIN (*seating herself in the chair that* MR. HYDE *took in the opening scene.*) It's called "Mama and the Hospital."

PAPA (*delighted*): You write about Mama?

KATRIN: Yes.

MAMA: But I thought . . . I thought you say . . . I tell you . . . (*She gestures at* PAPA, *behind his back.*).

KATRIN: I know, Mama, but . . . well, that's how it came out.

(DAGMAR *comes in.*)

DAGMAR: What is it? What do you want?

MAMA: Katrin write story for magazine. They pay her five hundred dollar to print it.

DAGMAR (*completely uninterested*): Oh. (*She starts back for the pantry.*)

MAMA (*stopping her*): She read it to us. I want you should listen. (DAGMAR *sits on the floor* at MAMA's *feet.*) You are ready, Katrin?

KATRIN: Sure.

MAMA: Then read.

KATRIN (*reading*): "For as long as I could remember, the house on Steiner Street had been home. All of us were born there. Nels, the oldest and the only boy . . ." (NELS *looks up, astonished to be in a story.*) "my sister, Christine . . ." (CHRISTINE *does likewise*) "and the littlest sister, Dagmar. . . ."

DAGMAR: Am I in the story?

MAMA: Hush, Dagmar. We are all in the story.

KATRIN: "But first and foremost, I remember MAMA." (*The lights begin to dim and the curtain slowly to fall. As it descends, we hear her voice continuing.*) "I remember that every Saturday night Mama would sit down by the kitchen table and count out the money Papa had brought home in the little envelope . . ."

(*By now, the curtain is down.*)

★ ★ ★ ★ ★

Talking It Through

1. "I Remember Mama" is largely a character study of Mama as seen through Katrin's loving and appreciative eyes. What do we learn about Mama from the scene in the soda fountain? What are her values? How does the playwright express them both through action and dialogue?

2. Like the son in "My Father Sits in the Dark" Katrin rarely hears her mother speak of the old country, and we feel it is part of Katrin's "treat" to hear her mother do so. How does Mama feel about Norway now? How do we know that an important part of her is still there, even though she claims, "I would be like a tourist now"?

3. What is Katrin's dream? Are her values the same as her mother's or different?

4. What is Mama's reaction when Katrin's tenth story is rejected by a publisher? How might other parents react in the situation? What does this say about Mama's character?

5. What information from the newspaper does Mama use to devise her plan to meet Florence Dana Moorhead? How does she use the old country to help her daughter realize her dreams in the new?

6. Reread the dialogue between Mama and the writer, and what Mama has to say about the visit when she returns. What strategies did Mama use to cajole Moorhead into reading Katrin's work? How successful has she been? Explain.

7. What advice does Florence Dana Moorhead have to give about writing? Why do you think Katrin ignored the same advice from her teacher? How does Katrin come to understand what it means and use it in her writing? What is the outcome?

Writer's Workshop

1. Take F. D. Moorhead's advice, and write about what you know best. When Katrin first considers writing about her family, she thinks, "What's ever happened to *any* of us?" Yet she comes to realize her own experience is her best material.

   Write a dialogue in play form about an incident that you feel illuminates important qualities about a friend or family member you admire. Who are your other characters? How will you convey the situation and setting through the dialogue? What is the conflict or difficulty being confronted? (It could be serious or humorous.) How is it resolved, and what does it reflect about your main character?

2. Write a character study of Mama, based on the scenes you have read or on a more complete reading of the play. What adjectives would you use to describe her? Is she generous or stingy? Does she love her husband or merely tolerate him? Is she supportive or pushy, happy with her life or disgruntled? For each quality you find in her, give evidence from the play to support your view.

3. "I Remember Mama" and "Rules of the Game" are about immigrant mothers as seen through the eyes of their daughters. Both mothers successfully use their old culture to help their daughters "get ahead" in America. Write an essay in which you compare Mrs. Jong and Mama. Which one has been the more successful parent, in your opinion?

In the ★ *American* ★ *Society*

G I S H   J E N

Gish Jen, who lives in Cambridge, Massachusetts, has written many short stories that have appeared in magazines and which have been widely anthologized. Her latest book is called Typical American *and was published in 1991.*

I. His Own Society

When my father took over the pancake house, it was to send my little sister Mona and me to college. We were only in junior high at the time, but my father believed in getting a jump on things. "Those Americans always saying it," he told us. "Smart guys thinking in advance." My mother elaborated, explaining that businesses took bringing up, like children. They could take years to get going, she said, years.

In this case, though, we got rich right away. At two months we were breaking even, and at four, those same hotcakes that could barely withstand the weight of butter and syrup were supporting our family with ease. My mother bought a station wagon with air conditioning, my father an oversized, red vinyl recliner for the back room; and as time went on and the business continued to thrive, my father started to talk about his grandfather and the village he had reigned over in China—things my father had never talked about when he worked for other people. He told us about the bags of rice his family would give out to the poor at New Year's, and about the people who came to beg, on their hands and knees, for his grandfather to intercede for the more wayward of their relatives. "Like that Godfather in the movie," he would tell us as, his feet up, he distributed paychecks. Sometimes an employee would get two green envelopes instead of one, which meant that Jimmy needed a tooth pulled, say, or that Tiffany's husband was in the clinker again.

"It's nothing, nothing," he would insist, sinking back into his chair. "Who else is going to take care of you people?"

My mother would mostly just sigh about it. "Your father thinks this is China," she would say, and then she would go back to her mending. Once in a while, though, when my father had given away a particularly large sum, she would exclaim, outraged, "But this here is the U—S—of—A!"— this apparently having been what she used to tell immigrant stock boys when they came in late.

She didn't work at the supermarket anymore; but she had made it to the rank of manager before she left, and this had given her not only new words and phrases, but new ideas about herself, and about America, and about what was what in general. She had opinions, now, on how downtown should be zoned; she could pump her own gas and check her own oil; and for all she used to chide Mona and me for being "copycats," she herself was now interested in espadrilles, and wallpaper, and most recently, the town country club.

"So join already," said Mona, flicking a fly off her knee.

My mother enumerated the problems as she sliced up a quarter round of watermelon: There was the cost. There was the waiting list. There was the fact that no one in our family played either tennis or golf.

"So what?" said Mona.

"It would be waste," said my mother.

"Me and Callie can swim in the pool."

"Plus you need that recommendation letter from a member."

"Come *on*," said Mona. "Annie's mom'd write you a letter in *sec*."

My mother's knife glinted in the early summer sun. I spread some more newspaper on the picnic table.

"Plus you have to eat there twice a month. You know what that means." My mother cut another, enormous slice of fruit.

"No, I *don't* know what that means," said Mona.

"It means Dad would have to wear a jacket, dummy," I said.

"Oh! Oh! Oh!" said Mona, clasping her hand to her breast. "Oh! Oh! Oh! Oh! Oh!"

We all laughed: my father had no use for nice clothes, and would wear only ten-year-old shirts, with grease-spotted pants, to show how little he cared what anyone thought.

"Your father doesn't believe in joining the American society," said my mother. "He wants to have his own society."

"So go to dinner without him." Mona shot her seeds out in long arcs over the lawn. "Who cares what he thinks?"

But of course we all did care, and knew my mother could not simply up and do as she pleased. For in my father's mind, a family owed its head a degree of loyalty that left no room for dissent. To embrace what he embraced was to love; and to embrace something else was to betray him.

He demanded a similar sort of loyalty of his workers, whom he treated more like servants than employees. Not in the beginning, of course. In the beginning all he wanted was for them to keep on doing what they used to do, and to that end he concentrated mostly on leaving them alone. As the months passed, though, he expected more and more of help, with the result that for all his largesse, he began having trouble keeping them. The cooks and busboys complained that he asked them to fix radiators and trim hedges, not only at the restaurant, but at our house; the waitresses that he sent them on errands and made them chauffeur him around. Our head waitress, Gertrude, claimed that he once even asked her to scratch his back.

"It's not just the blacks don't believe in slavery," she said when she quit.

My father never quite registered her complaint, though, nor those of the others who left. Even after Eleanor quit, then Tiffany, then Gerald, and Jimmy, and even his best cook, Eureka Andy, for whom he had bought new glasses, he remained mostly convinced that the fault lay with them.

"All they understand is that assembly line," he lamented. "Robots, they are. They want to be robots."

There *were* occasions when the clear running truth seemed to eddy, when he would pinch the vinyl of his chair up into little peaks and wonder if he was doing things right. But with time he would always smooth the peaks back down; and when business started to slide in the spring, he kept on like a horse in his ways.

By the summer our dishboy was overwhelmed with scraping. It was no longer just the hashbrowns that people were leaving for trash, and the service was as bad as the food. The waitresses served up French pancakes instead of German, apple juice instead of orange, spilt things on laps, on coats. On the Fourth of July some greenhorn sent an entire side of fries slaloming down a lady's *massif centrale*. Meanwhile in the back room, my father labored through articles on the economy.

"What is housing starts?" he puzzled. "What is GNP?"

Mona and I did what we could, filling in as busgirls and bookkeepers and, one afternoon, stuffing the comments box that hung by the cashier's desk. That was Mona's idea. We rustled up a variety of pens and pencils, checked boxes for an hour, smeared the cards up with coffee and grease, and waited. It took a few days for my father to notice that the box was full, and he didn't say anything about it for a few days more. Finally, though, he started to complain of fatigue; and then he began to complain that the staff was not what it could be. We encouraged him in this—pointing out, for instance, how many dishes got chipped—but in the end all that happened was that, for the first time since we took over the restaurant, my father got it into his head to fire someone. Skip, a skinny busboy who was saving up for a sports car, said nothing as my father mumbled on about the price of dishes. My father's hand shook as he wrote out the severance check; and he spent the rest of the day napping in his chair once it was over.

As it was going on midsummer, Skip wasn't easy to replace. We hung a sign in the window and advertised in the paper, but no one called the first week, and the person who called the second didn't show up for his interview. The third week, my father phoned Skip to see if he would come back, but a friend of his had already sold him a Corvette for cheap.

Finally a Chinese guy named Booker turned up. He couldn't have been more than thirty, and was wearing a lighthearted seersucker suit, but he looked as though life had him pinned: his eyes were bloodshot and his chest sunken, and the muscles of his neck seemed to strain with the effort of holding his head up. In a single dry breath he told us that he had never bussed tables but was willing to learn, and that he was on the lam from the deportation authorities.

"I do not want to lie to you," he kept saying. He had come to the United States on a student visa, had run out of money, and was now in a bind. He was loath to go back to Taiwan, as it happened—he looked up at this point, to be sure my father wasn't pro-KMT—but all he had was a phony social security card and a willingness to absorb all blame, should anything untoward come to pass.

"I do not think, anyway, that it is against the law to hire me, only to be me," he said, smiling faintly.

Anyone else would have examined him on this, but my father conceived of laws as speed bumps rather than curbs. He wiped the counter with his sleeve, and told Booker to report the next morning.

"I will be good worker," said Booker.

"Good," said my father.

"Anything you want me to do, I will do."

My father nodded.

Booker seemed to sink into himself for a moment. "Thank you," he said finally. "I am appreciate your help. I am very, very appreciate for everything." He reached out to shake my father's hand.

My father looked at him. "Did you eat today?" he asked in Mandarin.

Booker pulled at the hem of his jacket.

"Sit down," said my father. "Please, have a seat."

My father didn't tell my mother about Booker, and my mother didn't tell my father about the country club. She would never have applied, except that Mona, while over at Annie's, had let it drop that our mother wanted to join. Mrs. Lardner came by the very next day.

"Why, I'd be honored and delighted to write you people a letter," she said. Her skirt billowed around her.

"Thank you so much," said my mother. "But it's too much trouble for you, and also my husband is . . ."

"Oh, it's no trouble at all, I tell you." She leaned forward so that her chest freckles showed. "I know just how it is. It's a secret of course, but you know, my natural father was Jewish. Can you see it? Just look at my skin."

"My husband," said my mother.

"I'd be honored and delighted," said Mrs. Lardner with a little wave of her hands. "Just honored and delighted."

Mona was triumphant. "See, Mom," she said, waltzing around the kitchen when Mrs. Lardner left. "What did I tell you? 'I'm just honored and delighted, just honored and delighted.' " She waved her hands in the air.

"You know, the Chinese have a saying," said my mother. "To do nothing is better than to overdo. You mean well, but you tell me now what will happen."

"I'll talk Dad into it," said Mona, still waltzing. "Or I bet Callie can. He'll do anything Callie says."

"I can try, anyway," I said.

"Did you hear what I said?" said my mother. Mona bumped into the broom closet door. "You're not going to talk anything; you've already made enough trouble." She started on the dishes with a clatter.

Mona poked diffidently at a mop.

I sponged off the counter. "Anyway," I ventured. "I bet our name'll never even come up."

"That's if we're lucky," said my mother.

"There's all these people waiting," I said.

"Good," she said. She started on a pot.

I looked over at Mona, who was still cowering in the broom closet. "In fact, there's some black family's been waiting so long, they're going to sue," I said.

My mother turned off the water. "Where'd you hear that?"

"Patty told me."

She turned the water back on, started to wash a dish, then put it back down and shut the faucet.

"I'm sorry," said Mona.

"Forget it," said my mother. "Just forget it."

Booker turned out to be a model worker, whose boundless gratitude translated into a willingness to do anything. As he also learned quickly, he soon knew not only how to bus, but how to cook, and how to wait table, and how to keep the books. He fixed the walk-in door so that it stayed shut, reupholstered the torn seats in the dining room, and devised a system for tracking inventory. The only stone in the rice was that he tended to be sickly; but, reliable even in illness, he would always send a friend to take his place. In this way we got to know Ronald, Lynn, Dirk, and Cedric, all of whom, like Booker, had problems with their legal status and were anxious to please. They weren't all as capable as Booker, though, with the exception of Cedric, whom my father often hired even when Booker was well. A round wag of a man who called Mona and me *shou hou*—skinny monkeys—he was a professed non-smoker who was nevertheless always begging drags off of other people's cigarettes. This last habit drove our head cook, Fernando, crazy, especially since, when refused a hit, Cedric would occasionally snitch one. Winking impishly at Mona and me, he would steal up to an ashtray, take a quick puff, and then break out laughing so that the smoke came rolling out of his mouth in a great incriminatory cloud. Fernando accused him of stealing fresh cigarettes too, even whole packs.

"Why else do you think he's weaseling around in the back of the store all the time," he said. His face was blotchy with anger. "The man is a frigging thief."

Other members of the staff supported him in this contention and joined in on an "Operation Identification," which involved numbering an initialing their cigarettes—even though what they seemed to fear for wasn't so much their cigarettes as their jobs. Then one of the cooks quit; and rather than promote someone, my father hired Cedric for the position. Rumors flew that he was taking only half the normal salary, that Alex had been pressured to resign, and that my father was looking for a position with which to placate Booker, who had been bypassed because of his health.

The result was that Fernando categorically refused to work with Cedric.

"The only way I'll cook with that piece of slime," he said, shaking his huge tattooed fist, "is if it's his ass frying on the grill."

My father cajoled and cajoled, to no avail, and in the end was simply forced to put them on different schedules.

The next week Fernando got caught stealing a carton of minute steaks. My father would not tell even Mona and me how he knew to be standing by the back door when Fernando was on his way out, but everyone suspected Booker. Everyone but Fernando, that is, who was sure Cedric had been the tip-off. My father held a staff meeting in which he tried to reassure everyone that Alex had left on his own, and that he had no intention of firing anyone. But though he was careful not to mention Fernando, everyone was so amazed that he was being allowed to stay that Fernando was incensed nonetheless.

"Don't you all be putting your bug eyes on me," he said. *"He's* the frigging crook." He grabbed Cedric by the collar.

Cedric raised an eyebrow, "Cook, you mean," he said.

At this Fernando punched Cedric in the mouth; and the words he had just uttered notwithstanding, my father fired him on the spot.

With everything that was happening, Mona and I were ready to be getting out of the restaurant. It was almost time: the days were still stuffy with summer, but our window shade had started flapping in the evening as if gearing up to go out. That year the breezes were full of salt, as they sometimes were when they came in from the East, and they blew anchors and docks through my mind like so many tumbleweeds, filling my dreams with wherries and lobsters and grainy-faced men who squinted, day in and day out, at the sky.

It was time for a change, you could feel it; and yet the pancake house was the same as ever. The day before school started my father came home with bad news.

"Fernando called police," he said, wiping his hand on his pant leg.

My mother naturally wanted to know what police; and so with much coughing and hawing, the long story began, the latest installment of which had the police calling immigration, and immigration sending an investigator. My mother sat stiff as whalebone as my father described how the man summarily refused lunch on the house and how my father had admitted, under pressure, that he knew there were "things" about his workers.

"So now what happens?"

My father didn't know. "Booker and Cedric went with him to the jail," he said. "But me, here I am." He laughed uncomfortably.

The next day my father posted bail for "his boys" and waited apprehensively for something to happen. The day after that he waited again, and the day after that he called our neighbor's law student son, who suggested my father call the immigration department under an alias. My father took his advice; and it was thus that he discovered that Booker was right: it was illegal for aliens to work, but it wasn't to hire them.

In the happy interval that ensued, my father apologized to my mother, who in turn confessed about the country club, for which my father had no choice but to forgive her. Then he turned his attention back to "his boys."

My mother didn't see that there was anything to do.

"I like to talking to the judge," said my father.

"This is not China," said my mother.

"I'm only talking to him. I'm not give him money unless he wants it."

"You're going to land up in jail."

"So what else I should do?" My father threw up his hands. "Those are my boys."

"Your boys!" exploded my mother. "What about your family? What about your wife?"

My father took a long sip of tea. "You know," he said finally, "in the war my father sent our cook to the soldiers to use. He always said it—the province comes before the town, the town comes before the family."

"A restaurant is not a town," said my mother.

My father sipped at his tea again. "You know, when I first come to the United States, I also had to hide-and-seek with those deportation guys. If people did not helping me, I'm not here today."

My mother scrutinized her hem.

After a minute I volunteered that before seeing a judge, he might try a lawyer.

He turned. "Since when did you become so afraid like your mother?"

I started to say that it wasn't a matter of fear, but he cut me off.

"What I need today," he said, "is a son."

My father and I spent the better part of the next day standing in lines at the immigration office. He did not get to speak to a judge, but with much persistence he managed to speak to a judge's clerk, who tried to persuade him that it was not her place to extend him advice. My father, though, shamelessly plied her with compliments and offers of free pancakes until she finally conceded that she personally doubted anything would happen to either Cedric or Booker.

"Especially if they're 'needed workers,' " she said, rubbing at the red marks her glasses left on her nose. She yawned. "Have you thought about sponsoring them to become permanent residents?"

Could he do that? My father was overjoyed. And what if he saw to it right away? Would she perhaps put in a good word with the judge?

She yawned again, her nostrils flaring. "Don't worry," she said. "They'll get a fair hearing."

My father returned jubilant. Booker and Cedric hailed him as their savior, their Buddha incarnate. He was like a father to them, they said; and laughing and clapping, they made him tell the story over and over, sorting over the details like jewels. And how old was the assistant judge? And what did she say?

That evening my father tipped the paperboy a dollar and bought a pot of mums for my mother, who suffered them to be placed on the dining room table. The next night he took us all out to dinner. Then on Saturday, Mona found a letter on my father's chair at the restaurant.

> Dear Mr. Chang,
>
> You are the grat boss. But, we do not like to trial, so will runing away now. Plese to excus us. People saying the law in America is fears like dragon. Here is only $140. We hope some day we can pay

back the rest bale. You will getting intrest, as you diserving, so grat
a boss you are. Thank you for every thing. In next life you will be
burn in rich family, with no more pancaks.

Yours truley,

Booker + Cedric

In the weeks that followed my father went to the pancake house for crises,
but otherwise hung around our house, fiddling idly with the sump pump
and boiler in an effort, he said, to get ready for winter. It was as though
he had gone into retirement, except that instead of moving south, he had
moved to the basement. He even took to showering my mother with little
attentions, and to calling her ''old girl,'' and when we finally heard that
the club had entertained all the applications it could for the year, he was
so sympathetic that he seemed more disappointed than my mother.

II. In the American Society

Mrs. Lardner tempered the bad news with an invitation to a bon
voyage ''bash'' she was throwing for a friend of hers who was going to
Greece for six months.

''Do come,'' she urged. ''You'll meet everyone, and then, you know,
if things open up in the spring . . .'' She waved her hands.

My mother wondered if it would be appropriate to show up at a party
for someone they didn't know, but ''the honest truth'' was that this was
an annual affair. ''If it's not Greece, it's Antibes,'' sighed Mrs. Lardner.
''We really just do it because his wife left him and his daughter doesn't
speak to him, and poor Jeremy just feels so *unloved.*''

She also invited Mona and me to the goings on, as ''*demi*-guests'' to keep
Annie out of the champagne. I wasn't too keen on the idea, but before I
could say anything, she had already thanked us for so generously agreeing
to honor her with our presence.

''A pair of little princesses, you are!'' she told us. ''A pair of princesses!''

The party was that Sunday. On Saturday, my mother took my father out
shopping for a suit. As it was the end of September, she insisted that he buy
a worsted rather than a seersucker, even though it was only ten, rather than
fifty percent off. My father protested that it was as hot out as ever, which
was true—a thick Indian summer had cozied murderously up to us—but
to no avail. Summer clothes, said my mother, were not properly worn after
Labor Day.

The suit was unfortunately as extravagant in length as it was in price,
which posed an additional quandary, since the tailor wouldn't be in until

Monday. The salesgirl, though, found a way of tacking it up temporarily.

"Maybe this suit not fit me," fretted my father.

"Just don't take your jacket off," said the salesgirl.

He gave her a tip before they left, but when he got home refused to remove the price tag.

"I like to asking the tailor about the size," he insisted.

"You mean you're going to *wear* it and then *return* it?" Mona rolled her eyes.

"I didn't say I'm return it," said my father stiffly. "I like to asking the tailor, that's all."

The party started off swimmingly, except that most people were wearing bermudas or wrap skirts. Still, my parents carried on, sharing with great feeling the complaints about the heat. Of course my father tried to eat a cracker full of shallots and burnt himself in an attempt to help Mr. Lardner turn the coals of the barbeque; but on the whole he seemed to be doing all right. Not nearly so well as my mother, though, who had accepted an entire cupful of Mrs. Lardner's magic punch, and seemed indeed to be under some spell. As Mona and Annie skirmished over whether some boy in their class inhaled when he smoked, I watched my mother take off her shoes, laughing and laughing as a man with a beard regaled her with navy stories by the pool. Apparently he had been stationed in the Orient and remembered a few words of Chinese, which made my mother laugh still more. My father excused himself to go to the men's room then drifted back and weighed anchor at the hors d'oeuvres table, while my mother sailed on to a group of women, who tinkled at length over the clarity of her complexion. I dug out a book I had brought.

Just when I'd cracked the spine, though, Mrs. Lardner came by to bewail her shortage of servers. Her caterers were criminals, I agreed; and the next thing I knew I was handing out bits of marine life, making the rounds as amiably as I could.

"Here you go, Dad," I said when I got to the hors d'oeuvres table.

"Everything is fine," he said.

I hesitated to leave him alone; but then the man with the beard zeroed in on him, and though he talked of nothing but my mother, I thought it would be okay to get back to work. Just that moment, though, Jeremy Brothers lurched our way, an empty, albeit corked, wine bottle in hand. He was a slim, well-proportioned man, with a Roman nose and small eyes and a nice manly jaw that he allowed to hang agape.

"Hello," he said drunkenly. "Pleased to meet you."

"Pleased to meeting you," said my father.

"Right," said Jeremy. "Right. Listen. I have this bottle here, this most recalcitrant bottle. You see that it refuses to do my bidding. I bid it open sesame, please, and it does nothing.'' He pulled the cork out with his teeth, then turned the bottle upside down.

My father nodded.

"Would you have a word with it please?'' said Jeremy. The man with the beard excused himself. "Would you please have a goddamned word with it?''

My father laughed uncomfortably.

"Ah!'' Jeremy bowed a little. "Excuse me, excuse me, excuse me. You are not my man, not my man at all.'' He bowed again and started to leave, but then circled back. "Viticulture is not your forte, yes I can see that, see that plainly. But may I trouble you on another matter? Forget the damned bottle.'' He threw it into the pool, and winked at the people he splashed. "I have another matter. Do you speak Chinese?''

My father said he did not, but Jeremy pulled out a handkerchief with some characters on it anyway, saying that his daughter had sent it from Hong Kong and that he thought the characters might be some secret message.

"Long life,'' said my father.

"But you haven't looked at it yet.''

"I know what it says without looking.'' My father winked at me.

"You do?''

"Yes, I do.''

"You're making fun of me, aren't you?''

"No, no, no,'' said my father, winking again.

"Who are you anyway?'' said Jeremy.

His smile fading, my father shrugged.

"*Who are you?*''

My father shrugged again.

Jeremy began to roar. "This is my party, *my party,* and I've never seen you before in my life.'' My father backed up as Jeremy came toward him. "*Who are you? WHO ARE YOU?*''

Just as my father was going to step back into the pool, Mrs. Lardner came running up. Jeremy informed her that there was a man crashing his party.

"Nonsense,'' said Mrs. Lardner. "This is Ralph Chang, who I invited extra especially so he could meet you.'' She straightened the collar of Jeremy's peach-colored polo shirt for him.

"Yes, well, we've had a chance to chat,'' said Jeremy.

She whispered in his ear; he mumbled something; she whispered something more.

"I do apologize,'' he said finally.

My father didn't say anything.

"I do." Jeremy seemed genuinely contrite. "Doubtless you've seen drunks before, haven't you? You must have them in China."

"Okay," said my father.

As Mrs. Lardner glided off, Jeremy clapped his arm over my father's shoulders. "You know, I really am quite sorry, quite sorry."

My father nodded.

"What can I do, how can I make it up to you?"

"No thank you."

"No, tell me, tell me," wheedled Jeremy. "Tickets to casino night?" My father shook his head. "You don't gamble. Dinner at Bartholomew's?" My father shook his head again. "You don't eat." Jeremy scratched his chin. "You know, my wife was like you. Old Annabelle could never let me make things up—never, never, never, never, never."

My father wriggled out from under his arm.

"How about sport clothes? You are rather overdressed, you know, excuse me for saying so. But here." He took off his polo shirt and folded it up. "You can have this with my most profound apologies." He ruffled his chest hairs with his free hand.

"No thank you," said my father.

"No, take it, take it. Accept my apologies." He thrust the shirt into my father's arms. "I'm so very sorry, so very sorry. Please, try it on."

Helplessly holding the shirt, my father searched the crowd for my mother.

"Here, I'll help you off with your coat."

My father froze.

Jeremy reached over and took his jacket off. "Milton's, one hundred twenty-five dollars reduced to one hundred twelve-fifty," he read. "What a bargain, what a bargain!"

"Please give it back," pleaded my father, "Please."

"Now for your shirt," ordered Jeremy.

Heads began to turn.

"Take off your shirt."

"I do not take orders like a servant," announced my father.

"Take off your shirt, or I'm going to throw this jacket right into the pool, just right into this little pool here." Jeremy held it over the water.

"Go ahead."

"One hundred twelve-fifty," taunted Jeremy. "One hundred twelve . . ."

My father flung the polo shirt into the water with such force that part of it bounced back up into the air like a fluorescent fountain. Then it settled into a soft heap on top of the water. My mother hurried up.

"You're a sport!" said Jeremy, suddenly breaking into a smile and slapping my father on the back. "You're a sport! I like that. A man with spirit, that's what you are. A man with panache. Allow me to return to you your jacket." He handed it back to my father. "Good value you got on that, good value."

My father hurled the coat into the pool too. "We're leaving," he said grimly. "Leaving!"

"Now, Ralphie," said Mrs. Lardner, bustling up; but my father was already stomping off.

"Get your sister," he told me. To my mother: "Get your shoes."

"That was *great,* Dad," said Mona as we walked down to the car. "You were *stupendous.*"

"Way to show 'em," I said.

"What?" said my father offhandedly.

Although it was only just dusk, we were in a gulch, which made it hard to see anything except the gleam of his white shirt moving up the hill ahead of us.

"It was all my fault," began my mother.

"Forget it," said my father grandly. Then he said, "The only trouble is I left those keys in my jacket pocket."

"Oh *no,*" said Mona.

"Oh no is right," said my mother.

"So we'll walk home," I said.

"But how're we going to get into the *house,*" said Mona.

The noise of the party churned through the silence.

"Someone has to going back," said my father.

"Let's go to the pancake house first," suggested my mother. "We can wait there until the party is finished, and then call Mrs. Lardner."

Having all agreed that that was a good plan, we started walking again.

"God, just think," said Mona. "We're going to have to *dive* for them."

My father stopped a moment. We waited.

"You girls are good swimmers," he said finally. "Not like me."

Then his shirt started moving again, and we trooped up the hill after it, into the dark.

★ ★ ★ ★ ★

Talking It Through

1. Gish Jen's story is divided into two parts. The first is entitled "His Own Society," the second, "In the American Society." Even in Part I, however, there are many examples of this Chinese-American family's transplantings.

Make a list of particularly American emblems that are mentioned. Even the pancake business itself is very unlike the Chinese restaurant where the action of *FOB* takes place. Discuss the assimilation of the Changs. Which family members have adopted the customs of American society? How does the author let us know this?

2. In what ways does Ralph Chang create "his own society"? What ties with Chinese culture are there in his treatment of employees in the pancake house?

3. Mr. Chang hires the illegal alien, Booker, and his fellow undocumented emigrés. Eventually this causes dissension in the restaurant and, ultimately, an investigation by immigration authorities. Their employer comes to the aid of Booker and Cedric in his own fashion. What, specifically, does he do, and how does the issue of the immigration hearing at first seem destined for a happy ending? Compare Booker's and Cedric's need for valid permanent status papers with that of other newcomers you have previously read about.

4. Booker and Cedric decide they don't want to face a trial, and so write to Mr. Chang, explaining their next move. Why does Gish Jen reproduce their letter in its entirety in her story? What is the effect of the fractured English here? Does she expect the reader to be amused by it? How does it relate to the overall tone of this piece? Why do you think Part I ends here?

5. The wish of Mrs. Chang to join the local country club is another strand of this story. Why is his wife reluctant to discuss the matter with Mr. Chang? What does the country club membership symbolize? What is ironic about Mrs. Lardner's sponsorship of the Chang's application? Notice the parallelism of her sponsorship with Ralph Chang's sponsorship of his immigrant workers.

6. In Part II, Mrs. Lardner invites the Changs to a bon voyage party as consolation for not having made it into the country club. Father buys an ill-fitting new suit for the occasion. The Changs mingle fairly successfully until the drunken guest of honor has an exchange with Mr. Chang, challenging his presence at the party. Although Jeremy Brothers apologizes for his behavior, he continues to harass and goad Mr. Chang, who ultimately throws Brothers' sport shirt and his own still-tagged suit jacket into the swimming pool.

   Why do Chang's wife, daughters, and even Jeremy Brothers admire his actions? What does this act have to do with being in American society? What does it have to do with being transplanted?

7. What is the story's final irony? How does the author leave you feeling at the end? What is the significance of Mr. Chang's final statement: "You girls are good swimmers . . . Not like me"?

Writer's Workshop

1. Write a letter on behalf of the Changs recommending them as prospective members of the country club. What will make their application be viewed favorably? Be sure to tell the members of the country club board why you think the Changs will fit in. Provide the board members with information about the Changs you think will impress them.

2. Write an essay discussing the symbols of "American Society" used in this story and in other pieces in this anthology. How are the symbols viewed by the immigrants who encounter them? To some they seem desirable; others reject them. Try to analyze reasons for individual attitudes. Conclude your essay by providing your own list of contemporary American symbols and their significance to you.

3. At the end of the story, Mrs. Chang acknowledges that she will have to telephone Mrs. Lardner as soon as the Changs reach their restaurant. Write the episode of the story that documents that phone conversation. How would Mrs. Chang feel about making her call? How would she begin the conversation? Remember, it is Callie who is the narrator, and the events are told through her eyes. Keep her voice in your own narrative.

⋆ *Delia* ⋆

MARY GORDON

This story takes place in the early decades of the twentieth century. It concerns a group of four Irish Catholic sisters the youngest of whom, Delia, has married an "outsider." Mary Gordon's novels Final Payments *and* The Company of Women *have achieved wide acclaim.*

People talked about how difficult it was to say which of the O'Reilley girls was the best-looking. Kathleen had the green eyes. She came over by herself at seventeen. She worked as a seamstress and married Ed Derency. The money that she earned, even with all the babies—one a year until she was thirty-five—was enough to bring over the three other girls. Bridget had black hair and a wicked tongue. She married a man who was only five feet tall. She had no children for seven years; then she had a red-haired boy. Some believed he was the child of the policeman. Nettie was small; her feet and her ankles were as perfect as a doll's. She married Mr. O'Toole, who sang in the choir and drank to excess. She had only daughters. Some thought Delia the most beautiful, but then she was the youngest. She married a Protestant and moved away.

In defense of her sister, Kathleen pointed out that John Taylor looked like an Irishman.

"He has the eyes," Kathleen said to Nettie and to Bridget. "I never saw a Protestant with eyes like that."

"Part of the trouble with Delia all along is you babied her, Kathleen," Bridget said. "You made her believe she could do no wrong. What about the children? Is it Protestant nephews and nieces you want?"

"He signed the form to have them baptized," said Nettie.

"And what does that mean to a Protestant?" Bridget said. "They'll sign anything."

"He's good to the children. My children are mad for him," said Kathleen.

"Your children are mad entirely. Hot-blooded," said Bridget. "It's you have fallen for the blue eyes yourself. You're no better than your sister."

"He's kind to my Nora," said Kathleen.

Then even Bridget had to be quiet. Nora was Kathleen's child born with one leg shorter than the other.

"There was never any trouble like that in our family," Bridget had said when she first saw Nora. "It's what comes of marrying outsiders."

John Taylor would sit Nora on his lap. He told her stories about the West.

"Did you see cowboys?" she would ask him, taking his watch out of the leather case he kept it in. The leather case smelled like soap; it looked like a doll's pocketbook. When Nora said that it looked like a doll's pocketbook, John Taylor let her keep it for her doll.

"Cowboys are not gentlemen," said John Taylor.

"Is Mr. du Pont a gentleman?" asked Nora.

"A perfect gentleman. A perfect employer."

John Taylor was the chauffeur for Mr. du Pont. He lived in Delaware. He told Nora about the extraordinary gardens on the estate of Mr. du Pont.

"He began a poor boy," said John Taylor.

"Go on about the gardens. Go on about the silver horse on the hood of the car."

Delia came over and put her hands on top of her husband's. Her hands were cool-looking and blue-white, the color of milk in a bowl. She was expecting her first baby.

"Some day you must come and visit us in Delaware, when the baby's born," she said to Nora. She looked at her husband. Nora knew that the way they looked at each other had something to do with the baby. When her mother was going to have a baby, she got shorter; she grew lower to the ground. But Delia seemed to get taller; she seemed lighter and higher, as though she were filled, not with a solid child like one of Nora's brothers or sisters, but with air. With bluish air.

Delia and John Taylor would let her walk with them. She would walk between them and hold both their hands. Their hands were very different. Delia's was narrow and slightly damp; John Taylor's was dry and broad. It reminded Nora of his shoes, which always looked as if he were wearing them for the first time. They knew how to walk with her. Most people walked too slowly. She wanted to tell them they did not have to walk so slowly for her. But she did not want to hurt their feelings. John Taylor and Delia knew just how to walk, she thought.

After only two weeks, they went back to Delaware.

"She's too thin entirely," said Bridget.

"She's beautiful," said Nora. Her mother clapped her hand over Nora's mouth for contradicting her aunt.

Delia never wrote. Nora sent her a present on her birthday, near Christmas. She had made her a rose sachet: blue satin in the shape of a heart, filled with petals she had saved in a jar since the summer. She had worked with her mother to do the things her mother had told her would keep the smell.

Delia sent Nora a postcard. "Thank you for your lovely gift. I keep it in the drawer with my linen."

Linen. Nora's mother read the card to her when the aunts were to tea at their house.

"Fancy saying 'linen' to a child," said Bridget. "In a postcard."

"She has lovely underthings," said Nettie.

"Go upstairs. See to your little brother, Nora," said her mother.

"When they came back to New York, he gave her twenty-five dollars, just to buy underthings. Hand-hemmed, all of them. Silk ribbons. Ivory-colored," said Nettie.

"Hand-done by some greenhorn who got nothing for it," said Bridget.

Now Nora knew what Delia meant by linen. She had thought before it was tablecloths she meant, and that seemed queer. Why would she put her good sachet in with the tablecloths? Now she imagined Delia's underclothes, white as angels, smelling of roses. Did John Taylor see her in her underclothing? Yes. No. He was her husband. What did people's husbands see?

She was glad the aunts had talked about it. Now she could see the underclothes more clearly. Ivory ribbons, Nettie had said. Delia's stomach swelled in front of her, but not as much as Nora's mother's. And Nora's mother was going to have a baby in May, which meant Delia would have hers first. March, they had said. But Delia's stomach was light/hard, like a balloon. Nora's mother's was heavy/hard, like a turnip. Why was that, Nora wondered. Perhaps it was because her mother had had five babies, and this was Delia's first.

When her mother wrote to Delia, Nora dictated a note to her too. She asked when John Taylor's birthday was. She thought it was in the summer. She would make him a pillow filled with pine needles if it was in the summer. In July, the family went to the country for a week, and her mother would give her an envelope so she could fill it with pine needles for her Christmas gifts.

March came and went and no one heard anything of Delia's baby. Nora's mother wrote, Nettie wrote, even Bridget wrote, but no one heard anything.

"She's cut herself off," said Bridget. "She hasn't had the baby baptized, and she's afraid to face us."

"First babies are always late," said Kathleen. "I was four weeks overdue with Nora."

"Perhaps something's happened to the baby. Perhaps it's ill and she doesn't want to worry us," said Nettie.

"Nothing like that used to happen in our family," said Bridget, sniffing. "Or anyone we knew in the old country."

"What about Tom Hogan? He had three daft children. And Mrs. Kelly had a blind boy," said Nettie.

"If you'd say a prayer for your sister instead of finding fault with her, you might do some good with your tongue, Bridget O'Reilley, for once in your life," said Kathleen.

"If she'd of listened to me, she wouldn't be needing so many prayers," said Bridget.

"God forgive you, we all need prayers," said Kathleen, crossing herself.

"What's the weather in Delaware?" said Nettie.

"Damp," said Bridget. "Rainy."

"They live right on the estate," said Kathleen. "They eat the same food as Mr. du Pont himself."

"Yes, only not at the same table," said Bridget. "Downstairs is where the servants eat. I'd rather eat plain food at my own table than rich food at a servant's board."

"Will we not write to her, then?" said Nettie, to Kathleen mainly.

"Not if she's not written first. There must be some reason," said Kathleen.

"It's her made the first move away," said Bridget.

"If something was wrong, we'd hear. You always hear the bad. She must be all wrapped up. Probably the du Ponts have made a pet of her," said Kathleen.

Nora remembered that John Taylor had said that on Mrs. du Pont's birthday there was a cake in the shape of a swan. And ices with real strawberries in them, although it was the middle of November. And the ladies wore feathers and looked like peacocks, Delia had said. "They're beautiful, the ladies," John Taylor had said. "You should know, tucking the lap robes under them," Delia had said, standing on one foot like a bird. "God knows where you'd of been if I hadn't come along to rescue you in good time." "You've saved me from ruin," John Taylor had said, twirling an imaginary moustache.

Nora remembered how they had laughed together. John and Delia were the only ones she knew who laughed like that and were married.

"Do you think we'll never see Delia and John again?" said Nora to her mother.

"Never say never, it's bad luck," her mother said. She put her hand to her back. The baby made her back ache, she said. Soon, she told Nora, she would have to go to bed for the baby.

"And then you must mind your Aunt Bridget and keep your tongue in your head."

"Yes, ma'am," said Nora. But her mother knew she always minded; she never answered back. Only that once, about Delia, had she answered back.

When Nora's mother went to bed to have the baby, the younger children went to Nettie's, but Nora stayed home. "Keep your father company," her mother had said. "At least if he sees you it'll keep him from feeling in a house full of strangers entirely."

But even with her there, Nora's father walked in the house shyly, silently, as if he was afraid of disturbing something. He took her every evening, since it was warm, to the corner for an ice cream. She saw him so rarely that they had little to say to one another. She knew him in his tempers and in his fatigue. He would walk her home with a gallantry that puzzled her, and he went to sleep while it was still light. He woke in the morning before her, and he went away before she rose.

Bridget made Nora stay outside all day when her mother went into labor.

She sat on the front steps, afraid to leave the area of the house, afraid to miss the first cry or the news of an emergency. Children would come past her, but she hushed them until they grew tired of trying to entice her away. She looked at her hands; she looked down at her white shoes, one of which was bigger than the other, her mother had said, because God had something special in mind for her. What could He have in mind? Did God change His mind? Did He realize He had been mistaken? She counted the small pink pebbles in the concrete banister. She could hear her mother crying out. Everyone on the block could, she thought, with the windows open. She swept the sand on the middle step with the outside of her hand.

Then in front of her were a man's brown shoes. First she was frightened, but a second later, she recognized them. She did not have to look up at the face. They were John Taylor's shoes; they were the most beautiful shoes she had ever seen.

"Hello, Nora," he said, as if she should not be surprised to see him.

"Hello," she said, trying not to sound surprised, since she knew he did not want her to.

"Is your mother in?"

"She's upstairs in bed."

"Not sick, I hope."

"No. She's having another baby."

John Taylor sucked breath, as if he had changed his mind about something. The air around him was brilliant as glass. He looked around him, wanting to get away.

"How is Delia?" said Nora, thinking that was what her mother would have said.

"She died," said John, looking over his shoulder.

"And the baby? Is it a boy or a girl?"

"Dead. Born dead."

"Do you still drive a car for that man?" she said, trying to understand what he had told her. Born dead. It did not sound possible. And Delia dead. She heard her mother's voice from the window.

"I'm on holiday," said John, reaching into his pocket.

She was trying to think of a way to make him stay. If she could think of the right thing, he would take her for a walk, he would tell her about the cars and the gardens.

"How've you been, then?" she said.

"Fine," said John Taylor.

But he did not say it as he would have to an adult, she knew. He did not say it as if he were going to stay.

"Nora," he said, bending down to her. "Can we have a little secret? Can I give you a little present?"

"Yes," she said. He was going away. She could not keep him. She wanted something from him. She would keep his secret; he would give her a gift.

He reached into his pocket and took out a silver dollar. He put it in her hand and he closed her hand around it.

"Don't tell anyone I was here. Or what I said. About Delia, or about the baby."

It was very queer. He had come to tell them, and now she must not tell anyone, she thought. Perhaps he had come this way only to tell her. That was it: he had come from Delaware to tell her a secret, to give her a gift.

"I won't say anything," she said. She looked into his eyes; she had never looked into the eyes of an adult before. She felt an itching on the soles of her feet from the excitement of it.

"I'll count on you, then," he said, and walked quickly down the street, looking over his shoulder.

She went into the house. Upstairs, she could hear Bridget's voice, and her mother's voice in pain, but not yet the voice of the baby. She lifted her skirt. She put the silver dollar behind the elastic of her drawers. First it was cold against her stomach, but then it became warm from the heat of her body.

★ ★ ★ ★ ★

Talking It Through

1. What does Mary Gordon tell us about each O'Reilley sister in her opening paragraph? What aspects of their lives does she stress? Which of the sisters is probably the least happily married?

2. The story is largely told through the eyes of Kathleen's daughter Nora, who has a limp. What else do we know about Nora, her parents, and the social customs that prevailed in her house? Give an example of something we see through Nora's eyes. How would Gordon have described the scene differently had it been perceived by an adult?

3. Bridget is the sister who most disapproves of Delia's marriage to a Protestant "outsider." What are her specific complaints about Delia and her husband? Why does she assume that Delia never wrote to them? What is her explanation of why Nora has a limp?

4. Why does Nora establish such close ties with Delia and her husband? How does she perceive their marriage and why is it different from others she has observed?

5. Why does John Taylor leave before telling the entire family his news? How

do you think Nora understands the situation? What does the silver dollar represent, in your opinion?

6. Immigrant families are frequently torn between their desires to keep their old values intact and their desires to assimilate into the new culture. What has caused stress among the sisters? Bridget says of Delia, "It's her made the first move away." Were the family ties broken in this story, and if so, by whom—Delia or her sisters?

Writer's Workshop

1. Mary Gordon has carefully told this story through Nora's eyes. Retell the story from Bridget's point of view. How would she interpret events? What explanation might she give for Delia's fate? How would the tone and voice of the story change?

2. This story ends on a fragile moment in time. Continue Nora's story where Gordon leaves off. How do the sisters finally learn of Delia's fate? What effect has Delia had on Nora in terms of the girl's future life? How do you envision Nora as a grown woman?

⋆ *The Secret Lion* ⋆

A L B E R T O   A L V A R O   R Í O S

Alberto Ríos was born in Nogales, Arizona, a few miles from the Mexican border. He is a prize-winning poet who has used his Mexican origins as source material in both his poetry and prose. This selection is from his short story collection, The Iguana Killer. *Ríos writes of discovering a childhood paradise, if only temporarily, on the other side of an arroyo.*

I WAS TWELVE AND IN JUNIOR HIGH SCHOOL AND SOMETHING HAPPENED THAT we didn't have a name for, but it was there nonetheless like a lion, and roaring, roaring that way the biggest things do. Everything changed. Just that. Like the rug, the one that gets pulled—or better, like the tablecloth those magicians pull where the stuff on the table stays the same but the gasp! from the audience makes the staying-the-same part not matter. Like that.

What happened was there were teachers now, not just one teacher, teach-erz, and we felt personally abandoned somehow. When a person had all these teachers now, he didn't get taken care of the same way, even though six was more than one. Arithmetic went out the door when we walked in. And we saw girls now, but they weren't the same girls we used to know because we couldn't talk to them anymore, not the same way we used to, certainly not to Sandy, even though she was my neighbor, too. Not even to her. She just played the piano all the time. And there were words, oh there were words in junior high school, and we wanted to know what they were, and how a person did them—that's what school was supposed to be for. Only, in junior high school, school wasn't school, everything was backward-like. If you went up to a teacher and said the word to try and find out what it meant you got in trouble for saying it. So we didn't. And we figured it must have been that way about other stuff, too, so we never said anything about anything—we weren't stupid.

But my friend Sergio and I, we solved junior high school. We would come home from school on the bus, put our books away, change shoes, and go across the highway to the arroyo.[1] It was the one place we were not supposed to go. So we did. This was, after all, what junior high had at least shown us. It was our river, though, our personal Mississippi, our friend from long back, and it was full of stories and all the branch forts we had built in it when we were still the Vikings of America, with our own symbol, which we had carved everywhere, even in the sand, which let the water take it. That was good, we had decided; whoever was at the end of this river would know about us.

At the very very top of our growing lungs, what we would do down there was shout every dirty word we could think of, in every combination we could come up with, and we would yell about girls, and all the things we wanted to do with them, as loud as we could—we didn't know what we wanted to do with them, just things—and we would yell about teachers, and how we loved some of them, like Miss Crevelone, and how we wanted to dissect some of them, making signs of the cross, like priests, and we would yell this stuff over and over because it felt good, we couldn't explain why, it just felt good and for the first time in our lives there was nobody to tell us we couldn't. So we did.

---

[1] *arroyo:* small stream; more usually a dry river bed.

One Thursday we were walking along shouting this way, and the railroad, the Southern Pacific, which ran above and along the far side of the arroyo, had dropped a grinding ball down there, which was, we found out later, a cannonball thing used in mining. A bunch of them were put in a big vat which turned around and crushed the ore. One had been dropped, or thrown—what do caboose men do when they get bored—but it got down there regardless and as we were walking along yelling about one girl or another, a particular Claudia, we found it, one of these things, looked at it, picked it up, and got very very excited, and held it and passed it back and forth, and we were saying "Guythisis, this is, geeGuythis . . .": we had this perception about nature then, that nature is imperfect and that round things are perfect: we said "GuyGodthis is perfect, thisisthis is perfect, it's round, round and heavy, it'sit's the best thing we'veeverseen. Whatisit?" We didn't know. We just knew it was great. We just, whatever, we played with it, held it some more.

And then we had to decide what to do with it. We knew, because of a lot of things, that if we were going to take this and show it to anybody, this discovery, this best thing, was going to be taken away from us. That's the way it works with little kids, like all the polished quartz, the tons of it we had collected piece by piece over the years. Junior high kids too. If we took it home, my mother, we knew, was going to look at it and say "throw that dirty thing in the, get rid of it." Simple like, like that. "But ma it's the best thing I" "Getridofit." Simple.

So we didn't. Take it home. Instead, we came up with the answer. We dug a hole and we buried it. And we marked it secretly. Lots of secret signs. And came back the next week to dig it up and, we didn't know, pass it around some more or something, but we didn't find it. We dug up that whole bank, and we never found it again. We tried.

Sergio and I talked about that ball or whatever it was when we couldn't find it. All we used were small words, neat, good. Kid words. What we were really saying, but didn't know the words, was how much that ball was like that place, that whole arroyo: couldn't tell anybody about it, didn't understand what it was, didn't have a name for it. It just felt good. It was just perfect in the way it was that place, that whole going to that place, that whole junior high school lion. It was just iron-heavy, it had no name, it felt good or not, we couldn't take it home to show our mothers, and once we buried it, it was gone forever.

The ball was gone, like the first reasons we had come to that arroyo years earlier, like the first time we had seen the arroyo, it was gone like everything else that had been taken away. This was not our first lesson. We stopped going to the arroyo after not finding the thing, the same way we had stopped going there years earlier and headed for the mountains. Nature seemed to keep pushing us around one way or another, teaching us the same thing every place we ended up. Nature's gang was tough that way, teaching us stuff.

When we were young we moved away from town, me and my family. Sergio's was already out there. Out in the wilds. Or at least the new place seemed like the wilds since everything looks bigger the smaller a man is. I was five, I guess, and we had moved three miles north of Nogales where we had lived, three miles north of the Mexican border. We looked across the highway in one direction and there was the arroyo; hills stood up in the other direction. Mountains, for a small man.

When the first summer came the very first place we went to was of course the one place we weren't supposed to go, the arroyo. We went down in there and found water running, summer rain water mostly, and we went swimming. But every third or fourth or fifth day, the sewage treatment plant that was, we found out, upstream, would release whatever it was that it released, and we would never know exactly what day that was, and a person really couldn't tell right off by looking at the water, not every time, not so a person could get out in time. So, we went swimming that summer and some days we had a lot of fun. Some days we didn't. We found a thousand ways to explain what happened on those other days, constructing elaborate stories about the neighborhood dogs, and hadn't she, my mother, miscalculated her step before, too? But she knew something was up because we'd come running into the house those days, wanting to take a shower, even—if this can be imagined—in the middle of the day.

That was the first time we stopped going to the arroyo. It taught us to look the other way. We decided, as the second side of summer came, we wanted to go into the mountains. They were still mountains then. We went running in one summer Thursday morning, my friend Sergio and I, into my mother's kitchen, and said, well, what'zin, what'zin those hills over there—we used her word so she'd understand us—and she said nothing-don'tworryaboutit. So we went out, and we weren't dumb, we thought with our eyes to each other, ohhoshe'stryingtokeepsomethingfromus. We knew adult.

We had read the books, after all; we knew about bridges and castles and wildtreacherousraging alligatormouth rivers. We wanted them. So we were going to go out and get them. We went back that morning into that kitchen and we said "We're going out there, we're going into the hills, we're going away for three days, don't worry." She said, "All right."

"You know," I said to Sergio, "if we're going to go away for three days, well, we ought to at least pack a lunch."

But we were two young boys with no patience for what we thought at the time was mom-stuff: making sa-and-wiches. My mother didn't offer. So we got our little kid knapsacks that my mother had sewn for us, and into them we put the jar of mustard. A loaf of bread. Knivesforksplates, bottles of Coke, a can opener. This was lunch for the two of us. And we were weighed down, humped over to be strong enough to carry this stuff. But we started walking, anyway, into the hills. We were going to eat berries and stuff otherwise. "Goodbye." My mom said that.

After the first hill we were dead. But we walked. My mother could still see us. And we kept walking. We walked until we got to where the sun is straight overhead, noon. That place. Where that is doesn't matter; it's time to eat. The truth is we weren't anywhere close to that place. We just agreed that the sun was overhead and that it was time to eat, and by tilting our heads a little we could make that the truth.

"We really ought to start looking for a place to eat."

"Yeah. Let's look for a good place to eat." We went back and forth saying that for fifteen minutes, making it lunchtime because that's what we always said back and forth before lunchtimes at home. "Yeah, I'm hungry all right." I nodded my head. "Yeah, I'm hungry all right too, I'm hungry." He nodded his head. I nodded my head back. After a good deal more nodding, we were ready, just as we came over a little hill. We hadn't found the mountains yet. This was a little hill.

And on the other side of this hill we found heaven.

It was just what we thought it would be.

Perfect. Heaven was green, like nothing else in Arizona. And it wasn't a cemetery or like that because we had seen cemeteries and they had gravestones and stuff and this didn't. This was perfect, had trees, lots of trees, had birds, like we had never seen before. It was like "The Wizard of Oz," like when they got to Oz and everything was so green, so emerald, they had to wear those glasses, and we ran just like them, laughing, laughing that way we did that moment, and we went running down to this clearing in it all, hitting each other that good way we did.

We got down there, we kept laughing, we kept hitting each other, we unpacked our stuff, and we started acting "rich." We knew all about how to do that, like blowing on our nails, then rubbing them on our chests for the shine. We made our sandwiches, opened our Cokes, got out the rest of the stuff, the salt and pepper shakers. I found this particular hole and I put my coke right into it, a perfect fit, and I called it my Coke-holder. I got down next to it on my back, because everyone knows that rich people eat lying down, and I got my sandwich in one hand and put my other arm around the Coke in its holder. When I wanted a drink, I lifted my neck a little, put out my lips, and tipped my Coke a little with the crook of my elbow. Ah.

We were there, lying down, eating our sandwiches, laughing, throwing bread at each other and out for the birds. This was heaven. We were laughing and we couldn't believe it. My mother *was* keeping something from us, ah ha, but we had found her out. We even found water over at the side of the clearing to wash our plates with—we had brought plates. Sergio started washing his plates when he was done, and I was being rich with my Coke, and this day in summer was right.

When suddenly these two men came, from around a corner of trees and the tallest grass we had ever seen. They had bags on their backs, leather bags, bags and sticks.

We didn't know what clubs were, but I learned later, like I learned about the grinding balls. The two men yelled at us. Most specifically, one wanted me to take my Coke out of my Coke-holder so he could sink his golf ball into it.

Something got taken away from us that moment. Heaven. We grew up a little bit, and couldn't go backward. We learned. No one had ever told us about golf. They had told us about heaven. And it went away. We got golf in exchange.

We went back to the arroyo for the rest of that summer, and tried to have fun the best we could. We learned to be ready for finding the grinding ball. We loved it, and when we buried it we knew what would happen. The truth is, we didn't look so hard for it. We were two boys and twelve summers then, and not stupid. Things get taken away.

We buried it because it was perfect. We didn't tell my mother, but together it was all we talked about, till we forgot. It was the lion.

★ ★ ★ ★ ★

Talking It Through

1. The narrator tells of a time when he was twelve and in junior high school when "Everything changed." What are some of the big changes he observes? Do they seem true to life to you? Here the author talks about a quite separate culture from ethnic culture. It is the school culture. Try to define your school culture as he does. What are its specific components? When may a student find herself or himself transplanted?

2. The boy in the story and his friend Sergio "solved" junior high school. How did they do this? Why is the grinding ball they discover so precious? Why do they wish to keep it a secret?

3. The writer describes the boys' first explorations of the arroyo at the age of five. Why do they switch from the arroyo to the "mountains"? Note how

Ríos reports some conversations in an unpunctuated run-on flow of words. What is his purpose in doing so? Do you think it is a good technique? Explain.

4. In typical kid fashion, the boys pack a lunch for their adventure in the "mountains." And in typical fashion they can barely wait for lunchtime to eat it. Just as they are ready, on the other side of the hill they find "heaven." It is green "like nothing else in Arizona." It even has a "Coke-holder," and a source of water at a time of year when everything else would be parched. Then culture shock sets in.

   Why are the boys so unprepared for the reality of their environment? Do you think their amazement is more than childish naivete? How is their experience related to that of the Changs of "In the American Society"?

5. What does Alberto Ríos mean by "The Secret Lion" of the title? Does everyone have a secret lion? How might it be related to the immigrant experience?

Writer's Workshop

1. Have you ever, as the boys did, misperceived a circumstance in which you found yourself? Describe what you thought your situation was and your reactions when you learned of your misunderstanding. Think about ways of making your account suspenseful for the reader. What tone will your piece have? Will it emphasize the humor of the occasion, your astonishment, or your embarrassment? How will you contrast the imagined with the real?

2. Consider the importance of scale in descriptive writing. Choose one place to observe carefully. Take notes if it will help you to get details firmly and accurately placed. You may wish to take with you either a magnifying lens or a pair of inexpensive binoculars if they are available. After you have researched your location, write about it, first, as if you were a child of five (about three-and-a-half feet tall), and then from the perspective of a professional basketball player (about 6′6″).

3. What is your "secret lion"? If you feel comfortable discussing it, write about it so the reader understands its meaning and importance to you. You may treat the subject anecdotally as does Ríos, or write in essay form.

★ *Los New Yorks* ★

VICTOR HERNANDEZ CRUZ

*Victor Hernandez Cruz was born in 1949 in Puerto Rico in the tiny town of
Aguas Buenas and came to the United States as a small child. Several
collections of his poetry have been published. This poem uses both Spanish
and English words to give the flavor of a transplanted Puerto Rican life in
New York City.*

In the news that sails through the air
Like the shaking seeds of maracas[1]
I find you out

Suena[2]

You don't have to move here   5
Just stand on the corner
Everything will pass you by
Like a merry-go-round the red
bricks will swing past your eyes
They will melt   10
So old
will move out by themselves

Suena

I present you the tall skyscrapers
as merely huge palm trees with lights   15

---

[1] *maracas:* dried gourds on sticks; the inner seeds make a sound when the gourds are
shaken. Maracas are used as percussion instruments in Latino music.

[2] *suena:* Spanish verb, literally meaning "It sounds," from the infinitive "sonar," to
sound or to ring.

Suena

The roaring of the trains is a fast
guaguanco³
dance of the ages

Suena   20

Snow falls
Coconut chips galore
Take the train to Caguas⁴
and the bus is only ten cents
to Aguas Buenas⁵   25

Suena

A tropical wave settled here
And it is pulling the sun
with a romp
No one knows what to do   30

Suena

I am going home now
I am settled there with my fruits
Everything tastes good today
Even the ones that are grown here   35
Taste like they're from outer space
Walk y Suena
Do it strange
Los New Yorks.

Talking It Through

1. In "Los New Yorks," the poet deliberately intersperses Spanish words with
   English. Why does he do this? Try to think of more than one effect this has.
   This device was also used in the poem "Grandma's Primo" in an earlier
   unit. Look back to see if both poets have the same intentions.

³*guaguanco:* a musical form created in Cuba with roots in Africa.

⁴*Caguas:* location in Puerto Rico; a rival town.

⁵*Aguas Buenas:* the poet's home town.

This poem of seven stanzas has no punctuation except for the period at the very end. How does the poet substitute for punctuation and get you to pause appropriately? Read the poem aloud to see where the stresses and the pauses are located.

2. The poem "Los New Yorks" repeats the word *"suena"* (pronounced *swayna*) which is the Spanish verb for "sounds" between each stanza. What do you feel is the purpose of using words to convey sound images? Victor Cruz also makes use of the musicality of the Spanish language which has many open vowel sounds. There is also a comparison to be made to the refrain of a song in the repetition of the word. In the last stanza, there is a play on the word *suena*. *Sueña* (with a tilde mark) means "dream" in Spanish.

3. Cruz uses similes and metaphors to compare his native Puerto Rico with New York. How do his choices of imagery convey a sense of the island from which he has emigrated?

4. In his final stanza, Cruz talks of going home where he is settled "with my fruits." Compare his poem to that of Claude McKay's "The Tropics in New York" in the previous unit. What is similar in the two poems? How does Cruz indicate he has come to terms with being on the island of Manhattan instead of the tropical island of Puerto Rico?

Writer's Workshop

1. Create a poem of your own which contrasts two different places you know. Use a single word repetitively between stanzas in the manner of Victor Cruz. Create your own consistent similes and metaphors to compare the two locales. Put yourself into the poem as he does.

2. Write an essay comparing Claude McKay's "The Tropics in New York" with Victor Cruz's "Los New Yorks." Compare theme as well as style. McKay's poem is rhymed. Cruz's is not. Before you begin your essay, make a list of similarities and differences.

3. Buy a tropical fruit in your local market. Examine its texture, color, odor, taste. Cut it open and examine the pattern of its interior including its seeds. Use an encyclopedia or botany book to investigate its growth habits and environmental needs. Then write a poem or short description about it. Think of strong, original similes and metaphors to compare it to things it reminds you of.

★ *America* ★

STEPHEN SONDHEIM

Stephen Sondheim, who wrote the lyrics to Leonard Bernstein's score for West
Side Story, *has written both words and music for an amazing string of
award-winning Broadway musicals, including* Follies, Company, Pacific
Overtures, *and* A Little Night Music. *Here the vibrant female ensemble from*
West Side Story *tackles "America" from their Puerto Rican perspective.*

ROSALIA
Puerto Rico . . .
You lovely island . . .
Island of tropical breezes.
Always the pineapples growing,   5
Always the coffee blossoms blowing . . .

ANITA *(mockingly)*
Puerto Rico . . .
You ugly island . . .
Island of tropic diseases.   10
Always the hurricanes blowing,
Always the population growing . . .
And the money owing,
And the babies crying,
And the bullets flying.   15
I like the island Manhattan —
Smoke on your pipe and put that in!

OTHERS *(except Rosalia)*
I like to be in America!
Okay by me in America!   20
Everything free in America
For a small fee in America!

ROSALIA
I like the city of San Juan.

ANITA   25
I know a boat you can get on.

ROSALIA
Hundreds of flowers in full bloom.

ANITA
Hundreds of people in each room!   30

ALL (*except Rosalia*)
Automobile in America,
Chromium steel in America,
Wire-spoke wheel in America,
Very big deal in America!   35

ROSALIA
I'll drive a Buick through San Juan.

ANITA
If there's a road you can drive on.

ROSALIA   40
I'll give my cousins a free ride.

ANITA
How you get all of them inside?

ALL (*except Rosalia*)
Immigrant goes to America,   45
Many hellos in America,
Nobody knows in America
Puerto Rico's in America!

(*The girls dance around Rosalia.*)

ROSALIA   50
I'll bring a TV to San Juan.

ANITA
If there's a current to turn on!

ROSALIA
I'll give them new washing machine.   55

ANITA
What have they got there to keep clean?

ALL (*except Rosalia*)
I like the shores of America!

Comfort is yours in America!   60
Knobs on the doors in America,
Wall-to-wall floors in America!

(They dance)

ROSALIA
When I will go back to San Juan —   65

ANITA
When you will shut up and get gone!

ROSALIA
Ev'ryone there will give big cheer!

ANITA   70
Ev'ryone there will have moved here!

(More dancing)

Talking It Through

1. *West Side Story,* based on Shakespeare's *Romeo and Juliet,* tells the story of the Jets, an American gang, and the Sharks, their rivals, who have recently come from Puerto Rico. The Romeo here is Tony, a member of the Jets who has fallen in love with Maria, his Juliet, who is a sister of the leader of the Sharks.

   In the song "America," sung near the close of the first act of the play, Rosalia sings of her dreams of returning to her home island of Puerto Rico, while her New-York-wise friends counter with attributes of American culture. Make a list of what Rosalia misses in America and of what the other girls see as Puerto Rico's shortcomings.

2. What do Rosalia's companions admire about America?

3. Compare the lyrics of "America" with "Los New Yorks." Are the spokespeople in the two concerned with the same components of mainland American life?

Writer's Workshop

1. Analyze the rhyme scheme and meter used by Stephen Sondheim in "America." Then write additional verses and choruses to the song to bring the lyrics up to date. The musical was written in the late 1950s. What things would the girls find desirable now in America and what would the

chorus sing about that would not have been available then? Think of such items as personal computers, CD's, microwaves, space satellites, lasers, camcorders, VCRs, none of which had been invented in 1957.

2. Write a song lyric in your own style that deals with the subject of American culture. Will your subjects come from sports, entertainment, politics, or the natural landscape? You might want to create verses to deal with each and with others that may occur to you. When your song is written, either as a solo or with a group of friends, orchestrate it and perform it for the class.

⋆ *Donald Duk* ⋆

FRANK CHIN

Frank Chin is a Chinese-American playwright, editor, and novelist. This excerpt is the beginning of his novel about a second generation twelve-year-old boy who despite his sophisticated American tastes must come to terms with his Chinese heritage.

WHO WOULD BELIEVE ANYONE NAMED DONALD DUK DANCES LIKE FRED Astaire? Donald Duk does not like his name. Donald Duk never liked his name. He hates his name. He is not a duck. He is not a cartoon character. He does not go home to sleep in Disneyland every night. The kids that laugh at him are very smart. Everyone at his private school is smart. Donald Duk is smart. He is a gifted one, they say.

No one in school knows he takes tap dance lessons from a man who calls himself ''The Chinese Fred Astaire.'' Mom talks Dad into paying for the lessons and tap shoes.

Fred Astaire. Everybody everywhere likes Fred Astaire in the old black-and-white movies. Late at night on TV, even Dad smiles when Fred Astaire dances. Mom hums along. Donald Duk wants to live the late night life in old black-and-white movies and talk with his feet like Fred Astaire, and smile Fred Astaire's sweet lemonade smile.

The music teacher and English teacher in school go dreamy eyed when they talk about seeing Fred Astaire and Ginger Rogers on the late-night TV. "Remember when he danced with Barbara Stanwyck? What was the name of that movie . . .?"

"Barbara Stanwyck?"

"Did you see the one where he dances with Rita Hayworth?"

"Oooh, Rita Hayworth!"

Donald Duk enjoys the books he read in schools. The math is a curious game. He is not the only Chinese in the private school. But he is the only Donald Duk. He avoids the other Chinese here. And the Chinese seem to avoid him. This school is a place where the Chinese are comfortable hating Chinese. "Only the Chinese are stupid enough to give a kid a stupid name like Donald Duk," Donald Duk says to himself. "And if the Chinese were that smart, why didn't they invent tap dancing?"

Donald Duk's father's name is King. King Duk. Donald hates his father's name. He hates being introduced with his father. "This is King Duk, and his son Donald Duk." Mom's name is Daisy. "That's Daisy Duk, and her son Donald." Venus Duk and Penny Duk are Donald's sisters. The girls are twins and a couple of years older than Donald.

His own name is driving him crazy! Looking Chinese is driving him crazy! All his teachers are making a big deal about Chinese stuff in their classes because of Chinese New Year coming on soon. The teacher of California History is so happy to be reading about the Chinese. "The man I studied history under at Berkeley[1] authored this book. He was a spellbinding lecturer," the teacher throbs. Then he reads, "The Chinese in America were made passive and nonassertive by centuries of Confucian thought[2] and Zen mysticism.[3] They were totally unprepared for the violently individualistic and democratic Americans. From their first step on American soil to the middle of the twentieth century, the timid, introverted Chinese have been helpless against the relentless victimization by aggressive, highly competitive Americans.

"One of the Confucian concepts that lends the Chinese vulnerable to the

[1]*Berkeley:* branch of the University of California near San Francisco.

[2]*Confucian thought:* Confucius was a Chinese philosopher who lived around 500 B.C. His maxims and ideas have influenced Chinese (and Japanese) family and public life down to our time. Confucianism emphasizes "filial piety," respect for one's elders, and a strict hierarchy among members of society.

[3]*Zen mysticism:* Zen is a sect of the Buddhist religion that emphasizes meditation, contemplation, and austerity.

assertive ways of the West is 'the mandate of heaven.'[4] As the European kings of old ruled by divine right, so the emperors of China ruled by the mandate of heaven.'' The teacher takes a breath and looks over his spellbound class. Donald wants to barf pink and green stuff all over the teacher's teacher's book.

''What's he saying?'' Donald Duk's pal Arnold Azalea asks in a whisper.

''Same thing as everybody—Chinese are artsy, cutesy and chickendick.'' Donald whispers back.

Oh, no! Here comes Chinese New Year again! It is Donald Duk's worst time of year. Here come the stupid questions about the funny things Chinese believe in. The funny things Chinese do. The funny things Chinese eat. And, ''Where can I buy some Chinese firecrackers?''

And in Chinatown it's *Goong hay fot choy*[5] everywhere. And some gang kids do sell firecrackers. And some gang kids rob other kids looking for firecrackers. He doesn't like the gang kids. He doesn't like speaking their Chinese. He doesn't have to—this is America. He doesn't like Chinatown. But he lives here.

The gang kids know him. They call him by name. One day the Frog Twins wobble onto the scene with their load of full shopping bags. There is Donald Duk. And there are five gang boys and two girlfriends chewing gum, swearing and smirking. The gang kids wear black tanker jackets, white tee shirts and baggy black denim jeans. It is the alley in front of the Chinese Historical Society Museum. There are fish markets on each side of the Chinatown end of the alley. Lawrence Ferlinghetti's[6] famous City Lights Bookstore is at the end that opens on Columbus Street. Suddenly there are the Frog Twins in their heavy black overcoats. They seem to be wearing all the clothes they own under their coats. Their coats bulge. Under their skirts they wear several pairs of trousers and slacks. They wear one knit cap over the other. They wear scarves tied over their heads and shawls over their shoulders.

That night, after he is asleep, Dad comes home from the restaurant and wakes him up. ''You walk like a sad softie,'' Dad says. ''You look like you want everyone to beat you up.''

''I do not!'' Donald Duk says.

''You look at yourself in the mirror,'' Dad says, and Donald Duk looks at himself in his full-length dressing mirror. ''Look at those slouching

---

[4]*Mandate of Heaven:* In Confucian thought the emperor was granted a mandate or right to rule by the Gods, but only if he ruled justly. He was supposed to be a father to his country.

[5]*Goong hay fot choy:* Chinese for ''Happy New Year.''

[6]*Lawrence Ferlinghetti:* Well-known ''Beat'' poet of the late 1950s in San Francisco.

shoulders, that pouty face. Look at those hands holding onto each other. You look scared!'' Dad's voice booms and Donald hears everyone's feet hit the floor. Mom and the twins are out in the hall looking into his open door.

"I am scared!" Donald Duk says.

"I don't care if you are scared," Dad says. His eyes sizzle into Donald Duk's frightened pie-eyed stare. "Be as scared as you want to be, but don't look scared. Especially when you walk through Chinatown.''

"How do I look like I'm not scared if I *am* scared?" Donald Duk asks.

"You walk with your back straight. You keep your hands out of your pockets. Don't hunch your shoulders. Think of them as being down. Keep your head up. Look like you know where you're going. Walk like you know where you're going. And you say, 'Don't mess with me, horesepuckie? Don't mess with me!' But you don't say it with your mouth. You say it with your eyes. You say it with your hands where everybody can see them. Anybody get two steps in front of you, you zap them with your eyes, and they had better nod at you or look away. When they nod, you nod. When you walk like nobody better mess with you, nobody will mess with you. When you walk around like you're walking now, all rolled up in a little ball and hiding out from everything, they'll get you for sure.''

Donald does not like his dad waking him up like that and yelling at him. But what the old man says works. Outside among the cold San Francisco shadows and the early morning shoppers, Donald Duk hears his father's voice and straightens his back, takes his hands out of his pockets, says "Don't mess with me!" with his eyes and every move of his body. And, yes, he's talking with his body the way Fred Astaire talks, and shoots every gang kid who walks toward him in the eye with a look that says, "Don't mess with me." And no one messes with him. Dad never talks about it again.

Later, gang kids laugh at his name and try to pick fights with him during the afternoon rush hour, Dad's busy time in the kitchen. Donald is smarter than these lowbrow beady-eyed goons. He has to beat them without fighting them because he doesn't know how to fight. Donald Duk gets the twins to talk about it with Dad while they are all at the dining room table working on their model airplanes.

Dad laughs. "So he has a choice. He does not like people laughing at his name. He does not want the gangsters laughing at his name to beat him up. He mostly does not want to look like a sissy in front of them, so what can he do?''

"He can pay them to leave him alone," Venus says.

"He can not! That is so chicken it's disgusting!" Penelope says.

"So, our little brother is doomed."

"He can agree with them and laugh at his name," Dad says. "He can tell them lots of Donald Duk jokes. Maybe he can learn to talk that quack-quack Donald Duck talk.''

"Whaaat?" the twins ask in one voice.

"If he keeps them laughing," Dad says, "even if he can just keep them listening, they are not beating him up, right? And they are not calling him a sissy. He does not want to fight? He does not have to fight. He has to use his smarts, okay? If he's smart enough, he makes up some Donald Duck jokes to surprise them and make them laugh. They laugh three times, he can walk away. Leave them there laughing, thinking Donald Duk is one terrific fella.''

"So says King Duk," Venus Duk flips. The twins often talk as if everything they hear everybody say and see everybody do is dialog in a memoir they're writing or action in a play they're directing. This makes Mom feel like she's on stage and drives Donald Duk crazy.

"Is that Chinese psychology, dear?" Daisy Duk asks.

"Daisy Duk inquires," says Penelope Duk.

"And little Donnie Duk says, *Oh, Mom!* and sighs.''

"I do not!" Donald Duk yelps at the twins.

"Well, then, say it," Penelope Duk says. "It's a good line. So *you* you, you know.''

"Thank you," Venus says.

"Oh goshes, you all, your sympathy is so . . . so . . . so literary. So dramatic," Donald Duk says. "It is truly depressing.''

"I thought it was narrative," Venus says.

"Listen up for some Chinese psychology, girls and boys," Daisy Duk says.

"No, that's not psychology, that's Bugs Bunny," Dad says.

"You don't mean, Bugs Bunny, dear. You always make that mistake.''

"Br'er Rabbit!"[7] Dad says.

"What does that mean?" Donald Duk asks the twins. They shrug their shoulders. Nobody knows what Br'er Rabbit has to do with Dad's way of avoiding a fight and not being a fool, but it works.

One bright and sunny afternoon, a gang boy stops Donald and talks to him in the quacking voice of Walt Disney's Donald Duck. The voice breaks Donald Duk's mind for a flash, and he is afraid to turn on his own Donald Duck voice. He tries telling a joke about Donald Duck not wearing trousers or shoes, when the gangster—in black jeans, black tee shirt, black jacket,

---

[7] *Br'er Rabbit:* character in famous trickster tale of African American origin. It was retold by Joel Chandler Harris. Br'er Rabbit fooled Br'er Fox by creating a tar baby to which Br'er Fox got stuck.

black shades—says in a perfect Donald Duck voice, "Let's take the pants off Donald Duk!"

"Oh oh! I stepped in it now!" Donald Duk says in his Donald Duck voice and stuns the gangster and his two gangster friends and their three girlfriends. Everything is seen and understood very fast. Without missing a beat, his own perfect Donald Duck voice cries for help in perfect Cantonese *Gow meng ahhhh!* and they all laugh. Old women pulling little wire shopping carts full of fresh vegetables stop and stare at him. Passing children recognize the voice and say Donald Duck talks Chinese.

"Don't let these monsters take off my pants. I may be Donald Duk, but I am as human as you," he says in Chinese, in his Donald Duck voice, "I know how to use chopsticks. I use flush toilets. Why shouldn't I wear pants on Grant Street in Chinatown?" They all laugh more than three times. Their laughter roars three times on the corner of Grant and Jackson, and Donald Duk walks away, leaving them laughing, just the way Dad says he can. He feels great. Just great!

Donald Duk does not want to laugh about his name forever. There has to be an end to this. There is an end to all kidstuff for a kid. An end to diapers. An end to nursery rhymes and fairy tales. There has to be an end to laughing about his name to get out of a fight. Chinese New Year. Everyone will be laughing. He is twelve years old. Twelve years old is special to the Chinese. There are twelve years in the Asian lunar zodiac. For each year there is an animal. This year Donald will complete his first twelve-year cycle of his life. To celebrate, Donald Duk's father's old opera mentor, Uncle Donald Duk, is coming to San Francisco to perform a Cantonese opera. Donald Duk does not want Chinese New Year. He does not want his uncle Donald Duk to tell him again how Daddy was a terrible man to name his little boy Donald Duk, because all the *bok gwai*, the white monsters, will think he is named after that barebutt cartoon duck in the top half of a sailor suit and no shoes.

★ ★ ★ ★ ★

Talking It Through

1. Fred Astaire, the debonair dancer and star of 1930s movie musicals, is Donald Duk's idol. The film star epitomizes grace, geniality, and sophistication. Donald hates his name, puts down his Chinese traditions, and deplores the arrival of another Chinese New Year celebration. Why do you think Donald seems embarrassed by his family's Chinese roots? What do we learn about the Duk family from this selection? How assimilated is

Donald? Why do you think he is so upset with his teacher of California history?

2. Frank Chin tells this story with a stand-up comic's staccato delivery. Despite the author's humorous tone, there is an underlying seriousness of theme. What is it? Also try to define the components of the comedy in this chapter.

3. What advice does Donald's father offer to prevent the gang kids from picking on Donald? Does the advice work? Is his problem different from that of the family in the Halper piece ("Prelude," p.173) who also fear a gang?

4. Do you think self-mockery is an effective way to cope with teasing? Explain. Is Donald's problem universal or the result of his ethnic background? Does it stem from the fact that he is more successfully transplanted than the teenagers who torment him? Give reasons for your opinions.

5. The end of this chapter refers to the Chinese New Year and the Asian lunar calendar. It also mentions Donald's completion of the first twelve-year cycle of his life. This is an important time for Donald, a rite of passage. What does Donald hope for? What other cultures that you know about have coming-of-age rituals? Does American society have such rites of passage? What would they be?

6. Does Donald Duk see himself as being "in the American society"? What does it tell about the Duk family that his uncle refers to Americans as *bok gwai*, white monsters, who will confuse his namesake with the Disney cartoon character?

7. Compare Donald Duk with the other Chinese-American characters encountered in this volume. There are the characters in David Hwang's play *FOB*, in Gish Jen's story, and in Amy Tan's novel. Which of them are the most successfully transplanted? What makes such a transplanting possible?

Writer's Workshop

1. Donald admires and wants to be like his movie hero, Fred Astaire. In fact, later in the book, he has imaginary conversations with him. Do you have such a hero or heroine from popular culture, someone whose manner you particularly like and would like to model yourself after? If so, write a piece to explain what makes him or her attractive to you. Is it movement? Looks? Dress? Speech pattern? Personality? Try to capture these qualities for the reader.

This may be easier to write if you refer to yourself by name and write in the third person as a way of objectifying your material.

2. Have you ever been teased or intimidated? Write a story based on personal experiences of being threatened by a group of your contemporaries. This threat may only be implied or in the mind of your character. Before you begin, briefly outline the incidents that will give your story its plot. What will lead up to the conflict? How will it reach its climax? How will your story end? Use conversation in your piece to give the personality of the characters as Chin does with the Duk family.

3. Choose among the young people depicted in this anthology and decide which of them are successfully transplanted according to your understanding of the term. First list your criteria so you can start your essay with a definition of terms you will use. Then list the people you will use and place beside them the attributes you see as being essential to taking root in a new environment. Finally write an essay to defend your choices. Use paragraphs that compare and contrast, show cause and effect, and ones that extend your thesis or argument.

★ *Little Song* ★

L A N G S T O N   H U G H E S

Langston Hughes, perhaps our most widely read African American poet, has written in moving terms of his African ancestry and of the hardships of the Negro, as African Americans were then called, in the United States. Here he concludes this unit on a more positive note of his hopes for the future.

Carmencita loves Patrick.
Patrick loves Si Lan Chen.
Xenophon loves Mary Jane.
Hildegarde loves Ben.

Lucienne loves Eric.   5
Giovanni loves Emma Lee.
Natasha loves Miguelito—
And Miguelito loves me.

Ring around the Maypole!
Ring around we go—   10
Weaving our bright ribbons
Into a rainbow!

Talking It Through

1. This rhymed poem of three stanzas uses names from different ethnic groups
   in two of them. What countries of origin do you associate with the names
   Langston Hughes has chosen? Look up in a glossary of proper names or
   in a dictionary some of those less familiar to you.

   Recite and tap out the rhythm of these stanzas. The cadences resemble
   those of jump-rope rhymes or of a skipping song. What effect does this
   give?

2. The third stanza differs from the others. What does the Maypole symbolize?
   What do the "bright ribbons" stand for? Jesse Jackson used the image of
   a rainbow in his 1988 presidential campaign. Do you think Langston
   Hughes would have supported Jackson's "Rainbow Coalition"? Use "Little
   Song" to explain your opinion.

3. What do you think it would take to bring about a world in which Hughes's
   optimism as expressed here would be justified?

Writer's Workshop

1. Using names as Langston Hughes does here, write a song or a poem of
   your own. Try listing names first according to countries or regions of origin.
   Can you think of some areas Hughes neglected to include? Then group
   those that rhyme with each other. What will your refrain be? What will
   you repeat? Try making Hughes's point using other symbols for unity in
   diversity.

2. How are we defined by our names? Does a name confer status? Can it stigmatize or stereotype you? Write an essay developing the theme of one's name.

   You might want to consider what associations a name can carry either as personal or societal baggage, how brand names evoke specific experiences and serve as social common denominators, or how celebrity names trigger associations to create a common cultural base.

3. You may be aware that new names were often conferred on emigrés by immigration officials when making out identity papers if a person's surname seemed too difficult to pronounce or write down. Often a Smith or Jones was substituted for the original surname. What would it be like to suddenly be given a new and different name, especially for someone who didn't speak the new language? Imagine such a situation and write the story it may suggest to you.

GLOSSARY OF LITERARY TERMS

Action: the events which occur in a story, novel, or play as the plot unfolds.

Allegory: a narrative in which the characters, action, and setting have a second level of meaning in addition to the apparent one. Thus the elements in the story function as symbols through which the author expresses universal truths.

Alliteration: the repetition of the same first letter in closely positioned words in a phrase or line of verse.

Allusion: a reference to a person, place, or event having significance in history, mythology, literature, or geography.

Antagonist: the person in a work of literature who opposes the protagonist (main character).

Apostrophe: a figure of speech in which an absent person, animal, or quality is addressed as if present and personified.

Archetype: a symbol that is typical or universal.

Assonance: the recurrence of similar vowel sounds in words which are close together in a phrase or line of verse.

Atmosphere: the mental and emotional feeling conveyed by the overall mood of a story, poem, or play.

Audience: the reader or listener for whom the work is intended. The voice of the writer frequently depends on the effect he or she wishes to have on the audience.

Characterization: the techniques used by the author to convey the personality and values of a fictional character.

Cliché: an expression that has become stale through overuse.

Climax: the point of greatest emotional intensity in a work of literature that is usually the turning point of the plot.

Conflict: a struggle between opposing forces in a work of literature. The conflict can exist between one character and another, between one character and outside forces in the society, or within one character (inner conflict).

Connotation: the meaning a word is intended to evoke in the reader, in addition to its denotative or literal one.

Denouement: see *resolution*.

Dialect: the speech patterns, including word usage and accent, characteristic of a geographical region or particular group of people.

Figures of speech: a general term for a variety of literary and poetic devices used to create more vivid expression than literal language could achieve. For examples, see *allusion, hyperbole, metaphor, personification, simile.*

Flashback: a scene interrupting the chronological flow of a story to narrate an event(s) which happened in the past.

Foot: a unit used to measure the rhythm in a line of verse. Each foot usually contains at least one stressed and one unstressed syllable.

Foreshadowing: a technique whereby the author hints at events to come. Foreshadowing helps to build suspense and unify the story.

Free verse: poetry that is written without regard to formal patterns of rhyme and rhythm.

Genre: a class or type of literary work such as poetry, drama, novel, or short story.

Hyperbole: a deliberate and obvious exaggeration, used for its effect.

Imagery: an image or picture evoked in words, especially through the use of sensory details and figures of speech.

Irony: a mode of expression in which the author says one thing, but means its opposite. Irony may also arise when the outcome of events is the opposite of what is expected.

Locale: the particular place in which the events of a story unfold.

Metaphor: a figure of speech in which an implied comparison is made, without the use of *like* or *as*.

Meter: a rhythmic pattern created by the regular repetition of stressed and unstressed syllables, or feet.

Monologue: a long speech delivered by one person.

Motivation: the cause of a character's behavior, either internal or external.

Myth: the framework of shared cultural symbols as conveyed in story, character, and ideals.

Narrative voice: the point of view used by the author to tell the story. First person point of view in narrative voice: the narrative is told by a character in the story, using the pronoun "I."

Omniscient point of view: the narration is told by an all-knowing narrator, who can relate what every character sees or thinks.

Omniscient third person point of view: the narration is told by an all-knowing observer, but events are seen through the eyes of only one of the characters. The author refers to the characters as "he," "she," or "they."

Onomatopoeia: a word or phrase which imitates the sounds of what it describes. Examples are *buzz, bang, hiss*.

Oratory: skill or eloquence in public speaking.

Oxymoron: a figure of speech in which opposite or contradictory ideas or terms are combined, e.g., "thunderous silence."

Paraphrase: explaining the meaning of a work in one's own words.

Parody: an imitation which gently makes fun of another work, or person, by exaggerating distinctive features.

Persona: the character of the narrator when the narrator speaks as if he or she is another person.

Personification: a figure of speech in which animals, inanimate objects, or ideas are endowed with human form or characteristics.

Plot: the sequenced pattern of events in a work of literature. These include the situation(s) giving rise to the conflict, the rising action, climax, and resolution.

Point of view: the perspective through which the narration is told. See *narrative voice*.

Propaganda: writing intended to convince the reader of a particular viewpoint, often through the use of oversimplification.

Protagonist: the main character in a work of drama or fiction.

Realism: the attempt to depict people and events as they really are, without romanticizing or idealizing them.

Resolution: the events that follow the climax and resolve the plot, also referred to as *falling action* or *denouement*.

Rhetorical question: a question asked for its effect, rather than for an answer.

Rhyme: in poetry, a regular recurrence of similar sounds, especially at the ends of lines.

Rhythm: in poetry, the regular recurrence of stressed and unstressed syllables. When a strict pattern is adhered to, it can be measured in meters, which are composed of feet (see *foot* and *meter*).

Romantic: a literary style that expresses emotion and idealism and often attributes these qualities to nature.

Satire: the use of sarcasm, ridicule, or irony to expose or attack human vices or folly.

Setting: the time and place which provide the backdrop for the events in a piece of literature.

Soliloquy: a speech delivered by one character in a play, spoken directly to the audience.

Stage directions: in a play, words or phrases (usually in italics or parentheses) explaining to the actors or director how the play should be staged.

Stanza: a group of lines of verse which form one of the divisions of a poem. In formal poetry, a stanza will usually contain four or more lines that repeat the rhythmic and rhyme schemes.

Stereotype: a generalized and standardized preconception of the way people or a group of people behave, lacking in accuracy.

Style: the distinctive way in which an author writes that makes his or her writing unique.

Symbol: something which on a literal level represents itself, but is also used to represent an abstract idea or quality.

Synecdoche: a figure of speech in which a part represents the whole. Example: *bread* for *food*.

Theme: the main idea of a literary work, either explicitly stated, or implied.

Tone: the feeling and mood conveyed by a work of literature which reflects the author's attitude toward his or her subject matter and audience.

Verse: poetry composed in meter.

334 ACKNOWLEDGMENTS

"America" from WEST SIDE STORY. Music by Leonard Bernstein; Lyrics by Stephen Sondheim. Copyright © 1956, 1957 (Renewed) by Leonard Bernstein and Stephen Sondheim. Jalni Publications, Inc., U.S. and Canadian Publisher. G. Schirmer, Inc., worldwide print rights and Publisher for the rest of the World. International Copyright Secured. All Rights Reserved. Used by Permission.

"Rules of the Game" from THE JOY LUCK CLUB by Amy Tan. Reprinted by permission of The Putnam Publishing Group for THE JOY LUCK CLUB by Amy Tan. Copyright © 1989 by Amy Tan.

"Tears of Autumn" from AMERICAN MOSAIC by Yoshiko Uchida. Published by Graywolf Annual Editions, Saint Paul, 1990. Reprinted by permission of the Estate of Yoshiko Uchida.

Excerpts from I REMEMBER MAMA—A PLAY IN 2 ACTS, copyright 1945 by John Van Druten and renewed 1972 by Fulton Brylawski. Reprinted by permission of Harcourt Brace Jovanovich, Inc.

"My Father Sits in the Dark" by Jerome Weidman. From MY FATHER SITS IN THE DARK AND OTHER STORIES. Copyright 1934, copyright renewed © 1961. Reprinted by permission of Brandt & Brandt Literary Agents, Inc.

"I Learned to Sew" by Mitsuye Yamada, in DESERT RUN: POEMS AND STORIES, published by Kitchen Table: Women of Color Press, Latham, NY, 1988. Reprinted by permission of the author.

"Nothing in Our Hands But Age" by Rachel Puig Zaldívar from HISPANICS IN THE UNITED STATES: AN ANTHOLOGY OF CREATIVE LITERATURE, edited by Gary D. Keller and Francisco Jiménez (1980). Reprinted by permission of Bilingual Press.

INDEX OF AUTHORS AND TITLES